GWT in Practice

D1473219

GWT in Practice

ROBERT COOPER
CHARLES COLLINS

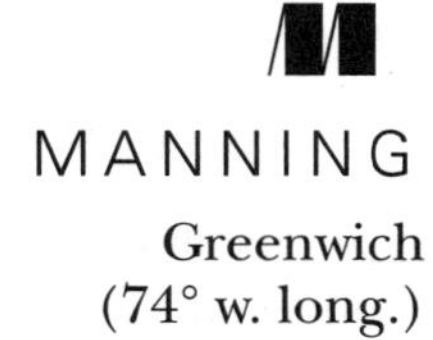

MANNING
Greenwich
(74° w. long.)

For online information and ordering of this and other Manning books, please visit www.manning.com. The publisher offers discounts on this book when ordered in quantity. For more information, please contact:

Special Sales Department
Manning Publications Co.
Sound View Court 3B   Fax: (609) 877-8256
Greenwich, CT 06830   email: orders@manning.com

©2008 by Manning Publications Co. All rights reserved.

No part of this publication may be reproduced, stored in a retrieval system, or transmitted, in any form or by means electronic, mechanical, photocopying, or otherwise, without prior written permission of the publisher.

Many of the designations used by manufacturers and sellers to distinguish their products are claimed as trademarks. Where those designations appear in the book, and Manning Publications was aware of a trademark claim, the designations have been printed in initial caps or all caps.

♾ Recognizing the importance of preserving what has been written, it is Manning's policy to have the books we publish printed on acid-free paper, and we exert our best efforts to that end. Recognizing also our responsibility to conserve the resources of our planet, Manning books are printed on paper that is at least 15% recycled and processed elemental chlorine-free

Manning Publications Co.   Copyeditor: Andy Carroll
Sound View Court 3B   Typesetters: Denis Dalinnik
Greenwich, CT 06830   Cover designer: Leslie Haimes

ISBN 1-933988-29-0
Printed in the United States of America
1 2 3 4 5 6 7 8 9 10 – VHG – 12 11 10 09 08

contents

preface *xi*
acknowledgments *xii*
about this book *xiii*
about the cover illustration *xvii*

PART 1 GETTING STARTED 1

1 *Introducing GWT* *3*

1.1 Why GWT 5

History *5* ▪ *Why Ajax matters* *6* ▪ *Leveraging the web* *7*
Tooling and testing *7* ▪ *A single code base* *8* ▪ *Limitations* *8*

1.2 What GWT includes 9

GWT compiler *9* ▪ *User Interface layer* *10* ▪ *Remote Procedure Calls* *10* ▪ *Additional utilities* *11* ▪ *GWT shell* *12*

1.3 GWT basics 13

Modules and inheritance *13* ▪ *Host pages* *14*
Entry point classes *16*

1.4 Working with the GWT shell 16

The logging console *17* ▪ *The hosted mode browser* *18*

1.5 Understanding the GWT compiler 19

JavaScript output style 20 ▪ Additional compiler nuances 23 The compiler lifecycle 24

1.6 Summary 30

2 ***A New Kind of Client 32***

2.1 Basic project structure and components 33

Generating a project 34 ▪ The standard directory structure 35 GWT starting point files 36 ▪ Host pages 37 ▪ Modules 38 Entry points 40

2.2 Design patterns and GWT 40

MVC and GWT 41 ▪ Creating a widget 42 ▪ Communicating by observing events 46 ▪ Operator strategy 48 ▪ Controlling the action 51

2.3 Styling a GWT component 54

Providing a CSS file 54 ▪ Connecting style names with Java 56

2.4 Running a completed project 56

Hosted mode and the GWT shell 57 ▪ Web mode and the GWT compiler 58

2.5 Summary 59

3 ***Communicating with the Server 61***

3.1 Making GWT Remote Procedure Calls 62

Starting the HelloServer project 62 ▪ Defining GWT serializable data 64 ▪ Creating RPC services 66 Expanding on RemoteServiceServlet 69 ▪ Calling the server from the client 70 ▪ Troubleshooting server communication 74

3.2 The development server—Tomcat Lite 75

The web.xml file 75 ▪ The context.xml file 77

3.3 Using an external development server 79

3.4 Summary 80

PART 2 TASK-SPECIFIC ISSUES 83

4 ***Core Application Structure 85***

4.1 Building a model 86

4.2 Building view components 90

Extending widgets 90 ▪ Extending composite 93
Binding to the model with events 95

4.3 The controller and service 98

Creating a simple controller 99 ▪ JPA-enabling the model 100
Creating a JPA-enabled service 104

4.4 Summary 106

5 ***Other Techniques for Talking to Servers 107***

5.1 Web development methods and security 108

Dealing with browser security 108 ▪ Understanding XMLHttpRequest 110 ▪ Coding asynchronously 110
Developing GWT applications in NetBeans 111

5.2 Enabling REST and POX communications 112

Making basic HTTP requests with GWT 112 ▪ Making advanced HTTP requests with GWT 114 ▪ Working with XML 115

5.3 Understanding Java-to-JavaScript interaction 116

Using GWT JavaDoc annotations to serialize collections 116
Using JSON 119

5.4 Creating a cross-domain SOAP client with Flash 121

Using Flash as a SOAP client 121 ▪ Setting a Flash security context 130 ▪ Drawbacks and caveats 131

5.5 Incorporating applets with GWT 131

Using Java as a SOAP client 131 ▪ Signing JARs for security bypass 136

5.6 Streaming to the browser with Comet 137

5.7 Summary 147

6 ***Integrating Legacy and Third-Party Ajax Libraries 148***

6.1 A closer look at JSNI 149

JSNI basics revisited 149 ▪ Potential JSNI pitfalls 151
Configuring IntelliJ IDEA 153

6.2 Wrapping JavaScript libraries 155

Creating a JavaScript module 156 ▪ Creating wrapper classes 156 ▪ Using the wrapped packages 159

6.3 Managing GWT-JavaScript interaction 162

Maintaining lookups 162 ▪ Daisy-chaining Java listeners into JavaScript closures 166 ▪ Maintaining listeners in Java 168 ▪ Conversion between Java and JavaScript 172

6.4 Wrapping JavaScript with GWT-API-Interop 178

6.5 Summary 181

7 ***Building, Packaging, and Deploying 183***

7.1 Packaging GWT modules 184

Building and packaging modules 184 ▪ Sharing modules 186

7.2 Building and deploying applications 187

The client side 188 ▪ The server side 188 ▪ Manually building a WAR file 189

7.3 Automating the build 191

Extending the Ant build 191 ▪ Using Maven 195

7.4 Managing Tomcat Lite from the build 205

7.5 Summary 210

8 ***Testing and Continuous Integration 211***

8.1 GWT testing 212

Knowing what to test 212 ▪ How GWT testing works 213 Testing gotchas 214 ▪ Basic GWT tests 217 ▪ Testing outside of GWT 224

8.2 Advanced testing concepts 226

Benchmarking 227 ▪ Remote testing 229 Code coverage 231 ▪ Coverage in an automated build 234

8.3 Continuous integration 239

Adding a GWT project to Hudson 240

8.4 Summary 245

PART 3 FULLY FORMED APPLICATIONS........................247

9 ***Java Enterprise Reinvented 249***

9.1 Constructing two models 251

9.2 Mapping to DTOs 257

9.3 Wiring applications with Spring 260

9.4 Constructing the client application 265

The controller and global model 266 ▪ The basic CRUD wrapper 269 ▪ The BookEdit widget 272

9.5 Summary 279

10 ***Building the Storefront 281***

10.1 Securing GWT applications 282

10.2 Building a drag-and-drop system 289

Enabling dragging 290 ▪ Handling drops 293

10.3 JSNI special effects 296

10.4 Summary 299

11 ***Managing Application State 300***

11.1 Overview of the sample application 301

11.2 Creating a basic messaging service 304

11.3 Handling messages on the client and server 310

Messages and CometEvents 310 ▪ Streaming messages to the client 312 ▪ Receiving images 315

11.4 Recording and playing back conversations 317

Capturing changes to the model layer 320 ▪ Handling deep links 325 ▪ When to use hyperlinks rather than history 326

11.5 Dealing with state on the server side 327

11.6 Adding a UI and cleaning up 330

Displaying events 330 ▪ Sending events 331 Cleaning up 333

11.7 Summary 334

appendix A Notable GWT Projects 335

appendix B Quick Reference 338

index 351

preface

At the Sun JavaOne conference in 2006, where GWT was first showcased, the lights immediately went on. I was in attendance, and I instantly understood, as did many others, what GWT creators Bruce Johnson and Joel Webber were showing the world. GWT was something different. It was not just another web framework at a Java conference but a new approach. An approach that embraced the treatment of JavaScript in the browser as the "assembly language" of the web, as Arno Puder of the XML11 project once put it, and that did so by starting from Java, in order to iron out some of the terrain of the browser landscape.

I was excited about leveraging this new technology in the real world, and I brought it back to the company I worked for, where my longtime friend Charlie Collins also worked. There, in Atlanta, Georgia, where the GWT team is also based, we started cranking away on several GWT applications, some tools to help support our development (such as GWT-Maven), and a framework approach to using GWT. Along the way, we got involved in the GWT community on the project-issue tracker and discussion boards, we pondered GWT at JUG meetings, and we discussed some of the finer points with the GWT team on a few special occasions.

Early on, I posted a series of articles about GWT online that became rather popular. That response, coupled with our practical knowledge of GWT and of web application design in general (having been involved in that field since the Servlet API itself arrived), led us to think that the time was right for a hands-on GWT "how to" book. We took the concept to several book publishers and decided that Manning was right for the project based on our general fondness for their books and the fact that they had a new "in Practice" series that they thought would be a perfect fit for our proposal.

The rest is history, as they say. A lot of long nights and weekends, and close to two years later, *GWT in Practice* is an actual book! The experience we have with GWT, which is captured in the book, will be helpful whether you are new to GWT or you have already used GWT and are seeking some problem-solving advice. We hope this book will help you find the same kind of success we have had in creating impressive and successful web applications using GWT.

ROBERT COOPER

acknowledgments

It may seem obvious that writing a book is no small endeavor, but it would probably also surprise a lot of people to know just how much work goes into the process. Although there are only two names listed on the cover of this book, a host of dedicated, talented professionals, working behind the scenes, made this book possible.

We would like to thank the entire staff at Manning for making *GWT in Practice* a reality: publisher Marjan Bace, acquisitions editor Mike Stephens, development editor Cynthia Kane, copy editor Andy Carroll, as well as Mary Piergies, Karen Tegtmayer, Dottie Marisco, Elizabeth Martin, Denis Dalinnik, Ron Tomich, and Megan Yockey.

Many reviewers also provided essential feedback. The book was honed over a series of reviews thanks to their invaluable suggestions. We would like to thank the following individuals for their time and effort in the review process: Martyn Fletcher, Todd Hoff, Devon Hillard, Jason Kolter, Adam Tacy, Robert Hanson, Andrew C. Oliver, Sandy McArthur, Carl Hume, Edmon Begoli, Eric Raymond, Andrew Grothe, Mark Bauer, Carlo Bottiglieri, Julian Seidenberg, Deepak Vohra, Bill Fly, Peter Pavlovich, Marcin Leszczyński and Massimo Perga. Special thanks to Valentin Crettaz, who did one last technical review of the final manuscript shortly before it went to press.

Robert Cooper

I want to begin by dedicating this to Fraser and Leslie Wylie in congratulations on their recent nuptials. I love you both.

Thanks to Charlie for trying to keep me honest in this effort and to Chris Adamson for prodding me to write more at every turn. Thanks to my friends Kevin Mitchell, Chris Drobny, and Brian Gregory for their support through this process and their friendship. Finally, a big thanks to the GWT team for reigniting my love for the web.

Charlie Collins

To begin with, I would like to thank my coauthor, Robert Cooper. "Cooper," as he is affectionately known to friends, not only proposed this project and brought a large part of it to fruition, but he also brought me into the fold and provided the bulk of my early exposure to GWT.

I would also like to thank the open source software community in general for providing me with many of the tools and software applications I used to write this book, from OpenOffice, ArgoUML, Subversion, and GIMP to Apache Tomcat, Eclipse, now Java, and, of course, GWT itself. Many thanks go to the GWT team, all of the GWT contributors, the GWT community, and to Google. Not only did I enjoy writing the book, but I also appreciate working with the toolkit on a day-to-day basis and building software with it.

Lastly, I want to thank my family: my wife Erin and my daughters Skylar and Delaney, who not only put up with me in general, but also showed incredible understanding when I had to spend yet another evening or weekend at the keyboard instead of with them; and my parents, who have been supportive and helpful in everything, always.

about this book

Welcome to *GWT in Practice*. This book is intended to serve as a practical field guide for developers working with the Google Web Toolkit. While it includes some introductory information, it is not a complete introduction to all the classes and libraries included with GWT. It is, however, a guide to working around common issues developers encounter when building GWT applications, and to working with other Java EE technologies.

When getting started with GWT, there are a lot of things that will seem alien to traditional web developers in the Java world. This begins with GWT's tooling—a specialized version of Tomcat for debugging and testing your Ajax applications—and continues into the design approach—an expression of the Model View Controller (MVC) pattern more akin to desktop application development than the web frameworks you may be familiar with. Hopefully this book will smooth the glide path for you as you move into development with GWT.

GWT in Practice also looks at working with technologies you may be familiar with, but that have different usage patterns in the GWT world. These include using the Java Persistence API with Hibernate or TopLink, working with build tools, testing, and continuous integration. These are at the core of modern enterprise application development but can be problematic for new GWT developers. We'll give you what you need to integrate GWT applications into your enterprise development environment.

Who should read this book

Ajax development brings advantages to both users and application providers; GWT brings the advantages of Ajax and the benefits of Java to developers. This book will be of most help to Java developers coming to GWT's style of Ajax development.

While you don't need to understand everything in this book to get value from it, you should have some basic experience with web development in a Java EE environment and some experience working with Java application servers. Obviously, a working knowledge of HTML and CSS is important, as is a basic understanding of the browser DOM. Some experience with JavaScript or Ajax is also beneficial.

We have made an effort to cover as many tools in our examples as possible. Whether you use Eclipse, NetBeans, or IntelliJ IDEA to edit code, and Ant or Maven to build your projects, you will find at least one chapter that deals with your tools. Of course, this means many of the chapters will include discussions of tools that are not your own. We expect you to be familiar enough with your tooling to work around the parts you don't care about specifically.

You should find this book to be helpful and a good ongoing reference while you are developing your applications. If your needs are task-specific, chances are good that at least one or two chapters cover what you are looking for. However, if you have limited experience with web technologies in general, we recommend you start with *GWT in Action*, available from Manning as well.

Roadmap

This book is divided into three parts. Part 1 is a quick introduction to the "GWT way," which includes tools and concepts the rest of the book relies upon. Part 2 includes a series of practical examples laid out in a problem, solution, and discussion format. Part 3 dives into a larger hands-on sample application that puts all of the GWT pieces together.

In chapter 1 we take a brief historical tour and explore the roots of Ajax itself, and then address why it's important and how GWT can help. We also cover the basic tools and terminology involved in GWT.

Chapter 2 starts with an exclusively client-side example that reinforces some of the basic GWT tenets and stresses a few new points, such as the fact that in GWT a lot more than the view exists on the client. This is where GWT differs from many other web toolkits—it allows a true Model View Controller (MVC) architectural approach to be used in a browser-based application.

From there the logical step is to create a full-featured client with server resources. In chapter 3 we use GWT Remote Procedure Calls (RPCs), demonstrate what serializable types are, and show how talking to servers works with GWT RPC. We also cover some of the details of the GWT hosted mode development shell, which uses an embedded version of Apache Tomcat.

Those first three chapters form the foundation of the book. We then move into part 2. In chapter 4, we go a bit deeper into what a canonical GWT application involves, including data binding and using the Java Persistence API (JPA) with GWT to persist data in a database.

Chapter 5 concentrates on talking to servers using mechanisms other than GWT RPC. Here we discuss JavaScript-to-Java details, the usage of JavaScript Object Notation (JSON), browser security, and the same-origin policy. This is also where we utilize Representational State Transfer (REST) and XML over HTTP. We conclude by running a Simple Object Access Protocol (SOAP) example from a GWT client (using Flash), and incorporating applets. This chapter runs the gamut in terms of ways to expose GWT clients to data, and it demonstrates the flexibility you have when working with GWT in general.

Chapter 6 then goes on to take a close look at the GWT JavaScript Native Interface (JSNI) mechanism, and the GWT-API-Interop library. Both of these are used to integrate existing JavaScript libraries with GWT.

In chapter 7 we focus on building, packaging, and deploying GWT applications with both client- and server-side components. Here we discuss creating and sharing GWT projects as libraries and creating deployable Web Application Archive (WAR) files. This is also where we first touch on using an automated build with GWT, and we cover the use of both Ant and Maven.

We put the automated build technique to further use in chapter 8, where we cover continuous integration and testing. Testing has some unique aspects in GWT, and some complications involving performance, code coverage, and remote testing, all of which are addressed here.

Then we move on to the third part of the book, "Dirty Hands." As the title of this part implies, this is where we roll up our sleeves and crank out some non-trivial example applications. In chapter 9 we cover the use of Data Transfer Objects (DTOs) as part of the GWT application model. Here we discuss the integration of server-side libraries such as Spring, and we build out an Ajax-enabled administrative CRUD (Create Read Update Delete) interface for a bookstore.

In chapter 10 we continue the sample application from chapter 9 and add the user-facing storefront. We further discuss security and the concept of roles, and then we add some eye candy by creating a drag-and-drop system for GWT. We also discuss JSNI special effects.

In chapter 11 we get into another sample application, this time a screen-sharing example that utilizes the Comet push technique. In this example, we deal with application state using the GWT history mechanism, and we also cope with state on the server side.

Finally, we conclude the book with two appendices that provide valuable reference information. Appendix A describes many impressive third-party GWT applications or libraries that you can use to enhance or extend your own applications. Appendix B is a general reference that includes GWT tools and options, definitions for GWT module descriptor and host page elements, a list of emulated JRE classes available with GWT, a description of GWT serializable types, and a list of common user interface widgets and the event handling they support.

Code conventions

In the text, the names of classes, keywords, interfaces, XML elements, code, and other code-related terms are presented in a `monospace font`. In longer code examples, some lines have been reformatted to fit within the available space on the page. Additionally, some lines of code were so long that they simply couldn't be represented and we have truncated them with the `[...]` signifier and noted them.

Code annotations are used in place of inline comments in the code. These highlight important concepts or areas of the code. Some annotations appear with numbered bullets that are referenced later in the text. The original source code also contains additional comments you might find of value.

Code downloads

All the code referenced in this book is available for download from www.manning.com/GWTinPractice or www.manning.com/cooper. We expect that if you are working through the book as a practical exercise, you will download and have this code available, as not all the code needed to run the projects is included in the text of the book.

Once you have unzipped the example source distribution, you will find it organized by chapter. Each chapter's folder contains a readme.txt file that provides specific setup instructions or considerations for working with that code. There is also a top-level file that provides a detailed overview of the project layout conventions.

The example code works for Mac, Windows, and Linux users. To get started, you should set up two environment variables: `JAVA_HOME` (if you don't have it set by default), and `GWT_HOME`. These can be set using the `set` command on Windows, or `export` on Mac OS X or Linux.

Author Online

The purchase of *GWT in Practice* includes free access to a private forum run by Manning Publications where you can make comments about the book, ask technical questions, and receive help from the authors and other users. You can access and subscribe to the forum at www.manning.com/GWTinPractice. This page provides information on how to get on the forum once you are registered, what kind of help is available, and the rules of conduct in the forum.

Manning's commitment to our readers is to provide a venue where a meaningful dialogue between individual readers and between readers and the authors can take place. It's not a commitment to any specific amount of participation on the part of the authors, whose contribution to the book's forum remains voluntary (and unpaid). We suggest you try asking the authors some challenging questions, lest their interest stray!

The Author Online forum and the archives of previous discussions will be accessible from the publisher's website as long as the book is in print.

about the cover illustration

The figure on the cover of *GWT in Practice* is a "Janissary in Ceremonial Dress." Janissaries were an elite corps of soldiers in the service of the Ottoman Empire, loyal only to the Sultan. The illustration is taken from a collection of costumes of the Ottoman Empire published on January 1, 1802, by William Miller of Old Bond Street, London. The title page is missing from the collection and we have been unable to track it down to date. The book's table of contents identifies the figures in both English and French, and each illustration bears the names of two artists who worked on it, both of whom would no doubt be surprised to find their art gracing the front cover of a computer programming book...two hundred years later.

The collection was purchased by a Manning editor at an antiquarian flea market in the "Garage" on West 26th Street in Manhattan. The seller was an American based in Ankara, Turkey, and the transaction took place just as he was packing up his stand for the day. The Manning editor did not have on his person the substantial amount of cash that was required for the purchase and a credit card and check were both politely turned down. With the seller flying back to Ankara that evening the situation was getting hopeless. What was the solution? It turned out to be nothing more than an old-fashioned verbal agreement sealed with a handshake. The seller simply proposed that the money be transferred to him by wire and the editor walked out with the bank information on a piece of paper and the portfolio of images under his arm. Needless to say, we transferred the funds the next day, and we remain grateful and impressed by this unknown person's trust in one of us. It recalls something that might have happened a long time ago.

The pictures from the Ottoman collection, like the other illustrations that appear on our covers, bring to life the richness and variety of dress customs of two centuries ago. They recall the sense of isolation and distance of that period—and of every other historic period except our own hyperkinetic present.

Dress codes have changed since then and the diversity by region, so rich at the time, has faded away. It is now often hard to tell the inhabitant of one continent from another. Perhaps, trying to view it optimistically, we have traded a cultural and visual diversity for a more varied personal life. Or a more varied and interesting intellectual and technical life.

We at Manning celebrate the inventiveness, the initiative, and, yes, the fun of the computer business with book covers based on the rich diversity of regional life of two centuries ago, brought back to life by the pictures from this collection.

Part 1

Getting Started

Chances are if you have picked up this book, you are using GWT in your applications now, or maybe you are coming to GWT for the first time. In chapters 1-3 we are going to make a run through the basics, and help you sidestep land mines along the way. By the time you get through part 1, you should be fluent in the GWT core technologies, and the application design we are going to use and reuse throughout this book.

We will begin with a look at the tried-and-true Model View Controller (MVC) pattern. We are going to harp on this a lot, so you would be well served to see where we are coming from. If you, like many other developers, have used MVC in the context of web development and have done minimal desktop application development, this is an important shift in perspective. We will continue looking at the core GWT tools, including the compiler, the debugging shell and the utility scripts that come with the system. Finally we will step through the GWT Remote Procedure Call (RPC) mechanism in some detail to make sure you have a handle on the full suite of GWT tools and technologies. What we aren't going to do is rehash the GWT documentation. There are a lot of classes for UI construction available to you, as well as a lot of utility classes, but these are best left to the JavaDoc. We are going to take a look at only what you need to know to get up and running smoothly in your development efforts.

1 Introducing GWT

This chapter covers

- The history and purpose of GWT
- The components of GWT
- GWT basics
- Working with the GWT shell and GWT compiler

The man of virtue makes the difficulty to be overcome his first business, and success only a subsequent consideration.

—Confucius

Asynchronous JavaScript and XML (Ajax) development is hard. Not ascending-Everest hard, maybe not even calculating-your-taxes hard, but hard. This is true for a number of reasons: JavaScript can require a lot of specialized knowledge and discipline, browsers have slightly different implementations and feature sets, tooling is still immature, and debugging in multiple environments is problematic. All of these factors add up to developers needing a vast knowledge of browser oddities and tricks to build and manage large Ajax projects.

To help deal with these problems, a number of toolkits and libraries have emerged. Libraries like Dojo, Script.aculo.us, Ext JS, and the Yahoo User Interface

Library (YUI) have sought to provide enhanced core features and general ease of use to JavaScript. In addition, projects like Direct Web Remoting (DWR) have sought to simplify communications between the client and the server. Even more advanced techniques, like those used by XML11 and Echo2, create an entire rendering layer in the browser while executing application code on the server side. These are all valid approaches, but the Google Web Toolkit (GWT) represents something different.

GWT is a Java to JavaScript cross-compiler. That is, it takes Java code and compiles it into JavaScript to be run in a browser, as figure 1.1 depicts.

There are many reasons GWT was engineered to start with the statically compiled, strongly typed Java language, which has generous tooling and testing support, and then emits JavaScript application versions for all the major browsers in one compilation step. Chief among these reasons is the simple fact that JavaScript is what is available in a browser: starting from a single code base and generating all the required variations makes life a lot easier for the developer, and more consistent, stable, and performant for the user.

Other aspects that set GWT apart include a harness for debugging Java bytecode directly as it executes in a simulated browser environment, a set of core UI and layout widgets with which to build applications, a Remote Procedure Call (RPC) system for handling communications with a host web server, internationalization support, and testing mechanisms.

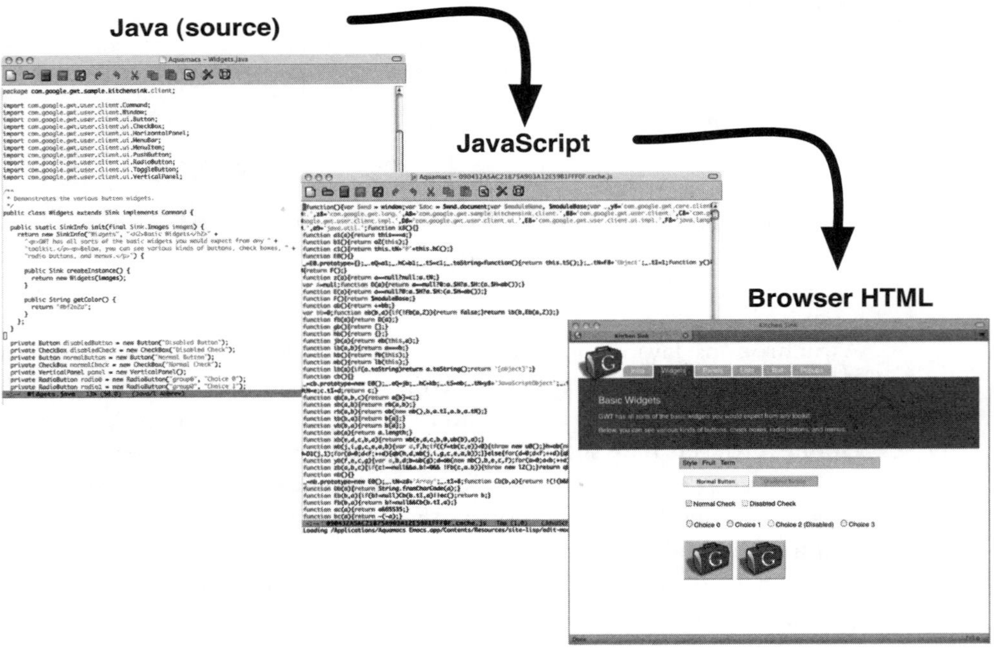

Figure 1.1 An overview of the GWT approach. Java source code is compiled into JavaScript, which is then run in a web browser as JavaScript/HTML/CSS.

GWT provides a platform for creating true "Rich" Internet Applications (RIAs)—rich in the sense of allowing the client to maintain state and even perform computations locally, with a full data model, without requiring a trip to the server for every update to the interface. This has many advantages for both the user and the developer. The user gets a more responsive application, and the developer can distribute the load of the application. GWT also provides a rich platform in terms of a wide variety of UI elements and capabilities: sliders, reflections, drag-and-drop support, suggest boxes, data-bound tables, and more. This rich client platform, ultimately utilizing only HTML, JavaScript, and Cascading Style Sheets (CSS), still has full access, in a variety of ways, to back-end server resources when needed.

In short, GWT makes Ajax development a lot easier. Not falling-off-a-log easy, maybe not even taking-candy-from-a-baby easy, but easier—and it makes Ajax applications better for users. With *GWT in Practice*, we hope to clarify some facets of GWT that might seem hard or confusing. Along the way, we'll also provide practical GWT development advice based on real-world experience.

If you're a Java web developer now, you'll need a change of perspective to build GWT applications well, and you'll need a good understanding of the core GWT tools and how they work in order to fit them into your environment. If you're an Ajax developer coming to Java, you'll need a bit of indoctrination in "The Java Way." Even if you're currently using or experimenting with GWT, you may want to increase your technical bag of tricks. It's our hope that you find all of this, and maybe even a little more, in this book.

1.1 Why GWT

The quick, but wrong, answer to why GWT was created and why it's gaining popularity is because it's new and shiny! Though GWT is no SOA or ESB on the buzz-meter yet, it's widely discussed. But does it deserve the attention and praise it receives? When we get past the hype, what are the reasons for its creation, and why might it make sense to use it?

In the next few sections, we'll address these questions and lay out the overall approach of GWT and look at why it was created, where it's applicable, and why it should matter to you as a software developer (or manager). We'll begin our discussion of what makes GWT significant with a brief trip back through the history of web development, and the patterns and techniques involved, in order to frame the concepts.

1.1.1 History

In the beginning, there was HTML. Originally, HTML was a semantic document markup language intended to help researchers on the Internet link related documents together. But soon after HTML use blossomed, forms came along. When forms were added to HTML, it transitioned from being strictly a document markup language to a UI design language. HTML still suffers in some ways from this legacy, but the ease with which it allowed web-based applications to be deployed became a driving factor in its use nonetheless.

As the world of web applications began to expand, developers supporting the basic form applications on the server side repurposed the Model View Controller (MVC) pattern so that it centered on the server and rendered to HTML. From simple Perl scripts to complete frameworks, development remained on the server, and things like application state became a complex problem with complex solutions—involving everything from Struts to JavaServer Faces (JSF) and Seam. Although these solutions made web applications more capable and development easier, they didn't provide the user experience of a full desktop-like fat client application, and they continued in the same render-call-render lifecycle that the web had used when forms were first added.

When Netscape introduced JavaScript to the web browser, the browser became something more than just a simple thin client. It became a platform on its own, capable of running small applications entirely within the scope of a page. This approach was widely used for simple things, such as field validation, but its use didn't spread to more advanced functionality until Microsoft introduced the XMLHttpRequest (XHR) object. This object made calls back to the server from the JavaScript environment easy, and the technique was soon adopted by all the major browsers. The frontiers and capabilities of web applications expanded even further when dynamic HTML and forms were combined with the server side via XHR, permitting only portions of browser windows to be redrawn. The Ajax era was born.

1.1.2 Why Ajax matters

Ajax changed the landscape because it finally broke the browser's render-call-render pattern and allowed browsers to update without making a visible, and often slow, trip back to the server for every page view. Ajax makes even the term *page* a bit of a relic. With Ajax, the browser is much closer to being able to support full blown *fat* or *rich* Internet applications.

Because GWT is Ajax and is easily extensible to new browsers, it provides a wider array of supported devices than many other RIA approaches. Silverlight, Flash, and the Java Applet Plugin all give developers the ability to create powerful, easy-to-use applications that run from a web browser, but their dependency on an environment outside of the browser means that they will always lag behind in deployment. GWT and other Ajax-based applications worked on Day Zero for both the Nintendo Wii and the iPhone, for instance. GWT's concise browser abstraction also makes it easy to update GWT applications when new versions of currently supported browsers are released, requiring only a recompile of the Java to support new devices.

Ajax is also significant in that applications that are native to the browser *feel* more natural to users. No matter how seamless the browser integration, there are typically some noticeable differences with plugin technologies. Such differences may include an install step; the treatment of browser constructs in a different manner, such as with bookmarks and navigation; and starkly different user interface elements compared with HTML, CSS, and JavaScript. GWT, and Ajax in general, is a form of RIA that embraces the parts of the web that do work well and that users are familiar with.

1.1.3 Leveraging the web

Users and developers have embraced the web because it offers centralized management and delivery, no local installation, instant updates to both functionality and content, and elements such as shareable bookmarks. Although the specifications that make up the web have needed to be adapted over the years to cope with drawbacks such as the stateless nature of HTTP, limited user input elements, and the render-call-render lifecycle, the advantages of the web have prevailed.

The desirable parts of the web, coupled with the implementation difficulties, are why RIA technologies exist in the first place, and this includes GWT. Some of these technologies, though, may go too far in their abstraction of the web layer, hiding the good as well as the bad.

GWT, happily, is designed with the web tier in mind. The centrally hosted distribution model that the web offers is fully leveraged, and updates to applications are transparent and seamless in this model. The URL is the application-download location, and the browser is the application platform. Concepts that users know and love are also present, and are intentionally not hidden or disabled. Browser buttons—even the infamous back button—can be put to work rather than disabled, and can do exactly what they're expected to do. Bookmarks are there and, again, they work, even when deep-linked into a particular area of the application.

Leveraging the parts of the web that do work well is intentional with GWT, as is GWT's extension of the RIA landscape to provide tooling and testing support.

1.1.4 Tooling and testing

Another of the reasons GWT is significant and is different from some other RIA offerings is that it provides tooling and testing support. GWT includes a powerful debugging shell that allows you to test and debug your code as it interacts with the native browser on your platform.

The testing support GWT provides is based on JUnit and on a few extensions the toolkit provides. Your GWT code can be tested as Java, from the shell. After you compile your code into JavaScript, the same test can be used again in that form by using further scaffolding provided by GWT. This allows you to test on various browser versions and, if desired, even on different platform and browser combinations.

The Java language also comes with first-class tooling support. Invaluable tools such as code parsers like PMD, static analysis tools like Checkstyle and FindBugs, advanced refactoring engines available in most Java Integrated Development Environments (IDEs), and debuggers and profilers all function perfectly normally within the context of the GWT shell.

Tooling support and testing facilities, which are front and center with GWT, are standard fare in traditional programming but aren't as common in for client-side web technologies. Along with this support, GWT provides a great deal of help for developers in other areas. One of the biggest advantages GWT offers is that it helps you cope with browser differences.

1.1.5 A single code base

Traditionally, web development has required a doctorate in browserology in order to cope with all of the differences in behavior among browser types and versions, even when you're just writing a standard web application using HTML and forms. Along with knowing details about multiple versions of HTML, the Document Object Model (DOM), CSS, JavaScript, and HTTP standards, developers have also needed to be aware of the way quirks and bugs affect each browser.

Add XML and XHR to the mix, along with more browser differences, and you can see why Ajax development has a well-deserved reputation on the street as being difficult. GWT doesn't avoid that difficulty directly, but it does encapsulate it and allow developers to worry about their application, rather than about the differences among browsers. GWT lets you work on a single code base, using Java, and then cross-compile that code into Ajax-enabled HTML and JavaScript for most of the major browser types and versions currently in use (Internet Explorer, Firefox, Safari, and Opera at present).

This is a huge benefit to developers. Imagine a world where browser makers actually adhere to standards and use the latest standard consistently—where you, as a developer, need create only one version of your application, which will work regardless of the user agent. That is a fantasy, of course, but the next best thing is to write application code once and then generate additional code to cope with the differences in the browser environment. This gives you, in effect, the same thing—one version of code to write and maintain instead of multiple versions. This is what GWT aims for.

The abstraction isn't always perfect, but it works well most of the time. And when there is a problem—a particular browser version has an issue in a particular scenario—it can usually be resolved quickly with open access to the source and the expertise of the community (and that expertise is put back into the toolkit, so that others avoid the same problem in the future).

1.1.6 Limitations

Along with the potentially leaky, but undeniably extremely useful, abstraction of the web layer, GWT has a few other potential limitations or drawbacks you should be aware of.

Don't call GWT a framework (even though in places the documentation does refer to it as such). GWT hasn't been here for years, and a lot of components people expect from "Framework" products aren't there. Java web frameworks, like Struts and WebWork, evolved from the lessons learned in traditional Java web development. As such, they come with a style, a set of patterns, and expected ways of working, all of which help developers see where to begin with their applications. GWT doesn't have that. When working with GWT as a developer, it's best to think of it as an analogue to the Java Abstract Windowing Toolkit (AWT). It's the basis for your application framework, not the framework itself.

This can be considered a limitation, but it can also be seen as a well-focused starting point. GWT doesn't try to dictate the development approach you'll use; rather, it aims to provide the components you can begin with to create Ajax applications, or frameworks, on your own. Through the course of this book, we'll demonstrate several patterns for development that should mitigate concerns in this area; the point here is that a toolkit isn't necessarily limiting—it's a starting point.

One area that is a limitation with GWT is that search engines have a hard time with JavaScript. Most search engine agents or robots don't speak JavaScript or know how to navigate an application that isn't composed of simple links. This means many GWT resources are nonexistent as far as such search engines are concerned. Of course, this applies to all of Ajax and JavaScript in general, not just GWT.

Many techniques can help you cope with this issue. Often the most useful and thorough is to have a native HTML-only version of your application alongside your GWT application, so that user agents that can't load JavaScript, whether or not they're search engine agents, can still access your data. The non-JavaScript version of your application need not be pretty; it should concentrate on core content and any degree of functionality you can provide. Be careful, though; make sure any non-JavaScript version of your site is an accurate representation. Providing "search engine only" content is known as *cloaking*, and it can get your site banned from search engine indexes.

When viewed in total, the benefits of GWT outweigh its limitations in many, but not all, cases. Overall, GWT provides a new approach to building Ajax web applications—starting from a single code base, generating the variations for all the major browsers, embracing the concepts of the web that are already familiar to users, and providing many tools and supporting features along the way.

Now that we have looked at the inspiration and reasoning behind GWT, we'll turn to addressing exactly what GWT includes.

1.2 What GWT includes

The Google Web Toolkit provides a number of technologies for building Ajax applications: the GWT compiler, a UI layer, an RPC system, several additional utilities that make the web tier easier to manage, and the GWT shell. We'll look briefly at each of them now, and then we'll step through them and highlight their usage. To begin, the compiler is at the core of GWT.

1.2.1 GWT compiler

The GWT Java compiler takes Java code and compiles it into JavaScript—that's all. It has some advanced rules for doing this, however. By defining GWT compile tasks into *modules*, which we'll cover in more detail in section 1.3, the compiler can perform more analysis on the code as it's processed, and branch into multiple compilation artifacts for different output targets. This means that when compiling a class, you can specify differing implementations based on known parameters. The obvious switch point is the user agent or client browser you're targeting. This feature drives the core of GWT's cross-browser compatibility.

Unlike most Ajax toolkits written in JavaScript, which have complex logic to adapt to different browser environments, GWT will switch out the implementation of core classes based on the user agent the compilation task is targeting. The bottom line is that each browser gets a lean, mean, and specific version of your application and isn't forced to download code for all the other browsers your application can support. It's through this mechanism that GWT implements a cross-browser UI toolkit.

1.2.2 User Interface layer

Built on top of GWT's intelligent compilation system is a cross-browser UI layer. The real magic here comes from implementing the UI elements in Java and then using a browser-specific implementation of the core DOM to build out the native browser elements as they're needed by the higher-level Java layer. Whereas some Ajax libraries have a lot of focus on UI widgets, GWT is intended to provide a core of UI functionality that users and the community can build upon.

The GWT UI layer provides a wide variety of layout-related panels, data representation constructs such as `Tree` and `Grid`, a set of user input elements, and more. The 1.4 release of GWT began to expand the UI toolkit to include some new advanced elements, like a rich text editor and a suggest box. This release also started to include some great new optimized UI elements that draw from the power of the plugin-capable compiler, such as the `ImageBundle`.

The `ImageBundle` takes static images in your application and merges them into a single graphic file. Then, by using the placed background mode in the CSS box model, it shows only the part of the large single image required at any point, as shown in figure 1.2. This means the client browser can make a single request to get all the images in your application, rather than negotiating multiple HTTP request-response cycles, thereby improving the startup time of your application.

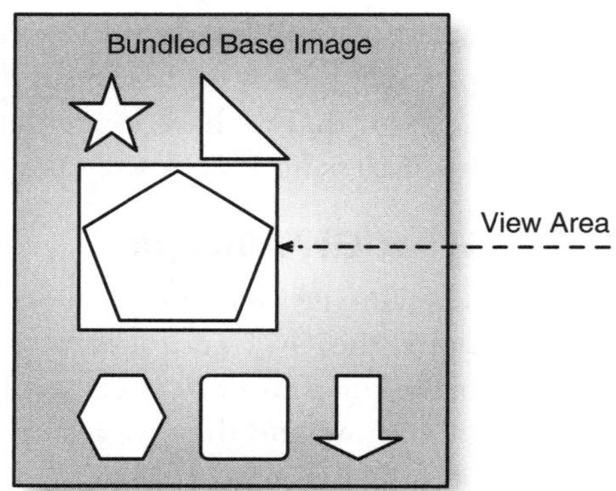

Figure 1.2 The `ImageBundle` merges many images into one large base image and then renders an individual image on the page by positioning the compiled image as a background behind a transparent view area image.

In addition to the core UI foundation and the subset of UI elements provided, GWT also includes several means for communicating with server resources. Chief among these methods is the GWT RPC mechanism.

1.2.3 Remote Procedure Calls

Another GWT core feature that draws heavily from the plugin capabilities of the compiler is the RPC functionality. This system allows for serialization and deserialization of

Java objects from server-side implementations of remote services, which can then be called asynchronously from the client.

To do this, the compiler generates code during the compilation step to handle the serialization at a low level. Serialized objects are versioned and mapped at compile time. This carries with it two major advantages. First, you can guarantee the client and server agreement as new versions are deployed. Second, the server implementation can compress the state of Java objects down to arrays of JavaScript primitives. This passing of simple arrays allows for even more concise data formatting than JavaScript Object Notation (JSON), which many laud for its simplicity and efficiency. We'll take a close look at the RPC functionality and communicating with servers in chapter 3.

Along with its own RPC system, GWT also includes a set of additional utilities that make development for the web simpler.

1.2.4 Additional utilities

Beyond the approach and the core elements, GWT also includes a number of utilities that are designed to make building applications for the web tier easier. These include support for additional ways to communicate with servers, internationalization (i18n) tools, a history management system, and testing support.

GWT provides several client-side libraries for going beyond the standard GWT RPC and instead communicating with XML and JSON-based services. These make it easy to integrate with many existing web APIs or to implement a completely non-Java-based backend. We'll explore these techniques in more detail in chapter 5.

There is also a compile-time-checked internationalization library that makes providing multilanguage support easy and reliable. This makes it not only possible, but straightforward, to internationalize your Ajax web applications. You'll see more about how this system works in section 1.5 when we delve into some compiler details.

The history management system makes bookmarking and deep-linking in your Ajax application pretty easy too. This system can also be overloaded when you need to seamlessly link between several deployed GWT applications. This can come in handy if you ever need to lazy load portions of your application for performance reasons or to reduce the initial download time (these occasions should be rare, because of all the other optimizations GWT provides).

Last, but not least, there is formal testing support. GWT gives you a means to test your code by writing test cases either as Java or as JavaScript. We'll cover this in more detail in chapter 8, which is devoted to testing and other aspects of code quality, such as continuous integration.

All of the additional utilities GWT provides are aimed at making the development cycle a little easier, and a little more predictable, on the web tier. Along these same lines, one of the main tools GWT provides is the GWT shell.

1.2.5 GWT shell

All of the great features GWT includes are built on the core of the architectural approach and the GWT compiler. But wait! There's more! GWT also includes a nice set of developer tools starting with the GWT shell and hosted mode browser, which is shown in figure 1.3.

The GWT shell allows you to test your application in a browser while executing the native Java bytecode. This gives you the ability to use all your favorite Java tools to inspect your application, including profilers, step-through debugging, and JTI-based monitors. This hosted mode browser, with an embedded Apache Tomcat server, is also what makes it possible to test your compiled JavaScript with JUnit. Because the shell is so central to all GWT development projects, we'll cover it in more detail in section 1.4, and we'll use it throughout the book.

We have looked at the reasons for the GWT architecture choices in general and at some of the tools and utilities provided. We'll now turn to the basic concepts of working with GWT and getting a project started.

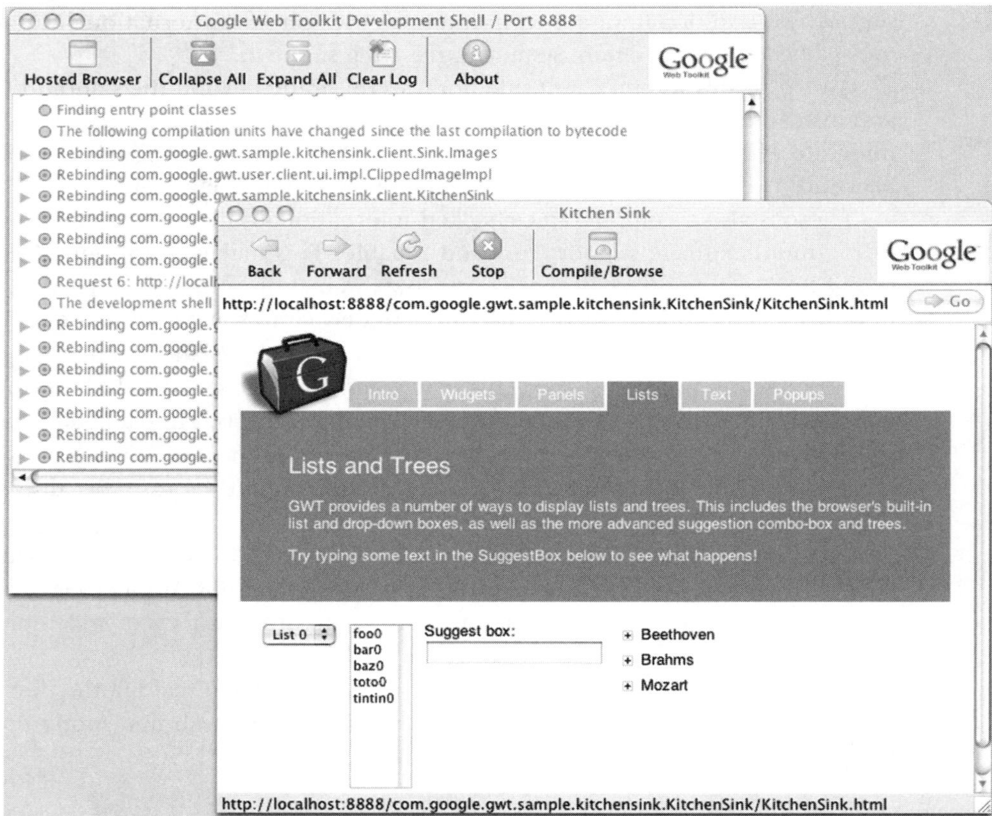

Figure 1.3 The GWT shell and hosted mode browser. The shell includes a hierarchical log view and a custom web browser.

1.3 GWT basics

Individual GWT projects are composed of a few key parts. We'll briefly touch on the main components of a GWT project to familiarize you with the concepts that you'll use over and over again when working with the toolkit.

First, GWT projects are defined in terms of modules, composed of resources, configuration, and source. The module configuration defines compile-time information about a project and specifies resources needed at runtime. Beyond configuration, modules also make possible a rich inheritance mechanism. Because of this capability, projects can be complete web applications, they can be of a pure library nature, or they can fall anywhere in between.

One thing a module defines is the starting point for a project's code, known as an *entry point*. Entry point classes are coded in Java and are referenced by a module definition and compiled to JavaScript. Modules themselves, and the entry points they define, are invoked through a `<script>` reference on an HTML page, known as a *host page*. Host pages invoke GWT projects and also support a few special `<meta>` tags that can be used to tweak things. At a high level, these are the three main components of a GWT project: a module configuration file, an entry point class, and an HTML host page.

In the next few sections, we'll introduce each of these components, beginning with modules and the inheritance they enable.

1.3.1 Modules and inheritance

Several aspects of GWT may seem alien to new users. The main one is the use of the module concept to define GWT applications. One of the core problems with web development over the years has been getting true reusability from applications and components. The GWT system of modules allows application components to package the client-side application code, server-side service implementations, and assets such as graphics and CSS files into an easily redistributable package. Modules, with their facilitation of inheritance, are also an important part of the GWT bootstrap and deployment process.

A module is defined by an XML file packaged with the Java source implementing the module. This XML file declares several primary elements: inherited modules, servlet deployments, compiler plugins, and entry points. Listing 1.1 shows a sample module file.

Listing 1.1 Calculator.gwt.xml module definition

```
<module>
   <inherits name='com.google.gwt.user.User'/>          ❶ Inherit core GWT classes
   <entry-point                                         ❷ Define EntryPoint
      class='com.manning.gwtip.calculator.client.Calculator'/>
   <stylesheet
      src='com.manning.gwtip.calculator.style.css'/>    ❸ Specify CSS file to use
</module>
```

This module file is pretty basic. It comes from the example application we'll create in chapter 2, a GWT-based calculator.

The `<inherits>` tag tells GWT to inherit the core User module ❶. This includes the GWT UI elements as well as the custom compiler elements that generate the appropriate versions for Firefox, Safari, Internet Explorer, and Opera. Remember, inheriting a module brings in all the elements of the module, not just source code. This is one of the main reasons for having the module system. Of course, the compiler can find additional Java sources referenced by your project, but the module system allows build-time and server-side behavior to be inherited as well.

Next is the declaration of an `<entry-point>` ❷. As mentioned previously, an entry point is the starting point for the code in a GWT project—we'll cover this in more detail in the next section.

Finally, a stylesheet is included for the application ❸. Although it isn't necessary to provide style information at this level, a stylesheet declared in the module follows the module through inheritance, making common formatting easier to carry from application to application as common components are reused.

This module definition makes a few core assumptions, the main one being the directory layout of the source folders. Although this layout is customizable, the default and conventional layout for GWT applications follows this format:

- The package folder (For example, com.manning)
  - `Module.gwt.xml` (The module definition file)
    - `client` The client package containing code that will be cross-compiled to JavaScript
    - `public` Folder containing assets used by the module (images, CSS files, other resources)
    - `server` The package containing server-side implementation code
    - `rebind` The package containing compile-time code (generators)

In the preceding example, a reference to com.manning.gwtip.calculator.style.css refers to the com.manning.gwtip.calculator.style.css file in the public folder of the module package. You can also see that the `<entry-point>` definition references a class in the client package.

We have only scratched the surface with regard to modules here. We'll come back to them later in this chapter when we discuss the GWT compiler, then in the next chapter when we build our first sample application, and throughout the book as we complete further examples. For now, we'll look more closely at entry points and at the GWT bootstrap process involving host pages.

1.3.2 Host pages

To run a GWT application, you start with an HTML page. The HTML host page, as it's known in GWT parlance, contains just a couple of special elements needed to activate a GWT application. First is a reference to a *nocache* JavaScript file that GWT generates for every module. This is a JavaScript file that detects the appropriate version of the application module, based on the user agent and other factors, and loads up the monolithically compiled application. Listing 1.2 shows an example HTML host page, again taken from the calculator example we'll build in the next chapter.

Listing 1.2 The calculator HTML host page

```
<html>
    <head>
        <title>Wrapper HTML for Calculator</title>
    </head>
    <body>
        <script language="javascript"
            src=
"com.manning.gwtip.calculator.Calculator.nocache.js"
            >
            </script>
        <iframe id="__gwt_historyFrame"
                style="width:0;height:0;border:0"></iframe>
        <h1>Calculator</h1>

    </body>
</html>
```

❶ Bootstrap JavaScript file

Special invisible iframe for history management

The important part here is that the host page includes the bootstrap JavaScript file that starts up the application ❶. When you compile your GWT application, you'll get two versions of this file, named [ModuleName].nocache.js, and [ModuleName]-xs.nocache.js, respectively. These two files typically represent the only part of your GWT application that you should send to the client without HTTP-level caching enabled. All of the other files GWT generates are named based on a hash of the source code that went into creating them, meaning that they can be cached indefinitely by the client with no ill effects. The two nocache files determine which hashed version needs to be loaded when the page is requested.

The cross-site *xs* version of the nocache file is for use by other domains that might include your application. This file allows those remote domains to communicate with your server-side resources, even if the HTML page that includes the script wasn't served from the same host as the server-side resources. This short-circuiting of the same-origin policy is dangerous: it opens up your application to possible Cross Site Scripting (XSS) security problems. It also makes your application more mashupable (which may, or may not, be desirable). You should use this script only if you know what you're doing. We'll discuss other aspects of the same-origin policy, and ways to work around it, in chapter 5.

When a module nocache script (either version—standard or cross-site) is loaded from a host page, the remainder of the GWT bootstrap process is invoked and an entry point class is loaded.

1.3.3 Entry point classes

An *entry point class* is a simple client-side class that implements the `com.google.gwt.core.client.EntryPoint` interface, which defines a single method: `onModuleLoad()`. This is the GWT equivalent of a class with the method `public static void main()` declared in Java—a place to begin. Again borrowing from the calculator example we'll build in chapter 2, listing 1.3 shows an example `EntryPoint` implementation.

Listing 1.3 The entry point for the `Calculator` class

```
public class Calculator implements EntryPoint {
    public void onModuleLoad() {
        RootPanel.get().add(
            new CalculatorWidget("calculator"));     ❶ Add CalculatorWidget to <body>
    }
}
```

The `onModuleLoad()` method is simple, but the operative element here is the use of GWT's `RootPanel` class. This is your application's access to the HTML host page. Calling `RootPanel.get()` returns a default container that is inserted just before the ending `</body>` tag in the HTML page ❶. If you want finer-grained control over where a GWT widget is injected into the page, you can call `RootPanel.get("ElementID")` where `ElementID` is a string value denoting the ID of an element on the HTML page, typically a `<div>` tag.

Modules, host pages, and entry points are the fundamental high-level concepts involved in any GWT project. We have touched on these concepts here to cover the basics, but don't worry if this introduction seems brief. We'll be using these components, and expanding on them, in the next chapter when we build our first GWT example application, and throughout the book in subsequent examples.

With our initial tour of these elements now complete, let's take a closer look at the tool you'll use most during development: the GWT shell.

1.4 Working with the GWT shell

The GWT shell, which we briefly introduced in section 1.2.5, is one of the most important components GWT provides, and one you'll use every day when developing GWT applications. We'll cover it in more detail here, and we'll touch on it again in other chapters when specific situations warrant it.

The shell is composed of three main parts: a logging console, an embedded Tomcat server, and the hosted mode browser. The GWT shell console provides an enhanced logging interface and centralized GUI as a GWT dashboard. The hosted mode browser is capable of invoking your Java classes directly on browser events, rather than requiring a compilation to JavaScript; thus you can use a standard Java debugger to work with your Ajax code, instead of relying solely on compiled JavaScript for testing and interaction. The development server, Tomcat Lite, facilitates local development and testing of server-based resources (this is covered in detail in chapter 3).

`GWTShell` supports several common command-line parameters you should be familiar with. The parameters are described in table 1.1:

```
GWTShell [-port port-number] [-noserver] [-whitelist whitelist-string]
[-blacklist blacklist-string] [-logLevel level] [-gen dir] [-out dir]
[-style style] [url]
```

Table 1.1 `GWTShell` parameters

Parameter	Description
`-port`	Runs an embedded Tomcat instance on the specified port (defaults to 8888).
`-noserver`	Prevents the embedded Tomcat server from running, even if a port is specified.
`-whitelist`	Allows the user to browse URLs that match the specified regular expressions (comma or space separated).
`-blacklist`	Prevents the user from browsing URLs that match the specified regular expressions (comma or space separated).
`-logLevel`	The logging level: `ERROR`, `WARN`, `INFO`, `TRACE`, `DEBUG`, `SPAM`, or `ALL`.
`-gen`	The directory into which generated files will be written for review.
`-out`	The directory to which output files will be written (defaults to current).
`-style`	Script output style: `OBF`[uscated], `PRETTY`, or `DETAILED` (defaults to `OBF`).
`url`	Launches the specified URL automatically.

We'll use many of these options in the examples throughout this book, and we'll go into more detail as we encounter each option. The first of these parameters that you may want to tweak is `-logLevel`, which changes the output level of the logging console. This is the first thing you notice when the GWT shell starts up.

1.4.1 The logging console

The GWT shell console is a hierarchical logging display with a few simple buttons that invoke the hosted mode browser and control logging output. The logging display is controlled by the `-logLevel` option on the `GWTShell` command line. Valid log levels are shown in table 1.2; the default level is `INFO`.

Table 1.2 `GWTShell -logLevel` options

Log Level	Description
`ERROR`	Shows only critical errors in the GWT shell code.
`WARN`	Shows uncaught exceptions in user code. `WARN` and `ERROR` information are displayed in red in the shell window.
`INFO`	(Default.) Shows server startup information and invocations into specific GWT modules. Most of the time, what you'll see in this mode is simply "Starting HTTP on port 8888."

Table 1.2 `GWTShell -logLevel` options (continued)

Log Level	Description
`TRACE`	Shows each request logged, as well as module instantiations, their locations on the class path, and the time. This is perhaps the most useful mode for day-to-day development. `TRACE` and `INFO` level information are displayed in gray in the shell window.
`DEBUG`	Shows the binding of classes inside the GWT shell for code invocations and URL mapping. This mode is also useful for debugging compilation errors into JavaScript, should you encounter them. `DEBUG` level information is displayed in green in the shell window.
`SPAM`	Shows all `ClassLoader` events and invocations to native JavaScript. `SPAM` level information is displayed in teal in the shell window.
`ALL`	Shows all logging information.

Figure 1.4 shows the buttons and some sample logging output in the GWT shell console component.

From the GWT shell console GUI, you also have the option to invoke the hosted mode browser. The hosted mode browser is what allows you to explore your Java application using a browser and browser-based events.

1.4.2 The hosted mode browser

The hosted mode browser operates as a test browser harness that directly invokes Java binary code in response to browser events. This allows you to skip the step of compiling to JavaScript and to immediately see changes to your code, as well as to perform step-through debugging of code between the client and server sides.

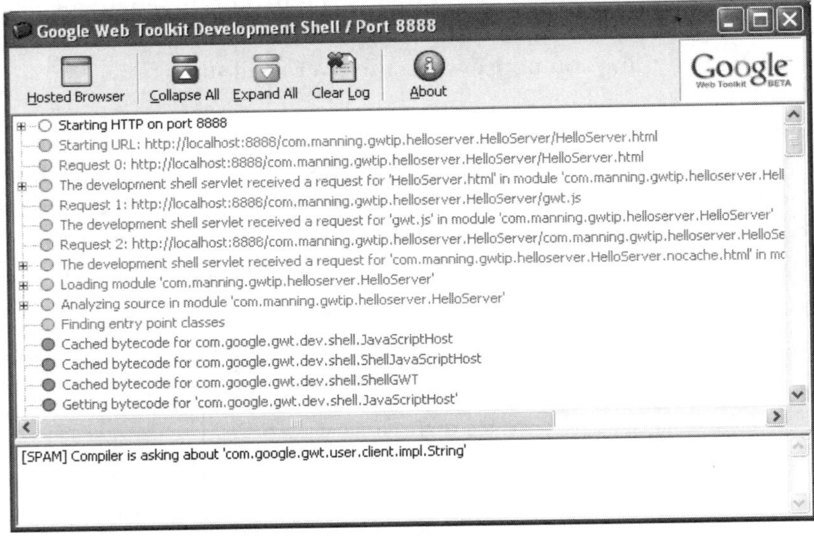

Figure 1.4 The GWT shell logging console shows different log level messages in different colors.

The hosted mode browser also provides a shortcut to executing the compiled JavaScript version of your application; this is known as *web mode.* While you're using the hosted browser from GWT, you can click the Compile/Browse button to perform a complete compilation of your Java to JavaScript and then browse your hosted application in the shell's development web server.

Note that it's important to make sure you have the `GWT_EXTERNAL_BROWSER` environment variable set before you click Compile/Browse. For example, on Linux you would set it like this:

```
export GWT_EXTERNAL_BROWSER=/usr/bin/firefox
```

This defines the command line that the GWT shell will invoke to launch a browser against the hosted Tomcat.

You can also use the hosted mode browser apart from the GWT shell's Tomcat instance with the `-noserver` option. This tells the shell not to use the embedded Tomcat instance in hosted mode, but rather to use an external server that you specify. Using an external web server, or Java container, can have several advantages. You can, for example, use the standalone browser to debug and test Java UI code that is talking to PHP or .NET backends that can't otherwise be run in the GWT shell. Or you can use a Java backend that may run in a different container than Tomcat. Using an external server with `-noserver` is covered further in chapter 3, when we look more closely at configuring the embedded Tomcat instance in general.

Regardless of which container you use, it's recommended that for hosted mode use you name your context path name the same as your module: for example, com.manning.gwtip.helloserver.HelloServer. Doing this will make it easier to map your service servlet calls later.

Along with the shell, and the hosted mode browser that it includes, the next key GWT tool that we need to look at is the GWT compiler.

1.5 Understanding the GWT compiler

The GWT compiler is the fulcrum of GWT. The entire approach GWT takes, encapsulating browser differences and compiling JavaScript from Java, is made possible by the design and architecture of the compiler. Because of the importance of the GWT compiler and its central role in virtually every aspect of GWT projects, we need to take a good look at the compiler here; we'll come back to it and fill in other details throughout the book.

The GWT compiler compiles Java into JavaScript, but it's important to understand that the compiler doesn't compile Java the same way javac does. The GWT compiler is really a *Java source to JavaScript source translator.*

The GWT compiler needs hints about the work that it must perform partly because it operates from source. These hints come in the form of the module descriptor, the marker interfaces that denote serializable types, the JavaDoc style annotations used in serializable types for collections, and more.

Although these hints may sometimes seem like overkill, they're needed because the GWT compiler will optimize your application at compile time. This doesn't just mean compressing the JavaScript naming to the shortest possible form; it also includes pruning unused classes, and even methods and attributes, from your code. The core engineering goal of the GWT compiler is summarized succinctly: you pay for what you use.

This optimization offers big advantages over other Ajax/JavaScript libraries, where a large initial download of a library may be needed even if just a few elements are used. In Java, serialization marked by the `java.io.Serializable` interface is handled at the bytecode level. GWT examines your code and only provides serialization for the classes where you explicitly need it.

Like `GWTShell`, `GWTCompiler` supports a set of useful command-line options. They're described in table 1.3:

```
GWTCompiler [-logLevel level] [-gen dir] [-out dir] [-treeLogger]
  [-style style] module
```

Table 1.3 `GWTCompiler` parameters

Option	Description
`-logLevel`	The logging level: `ERROR`, `WARN`, `INFO`, `TRACE`, `DEBUG`, `SPAM`, or `ALL`.
`-gen`	The directory into which generated files will be written for review.
`-out`	The directory to which output files will be written (defaults to the current directory).
`-treeLogger`	Logs output in a graphical tree view.
`-style`	The script output style: `OBF`[uscated], `PRETTY`, or `DETAILED` (defaults to `OBF`).
`module`	The name of the module to compile.

The `-gen` and `-out` command-line options specify where generated files and the final output directory are to be, respectively. And `-logLevel`, as in the case of `GWTShell`, is used to indicate the level of logging performed during the compilation. You can even use the `-treeLogger` option to bring up a window to view the hierarchical logging information you would see in the shell's console display.

The GWT compiler supports several styles of output, each of use in looking at how your code is executing in the browser.

1.5.1 JavaScript output style

When working with the GWT compiler, you can use several values with the `-style` command-line option to control what the generated JavaScript looks like. These options are as follows:

- `OBF`—Obfuscated mode. This is a non-human-readable, compressed version suitable for production use.
- `PRETTY`—Pretty-printed JavaScript with meaningful names.
- `DETAILED`—Pretty-printed JavaScript with fully qualified names.

To give you an idea of what these options mean, let's look at examples of `java.lang.StringBuffer` compiled in the three different modes. First, in listing 1.4, is the obfuscated mode.

Listing 1.4 `StringBuffer` in obfuscated compilation

```
function A0(){this.B0();return this.js[0];}
function C0(){if(this.js.length > 1)
{this.js = [this.js.join('')];this.length = this.js[0].length;}}
function D0(E0){this.js = [E0];this.length = E0.length;}
function Ez(F0,a1){return F0.yx(yZ(a1));}
function yB(b1){c1(b1);return b1;}
function c1(d1){d1.e1('');}
function zB(){}
_ = zB.prototype = new f();_.yx = w0;_.vB = A0;_.B0 = C0;_.e1 = D0;
_.i = 'java.lang.StringBuffer';_.j = 75;
function f1(){f1 = a;g1 = new iX();h1 = new iX();return window;}
```

Obfuscated mode is just that. This is intended to be the final compiled version of your application, which has names compressed and whitespace cleaned. Next is the pretty mode, shown in listing 1.5.

Listing 1.5 `StringBuffer` in pretty compilation

```
function _append2(_toAppend){
  var _last = this.js.length - 1;
  var _lastLength = this.js[_last].length;
  if (this.length > _lastLength * _lastLength) {
    this.js[_last] = this.js[_last] + _toAppend;
  }
   else {
    this.js.push(_toAppend);
  }
  this.length += _toAppend.length;
  return this;
}

function _toString0(){
  this._normalize();
  return this.js[0];
}

// Some stuff omitted.

function _$StringBuffer(_this$static){
  _$assign(_this$static);
  return _this$static;
}

function _$assign(_this$static){
  _this$static._assign0('');
}

function _StringBuffer(){
}
```

append() becomes _append2() to avoid collision

(1) toString() becomes _toString0()

```
_ = _StringBuffer.prototype = new _Object();
_._append = _append2;
_._toString = _toString0;
_._normalize = _normalize0;
_._assign0 = _assign;
_._typeName = 'java.lang.StringBuffer';     <-- _typeName holds name of original Java class
_._typeId = 75;
```

Pretty mode is useful for debugging as method names are somewhat preserved. However, collisions are resolved with suffixes, as the `_toString0()` method name shows ❶. Last, we have the detailed mode, as displayed in listing 1.6.

Listing 1.6 `StringBuffer` in detailed compilation

```
function java_lang_StringBuffer_append__Ljava_lang
        _String_2(toAppend){                     <-- ❶ Line broken for length
  var last = this.js.length - 1;
  var lastLength = this.js[last].length;
  if (this.length > lastLength * lastLength) {
    this.js[last] = this.js[last] + toAppend;
  }
   else {
    this.js.push(toAppend);
  }
  this.length += toAppend.length;                    Method names are fully qualified ❷
  return this;
}

function java_lang_StringBuffer_toString__(){
  this.normalize__();
  return this.js[0];
}

function java_lang_StringBuffer_normalize__(){
  if (this.js.length > 1) {
    this.js = [this.js.join('')];
    this.length = this.js[0].length;
  }
}

// . . . some stuff omitted

function java_lang_StringBuffer(){
}

_ = java_lang_StringBuffer.prototype = new java_lang_Object();
_.append__Ljava_lang_String_2 =
 java_lang_StringBuffer_append__Ljava_lang_String_2;
_.toString__ = java_lang_StringBuffer_toString__;
_.normalize__ = java_lang_StringBuffer_normalize__;
_.assign__Ljava_lang_String_2 =
 java_lang_StringBuffer_assign__Ljava_lang_String_2;
_.java_lang_Object_typeName = 'java.lang.StringBuffer';
_.java_lang_Object_typeId = 75;
```

Detailed mode preserves the full class name, as well as the method name ❷. For overloaded methods, the signature of the method is encoded into the name, as in the case of the `append()` method ❶.

There are some important concepts to grasp about this compilation structure, especially given the way GWT interacts with native JavaScript, through the JavaScript Native Interface (JSNI), which will be discussed in section 1.5.3. The names of your classes and methods in their JavaScript form aren't guaranteed, even for different compilations of the same application. Use of the special syntax provided with JSNI will let you invoke known JavaScript objects from your Java code and invoke your compiled Java classes from within JavaScript; but you can't freely invoke your JavaScript when using obfuscated style, predictably. This imposes certain limitations on your development:

- If you intend to expose your JavaScript API for external use, you need to create the references for calls into GWT code using JSNI registrations. We'll discuss how to do this in chapter 6.
- You can't rely on JavaScript naming in an object hash to give you java.lang.reflect.* type functionality, since the naming of methods isn't reliable.
- Although they're rare, you should consider potential conflicts with other JavaScript libraries you're including in your page, especially if you're publishing using the `PRETTY` setting.

In addition to being aware of the available compiler output options and how they affect your application, you should also be familiar with a few other compiler nuances.

1.5.2 Additional compiler nuances

Currently, the compiler is limited to J2SE 1.4 syntactical structures. This means that exposing generics or annotations in your GWT projects can cause problems. Other options are available for many of the purposes for which you might wish to use annotations. For example, you can often use JavaDoc-style annotations, to which GWT provides its own extensions.

Along with the J2SE 1.4 limitations, you also need to keep in mind the limited subset of Java classes that are supported in the GWT Java Runtime Environment (JRE) emulation library. This library is growing, and there are third-party extensions, but you need to be aware of the constructs you can use in client-side GWT code—the complete JRE you're accustomed to isn't available.

Of course, one of the great advantages of GWT's approach to compiling JavaScript from plain Java is that you get to leverage your existing toolbox while building your Ajax application. When you execute the hosted mode browser, you're running regularly compiled Java classes. This, again, means you can use all the standard Java tooling—static analysis tools, debuggers, IDEs, and the like.

These tools are useful for writing any code, but they become even more important in the GWT world because cleaning up your code means less transfer time to high-latency clients. Also, because JavaScript is a fairly slow execution environment, such cleanup can have a large impact on ultimate performance. The GWT compiler helps by optimizing the JavaScript it emits to include only classes and methods that are on the execution stack of your module and by using native browser functions where possible, but you should always keep the nature of JavaScript in mind. To that end, we'll now take a closer look at the lifecycle of a GWT compilation and at how this JavaScript is generated.

1.5.3 The compiler lifecycle

When the GWT compiler runs, it goes through several stages for building the final compiled project. In these stages, the need for the GWT module definition file becomes clear. First, the compiler identifies which combinations of files need to be built. Then, it generates any client-side code using the generator metaprogramming model. Last, it produces the final output. We'll look at each of these steps in the compiler lifecycle in more detail.

IDENTIFYING BUILD COMBINATIONS

One of the great strengths of GWT is that it builds specific versions of the application, each exactly targeted to what the client needs (user agent, locale, so on). This keeps the final download, and the operational overhead at the client level, very lean. A particular build combination is defined in the GWT module definition using a `<define-property>` tag. This establishes a base set of values that are used for the build. The first and very obvious property is the user agent that the JavaScript will be built for. Listing 1.7 shows the core GWT `UserAgent` module definition.

Listing 1.7 The GWT `UserAgent` definition

```
<define-property name="user.agent"
      values="ie6,gecko,gecko1_8,safari,opera"/>        ❶ Define valid options

<property-provider name="user.agent"><![CDATA[          Establish property-
    var ua = navigator.userAgent.toLowerCase();         provider JavaScript
    var makeVersion = function(result) {              ❷ implementation
        return (parseInt(result[1]) * 1000) +
        parseInt(result[2]);
    };

    if (ua.indexOf("opera") != -1) {                    Detect for Opera
      return "opera";
    } else if (ua.indexOf("webkit") != -1) {            Detect for Safari
      return "safari";
    } else if (ua.indexOf("msie") != -1) {              Detect for MSIE
      var result = /msie ([0-9]+)\.([0-9]+)/.exec(ua);
      if (result && result.length == 3) {
        if (makeVersion(result) >= 6000) {
          return "ie6";
        }
      }
    } else if (ua.indexOf("gecko") != -1) {             Detect for Gecko
      var result = /rv:([0-9]+)\.([0-9]+)/.exec(ua);
      if (result && result.length == 3) {
```

```
        if (makeVersion(result) >= 1008)
          return "gecko1_8";                    <— Detect for Gecko 1.8
        }
      return "gecko";
    }
    return "unknown";
]]></property-provider>
```

Here the <define-property> tag establishes a number of different builds that the final compiler will output ❶: in this case, ie6, gecko, gecko1_8, safari, and opera. This means each of these will be processed as a build of the final JavaScript that GWT emits. GWT can then switch implementations of classes based on properties using the <replace-with> tag in the module definition. As the GWT application starts up, the JavaScript snippet contained within the <property-provider> tag determines which of these implementations is used ❷. This snippet is built into the startup script that determines which compiled artifact is loaded by the client.

At the core of the GWT UI classes is the DOM class. This gets replaced based on the user.agent property. Listing 1.8 shows this definition.

Listing 1.8 Changing the DOM implementation by UserAgent

```
<inherits name="com.google.gwt.user.UserAgent"/>

<replace-with
  class="com.google.gwt.user.client.impl.DOMImplOpera">    <— DOM implementation for Opera
  <when-type-is class="com.google.gwt.user.client.impl.DOMImpl"/>
  <when-property-is name="user.agent" value="opera"/>
</replace-with>

<replace-with
  class=
"com.google.gwt.user.client.impl.DOMImplSafari">    <— DOM implementation for Safari
  <when-type-is class="com.google.gwt.user.client.impl.DOMImpl"/>
  <when-property-is name="user.agent" value="safari"/>
</replace-with>

<replace-with
  class="com.google.gwt.user.client.impl.DOMImplIE6">    <— DOM implementation for MSIE
  <when-type-is class="com.google.gwt.user.client.impl.DOMImpl"/>
  <when-property-is name="user.agent" value="ie6"/>
</replace-with>

<replace-with
  class=
"com.google.gwt.user.client.impl.DOMImplMozilla">    <— DOM implementation for Gecko 1.8
  <when-type-is class="com.google.gwt.user.client.impl.DOMImpl"/>
  <when-property-is name="user.agent" value="gecko1_8"/>
</replace-with>

<replace-with
  class=
"com.google.gwt.user.client.impl.DOMImplMozillaOld">    <— DOM implementation for Gecko
  <when-type-is class="com.google.gwt.user.client.impl.DOMImpl"/>
  <when-property-is name="user.agent" value="gecko"/>
</replace-with>
```

Now you can see the usefulness of this system. The basic DOM class is implemented with the same interface for each of the browsers, providing a core set of operations on which cross-platform code can easily be written. Classes replaced in this method can't be instantiated with simple constructors but must be created using the `GWT.create()` method. In practice, the DOM object is a singleton exposing static methods that are called by applications, so this `GWT.create()` invocation is still invisible. This is an important point to remember if you want to provide alternative implementations based on compile-time settings in your application. You can also define your own properties and property providers for switching implementations. We have found that doing this for different runtime settings can be useful. For example, we have defined debug, test, and production settings, and replacing some functionality in the application based on this property can help smooth development in certain cases.

This technique of identifying build combinations and then spinning off into specific implementations during the compile process is known in GWT terms as *deferred binding*. The GWT documentation sums this approach up as "the Google Web Toolkit answer to Java reflection." Dynamic loading of classes (dynamic binding) isn't truly available in a JavaScript environment, so GWT provides another way. For example, `obj.getClass().getName()` isn't available, but `GWT.getTypeName(obj)` is. The same is true for `Class.forName("MyClass")`, which has `GWT.create(MyClass)` as a counterpart. By using deferred binding, the GWT compiler can figure out every possible variation, or *axis*, for every type and feature needed at compile time. Then, at runtime, the correct permutation for the context in use can be downloaded and run.

Remember, though, that each axis you add becomes a combinatory compile. If you use 4 languages and 4 browser versions, you must compile 16 final versions of the application; and if you use several runtime settings, you end up with many more combinations in the mix. This concept is depicted in figure 1.5.

Compiling a new monolithic version of your application for each axis doesn't affect your end users negatively. Rather, this technique allows each user to download only the exact application version he needs, without taking any unused portion along for the ride. This is beneficial for users, but it slows compile time considerably, and it can be a painful point for developers.

Reducing the compile variants to speed up compile time

Even though GWT compile time can be long, keep in mind that the end result for users is well optimized. Also, the GWT module system allows you to tweak the compile time variants for the situation. During day-to-day development, you may want to use the `<set-property>` tag in your module definition to confine the compile to a single language, or single browser version, to speed up the compile step.

Another important use for module properties is in code generation, which is the next step of the compilation process.

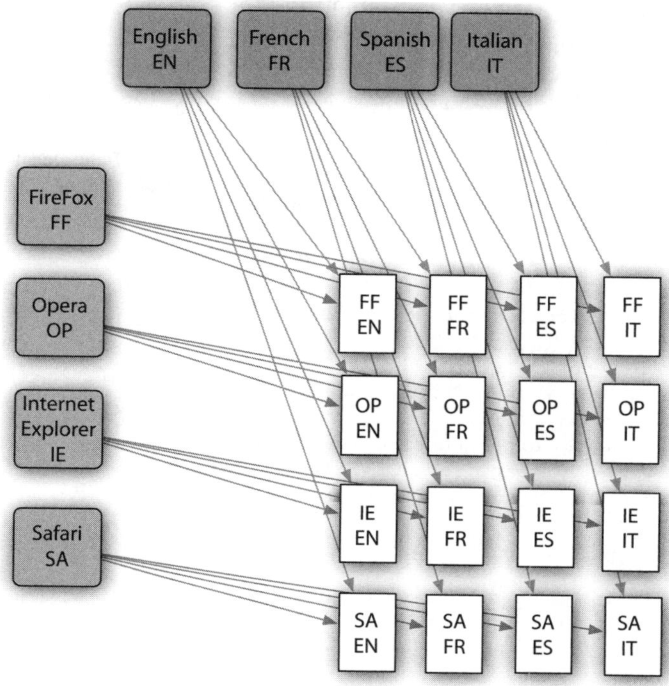

Figure 1.5 Multiple versions of a GWT application are created by the compiler for each axis or variant application property, such as user agent and locale.

GENERATING CODE

GWT's compiler includes a code generation or metaprogramming facility that allows you to generate code based on module properties at compile time. Perhaps the best example is the internationalization support. The i18n module defines several no-method interfaces that you extend to define `Constants`, `Messages` (which include in-text replacement), or `Dictionary` classes (which extract values from the HTML host page). The implementations of each of these classes are built at compile time using the code generation facility, producing a lean, custom version of your application in each language. The i18n module does this through the `<extend-property>` tag, which lets you add additional iterative values to a property in a module. Listing 1.9 demonstrates the use of this concept to add French and Italian support to a GWT application.

Listing 1.9 Defining French and Italian using `extend-property`

```
<extend-property name="locale" values="fr" />
<extend-property name="locale" values="it" />
```

When an application inherits the i18n module, the GWT compiler searches for interfaces that extend one of the i18n classes and generates an implementation for the class based on a resource bundle matching the language code. This is accomplished via the `<generate-with>` tag in the i18n module definition. Listing 1.10 shows this along with the <property-provider> tag, which is used for establishing which language will be needed at runtime.

Listing 1.10 The i18n module's `locale` property declarations

```
<define-property name="locale" values="default" />      ❶ Define locale property

<property-provider name="locale">      ❷ Establish property-provider
    <![CDATA[
    try {
      var locale;

      // Look for the locale as a url argument
      if (locale == null) {
        var args = location.search;
        var startLang = args.indexOf("locale");
        if (startLang >= 0) {
          var language = args.substring(startLang);
          var begin = language.indexOf("=") + 1;
          var end = language.indexOf("&");
          if (end == -1) {
            end = language.length;
          }
          locale = language.substring(begin, end);
        }
      }

      if (locale == null) {
        // Look for the locale on the web page
        locale = __gwt_getMetaProperty("locale")
      }

      if (locale == null) {
        return "default";
      }

      while (!__gwt_isKnownPropertyValue("locale",  locale)) {
        var lastIndex = locale.lastIndexOf("_");
        if (lastIndex == -1) {
           locale = "default";
          break;
        } else {
          locale = locale.substring(0,lastIndex);
        }
      }
      return locale;
    } catch(e) {
      alert("Unexpected exception in locale "+
            "detection, using default: "
             + e);
      return "default";
    }
    ]]>
</property-provider>

<generate-with
    class=
```

```
"com.google.gwt.i18n.rebind.LocalizableGenerator">      <-- ❸ Define generator for Localizable
    <when-type-assignable class=
"com.google.gwt.i18n.client.Localizable" />
</generate-with>
```

The module first establishes the `locale` property ❶. This is the property we extended in listing 1.9 to include `it` and `fr`. Next, the property provider is defined ❷. The value is checked first as a parameter on the request URL in the format `locale=xx` and then as a `<meta>` tag on the host page in the format `<meta name="gwt:property" content="locale=x_Y">`; finally, it defaults to `default`.

The last step is to define a generator class. Here it tells the compiler to generate implementations of all classes that extend or implement `Localizable` with the `LocalizableGenerator` ❸. This class writes out Java files that implement the appropriate interfaces for each of the user's defined `Constants`, `Messages`, or `Dictionary` classes.

Notice that, to this point, nowhere have we dealt specifically with JavaScript outside of small snippets in the modules. GWT will produce the JavaScript in the final step.

PRODUCING OUTPUT

It should be clear from the previous subsections that you can do a great deal from Java with the GWT module system, but you may need to get down to JavaScript-level implementations at some point if you wish to integrate existing JavaScript or extend or add lower-level components. For this, GWT includes JSNI. This is a special syntax that allows you to define method implementations on a Java class using JavaScript. Listing 1.11 shows a simple JSNI method.

Listing 1.11 A simple JSNI method

```
public class Alert {

    public Alert() {
        super();
    }
    public native void alert(String message)      <-- Define using native keyword
    /*-{                                          <-- Surround with special comment
        alert(message);
    }-*/;
}
```

In this listing, we first define the `alert()` method using the `native` keyword. Much like the Java Native Interface (JNI) in regular Java, this indicates that we are going to use a native implementation of this method. Unlike JNI, the implementation lives right in the Java file, surrounded by a special `/*- -*/` comment syntax. To reference Java code from JavaScript implementations, syntax similar to JNI is provided. Figure 1.6 shows the structure of calls back into Java from JavaScript.

GWT reuses the JNI typing system to reference Java types. We'll look at JSNI in more detail in chapter 6. As we mentioned previously, the final compiled output will have synthetic names for methods and classes, so the use of this syntax is important to ensure that GWT knows how to direct a call from JavaScript.

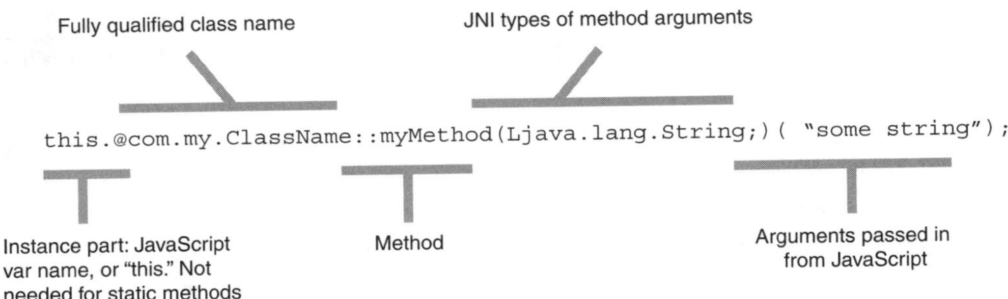

Figure 1.6 The structure of JSNI call syntax

In the final step of the compilation process, GWT takes all the Java files, whether provided or generated, and the JSNI method implementations, and examines the call tree, pruning unused methods and attributes. Then it transforms all of this into a number of unique JavaScript files, targeted very specifically at each needed axis. This minimizes both code download time and execution time in the client. Although this complex compilation process can be time consuming for the developer, it ensures that the end user's experience is the best it can possibly be for the application that is being built.

We'll come back to certain compiler aspects as we work through concrete examples throughout the book. For now, our discussion of the compiler lifecycle, deferred binding, generators, compiler output and JSNI, and some additional nuances completes our initial introduction to the core of GWT.

1.6 Summary

GWT is much more than another Ajax library or another web development tool. GWT adopts a fundamentally different approach by moving familiar development patterns around, providing a cross-compiler from Java to JavaScript and making greater use of the web browser as a "chubby client." This represents a step between the three-tier architecture of the 1980s fat clients and the thin client architecture of both the 1970s and 1990s.

GWT borrows from the approaches that have come before it and takes things in a new direction, expanding the web development frontiers. All the while, GWT maintains the advantages of traditional compiled-language development by starting out from Java; and it adopts the successful component-oriented development approach, applying these concepts to the web tier in a responsive Ajax fashion.

In addition to starting with Java, GWT also embraces the parts of the web that have worked well and allows developers and users to remain on familiar ground. This is an overlooked yet significant aspect of GWT. GWT doesn't try to hide the web from you, just to achieve the moniker "rich web application." Instead, GWT happily integrates with and uses HTML, JavaScript, and CSS.

Enhancing the tools for developing the rich web applications that Google is known for makes sense, but why share these tools with the world? This reasoning isn't complicated, but it's impressive and refreshing. Brett Taylor, the GWT product manager, sums it up nicely: "What's good for the web is good for Google." This sort of rising-tide approach makes sense for a web company such as Google.

In the next two chapters that round out part 1 of this book, we'll break down the components of GWT, which we've introduced in this chapter. Chapter 2 gets you up and running with a basic example of a client-side GWT application, which will reinforce the core concepts we have introduced here and illustrate important design patterns for utilizing the web browser in a new way—as a fully featured client. In chapter 3, we'll cover GWT RPCs, object serialization, and communicating with servers.

In part 2, we'll delve into practical details. We'll discuss building, packaging, and deploying GWT applications, and we'll look more closely at many of the GWT tools and features. These include examining a small but complete application to reinforce the front-to-back canonical GWT approach, other means for communicating with servers, using JSNI to integrate with JavaScript libraries and idioms, and testing and continuous integration.

In part 3, we'll present several complete example applications. They will further illustrate both client-side and server-side elements, including data binding, advanced UI concepts, streaming, and integration with traditional JEE components.

2 A New Kind of Client

This chapter covers

- Basic GWT project structure
- Design patterns and GWT
- Creating a client-side GWT application
- Using CSS with GWT

A beginning is the time for taking the most delicate care that the balances are correct.

—Frank Herbert

In the first chapter, we looked at the foundation and vocabulary we'll need to work with GWT. In this chapter, we'll be looking at how to build on top of that foundation. GWT provides a rather unique method for creating web applications, and some of its conventions may seem a bit foreign at first. Because of this, we'll take a look at a fairly basic project for our first example.

Our first *in Practice* foray into GWT will be a calculator project, where we'll restrict our focus to the client side of the picture. Using a simple and familiar construct such as this will allow us to revisit, and reinforce, some of the fundamental GWT concepts we looked at in chapter 1, such as project layout, modules, host

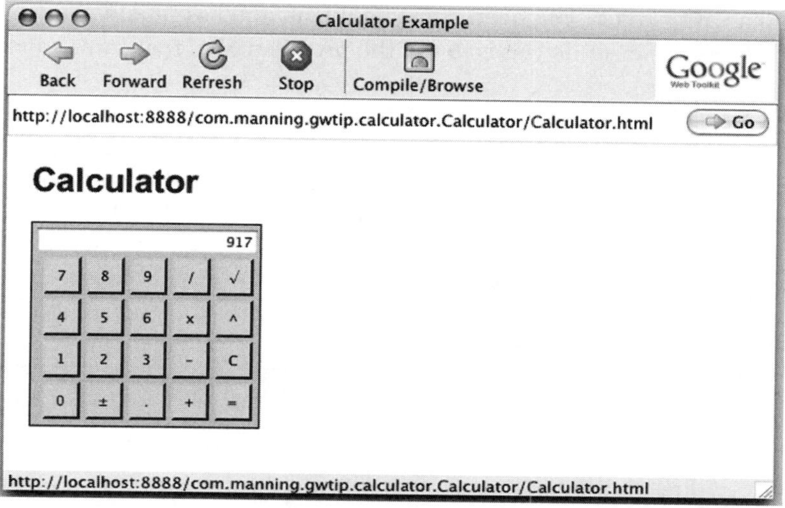

Figure 2.1 The GWT calculator example, demonstrating client-side autonomy for data, logic, and the UI

pages, entry points, and bootstrapping. Additionally, this project will allow us to introduce the use of several important architectural and design patterns in a GWT context, including MVC—an important pattern that you will see reused throughout the book. We'll also begin working with UI `Widget` classes and styling components using CSS.

Our completed GWT calculator will look like the one shown in figure 2.1. This first example is intentionally simple, but the patterns and approach we'll introduce are key to understanding how you can leverage GWT as a rich client platform.

As we build our calculator example, we'll not focus on using any particular tools other than GWT itself. We won't be using an IDE or any special build scripts this time. Instead, we'll concentrate on what is going on behind the scenes. Once we have covered that ground, we'll add the convenience of IDEs and other tools in later chapters. Such tools are very useful with GWT, and they can greatly enhance productivity, but it's important to understand the concepts themselves first. In this chapter we'll use the command line and a text editor.

We'll begin with a recap of project layout and the basic components, introduced in chapter 1. Though this is basic material, there are some subtleties involved, and it's important to know and understand it as part of the GWT foundation.

2.1 Basic project structure and components

Our first step is to consider and understand the project layout, and the basic components required—host pages, entry points, and modules, all of which were introduced in chapter 1. These are the core of every GWT project, and this is where we need to start, to fill in a bit more detail.

To begin a GWT project, you need to create the default layout and generate the initial files. The easiest way to do this is to use the provided `ApplicationCreator` tool.

2.1.1 Generating a project

`ApplicationCreator` is provided by GWT to create the default starting points and layout for a GWT project. `ApplicationCreator`, like the GWT shell and compiler, supports several command-line parameters, which are listed in table 2.1.

```
ApplicationCreator [-eclipse projectName] [-out dir] [-overwrite]
    [-ignore] className
```

Table 2.1 `ApplicationCreator` command-line parameters

Parameter	Description
`-eclipse`	Creates a debug launch configuration for the named eclipse project.
`-out`	The directory to which output files will be written (defaults to the current directory).
`-overwrite`	Overwrites any existing files.
`-ignore`	Ignores any existing files; does not overwrite.
`className`	The fully qualified name of the application class to be created.

To stub out our calculator project, we'll use `ApplicationCreator` based on a relative GWT_HOME path, and a `className` of `com.manning.gwtip.calculator.client.Calculator`, as follows:

```
mkdir [PROJECT_HOME]
cd [PROJECT_HOME]
[GWT_HOME]/applicationCreator
  com.manning.gwtip.calculator.client.Calculator
```

NOTE *GWT_HOME* It is recommended that you establish GWT_HOME as an environment variable referring to the filesystem location where you have unpacked GWT. Additionally, you may want to add GWT_HOME to your PATH for further convenience. Throughout this book, we'll refer to GWT_HOME when referencing the location where GWT is installed. We'll also use PROJECT_HOME to refer to the location of the current project.

PATH SEPARATORS For convenience, when referring to filesystem paths, we'll use forward slashes, which work for two-thirds of supported GWT platforms. If you are using Windows, please adjust the path separators to use backward slashes.

Running `ApplicationCreator` as described creates the default src directory structure and the starting-point GWT file resources. The next thing we need to do is take a look at this output and begin customizing and extending it to build our calculator.

2.1.2 The standard directory structure

Even though it's quite simple, the GWT layout is very important because the toolkit can operate in keeping with a Convention over Configuration design approach. As we'll see, several parts of the GWT compilation process make assumptions about the default layout. Because of this, not everything has to be explicitly defined in every instance (which cuts down on the amount of configuration required).

Taking a look at the output of the `ApplicationCreator` script execution, you will see a specific structure and related contents, as shown in listing 2.1. This represents the default configuration for a GWT project.

Listing 2.1 `ApplicationCreator` output, showing the default GWT project structure

```
src
src/com
src/com/manning
src/com/manning/gwtip
src/com/manning/gwtip/calculator
src/com/manning/gwtip/calculator/Calculator.gwt.xml
src/com/manning/gwtip/calculator/client                      ❶ Client source path
src/com/manning/gwtip/calculator/client/Calculator.java
src/com/manning/gwtip/calculator/public                      ❷ Public path
src/com/manning/gwtip/calculator/public/Calculator.html
Calculator-shell.sh
Calculator-compile.sh
```

The package name, `com.manning.gwtip.calculator`, is represented in the structure as a series of subdirectories in the src tree. This is the standard Java convention, and there are notably separate client and public subdirectories within.

The client directory is intended for resources that will be compiled into JavaScript ❶. Client items are *translatable*, or serializable, and will ultimately be downloaded to a client browser—these are Java resources in the source. The client package is known in GWT terminology as the *source path*.

The public directory denotes files that will also be distributed to the client, but that do *not* require compilation and translation to JavaScript ❷. This typically includes CSS, images, static HTML, and any other such assets that should not be translated, including existing JavaScript. The public package is known as the *public path*.

Note that our client-side example does not use any server resources, but GWT does include the concept of a server path/package for server-side resources. In chapter 3 we'll get into our first server-related example, where the server path will come into play.

Figure 2.2 illustrates this default GWT project layout.

Along with the structure that `ApplicationCreator` provides, you will notice that some new files have appeared. These files are the main starting points for any GWT project.

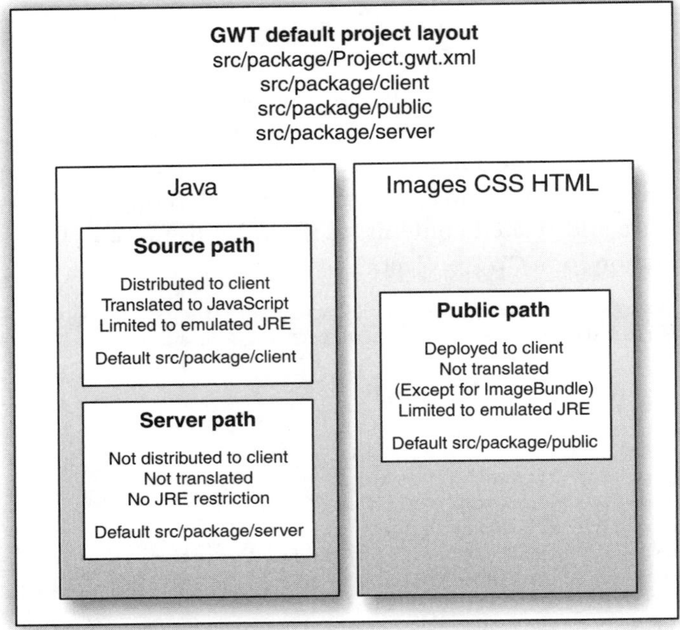

Figure 2.2 Default GWT project layout showing the separation of Java code for the client and server, and other non-Java assets

2.1.3 GWT starting point files

`ApplicationCreator` generates the structure and a required set of minimal files for a GWT project. The generated files include the XML configuration module definition, the entry point Java class, and the HTML host page. These are some of the basic GWT project concepts we first met in chapter 1. We'll revisit these briefly to add a bit more detail to the picture, and to complete the setup for our calculator project.

Along with the module definition, entry point, and host page, some shortcut scripts have also been created for use with the `GWTShell` and `GWTCompiler` tools. These scripts run the shell and compiler for the project. Table 2.2 lists all of the files created by `ApplicationCreator`: the basic resources and shortcut scripts needed for a GWT project.

The starting points `ApplicationCreator` provides essentially wire up all the moving parts for you and stub out your project. You take it from there and modify these generated files to begin building a GWT application. If the toolkit did not provide these files via `ApplicationCreator`, getting a project started, at least initially, would be much more time consuming and confusing. Once you are experienced in the GWT ways, you may wind up using other tools to kick off a project: an IDE plugin, a Maven "archetype," or your own scripts. `ApplicationCreator` is the helpful default. The contents and structure that `ApplicationCreator` provides are themselves a working GWT "Hello World" example. You get "Hello World" for free, out of the box.

"Hello World," however, is not that interesting. The connection of all the moving parts is what is really important; how a host page includes a module, how a module

Table 2.2 `ApplicationCreator`-generated initial project files that serve as a starting point for GWT applications

File	Name	Purpose
GWT module file	ProjectName.gwt.xml	Defines the project configuration.
Entry point class	ProjectName.java	Starting class invoked by the module.
Host page	ProjectName.html	Initial HTML page that loads the module.
`GWTShell` shortcut invoker script	ProjectName-shell.sh	Invokes `GWTShell` for the project.
`GWTCompiler` shortcut invoker script	ProjectName-compile.sh	Invokes `GWTCompiler` for the project.

describes project resources, and how an entry point invokes project code. These concepts are applicable to all levels of GWT projects—the basic ones and beyond. Understanding these parts is key to gaining an overall understanding of GWT. Next, we'll take a closer look at each of these concepts, beginning with the host page.

2.1.4 Host pages

A host page is the initial HTML page that invokes a GWT application. A host page, as we learned in chapter 1, contains a script tag that references a special GWT JavaScript file, Module.nocache.js. This JavaScript file, which the toolkit provides when you compile your project, kicks off the GWT application loading process. We saw the calculator project host page, Calculator.html, in chapter 1 (listing 1.2) as we introduced the basic GWT concepts.

Along with the script reference that loads the project resources, you can also specify several GWT-related `<meta>` tags in the host page. These tag options are not present in the default host page created by `ApplicationCreator`, nor are they used in our calculator example, but it's still important to be aware of them. The GWT `<meta>` tags that are supported in a host page are listed in table 2.3, as a reference.

Table 2.3 GWT `<meta>` tags supported in host pages

Meta tag	Syntax	Purpose
`gwt:module`	`<meta name="gwt:module" content="_module-name_">`	(Legacy, pre GWT 1.4.) Specifies the module to be loaded.
`gwt:property`	`<meta name="gwt:property" content="_name_=_value_">`	Statically defines a deferred binding client property.
`gwt:onPropertyErrorFn`	`<meta name="gwt:onPropertyErrorFn" content="_fnName_">`	Specifies the name of a function to call if a client property is set to an invalid value (meaning that no matching compilation will be found).

Table 2.3 GWT <meta> tags supported in host pages *(continued)*

Meta tag	Syntax	Purpose
`gwt:onLoadErrorFn`	`<meta name="gwt:onLoadErrorFn" content="_fnName_">`	Specifies the name of a function to call if an exception happens during bootstrapping or if a module throws an exception out of `onModuleLoad()`; the function should take a message parameter.

Thus, a host page includes a script reference that gets the GWT process started and refers to all the required project resources. The required resources for a project are assembled by the GWT compilation process, and are based on the module configuration.

2.1.5 Modules

GWT applications inhabit a challenging environment. This is partly because of the scope of responsibility GWT has elected to take on and partly because of the Internet landscape. Being a rich Internet-based platform and using only the basic built-in browser support for HTML, CSS, and JavaScript makes GWT quite impressive, but this is tough to achieve. Browsers that are "guided" by standards, but don't always stick to them, add to the pressure. Couple that environment with an approach that aims to bring static types, code standards, testing and debugging, inheritance, and reuse to the web tier, and you have a tall order.

To help with this large task, GWT uses modules as configuration and execution units that handle discreet areas of responsibility. Modules, which we introduced in chapter 1, enable the GWT compiler to optimize the Java code it gets fed, create variants for all possible situations from a single code base, and make inheritance and property support possible.

One of the most important resources generated by the `ApplicationCreator` is the Module.gwt.xml module descriptor for your project. This file exists in the top-level directory of your project's package and provides a means to define resource locations and structure.

In a default generated module file, there are only two elements: `<inherits>` and `<entry-point>`. To briefly recap our discussion in chapter 1, an `<inherits>` element simply includes the configuration for another named GWT module in the current definition, and `<entry-point>` defines a class that kicks things off and moves from configuration to code.

Table 2.4 provides an overview of the most common GWT module descriptor elements. These include some elements we have already seen, and several other additional items that are neither present in a default generated module file, nor used in our calculator, but again are included for reference.

Table 2.4 A summary of the most common elements supported by the GWT module descriptor

Module element	Description
`<inherits>`	Identifies additional GWT modules that should be inherited into the current module.
`<entry-point>`	Specifies which `EntryPoint` class should be invoked when starting a GWT project.
`<source>`	Identifies where the source code that should be translated into JavaScript by the GWT compiler is located.
`<public>`	Identifies where assets that are not translatable source code, such as images and CSS files, are located.
`<script>`	Injects a script element into a GWT module, ensuring it is present when inherited.
`<stylesheet>`	Injects a stylesheet into a GWT module, ensuring it is present when inherited.
`<servlet>`	Specifies the path to GWT RPC Service Servlet resources.
`<define-property>`	Initially defines properties.
`<set-property>`	Sets property values; for example, it is used in the `UserAgent` module to define the set of supported browsers.
`<extend-property>`	Specifies property value extensions; often used to specify locale information.
`<replace-with>`	Replaces components at runtime based on a decision process, such as different implementations for different browser versions.

The calculator module file from chapter 1 (listing 1.1) is a simple default module file, with the addition of an injected stylesheet via the `<stylesheet>` tag. By using either the `<script>` or `<stylesheet>` tags, you can guarantee that those resources will be available with your module when it's deployed. The difference between resource injection and simply adding a stylesheet reference, or script, to the HTML on your host page is that the module is in control. If you build libraries with GWT, or share entire projects (which we'll address in chapter 7), the host page is not distributed with your project. Users of your library will, therefore, not be using the same host page, and will not link to the same stylesheet. Script and stylesheet elements in host pages do work, but they are not certain to be present when others use your modules—injected resources are. Modules can bring other resources along with them, if needed.

Though the three lines of configuration in listing 1.1 may seem very simple, there is a bit more going on than meets the eye. GWT modules understand several default values for important properties. For example, the source path and public path locations are, by default, the client and public packages on the classpath, respectively. Because no other configuration is explicitly specified, our calculator project uses these defaults.

Modules are therefore significant on a number of fronts. In addition to setting configuration and properties, they also provide resources for projects, enable inheritance, give the compiler hints, and play a central role in the bootstrapping process. Once the bootstrap determines the correct permutation of an application, via the nocache script for a particular module, an entry point is invoked.

2.1.6 Entry points

An entry point class, as we have learned, is simply the first project-specific code every GWT application invokes. This is generally where the first browser-based element is accessed, and it's typically done with the static `RootPanel.get()` method. The `RootPanel`, as chapter 1 noted, is a default container that is inserted directly after the HTML `</body>` tag. With a reference to this panel, you can then compose your project and insert other elements from there.

We saw the entry point class of our calculator example in chapter 1 (listing 1.3). This class was a default `EntryPoint` implementation with the template "Hello World" code removed, and a new custom widget, `CalculatorWidget` (which we have yet to create), added.

With an entry point in place, our calculator project can now go from the HTTP request on the host page, through the configuration provided by the module descriptor, to additional JavaScript code (built from Java) included in the module.

This process is the same for every GWT project. Whether you are building an entire application with multiple module inheritance, or just a single widget in a single module, the bootstrap we have discussed, from configuration to code, is the same.

With configuration covered, and the GWT startup steps defined, our calculator example is ready to be implemented. We now need to create the `CalculatorWidget` referenced by the entry point class, and the rest of the calculator code. We'll do that next, and along the way we'll cover some important considerations for client-side design with GWT.

2.2 Design patterns and GWT

Since the calculator `EntryPoint` implementation (shown in listing 1.3) places a `CalculatorWidget` on the `RootPanel`, we now need to provide this widget. This will be our own widget, composed of basic GWT components. `CalculatorWidget` will contain the view for our calculator application, a simple data and logic layer as the model, and an intermediary controller between these layers. This, of course, means we'll be getting our first look at MVC and GWT together—keep in mind that all of these components will end up distributed to the client.

MVC will be the overarching pattern for the macro level of our application. Additionally, we'll use some other common object-oriented (OO) patterns on other levels because of the general benefits these approaches provide. For example, we'll use the Observer pattern for event handling as part of the mechanism of communication between our model and our view. We'll also use the Strategy pattern within the logic and operations parts of our model. We'll provide more detail about each of these patterns, and the reasoning behind their use in each situation, as we come to those portions of the application.

The most important pattern we need to consider is MVC itself. This pattern is the most useful we have found for creating GWT applications, while still keeping them manageable and testable.

2.2.1 MVC and GWT

MVC is a familiar pattern to many developers. The pattern was first described in the late 70s by Trygve Reenskaug, who was working on Smalltalk at the time, and it has since been adopted, in various forms, by a wide range of programmers using many languages. The pattern is intended to separate responsibilities and allow for reuse of the logic and data portion of an application—the *model*. The *view* layer represents the model graphically, as the UI. Delegation between these layers is handled by an intermediary that is invoked by the user's input, the *controller*. The basic MVC pattern is shown in figure 2.3.

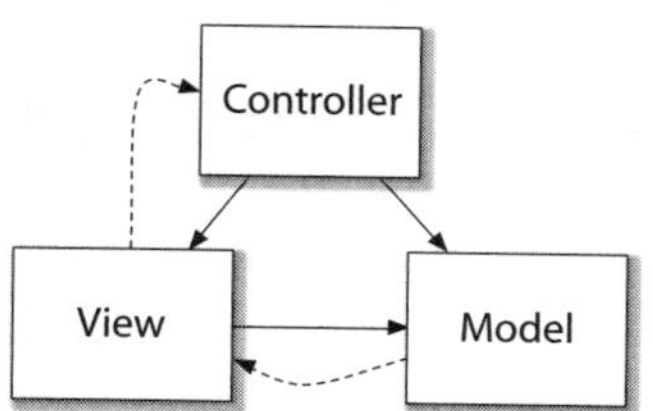

Figure 2.3 A basic model-view-controller architectural pattern diagram. The solid lines indicate a direct association, and the dashed lines indicate an indirect association, such as through an observer/observable relationship.

The key concepts to take away from MVC are the following: the model should be completely unaware of the view and controller, and the pattern can be applied on many different levels within an application.

In MVC, the model can be equipped to alert observers of changes within it, using the Observer pattern (something we'll look more closely at in section 2.2.3). This is shown by the dashed line in figure 2.3. In this way, any other layer observing the model can react to events coming from the model. Nevertheless, the model does not directly update the view, and this distinction is important. The model is the reusable part in all incarnations of MVC; if the model had any direct knowledge of the view, that tenet would break down. How the view and controller are linked together is often more variable.

The view typically has a reference to the controller, and may invoke controller methods directly, based on user input. The controller ideally will have no direct references back to the view, and should simply update the model. If the view is an observer of the model, this effectively updates the view without direct controller/view coupling. Alternatively, it's also common to see situations in which the controller and view are treated as a pair, with direct references from the controller to the view.

There are many ways to divide up the responsibilities, and the various approaches have their pros and cons. The important part, though, is that the separation of responsibilities makes the code clearer, and often also makes testing easier. We'll come back to the concept of testing, and how it relates to the MVC pattern, in chapter 8.

MVC can be applied with GWT, and it can happen on many different levels. An overall application may have a master domain, or model, and an overarching controller.

Individual widgets can have their own encapsulated MVC, and small elements, such as a button, can repeat the pattern on their own level.

The possible variations of MVC, and many somewhat similar GUI architectural patterns, such as Presentation Abstraction Control (PAC) and Model View Presenter (MVP), are very interesting but are beyond our scope here. Fortunately, entire tomes on the subject exist. For our purposes, we'll turn to concrete examples of MVC that we have found work well with GWT. To do this, we need to get into code and implement the pattern.

2.2.2 Creating a widget

The functional specifications for a calculator (at least a simple one) are fairly universal; they include a display, some buttons, and some mathematical operations defined by the likes of Pythagoras and Euclid. For our calculator, we'll make use of one GWT `TextBox` for the display and many GWT `Buttons` for, well, the buttons. We'll also use a layout derived from a `Panel` and a `Grid` to control the overall placement of the UI items. In terms of MVC, view elements are where all widgets begin, starting with the layout. The model and controller for our calculator will be implemented as separate classes that are referenced by the widget.

With GWT, you use widgets to create your application. These components are built from layout panels, input elements, events, data objects, and various combinations thereof. This is where GWT really departs from typical web applications and may seem somewhat foreign to those accustomed to standard server-side Java development. To create an application, you use widgets that are capable of being inserted or removed from the screen, in a single page, on the client side.

For our purposes, we'll extend the GWT-provided `VerticalPanel` component to build our view, and then include references to our separate controller and model, as shown in the class diagram in figure 2.4.

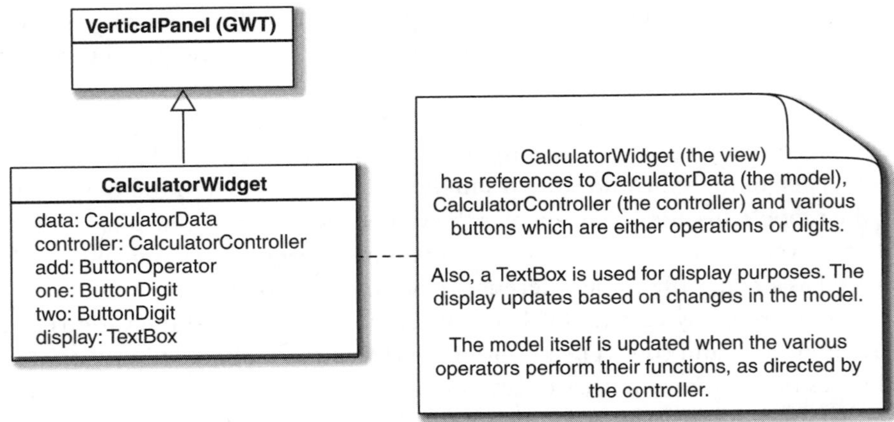

Figure 2.4 `CalculatorWidget` top-level class diagram showing the extension of GWT's `VerticalPanel` as the view, and the included model and controller references

It's worth noting that figure 2.4 does not display all the attributes or operations of the `CalculatorWidget` class. We have included just a representative sample of attributes to keep it concise. The code for the `CalculatorWidget` will be displayed in three parts in listings 2.2, 2.3, and 2.4. Listing 2.2 addresses the beginning of the class, showing what the class needs to import and how the class is derived from, and makes use of, other existing GWT classes.

Listing 2.2 CalculatorWidget.java, part one

```
package com.manning.gwtip.calculator.client;

import com.google.gwt.user.client.ui.Button;
import com.google.gwt.user.client.ui.ClickListener;
import com.google.gwt.user.client.ui.Grid;
import com.google.gwt.user.client.ui.TextBox;
import com.google.gwt.user.client.ui.VerticalPanel;

//. . . remainder of imports omitted

public class CalculatorWidget extends VerticalPanel {
    private TextBox display;

    public CalculatorWidget(final String title) {
        super();

        final CalculatorData data = new CalculatorData();

       final CalculatorController controller =
new CalculatorController(data);

//...
```

❶ Import existing GWT widgets
❷ Extend GWT VerticalPanel
❸ Instantiate CalculatorController

Within the first part of the `CalculatorWidget` class there are several important items. First of all, we're making use of some existing GWT `client.ui` classes to compose our view ❶. Our entire class is, in fact, a subclass of `VerticalPanel` ❷. This is significant in that we inherit all of the hierarchy of a GWT UI `Widget` automatically with this approach.

Directly extending a panel in this manner is simple (in this case, intentionally so), but it's also limiting. It's often better to use a GWT `Composite`. We're using direct subclassing here to keep things very basic, and we'll move on to `Composite` in due course.

In listing 2.2 we then go on to define a simple constructor, and within it we create an instance of `CalculatorController` ❸. `CalculatorController` itself will be addressed in section 2.2.5, after we complete the `CalculatorWidget` class. The controller we'll be using is a client-side component, which itself contains a reference to the data portion of our model, which is a single `CalculatorData` object.

That takes us to part two of the `CalculatorWidget` class: layout and buttons. These view elements are displayed in listing 2.3.

Listing 2.3 CalculatorWidget.java, part two

```
    VerticalPanel p = new VerticalPanel();
    p.setHorizontalAlignment(VerticalPanel.ALIGN_RIGHT);
    p.setStyleName(CalculatorConstants.STYLE_PANEL);

    Grid g = new Grid(4, 5);                                          ❶ Use GWT Grid
    g.setStyleName(CalculatorConstants.STYLE_GRID);                      for layout

    final Button zero =
new ButtonDigit(controller, "0");
    g.setWidget(3, 0, zero);
                                                   ❷ Add ButtonDigits
    final Button one =
new ButtonDigit(controller, "1");
    g.setWidget(2, 0, one);

    final Button two =
new ButtonDigit(controller, "2");
    g.setWidget(2, 1, two);

    //. . .

    final Button divide = new ButtonOperator(controller,
            new OperatorDivide());
    g.setWidget(0, 3, divide);                          Add ButtonOperators ❸

    final Button multiply = new ButtonOperator(controller,
            new OperatorMultiply());
    g.setWidget(1, 3, multiply);

    //. . .
                                                      ❹ Add standard
    final Button clear =                                  GWT Button
new Button(CalculatorConstants.CLEAR);
    clear.addClickListener(new ClickListener() {
            public void onClick(Widget sender) {
                controller.processClear();
            }
        });
    clear.setStyleName(CalculatorConstants.STYLE_BUTTON);
    g.setWidget(2, 4, clear);

  //...
```

In this second part of the `CalculatorWidget` class, we add components to our widget and add event handlers for those components. First, we create a GWT `Grid` ❶, a component made of rows and columns that ultimately will be implemented as an HTML table. We'll use this to lay out our calculator buttons. Then we add our two different types of buttons: `ButtonDigit` ❷ and `ButtonOperator` ❸. The digits on our calculator are implemented by our own class, `ButtonDigit`, which extends the GWT `Button` class. The operators are similarly implemented by our own `ButtonOperator` class. For the sake of brevity, we have not included the code for all the fairly self-explanatory buttons and operators (complete code for this and all other examples in the book is located on the Manning website).

We have yet to create ButtonDigit and ButtonOperator, which we'll do next, but the important thing to know at this point is that these classes both implement a ClickListener. This listener gets the control when the buttons are clicked, and it invokes a controller method. Listeners are common in component-oriented development and enable an event-driven approach. Various listeners, such as ClickListeners, OnChangeListeners, KeyboardListeners, and more are available in GWT. By using listeners in this way, the controller is notified to perform an appropriate action when any button or operator is pressed on our calculator.

> **NOTE** *About KeyboardListeners* In this example, we have not attached KeyboardListeners to our calculator, for brevity's sake. But, obviously, including them would be very useful for a calculator. They can be enabled by setting a default focus element and then attaching the listeners.

Finally, we also add a standard GWT Button for both our calculator's CLEAR and EQUALS functions ❹. These buttons directly invoke methods on our controller instance without our own Button subclass. This is done with regard to CLEAR and EQUALS because these are special cases in terms of calculator buttons, as we shall see when we get to the controller in the next section.

Before moving on, though, we need to implement the remainder of the CalculatorWidget, as shown in listing 2.4.

Listing 2.4 CalculatorWidget.java, part three

```
    // . . .
      display = new TextBox();                          ❶

      data.addChangeListener(
new CalculatorChangeListener() {                            ❷
              public void onChange(CalculatorData data) {
                  display.setText(
String.valueOf(data.getDisplay()));                 ◁─┐
              }                                       │
          });
      display.setText("0");
      display.setTextAlignment(TextBox.ALIGN_RIGHT);

      p.add(display);         │
      p.add(g);               │ ❸
      this.add(p);            │

    }
}
```

❶ Create TextBox for display
❷ Create anonymous CalculatorChangeListener
Update view on model changes
❸ Add display and grid to panel, panel to widget

The final part of the CalculatorWidget class creates a GWT TextBox for our calculator's display area ❶, and then adds that component and our Grid to an earlier created VerticalPanel, which is in turn added to the current instance of itself. This ensures that all of the items are visible when CalculatorWidget is used ❸.

Getting back to event handling, we have also introduced a custom listener—our own CalculatorChangeListener interface ❷. This is implemented as an anonymous inner class, and it connects our display widget (the view) to the data it represents (the model), through events.

These events are a manifestation of the Observer pattern. We'll now take a closer look at this relationship, because it's what facilitates the separate responsibilities in our MVC-powered GWT calculator.

2.2.3 Communicating by observing events

We need to briefly elaborate on the event handling we have just introduced via `CalculatorChangeListener`. The general pattern, Observer, is how our calculator's model and view will be connected. It's also how many of the examples we provide in this book, and default GWT components themselves, generally communicate.

In addition to MVC, many developers will be accustomed to event handling. Some non-GUI programmers may also have realized the power of this approach and may be using it on the server side. If you're already familiar with events, you may find our initial examples here primitive. This is because we're trying to simplify and demonstrate the concepts, rather than to create the most efficient or streamlined code. (For example, we're not using such standard Java event idioms as `PropertyChangeSupport` and related constructs. We'll step up to that in chapter 4.) This approach should bring those who have not yet encountered event-based and asynchronous programming, especially in relation to a GUI, up to speed quickly. We'll bring the pattern, illustrated in figure 2.5, to the forefront with our first manually driven example.

In our example, the `CalculatorChangeListener` is used to register our view component (our `CalculatorWidget` itself) with the data portion of our model (`CalculatorData`). This is basically the first half of an observer/observable relationship between these components. Our change listener interface is shown in listing 2.5.

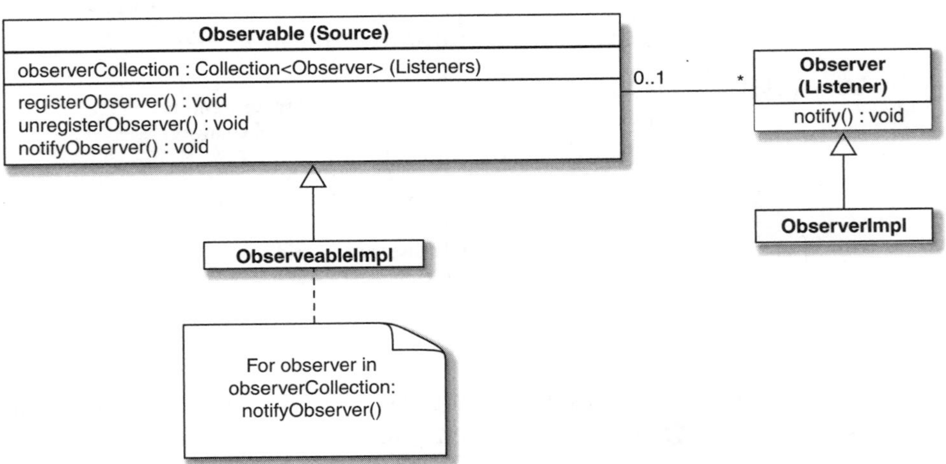

Figure 2.5 The Observer pattern, which is used in GWT to connect the model and view

Listing 2.5 CalculatorChangeListener.java

```
public interface CalculatorChangeListener {
    public void onChange(CalculatorData data);     <-- 1 Define single onChange callback method
}
```

CalculatorChangeListener has a single callback method, onChange() ❶. This is a fairly typical basic listener interface. Our CalculatorData model component, as we'll see in a bit, makes itself observable (available for listeners to listen to) by implementing another simple interface, CalculatorChangeNotifier. This change notifier interface is shown in listing 2.6.

Listing 2.6 CalculatorChangeNotifier.java

```
public interface CalculatorChangeNotifier {
    public void addChangeListener(
final CalculatorChangeListener listener);     <-- Define single addChangeListener method
}
```

CalculatorData, as shown in listing 2.7, therefore carries out the other half of the observer/observable relationship and notifies any listeners that come along when things change.

Listing 2.7 CalculatorData.java: the data portion of the model layer

```
public class CalculatorData implements CalculatorChangeNotifier {
    private String display;
    private double buffer;
    private boolean initDisplay;
    private boolean lastOpEquals;
    private CalculatorChangeListener listener;

    public CalculatorData() {
        this.clear();
    }

    public void addChangeListener(
final CalculatorChangeListener listener) {
        this.listener = listener;     <-- 1 Implement change notifier to register listener
    }

    public void clear() {
        this.display = "0";
        this.buffer = 0.0;
        this.initDisplay = true;
        this.lastOpEquals = false;
        if (listener != null) listener.onChange(this);
    }

    public double getBuffer() {
        return buffer;
    }

    public void setBuffer(double buffer) {
        this.buffer = buffer;
```

```
        listener.onChange(this);
    }
    public String getDisplay() {
        return display;
    }
    public void setDisplay(String display) {
        this.display = display;
        listener.onChange(this);
    }
    //...
```

Notify listener when things change

CalculatorData allows a single listener to register ❶, and then, when its own setters are invoked, it notifies that listener of the change. Again, keep in mind that we have simplified the approach here. In the real world, as is the case with GWT's own components that use this same pattern, you will likely see more than one listener attached to an observable in a collection, and hierarchies of specialized interfaces or abstract classes used for both observable and observer support (and you will need support to remove and clean up observers).

Along with the event mechanism, you probably have also noticed by now that the CalculatorWidget makes references to CalculatorConstants. This is a simple constants class that defines CSS styles and String constants such as: ADD, SUBTRACT, SQRT, and EQUALS.

Now that we have our CalculatorWidget in place and our event handling taken care of, we'll go back to the remainder of our example. This means we need to address ButtonDigit and ButtonOperator, where we'll meet the other half of our model, the logic.

2.2.4 Operator strategy

As we saw in the code in section 2.2.2, CalculatorWidget makes use of several custom button types. The buttons of a calculator handle the numeric and operator input. Buttons are, of course, view components, but the buttons we'll create to fill these roles are also backed by the logic portion of our model, our calculator's operators. We have used our own specific Java types, ButtonDigit and ButtonOperator, so that we can easily distinguish the logical types of buttons pressed, and so that we can further encapsulate the logic for each operation. Listing 2.8 shows our ButtonDigit implementation.

Listing 2.8 ButtonDigit.java

```
public class ButtonDigit extends Button {
    public ButtonDigit(
      final CalculatorController controller,
      final String label) {
        super(label);
        this.addClickListener(new ClickListener() {
                public void onClick(Widget sender) {
                    controller.processDigit(label);
```

❶ Construct ButtonDigit

❷ Propagate ClickListener click events

```
                }
            });
            this.setStyleName(CalculatorConstants.STYLE_BUTTON_DIGIT);
        }
    }
```

ButtonDigit is a very straightforward extension of the GWT Button class. It simply includes a CalculatorController object reference in its constructor ❶, and then invokes the controller's processDigit() method each time a ButtonDigit instance is clicked ❷. This is a repeat of the pattern we're using in the outer CalculatorWidget, using the same controller reference. This invocation is achieved via a ClickListener.

The primary point in this example, especially for server-oriented developers, is that extending the basic UI classes is not only possible, but desirable. Using OOP techniques to extend functionality allows for much cleaner separation and reuse of code. This is in contrast to HTML-based development, where the <input type="button" /> represents an opaque instruction. This fairly simple example just passes on a value, but you should note that the MVC pattern is present on multiple levels.

In listing 2.9 we see this pattern again with the ButtonOperator class. In this case, MVC comes into play on a micro level, while it's also used on a macro level with the entire outer Widget. ButtonOperator has a model, represented by the label; a view, managed by the parent class of Button, tweaked by the designation of a style to the button; and a controller layer represented by an AbstractOperator instance, which translates actions up to the larger scope controller for the calculator widget.

Listing 2.9 ButtonOperator.java

```
public class ButtonOperator extends Button {
    public ButtonOperator(final CalculatorController controller,
        final AbstractOperator op) {                          ❶ Define ButtonOperator constructor
        super(op.label);
        this.addClickListener(new ClickListener() {           ❷ Include ClickListener for event handling
                public void onClick(Widget sender) {
                    controller.processOperator(op);
                }
            });
        this.setStyleName(CalculatorConstants.STYLE_BUTTON_OPERATOR);
    }
}
```

ButtonOperator works in much the same way as ButtonDigit. It extends the GWT Button class and includes a CalculatorController object reference in its constructor ❶. Then it invokes the controller's processOperator() method each time a ButtonOperator instance is clicked ❷. The difference with ButtonOperator is that it includes a reference to an AbstractOperator class in its constructor.

Now that we have operator buttons, we obviously need operations to back these view components. To complete these components, we'll use the Strategy pattern to encapsulate the logic. Rather than a monolithic if/else logic block, we'll delegate each operation to a specified instance of an operator class (each an implementation

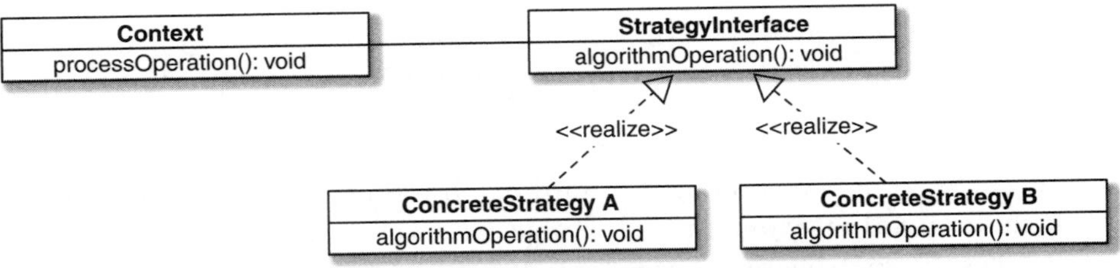

Figure 2.6 The Strategy pattern used in the GWT calculator example to implement operators

of `AbstractOperator`) and let those classes update our calculator's model. Using our operators in this manner makes our calculator easier to understand and allows for greater flexibility and extensibility. With this approach, we can add new operators later without affecting our existing logic. Figure 2.6 shows a diagram of the Strategy pattern.

The only exceptions to this strategic structure for operators are the `CLEAR` and `EQUALS` operations, which are handled directly by the calculator controller, not by operator subclasses. Doing it this way requires less code and makes things a bit clearer. (We have some global state information in the controller that `CLEAR` and `EQUALS` rely upon. A purist implementation could put this information in our model and make separate operators for `CLEAR` and `EQUALS` as well, but that would complicate the other operations just for the sake of the pattern, and we think that would be overkill in this instance.)

These concepts may seem slightly off the beaten GWT path, but they serve to demonstrate the important point that you can use many OO design principles within the context of the toolkit. This flexibility is one of the advantages of GWT. In addition, this approach provides a much more robust calculator at the end of the day.

To handle the individual operators for our calculator, we need to implement the `AbstractOperator` and the subclasses that will extend it. As we saw in listing 2.9, `ButtonOperator` includes a reference to `AbstractOperator`. This is because each operator needs to do something different within a calculator application; each has a unique behavior. `AbstractOperator`, the straightforward beginning of the hierarchy, is shown in listing 2.10.

Listing 2.10 AbstractOperator.java

```
public abstract class AbstractOperator {
    public String label;

    AbstractOperator(final String label) {
        this.label = label;
    }
    public abstract void operate(
        final CalculatorData data);         ❶ Define operate() method
}
```

`AbstractOperator` defines a single abstract method, `operate()`, which takes `CalculatorData` as input and updates it accordingly ❶. We further divide operators with abstract types that determine whether or not the operator being implemented is binary or unary. BinaryOperator and UnaryOperator are as follows:

```
public abstract class BinaryOperator extends AbstractOperator {
    BinaryOperator(final String label) {
        super(label);
    }

public abstract class UnaryOperator extends AbstractOperator {
    UnaryOperator(final String label) {
        super(label);
    }
}
```

With our operator abstractions in place, we'll now implement a simple concrete operator for addition. (We'll not explicitly cover all the concrete operators used in our CalculatorWidget in the text for the sake of brevity). Listing 2.11 displays OperatorAdd.

Listing 2.11 OperatorAdd

```
public class OperatorAdd extends BinaryOperator {

    public OperatorAdd() {
        super(CalculatorConstants.ADD);
    }

    public void operate(final CalculatorData data) {
        data.setDisplay(String.valueOf(data.getBuffer() +
                Double.parseDouble(data.getDisplay())));
        data.setInitDisplay(true);
    }
}
```

❶ Perform addition on data

❷ Set initDisplay to true

The binary addition operator adds the current buffer to the current display value, and then updates the display ❶. Binary operators in this context are basically responsible for updating the display, based on the values in the CalculatorData object. Also, this operator sets the initDisplay status to true ❷; this indicates that, when the next digit is entered, the display should start over rather than append digits to any possible existing value.

Now, with all of the other aspects of our CalculatorWidget in place, we can move on to the controller.

2.2.5 Controlling the action

The calculator's controller handles the interaction between the other calculator components. The controller is called upon by the various buttons to perform actions such as invoking an operator or otherwise manipulating the model or internal state.

The GWT CalculatorWidget controller component is significant for several reasons beyond just the separation of responsibilities derived from the MVC pattern itself. We'll write this component in Java, and it will be compiled into JavaScript by GWT along with our UI components, yet this has nothing to do with the interface. GWT allows you to create not only your UI but also any logic and data representations with client-side intentions. You can create classes, like we're about to do with our `CalculatorController` and have already done with our `CalculatorData`, which end up in the client browser as completely non-view-related items.

In the `CalculatorController`, which is presented in listing 2.12, notice that there are no references to GWT-related classes.

Listing 2.12 CalculatorController.java

```
public class CalculatorController {

    CalculatorData data;
    AbstractOperator lastOperator;
    Private double prevBuffer;

    public CalculatorController(
            final CalculatorData data) {        ❶ Include CalculatorData reference in constructor
        this.data = data;
    }

    public void processClear() {                ❷ Handle CLEAR and EQUALS locally
        data.clear();
        lastOperator = null;
    }

    public void processEquals() {
        if (lastOperator != null) {
            if (!data.isLastOpEquals()) {
                prevBuffer = Double.parseDouble(data.getDisplay());
            }
            lastOperator.operate(data);
            data.setBuffer(prevBuffer);
            data.setLastOpEquals(true);
        }
    }

    public void processOperator(                ❸ Call processOperator
                final AbstractOperator op) {
        if (op instanceof BinaryOperator) {
            if ((lastOperator == null) || (data.isLastOpEquals())) {
                data.setBuffer(Double.parseDouble(data.getDisplay()));
                data.setInitDisplay(true);
            } else {
                lastOperator.operate(data);
            }
                lastOperator = op;
        } else if (op instanceof UnaryOperator) {
            op.operate(data);
        }
        data.setLastOpEquals(false);
    }

    public void processDigit(final String s) {  ❹ Call processDigit
        if (data.isLastOpEquals()) {
            lastOperator = null;
        }
```

```
            if (data.isInitDisplay()) {
                if (data.isLastOpEquals()) {
                    data.setBuffer(0.0);
                } else {
                    data.setBuffer(Double.parseDouble(data.getDisplay()));
                }
                data.setDisplay(s);
                data.setInitDisplay(false);
            } else {
                if (data.getDisplay().indexOf(
                        CalculatorConstants.POINT) == -1) {
                    data.setDisplay(data.getDisplay() + s);
                } else if (!s.equals(CalculatorConstants.POINT)) {
                    data.setDisplay(data.getDisplay() + s);
                }
            }
            data.setLastOpEquals(false);
        }
    }
```

`CalculatorController` is instantiated with a new instance of `CalculatorData` ❶. Along with the data object member, our controller also has four main actions: `equals()` and `clear()`, which are used for the calculator operations of the same names ❷, and `processOperator()` ❸ and `processDigit()` ❹, which are used when their respective operator buttons are clicked.

Controller actions, such as the pressing of a digit or an operator, update the model, which fires the corresponding events. When the data in the model changes, in response to actions from the controller, components that are registered to listen will be notified. Our view, `CalculatorWidget`, is one such component. The controller also contains a reference to the `lastOperator` so that it can make decisions about what to do in the chain of operations it provides. Figure 2.7 shows an overview of the classes involved in our now-complete MVC-enabled calculator project.

This use of `CalculatorController` allows our client-side application, all by its lonesome, to handle state, logic, delegation, and the use of a separate model, along with the view. It's important to remember this expression of the MVC pattern, and where the responsibilities lie, as you will see it over and over again in this book. Java developers accustomed to the request-response cycle will be used to the view being rendered in a single, generally procedural action based on a single-state model. In GWT, as in well-designed desktop applications, the model can change independently of a singular view layer. This is notably different from a more transient view that performs a single operation and then goes away. Dealing with the state of the view, not just of the model, is something you will need to keep in mind during your development.

Now we have an event-driven GWT calculator in the form of a reusable `CalculatorWidget`. In addition, our code is fairly resilient to change and is extensible because we have used an OO approach with operators responsible for their own individual operations.

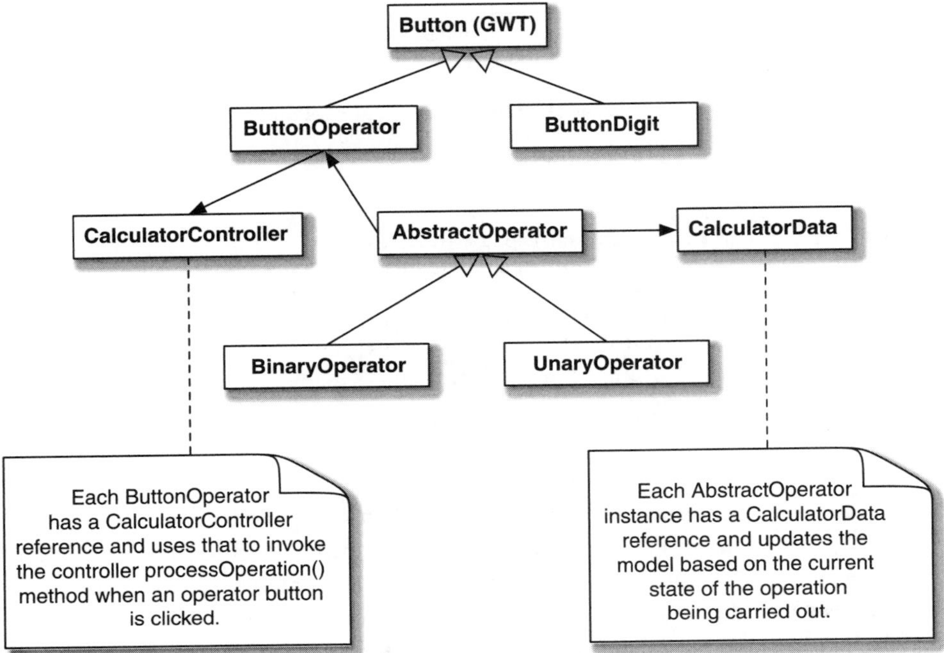

Figure 2.7 Overview of the classes involved with the GWT calculator example

Before we run and deploy our code, we'll first touch on the style-related elements within it, and on how we can make use of those elements to modify the look and feel of our new GWT `CalculatorWidget`.

2.3 Styling a GWT component

You can modify the look and feel of your GWT UI components with CSS. You can also integrate and make use of existing HTML, existing JavaScript including UI effects libraries, and standard web media such as images. This is a big plus. The good parts of the web, the UI elements that have been well received and are well understood, are not hidden.

To round out our example `CalculatorWidget`, we'll set up a stylesheet for our calculator and then explore graphics and other resources.

2.3.1 Providing a CSS file

As we discussed in section 2.1.5, CSS and other resources can be defined and injected through GWT module configuration. This is how we're going to do things in this example. In order for our widgets to have style, we have to do two things: establish style names for each portion of any widget we want to style, and associate a stylesheet with our project.

To associate a stylesheet with our calculator project, we'll add a single line to our Calculator.gwt.xml module file:

```
<stylesheet src='com.manning.gwtip.calculator.style.css'/>
```

Once we place this line in our GWT module file, our project will automatically look for this resource in the public path, and inject this reference into the host page. Recall that the public path defaults to the public subdirectory of our source tree, and resources there are copied to the output folder of our project when compiled and deployed.

Resource injection is handy, and it is the only way to guarantee that certain resources will be present with your module, but you need to be aware of possible naming collisions when using it. For example, if you are including a stylesheet that you expect implementers to use mostly unmodified, it is important that you choose a fairly unique name for the CSS file, or that you package it in a meaningful subdirectory of the .public package. Otherwise it might be inadvertently overridden. If you inject styles.css, you may unintentionally override another stylesheet referenced directly by the host page. This is why we have used a fully qualified Java style name for our stylesheet.

Since we now will have a project looking for an associated stylesheet, we need to provide that stylesheet. Listing 2.13 displays a portion of a stylesheet that can be used with our calculator project. This stylesheet is not very fancy, but it does demonstrate styling GWT elements.

Listing 2.13 com.manning.gwtip.calculator.style.css

```
body {
  background-color: #ffffff;
  color: #000000;
  font-size: 85%;
  font-weight: normal;
  font-family: Arial, sans-serif;
  margin: 20px 20px 20px 20px;
}
.calc-Button {
    border: 2px solid #000000;
    border-top-color: #cccccc;
    border-left-color: #cccccc;
    padding: 0.15em;
    background-color: #d3d3d3;
    color: #000000;
    width: 30px;
    height: 30px;
    font-weight: normal;
}
.calc-Grid {
    width: 160px;
}
.calc-Panel {
    padding: 0.15em;
```

```
    background-color: #a6c6a3;
    border: 1px solid #000000;
}
.calc-Cell {
}
.gwt-TextBox {
    background-color: #ffffff;
    width: 168px;
}
```

In our calculator, we're using some fairly simple CSS buttons. If we were really clever graphic designers, as opposed to design-challenged coders, we might have used some images for our calculator buttons and associated the images using CSS. Had we taken this approach, we would have included the images in the public path, so that they ended up as accessible resources in the deployed project.

Once we have defined and created our stylesheet, we simply need to associate our components with particular style classes or identifiers.

2.3.2 Connecting style names with Java

In our code examples for `CalculatorWidget`, you may have noticed the `setStyleName()` method we used in various places to connect a style name to a UI component. This method, and other related style methods such as `addStyleName()`, are made available in the base GWT class `UIObject`, from which `Grid`, `Button`, `Panel`, and every other GWT UI component is ultimately derived.

In addition to explicitly setting the style class name, you can also set limited individual style attributes with methods like `setVisible()`, `setHeight()`, and `setWidth()`. However, you do not have access to every CSS property in this manner. Therefore, it is often just easier, and arguably better design by loose coupling, to set the entire style class and then use actual CSS to perform your style actions.

You'll notice from our CSS example that we're using fairly explicit selector names based on a pattern of widget-element. These type names, such as `gwt-TextBox` and `calc-Button` are recommended so that anyone wishing to modify a style will easily be able to recognize which element is handled by which style name.

With our stylesheet in place, and our associated identifiers present in our Java classes, we now have a style-enabled calculator example. With all of our resources and code ready to go, it's time to use the GWT shell and GWT compiler to actually run the project!

2.4 Running a completed project

With the `CalculatorWidget` code in hand, styled and set, we're now ready to run our project and see what it can do. We briefly discussed the GWT shell and GWT compiler in chapter 1, and we mentioned them again earlier in this chapter when we identified all the files created by running `ApplicationCreator`. Here we'll put `GWTShell` and `GWTCompiler` to use with our calculator project.

First, we'll use `GWTShell` to get the lay of the land and launch the hosted mode browser. This is how you typically "run" and debug a project while in hosted mode during development. Then we'll move on to compiling things with `GWTCompiler`, which is what is normally used as part of a build process to turn your Java into JavaScript and create a deployable artifact for web mode.

2.4.1 Hosted mode and the GWT shell

When we ran `ApplicationCreator`, GWT created some shortcut scripts for invoking `GWTShell` and `GWTCompiler` with our project (as we noted in section 2.1). First we'll execute `GWTShell` using the `[PROJECT_HOME]/Calculator-shell` script (it will have a platform-dependent extension).

Whether you have been following along and manually building the code for the calculator sample in this chapter, or have downloaded it from the Manning web site, the next step is to ensure that your environment is configured as it needs to be to support GWT and the project itself, and then invoke `Calculator-shell`. This should successfully invoke the example in the shell as shown in figure 2.8.

The background window in figure 2.8 is the GWT shell, and the foreground is the hosted mode browser running `CalculatorWidget`. The GWT shell, as noted in chapter 1, includes a logging console where any problems will be displayed. This includes exceptions, which are passed up the call stack. The shell also includes buttons for manipulating the log and launching the hosted mode browser.

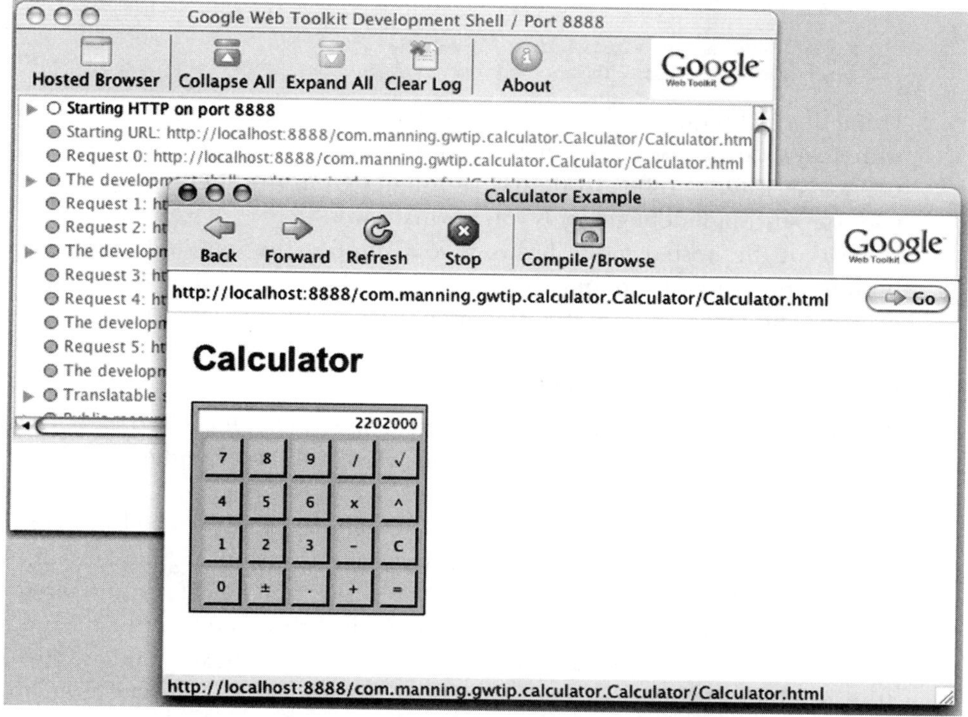

Figure 2.8 The GWT shell and hosted mode browser running `CalculatorWidget`

> **Can the GWT shell browser be specified?**
>
> When you launch the GWT shell, you'll notice that the hosted mode browser is the system browser for the platform you are using. This means Internet Explorer on Windows, Safari on Mac, and Mozilla Firefox on Linux. The hosted mode browser is actually based on SWT browser components, so it is not currently possible to specify or configure which browser is used when running the shell. (This will change in the near future with *out-of-process* hosted mode, which will allow you to use any supported browser on a platform.)

Recall that the shell and the hosted mode browser execute your project as Java bytecode, as opposed to JavaScript, when executed in web mode (which we'll get to in a moment). This means that from hosted mode, in addition to being able to quickly recompile your code with the Refresh button, you can also use Java debuggers and profilers, as you normally would with any Java project.

To connect to the GWT shell for the purposes of debugging, you can use the Java Platform Debugger Architecture (JPDA), which is built into most JVM implementations, and your favorite IDE. By invoking `com.google.gwt.dev.GWTShell` with the following command-line options, you can force the GWT shell to delay startup until a debugger has connected:

```
-Xdebug -Xnoagent -Djava.compiler=NONE
-Xrunjdwp:transport=dt_socket,server=y,address=8888,suspend=y
```

Using this technique, you can run the shell outside of your IDE, and then connect to it with Eclipse, or NetBeans, or such, at `localhost:8888`. Once this connection is made, the socket listener resets to the HTTP listener from the shell and you can continue your step-through debugging as you normally would.

Within the hosted mode browser, you'll notice the standard browser navigation buttons and a special Compile/Browse button that invokes the GWT compiler for the project. This takes you out of hosted mode (Java) and into web mode (JavaScript).

2.4.2 Web mode and the GWT compiler

`GWTCompiler`, which we addressed in some detail in chapter 1, is the GWT facility that compiles your Java source path code into JavaScript, and bundles it with your public path resources in a deployable project form.

The Compile/Browse button made available in the GWT shell will compile your project, deploy it in a stripped-down development version of Apache Tomcat on the local host (actually, the GWT shell also uses this mini Tomcat for any service servlets involved), and launch the project in the default configured browser for the machine. As the screenshot in figure 2.9 shows, the browser used for web mode can be specified (the machine default can be configured), so it can be different from the system browser that hosted mode must use inside the shell.

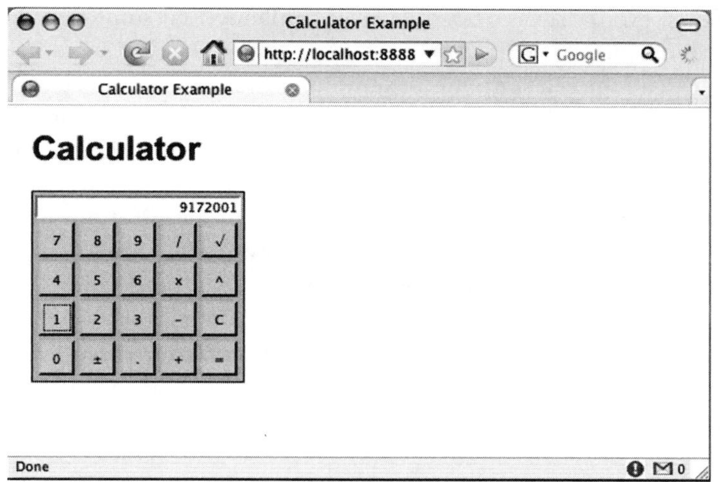

Figure 2.9 **`CalculatorWidget` running in web mode, using Firefox on a Mac, after clicking the Compile/Browse button in the GWT shell**

With the compile step, you are switching out of hosted mode and into web mode—running your code as JavaScript instead of directly as Java. In addition to the Compile/Browse button in the shell, the shortcut `ProjectName-compile` script, created by `ApplicationCreator`, can also be used to compile your project (which will place it by default in the [PROJECT_HOME]/www location).

You can, of course, also use the GWT compiler manually, or with an IDE plugin, or by using build tools such as Ant or Maven. Building and deploying projects, and the related tools, are concepts we'll address in chapter 8.

At this point we have a completed first project, which covered important basic GWT concepts and patterns for client-side development, and we have run it in both hosted and web modes.

2.5 Summary

In this chapter, we built a project with GWT the old fashioned way—on the command line using the provided GWT scripts and a text editor. Convenience and productivity are important, so we'll start using tools such as IDEs in the next chapter, but the steps we followed in this chapter should help you understand exactly what is going on behind the scenes when you use those tools. Going through the motions manually the first time, especially on a simple foundational project, will help your overall understanding in the long run.

You should now have a good general feel for the type of development possible with GWT, and what the default layout and basic components of a GWT application are. Understanding concepts such as modules, entry points, host pages, and the GWT compilation and bootstrapping process is essential when working on any GWT application. Although we stuck to the client side of the picture in this chapter, we still covered a lot of ground with our first example. By creating a calculator as a reusable component, we have demonstrated interface reuse. Within our calculator, we addressed layout, user input elements, event-driven design, and we implemented some very important patterns on the client side.

While a basic calculator is a simplified example of the overall concepts, as it has a minimal data model and very few actions to control, it does serve to demonstrate how GWT can be used on the web tier as an entirely new kind of client: a client that includes its own data and logic, and its own controller, in addition to a view. This client is independent of the server tier, though still capable of server communications for data purposes, and it is not based on pages rendered on a server and sent down with every user action. This type of development, and the MVC approach it employs, allows us to begin migrating toward a more robust and responsive browser-based application.

In the next chapter, we'll look at an example that communicates with a server using GWT RPC. This will follow up on the techniques presented in this chapter and the basic concepts we introduced in chapter 1.

3 Communicating with the Server

This chapter covers

- Making RPCs with GWT
- Using Tomcat Lite for development
- Using an external development server

In general, an implementation must be conservative in its sending behavior, and liberal in its receiving behavior.

—Jon Postel

In the last chapter, we examined the MVC architectural pattern on the client and created a simple client-side GWT application. Naturally, the next thing we need to do is learn how to communicate with server resources.

GWT provides a simple and asynchronous RPC and object-serialization mechanism that allows the client and server to talk. This RPC mechanism is the canonical means of enabling client-server communications within GWT, but it's not the only way. We'll stay focused on standard GWT RPC in this chapter, and we'll cover the other means in chapter 5, once we have a bit more background.

To work with the RPC support provided by the toolkit, we'll also need to revisit the core GWT tools, the GWT shell and GWT compiler. The shell drives RPC development by providing the server in which that development takes place—a stripped down version of Apache Tomcat 5.0.x that hosts server resources. This embedded Tomcat Lite can take some getting used to, even for experienced Tomcat users. The GWT compiler, in turn, provides all the support for translating Java code into JavaScript. This means that when we want to transfer a true object across the wire using RPC, rather than just using untyped `String`s, we need to know a bit about the compiler to do it most effectively.

To begin building a GWT application that can communicate with server resources, we'll start with a very simple "Hello World" RPC project. Once we set up the code portions of the project and lay out the GWT RPC details, we'll then step into the shell and compiler in turn. By the time we reach the end of the example, you should have a much better understanding of the core tools and RPC technologies you'll be working with in GWT. So let's get started with "Hello Server."

3.1 Making GWT Remote Procedure Calls

GWT enables client applications to communicate with server resources through its own RPC and object-serialization mechanism. This communication process involves each side of the conversation implementing a very straightforward GWT service interface and sending/receiving special GWT serialized data. The server side exposes resources, and the client side invokes those resources asynchronously.

GWT intentionally keeps things very basic and optimizes the translation of data from Java to JavaScript and vice versa. While this mechanism is really easy to work with and to understand, it's a GWTism. That is to say, GWT does not use a standard or existing idiomatic approach—no XML-RPC, SOAP, or REST is involved. But despite using its own approach, GWT can also communicate with existing services in additional ways to facilitate integration, such as using plain XML over HTTP (POX), or JSON. These are additional methods, though; the native mechanism for GWT client-server communication is GWT RPC.

3.1.1 Starting the HelloServer project

We'll use GWT RPC in our sample "Hello Server" application, aptly named HelloServer. We'll first define the data we want to pass across the wire, then create a server endpoint, which outlines a method that uses that data, and finally implement a client to complete the process. Figure 3.1 shows what our completed HelloServer application will look like.

In the last chapter, we used the GWT `ApplicationCreator` utility to create our basic project. We'll use the same approach here, but we'll also use the GWT `ProjectCreator` utility to make Eclipse project files. After we use `ApplicationCreator` and `ProjectCreator`, we'll build the example using Eclipse.

The `ProjectCreator` usage options are shown here and described in table 3.1.

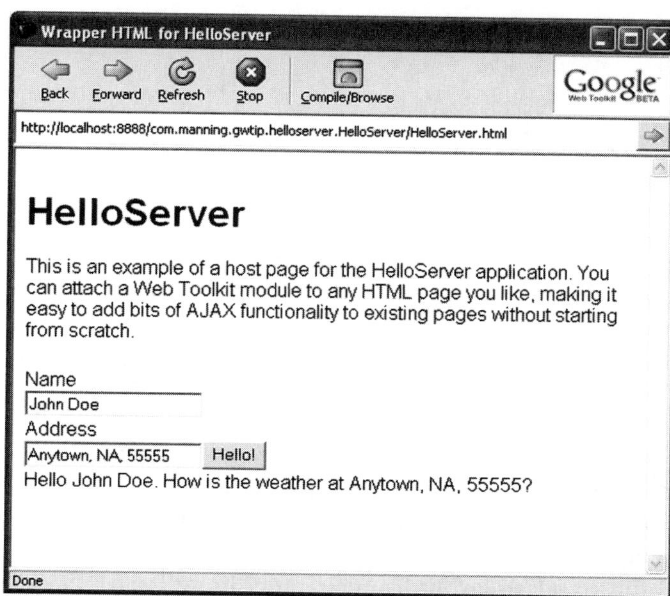

Figure 3.1
The HelloServer sample application demonstrating GWT server communications. The last line on the screen shows the server's response to the user's input.

```
ProjectCreator [-ant projectName] [-eclipse projectName] [-out dir]
   [-overwrite] [-ignore]
```

Let's start by creating our application with `ApplicationCreator`, and then obtaining our Eclipse project configuration with `ProjectCreator`, as follows:

```
mkdir [PROJECT_HOME]
cd [PROJECT_HOME]
[GWT_HOME]/ApplicationCreator \
   com.manning.gwtip.helloserver.client.HelloServer
[GWT_HOME]/ProjectCreator -eclipse HelloServer
```

Running `ApplicationCreator` and `ProjectCreator` as shown will create your default project template files and will create Eclipse-centric .project and .classpath files. From there, you can open Eclipse and use the File > Import > Existing Projects Into Workspace feature to import the HelloServer project.

Table 3.1 `ProjectCreator` parameters

Parameter	Description
`-ant`	Generates an Ant build file to compile source (.ant.xml will be appended).
`-eclipse`	Generates an Eclipse project.
`-out`	The directory to which output files will be written (defaults to the current directory).
`-overwrite`	Overwrites any existing files.
`-ignore`	Ignores any existing files; does not overwrite them.

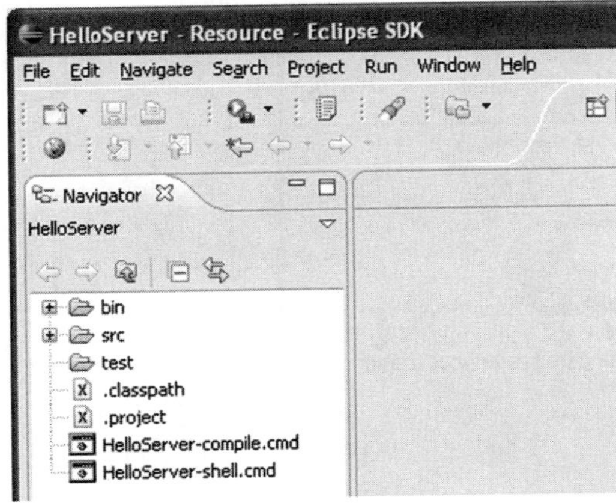

Figure 3.2
The HelloServer project layout in the Eclipse Resource perspective after `ProjectCreator` has generated the Eclipse project

Once you have the HelloServer project in your Eclipse Navigator, you should see the standard GWT layout within it. Figure 3.2 displays the imported HelloServer project in the Eclipse Resource perspective.

You should recall this standard layout from chapters 1 and 2, and the `-shell` and `-compile` script shortcuts should also be familiar. If you execute `HelloServer-shell`, you'll invoke `GWTShell` and you'll see the standard template, "Click Me—Hello World," which every default GWT project starts with.

With the basic project in place, we're ready to move on to implementing HelloServer. We'll start by defining our simple data model and looking at GWT's serialization mechanism.

3.1.2 *Defining GWT serializable data*

The first class we need to create is a simple data class, which we'll call `Person`. Before our `Person` objects can be passed from a GWT client application to an RPC service, they must be marked with either the `com.google.gwt.user.client.rpc.IsSerializable` or the `java.io.Serializable` interface. This is conceptually analogous to regular Java serialization, but in this case it's used in a manner specific to GWT. Also as in regular serialization, GWT will honor the transient modifier on class properties, allowing them to be omitted if they are not themselves serializable.

NOTE While `IsSerializable` doesn't define any methods, it's imperative that your `IsSerializable` implementations declare a no-arguments constructor.

The `IsSerializable` interface is both important and problematic. It's important because it gives the GWT compiler better information on what classes need to support serialization. It's problematic because it introduces a GWT-specific dependency into model classes, as you can see in listing 3.1, the `Person` class. While this is not a big problem if you're working entirely within the realm of your GWT application, it could quickly become a deal breaker if you wish to share object models with other Java projects in your organization.

Listing 3.1 The `Person` data object class

```
package com.manning.gwtip.helloserver.client;
import com.google.gwt.user.client.rpc.IsSerializable;
public class Person implements IsSerializable{

    public String name;
    public String address;

    public Person(){                         <-- Declare no-args constructor
        this(null, null);
    }

    public Person(String name, String address ) {
        super();
        this.name = name;
        this.address = address;
    }
}
```

Because of this GWT-dependency on `IsSerializable`, GWT 1.4 added support so that `java.io.Serializable` could be used in place of `IsSerializable`. This allows these two marker interfaces to act interchangeably in a GWT context. Generally, this helps to ensure that model classes can be created without direct GWT dependencies. Yet, it's important to understand that such model objects still need to be otherwise GWT translatable. That means they need no-argument constructors, and they cannot use Java 5 language features (for now).

Also, it's important to understand that the GWT implementation of `java.io.Serializable`, though convenient, is just a marker interface meaning the same thing as `IsSerializable`—this is not the same as actual Java serialization support. The documentation for the GWT version of `java.io.Serializable` puts it this way: "public interface `Serializable`: Provided for interoperability; RPC treats this interface synonymously with `IsSerializable`. The Java serialization protocol is explicitly not supported."

The bottom line is that you can use either `IsSerializable` or `Serializable`, and they mean exactly the same thing to GWT—this class is RPC translatable. The GWT `Serializable` emulation can help you avoid the GWT-specific `IsSerializable` dependency, but your model classes are still limited to what is possible with GWT. Because of this, we'll use the `IsSerializable` marker in this book's examples to make the association explicit. Keep in mind, though, that in real life you may be better off using `Serializable` as long as you're disciplined enough to remember the implicit GWT limitations.

In chapter 5, we'll cover serialization in more detail, including the use of collections and GWT JavaDoc style annotations to convey type information. We'll also look at using Data Transfer Objects (DTOs) to move between different object models in chapter 9. For this introductory example, though, we'll keep the model simple, with just our `Person` bean. We want to create our simple service infrastructure to illustrate the GWT RPC basics.

3.1.3 Creating RPC services

GWT includes a GWT RPC package for enabling communications with server resources. Constructing an RPC service entails building two interfaces and a service implementation.

You begin by creating a synchronous service interface, which extends the GWT `RemoteService` interface and defines the methods your service exposes. Next, you create an asynchronous interface based on the first synchronous one. This asynchronous interface will have the same name as the synchronous interface, but with an *Async* suffix. Importantly, the asynchronous interface does not extend `RemoteService` itself. The asynchronous interface must have all the same methods as the synchronous one, except that each of the asynchronous methods must declare a `void` return type, throw no exceptions, and have an additional final reference parameter of type `AsyncCallback`. These two interfaces—one synchronous, one asynchronous—are the client side of the picture. Finally, you must create a server-side implementation of your client-side synchronous `RemoteService` interface. This must extend the GWT `RemoteServiceServlet` class.

These three parts, the synchronous client service interface, asynchronous client service interface, and server implementation service servlet, are the backbone of GWT RPC. Table 3.2 restates these RPC components for reference.

In our example, we'll add one more element to the mix in order to decouple our implementation just a bit and make things more flexible. We're going to put our server-side `RemoteService` implementation in a separate class, apart from our `RemoteServiceServlet` implementation. This could be done in a single step—we could have a server-side implementation that both implements `RemoteService` and extends `RemoteServiceServlet` in one fell swoop. However, we'll separate these two as a best practice, because in a larger project you may want to use the service implementation outside of the context of your GWT classes. With the `RemoteServiceServlet` separated,

Table 3.2 Components involved in creating a GWT RPC service

Required interface	Extension	Purpose
`MyService`	`RemoteService`	Client side. Synchronous interface, used internally by GWT.
`MyServiceAsync`	None	Client side. Asynchronous interface which, by convention, backs the synchronous interface. It must have the same name with an *Async* suffix, must declare `void` return type on all methods, must throw no exceptions, and must include `AsyncCallback` as the last parameter in all methods.
`MyServiceImpl`	`RemoteServiceServlet`	Server side. An implementation of the client-side synchronous interface, which by convention will be accessible in the client through the asynchronous interface.

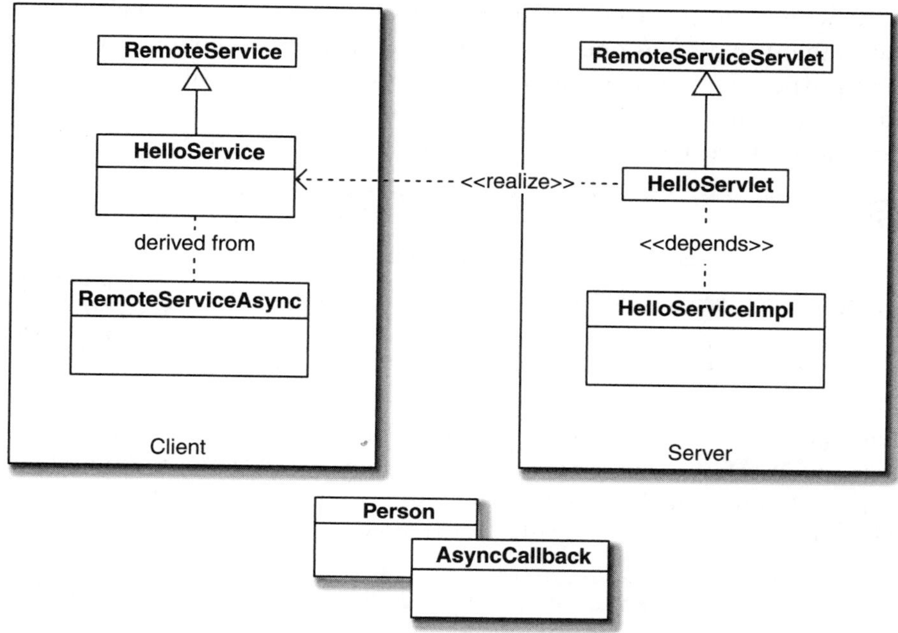

Figure 3.3 GWT RPC class diagram for HelloServer. Notice that the `RemoteServiceAsync` class is not directly related to our service implementation or servlet; it's associated by convention.

you're free to implement the `RemoteService` interface class itself in a Spring bean, an Enterprise JavaBean (EJB), or even through a SOAP service.

Figure 3.3 reinforces these points and also shows the structure we'll use for our HelloServer example.

It's important to remember that all of the classes you use as arguments or returns from the methods defined by your `RemoteService` interface must be GWT-serializable, as we discussed in section 3.1.2. In addition, your remote interface and all the data you wish to serialize must be part of your source path so that `GWTCompiler` finds these resources and creates the appropriate JavaScript versions.

Getting into the RPC code, we'll start with the client-side synchronous interface, `HelloService.java`, which is displayed in listing 3.2.

Listing 3.2 HelloService.java

```
package com.manning.gwtip.helloserver.client;

import com.google.gwt.user.client.rpc.RemoteService;

public interface HelloService extends RemoteService {
    String sayHello(Person p);
}
```

Return a String, accept Person as input

Next, we need to create our client-side asynchronous interface, which is almost identical to the synchronous one with the previously noted exceptions (*Async* suffix, `void` return type, `AsyncCallback` as a parameter—the callback will be used to return the value). Note that both of these client-side interfaces are in the default source path, the `.client` package. Listing 3.3 shows our `HelloServiceAsync.java` interface.

Listing 3.3 HelloServiceAsync.java

```
package com.manning.gwtip.helloserver.client;

import com.google.gwt.user.client.rpc.AsyncCallback;

public interface HelloServiceAsync {
    void sayHello(Person p, AsyncCallback callback);
}
```

Return type void, AsyncCallback parameter included

Last, we need to create the server-side implementation of our client-side `RemoteService` interface. Our service implementation is just going to be a plain old Java object (POJO), though again you could use many different techniques at this point. This code for `HelloServiceImpl.java` is shown in listing 3.4.

Listing 3.4 HelloServiceImpl.java

```
package com.manning.gwtip.helloserver.server;

import com.manning.gwtip.helloserver.client.HelloService;
import com.manning.gwtip.helloserver.client.Person;

public class HelloServiceImpl implements HelloService {
    public HelloServiceImpl() {
    }

    public String sayHello(Person p) {
        return "Hello " + p.name + ". How is the weather at " + p.address +
        "?";
    }
}
```

Place in server package

Note that even though we created two client-side interfaces, one synchronous and one asynchronous, GWT doesn't support synchronous communications with your client application. You'll never use the synchronous one.

The reason for this is browser-related, and technical, and you might be familiar with it if you have done Ajax work in the past. The `XMLHttpRequest` object is asynchronous; however, the JavaScript interpreter in many browsers is a single execution thread. This means that if you tried to send a request and "spin" while waiting for the callback event to execute, you'd spin forever. The callback event wouldn't fire while the JavaScript interpreter was spinning.

Now we have three classes, but we're not quite done yet. The final piece is our `RemoteServiceServlet` implementation. This is the actual servlet that the web application exposes, and with which the client-side classes communicate. Listing 3.5 shows the code for our service servlet, `HelloServlet.java`.

Listing 3.5 HelloServlet.java

```
package com.manning.gwtip.helloserver.server;

import com.google.gwt.user.server.rpc.RemoteServiceServlet;
import com.manning.gwtip.helloserver.client.HelloService;
import com.manning.gwtip.helloserver.client.Person;

public class HelloServlet
    extends RemoteServiceServlet
    implements HelloService {                                  <- Implement service interface
    private HelloService impl = new HelloServiceImpl();       <- Instantiate implementation

    public HelloServlet() {
        super();
    }

    public String sayHello(Person p) {
        return impl.sayHello(p);                               <- Pass through from servlet to implementation
    }
}
```

This completes our service: two simple interfaces on the client, one implementation class on the server, and a service servlet to host and invoke the server-side implementation. Now that we have a basic service, we'll explore the options available from the `RemoteServiceServlet` class.

3.1.4 Expanding on RemoteServiceServlet

While we're wrapping our implementation, there are certain features provided by the servlet specification we might want. Indeed, we might want to do a lot of things to a request before it goes to the actual service implementation. The `RemoteServiceServlet` includes several methods you can call from within your servlet to access these features. The important ones are outlined in table 3.3.

Table 3.3 Selected methods of the `RemoteServiceServlet`

Method	Function
`getThreadLocalRequest()`	Called from a service method to get the `HttpServletRequest`, and `HttpSession` objects. It can be used for server-side state with session or customizing responses.
`getThreadLocalResponse()`	Called from a service method to get the `HttpServletResponse` object. It can be used to customize the response, such as for setting custom headers.
`onBeforeRequestDeserialized (String)`	Called before the request objects are deserialized, with the serialization payload as an argument.
`onAfterResponseSerialized (String)`	Called before the response serialized object is returned to the client, with the serialized payload as an argument.

Table 3.3 Selected methods of the `RemoteServiceServlet` *(continued)*

Method	Function
`shouldCompressResponse (HttpServletRequest, HttpServletResponse, String)`	Called to determine whether Gzip compression should be used on the response. The default behavior is `true` if the client accepts it and the response is greater than 256 bytes.
`processCall(String)`	Called to deserialize incoming payloads, call the appropriate service method, and return a string response payload.

The most important of the methods in table 3.3 are the two `ThreadLocal` methods, which let you access the session state. For instance, if you were proxying the calls into the RPC service to a SOAP service, you could check the session and authenticate the user with the SOAP service on the first call, using the user information available in the `HttpServletRequest` object. From there, you could store the connect stub for the user in the `Session` object, giving each user his own instance of the actual business object.

NOTE We're skipping over service security in general in this section, for the sake of simplicity, as this is our first RPC example. However, it should be kept in mind—the old saw, "never trust the client," still applies. We'll cover more aspects of RPC security in part 3.

You might not need the other methods listed in table 3.3 often, but they can be useful. It's important to remember that the Google serialization classes are available to you in your application in the form of the `com.google.gwt.user.server.rpc.impl.ServerSerializationStreamReader` and `ServerSerializationStreamWriter`. If, for instance, you wish to change the service state based on information contained in the client request, you can overload the methods in table 3.3 and inspect the message to the server beforehand. Unfortunately these methods don't provide you with the option to filter or modify the serialization payload. To do that, you'd need to overload the entire `processCall()` method and then make your changes before invoking the superclass method.

All of this takes place on the server, but we also want to make calls from the client.

3.1.5 *Calling the server from the client*

In order to invoke our RPC services on the client, we need to get the asynchronous service interface from the static `GWT.create()` method, bind it to a relative URL for our `HelloServlet`, create a callback handler, and make our call. Listing 3.6 demonstrates this directly within the `EntryPoint` class, `HelloServer`. This class, now in our Eclipse project, was initially created by the `ApplicationCreator` utility. We have entirely replaced what was in the default HelloServer.java file with our code here. (For the purposes of this example, we're doing things directly in the entry point. We're not trying to develop with reuse in mind, as we did with our calculator example in chapter 2.)

Listing 3.6 HelloServer.java

```
public class HelloServer implements com.google.gwt.core.client.EntryPoint {
    private HelloServiceAsync service;
    private TextBox name = new TextBox();
    private TextBox address = new TextBox();
    private Label response = new Label();
    private AsyncCallback serviceCallback =
        new AsyncCallback() {
            public void onSuccess(Object result) {
                String string = (String) result;
                response.setText(string);
            }

            public void onFailure(Throwable caught) {
                Window.alert("There was an error: " + caught.toString());
            }
        };

    public HelloServer() {
        super();
    }

    public void onModuleLoad() {
        service = (HelloServiceAsync)
           GWT.create(HelloService.class);

        ServiceDefTarget endpoint = (ServiceDefTarget) service;
        endpoint.setServiceEntryPoint(
            GWT.getModuleBaseURL() +
            "/HelloService");

        RootPanel root = RootPanel.get();

        root.add(new Label("Name"));
        root.add(name);
        root.add(new Label("Address"));
        root.add(address);

        Button button = new Button("Hello!",
                new ClickListener() {
                    public void onClick(Widget sender) {
                        service.sayHello(new Person(name.getText(),
                                address.getText()), serviceCallback);
                    }
                });
        root.add(button);
        root.add(response);
    }
}
```

❶ Create callback for success and failure

❷ Obtain Async service for interface

Bind service to HTTP path

❸ Implement ClickListener to call service

Our `HelloServer` entry point is intended to wire together our example with UI and event handling. Within it, we create an `AsyncCallback` object to handle the return values from our service ❶. (This could also have been done anonymously.) Then we use the static `GWT.create()` method to obtain a runtime reference to our service ❷, and implement a `ClickListener` to connect the click on the `Button` with the `sayHello()` service call ❸.

The final step we need to complete is to set up our module file, HelloServer.gwt.xml, with our servlet mapped to /HelloService. If we take a look at the existing HelloServer.gwt.xml file created by ApplicationCreator, we can see a single <inherits> element and a single <entry-point> class element. We need to add to that a <servlet> element to represent our service, as shown in listing 3.7.

Listing 3.7 HelloServer.gwt.xml module with servlet entry added

```
<module>
      <inherits name='com.google.gwt.user.User'/>

    <entry-point
       class='com.manning.gwtip.helloserver.client.HelloServer'/>

    <servlet path="/HelloService"
       class=
"com.manning.gwtip.helloserver.server.HelloServlet"
       />
</module>
```

Add servlet entry to module

We now have a complete, working GWT application that makes a call back to the server! While our example is not visually impressive, you should now be familiar with all the moving parts involved in making an asynchronous invocation to server-side code.

To run this example in hosted mode, you can simply invoke GWTShell via the HelloServer-shell shortcut script. (This script was either created when you manually ran ApplicationCreator, if you have been following along and building the project, or is provided with the code for this example on the Manning web site.) When you run the example, the client will call the server, and, under the hood, Java objects are being converted to the GWT wire format and passed into JavaScript.

Figure 3.4 provides a visual overview of the entire RPC process: from the user to the client service interface, across the wire into the remote service servlet, and then to the service implementation—and then back again.

Figure 3.5 shows an example request in hexadecimal format so that you can see the special characters used during a service call invocation. While it's not important for you to have a complete understanding of the hexadecimal values, this demonstrates an important point about the operation of the compiler in relation to the server.

As you can see in figure 3.5, the class name is the important information used in the transfer and it's followed by the properties and a sequence to identify which values belong to which property. In GWT (and unlike JSON) property names on objects can change from compilation to compilation, but the GWT client will always know the Java class name of the object.

Now for the response:

```
{OK}[1,["Hello John Doe. How is the weather at Anytown, NA, 55555"],0,2]
```

First, we have the response code of the call to the server, followed by our single return value. Since we're returning a simple string value, it's returned in the native

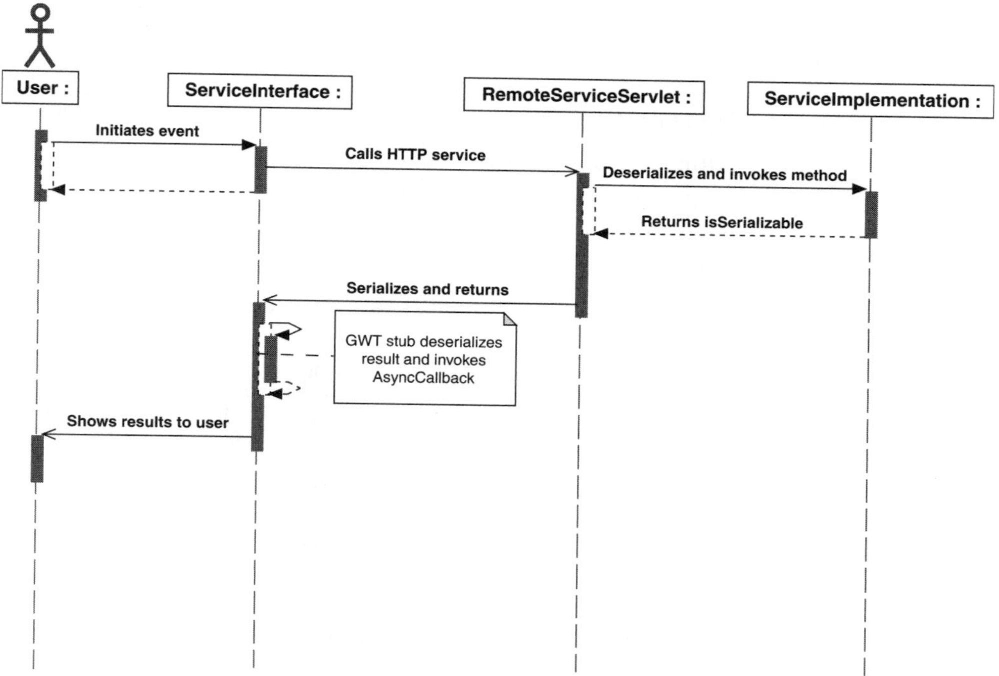

Figure 3.4 An overview of the complete RPC process. Notice that the user's browser lifeline is freed while the service call is executed; it's monopolized again as the call is returned.

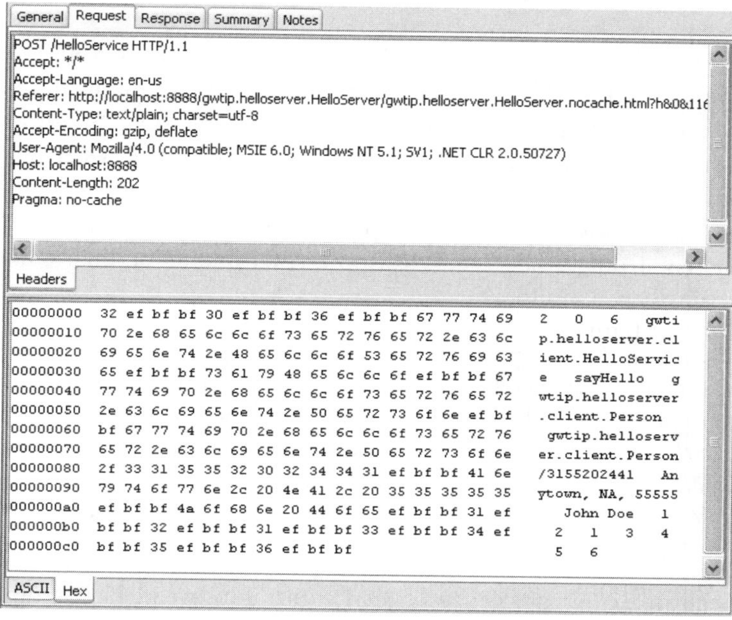

Figure 3.5 A GWT RPC request in hexadecimal format. Notice that the type information is passed for deserialization on the server, along with the attribute values.

JavaScript form. Once values are returned, they will frequently update the model level of your Ajax application.

3.1.6 Troubleshooting server communication

If you begin getting errors in the form of "Deferred binding result type 'module.client.MyService' is not instantiable" when you start creating GWT RPC services, try the following. First, turn your `-logLevel` option up on the shell logging console to provide additional clues as to what went wrong. Then, run through this checklist:

- Make sure you're casting your call to `GWT.create()` to `MyServiceAsync` and not `MyService`.
- Make sure your `MyService` interface extends `RemoteService`.
- Make sure your return types and arguments all implement `IsSerializable` or `Serializable`.
- Make sure the classes used as return types and arguments all have no-args constructors.
- Make sure the return types on methods in your `MyServiceAsync` class are all `void`.

In addition to the plumbing of GWT server communications and issues with regard to naming and types, you may also be curious about handling synchronization and multiple outstanding callbacks. Developers familiar with the issues surrounding asynchronous, message-based programming will possibly look at the asynchronous nature of Ajax messaging and overthink the issues of synchronization at the model level in their GWT applications.

One important thing to remember is that all JavaScript on a page is executed within the scope of a single thread. This means that while you might have multiple outstanding callbacks waiting for invocation, only one will be called at a time. Unlike invoking web services via the Java API for XML Web Services (JAX-WS) from a Swing application, there is no need to shift UI changes from the thread invoking the callback to the painting thread, since all JavaScript is executed on the painting thread. To borrow an analogy from Brian Glick (http://www.jroller.com/hifi78/entry/gwt_single_threaded_javascript_multi):

> *With the single threaded browser environment, I think about a colony of bees. (WARNING: Extremely strained metaphor coming!) The queen bee (the application) can tell the worker bees (XMLHttpRequest), "Go get me food." However, when the bees return, only one can give the food to the queen at a time. The rest have to sit in line and wait. From the bee keeper's standpoint, the environment is multi-threaded. All of these bees are swarming around at the same time. However, we need to look at it from the perspective of the queen, who only has to deal with one worker bee at a time.*

That is to say, the problems usually associated with multithreaded programming in Java don't apply. Your Java will always execute in a single thread. You'll never have multiple callbacks executing on the client at the same time. Attributes will never be modified outside of the current call stack. In opposition to the standard Servlet API, your client-side GWT code will be single threaded across all the instances you create in the code; it will be fundamentally static. There is no Swing event-dispatching thread. There are no daemon timers. There is a single execution thread that all code will run in, no matter the callback order.

Now that we have a working client/server communications example and have explored object serialization and noted some troubleshooting techniques, let's go back and take a closer look at the development mode server that makes GWT RPC work in the shell—Tomcat Lite.

3.2 The development server—Tomcat Lite

As we have seen previously, the GWT shell uses a stripped-down and somewhat customized version of the Apache Tomcat servlet container as its development mode server. While this is a Tomcat instance, GWT sets things up differently to automate certain elements and facilitate quick and easy development mode use and testing.

GWT's deployment of applications to the local Tomcat can be somewhat confusing. Saying that GWT uses Tomcat is much like saying that your favorite driver drives a Camaro in NASCAR races. It might look like a Camaro, people might even call it a Camaro, but driving it's not like driving the Camaro your local GM dealer will sell you. GWT's Tomcat has a custom deployment descriptor, web.xml, which includes the configuration for the special `GWTShellServlet`. This servlet is used in hosted mode only to automatically dispatch servlet entries from your module file into the appropriate classes.

In addition, GWT's Tomcat doesn't honor any Tomcat context-configuration information (context.xml) stored in your application. Instead, the GWT Tomcat instance uses ROOT.xml (its own variation of context.xml) and a set of pseudo-Tomcat home directories. This can be limiting and frustrating for developers who want to include additional container or application-level configuration for use inside Tomcat Lite. The first thing you're likely to want to modify to your own liking is web.xml.

3.2.1 The web.xml file

The Tomcat Lite development server won't honor your application's local web.xml deployment descriptor by default, so this is usually the first thing you have to deal with when it comes to setting up application-related parameters that you want in hosted mode. In order to enable such resources as filters or custom security constraints in your application in hosted mode, you can have your project's build file create or modify the appropriate [PROJECT_HOME]/tomcat structure.

The [PROJECT_HOME]/tomcat directory, where the GWT shell's development-mode Tomcat Lite server is installed by default, has the following default structure:

- [PROJECT_HOME]/tomcat
  - conf
    - web.xml (see listing 3.8)
    - gwt
      - localhost
        - ROOT.xml
  - webapps
    - ROOT
      - WEB-INF
        - web.xml (see listing 3.9)

With that structure in mind, we'll take a look at the files themselves to understand where to make modifications, should the need arise. The first web.xml file, shown in listing 3.8, is the one global to the whole server. By default, GWT sets this file up as a stripped-down version of the Tomcat base web.xml file that just includes some common MIME-type mappings. While the purist might argue that any MIME types you're going to use in your application should be included in your custom web.xml file, many people don't do this consistently.

Listing 3.8 The structure of the default server web.xml file

```
<?xml version="1.0" encoding="ISO-8859-1" ?>
<!-- A tweaked version of the default Tomcat web.xml file
to remove everything except the stuff we want to use -->
<web-app version="2.4">
   <mime-mapping>
       <extension>abs</extension>
       <mime-type>audio/x-mpeg</mime-type>
   </mime-mapping>

<!-- stuff omitted... -->

   <mime-mapping>
      <extension>zip</extension>
      <mime-type>application/zip</mime-type>
   </mime-mapping>
</web-app>
```

The second web.xml file, displayed in listing 3.9, is the GWT-generated mapping for servlets specified in the module's gwt.xml file through the previously noted special servlet, `GWTShellServlet`. This effectively proxies servlet mappings for use in hosted mode. (This servlet should never be deployed with your application—it's only useful for hosted mode.)

Listing 3.9 The special `GWTShellServlet` mapping web.xml file

```
<?xml version="1.0" encoding="ISO-8859-1" ?>
<web-app version="2.4">
    <servlet>
        <servlet-name>shell</servlet-name>
```

```
            <servlet-class>
                com.google.gwt.dev.shell.GWTShellServlet
            </servlet-class>
        </servlet>
        <servlet-mapping>
            <servlet-name>shell</servlet-name>
            <url-pattern>/*</url-pattern>
        </servlet-mapping>
    </web-app>
```

Working with these GWT-specific files and having your own web.xml configuration ignored in a development context is, of course, limiting in a number of ways. GWT won't honor your security parameters or filter chains. Nor will GWT inject resource references into your JNDI tree. Synchronizing the servlet entries in both your GWT module file and a separate deployment descriptor that will later be included with your deployed application is also a pain, and prone to "fat-finger" errors.

The solution is to somehow modify the Tomcat Lite web.xml files to include your application's local configuration information when you launch `GWTShell`. You can do this by hand, but it's much more convenient to have a build process that inspects a local web.xml file (one that's included in the source for your project, intended to be used outside of the hosted mode when you deploy) and includes your configuration information in the GWT files automatically.

Because you don't want to define servlet elements in two places, and you ultimately want to have a web.xml file that's deployed with your application that also matters to the GWT development server, you have a two-sided problem. That is, you may have GWT servlet elements defined in your module, and you may also have other application resources, such as security realm information, defined in your application's web.xml. Yet you need configuration information from both sources to be available in both places (in hosted mode for Tomcat Lite, and outside of hosted mode in standard container format when deployed). To accomplish this, you can inject your configuration into the Tomcat Lite web.xml for hosted mode use, and you can copy the `<servlet>` elements from your module file into your web.xml for standard deployment.

In order to make this happen, you can add some intelligence to your build process to create a new web.xml file for hosted mode use. You can then use this new file to replace the GWT default webapps/ROOT/web.xml file. We'll look into this and provide such an automated build process when we discuss using Ant and Maven to build GWT applications in chapter 7.

The important thing to keep in mind here is that, regardless of how you do it, you can modify the Tomcat Lite web.xml file for hosted mode configuration. You can also modify the Tomcat context.xml context descriptor in the same manner.

3.2.2 The context.xml file

If you want to include configuration resources at the Tomcat context level when working with the embedded Tomcat instance, and also have those resources available in hosted mode, you again have to manipulate the GWT Tomcat files. As an example, we'll deal with a common problem: defining JNDI `DataSource` entries at the context level. We provide a sample method for getting around the overall issue.

First off, let's talk about dependencies. `GWTShell`'s Tomcat instance does not include the libraries needed to load `DataSource` implementations into the JNDI tree on its own. If you want to use Tomcat's `DataSource` handling, you need to include (from the Jakarta Commons project, http://jakarta.apache.com) the Commons-DBCP and Commons-Pool JAR files in the startup classpath for your project. You also need to include the appropriate JDBC driver for your particular database.

Once you have the dependencies in place, you have to start `GWTShell` once to get it to write out a [PROJECT_HOME]/tomcat directory tree. This is effectively what you'd expect from `$CATALINA_HOME` in a regular Tomcat installation. Once this has happened, you can create or modify the main Tomcat Lite context file, which is renamed ROOT.xml in GWT. This file can be used to define your `DataSources`:

```
[PROJECT_HOME]/tomcat/conf/gwt/localhost/ROOT.xml
```

You can add your `DataSource` information to the ROOT.xml location, or copy a custom META-INF/context.xml from your project into that location and rename it. The configuration shown in listing 3.10 can be used as a reference.

Listing 3.10 Example `DataSource` configuration for Tomcat 5.0.x context.xml

```
<Resource name="jdbc/demogwt" auth="Container"
                  type="javax.sql.DataSource"/>
      <ResourceParams name="jdbc/demogwt">
        <parameter>
          <name>factory</name>
          <value>org.apache.commons.dbcp.BasicDataSourceFactory</value>
        </parameter>
        <parameter>
          <name>driverClassName</name>
          <value>com.mysql.jdbc.Driver</value>
        </parameter>
        <parameter>
          <name>url</name>
          <value>jdbc:mysql://localhost:3306/myDatabase</value>
        </parameter>
      </ResourceParams>
</Resource>
```

When you do this, of course, you're duplicating your context information and once again manipulating the Tomcat Lite files, rather than resources local to your project as you might normally expect. This is ugly, but it does get around the issue of including context resources and still makes development mode resources available as they would be in production, because they will be present once things are deployed. (This example is based on Tomcat 5.0.x. If you deploy to a newer version or a different platform, you'll have to deal with configuration differences.)

NOTE GWT will also let you specify a base Tomcat directory using the `catalina.base` system property. You can use this behavior to specify an alternative internal Tomcat location, which gives you many options with regard to creating and maintaining the internal Tomcat structure.

As an alternative to configuring the GWT-embedded Tomcat server, you can also use the hosted mode browser in standalone mode with an external servlet container by passing the `-noserver` switch to `GWTShell` on the command line.

3.3 Using an external development server

`GWTShell` includes the `-noserver` command-line option, which instructs the toolkit not to start or use the embedded Tomcat instance. If you use `-noserver`, you're essentially telling GWT that you'll handle the server-side resources on your own, like a baseball player in the outfield calling a fly ball—"I got this one."

There are pros and cons to this approach. On the plus side, it is very flexible, allowing you to run any servlet container you want, with any configuration you need, all within hosted mode. On the downside, the configuration is up to you, and it makes sharing projects that involve RPC more difficult when the embedded Tomcat is not utilized. Overall, using `-noserver` is a great way to extend the server-side possibilities, as long as you're aware of the difficulties it can pose.

If you want to use `-noserver`, you'll need to configure an external server and context, and host a few files for your project there. To operate with the shell in hosted mode, you'll need to copy four files, at a minimum, from the compiled version of your GWT module into your external context. These files are listed in table 3.4.

Table 3.4 Required external container files for `GWTShell -noserver` usage

File	Purpose
ModuleName.html	Host page
ModuleName.nocache.html	GWT nocache initialization script
gwt.js	Core GWT JavaScript (not application specific)
hosted.html	Core hosted mode JavaScript (not application specific)

With your external container and context in place, you then simply need to invoke `GWTShell` with the `-noserver` option and specify the correct port and path. This instructs the shell to point to the external server. Listing 3.11 shows a shell script for the Mac platform that demonstrates the use of these options.

Listing 3.11 Example shell script for use with an external container

```
#!/bin/sh

ENTRY_POINT=com.manning.gwtip.calculator.Calculator
HOST_PAGE=Calculator.html
```

```
APPDIR=`dirname $0`;
CPGWT=$APPDIR/src
CPGWT=$CPGWT:$GWT_HOME/gwt-user.jar
CPGWT=$CPGWT:$GWT_HOME/gwt-dev-mac.jar
java -XstartOnFirstThread        \
     -cp $CPGWT com.google.gwt.dev.GWTShell \
     -logLevel DEBUG -noserver -port 8080 "$@" \
     $ENTRY_POINT/$HOST_PAGE
```

Use XstartOfFirstThread on Macs only

Start shell with -noserver and -port 8080

When you start the shell in this manner, it will invoke the hosted mode browser and direct it to the specified path: http://localhost:8080/ENTRY_POINT/HOST_PAGE. If you wanted to, you could also not specify the port and path when you invoke the shell (simply start it with only `-noserver`), and then manually launch the hosted mode browser and type the correct URL in the address bar.

As the hosted mode browser connects to the HTML host page, it will look for a module bootstrap reference and execute the Java code it finds on its classpath. Be advised, though, that when using `-noserver`, server-side resources are completely out of the realm of GWT. This means server-side resources won't instantly update to changes like client-side resources do, and connecting a debugger, which can still be done, must be done outside the shell. Also remember that you have to set up server-side resources such as servlets, even for GWT RPC, on your own.

Throughout most of this book, we'll be using the Tomcat Lite instance as our host. While we think the `-noserver` switch can be helpful, we also feel that working with and understanding the embedded Tomcat instance is important. The reason not to abandon Tomcat Lite and always use other options is that once you're creating shared GWT projects that include server-side resources, you end up passing the configuration problem on. If you share GWT RPC resources, and they don't work in the stock toolkit, or in some automated fashion with the stock toolkit, the usability, acceptance, and adoption of your resources will likely plummet.

Later in the book, you'll see a detailed example of using `DataSources`, the Java Persistence API, and other common technologies within Tomcat Lite, and in chapter 7 we'll cover the automation for manipulating your hosted mode configuration.

3.4 Summary

Being able to communicate with servers in a statically typed and asynchronous manner is a great benefit of GWT development. Your Ajax application, which can use MVC on many layers (including on the client, as we saw in chapter 2), can include data transfer of typed objects, collections, and exceptions.

In this chapter we looked at communicating with server-side resources using GWT RPC, and at the GWT shell's Tomcat Lite instance, how you can use it to speed your own development, and how you can use an external server.

At this point, you should have a good working knowledge of the core technologies in the toolkit. The GWT shell will become your friend. It replaces your desktop servlet container and web browser while you're doing development tasks. And the GWT compiler is a technical tour de force, allowing you to work on, and with, your object model in Java, and still hand that off seamlessly to a JavaScript environment, making use of the browser platform and all the advantages it provides.

Beyond basic UI, client MVC, and GWT RPC, the toolkit also provides some useful features that help handle things like state in an Ajax application, the ability to integrate nicely with existing JavaScript tools and libraries, internationalization, and testing. In the next chapter, we'll take the technologies from the GWT world and look at how we can combine the MVC architectural pattern, RPC service, and your existing Java EE knowledge in a typical application.

Part 2

Task-specific Issues

Now that you have the basics down, we move on to more task-specific issues you will face. Getting GWT integrated into your existing development environment can seem daunting. To help you out we are going to look at a number of common integration points.

First we will look at using the Java Persistence API (JPA) to build a simple GWT application. Since this is step zero for much of a developer's job, it is important to get a handle on these issues. As we move through part 2, we will look at techniques and issues surrounding server communications, integration with legacy JavaScript code, building, unit testing and continuous integration of your projects. Along the way we will introduce GWT into your favorite development tools and IDEs. While the problem-solution format this part follows might give you the impression of a simple cookbook, we hope you will give it at least one good read through, as each chapter addresses not just the specific problems or tasks presented, but provides a grounding in the design issues associated with integration of GWT into your current environment.

4 Core Application Structure

This chapter covers

- Creating composite view components
- Data binding for the model and view
- The relationship of the controller to the RPC service layer
- Using JPA in the model
- Completing a front-to-back GWT application, client, and server

You must unlearn what you have learned.

—Yoda (*The Empire Strikes Back*)

You have been building web applications for years now. The flaws in the process are obvious, but if you are like us, coping with these flaws has become second nature. You know GWT provides a whole new metaphor for web development, and chapter 2's calculator example demonstrated that GWT development is much more like traditional desktop application development. Now you can hit rewind on your experiences and knowledge and look at web development in a new way. In this second part of the book, we will go beyond the introductory material you saw in the previous chapters, and look at more goal-oriented GWT techniques.

When working with GWT, you are, of course, no longer building navigation and pages in the way you did before. Even more module-centric web frameworks like JSF are still essentially page-based, with the model, view, and controller layers executing within the application server. Now you need to look at your application as having a series of widgets making up the view, a controller that orchestrates actions, and a smart model layer.

In this chapter, we will take a look at a basic use-case for a web application you have likely written many times before: user registration. We will move through the whole structure of this example and look at how these parts relate in GWT applications. We will start by building a model layer that is more intelligent than most of the models you have likely used in other web applications. Next, we will show how to construct the view components and connect them to the model. Finally, we will look at the controller, at how to use the controller layer to interact with services on the server, and at how to use the Java Persistence API (JPA) to store elements in the database.

4.1 Building a model

The model layer of a GWT application has to be a little bit smarter than the model in many traditional web applications. It needs to be responsible for notifying the view layer of changes, as well as for receiving updates to its own structure. In desktop Java development, this is accomplished through the use of `PropertyChangeEvents` and `PropertyChangeListeners` that bind the data from the model to the view components. The view layer "listens" for changes to the model and updates itself accordingly, using the Observer pattern. This can be done in GWT development as well. You saw a small example of this in chapter 2, with the calculator's model, and we will expand on that concept here, using a more formal and representative approach that demonstrates what you will need to do over and over.

Figure 4.1 shows a basic `User` class that we will work with. It is a simple class containing a user name and other common fields, as well as two `Address` objects (one shipping and one billing). To get started, we need to enable these for data binding.

PROBLEM

We need to enable data binding to user interface elements in our model.

SOLUTION

The basis of data binding between the model and the view is triggering events in the model that notify the view of changes, and vice versa. In the calculator example from chapter 2, we built an event system from scratch. We did this in order to be explicit and not involve additional concepts and dependencies in our first example. Nevertheless, this manual method is somewhat inconvenient.

Here we will use the `java.beans.PropertyChangeSupport` class. This isn't a class provided by GWT yet, but it is available as part of the GWTx project (http://code.

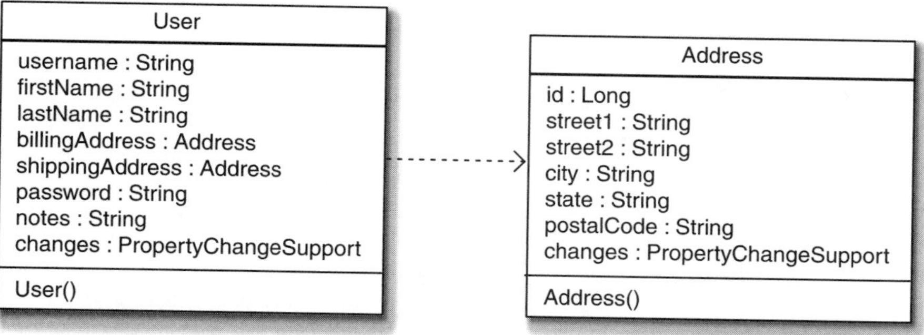

Figure 4.1 The `User` and `Address` classes serving as the model. Notice the `PropertyChangeSupport` attribute, which we will use to notify the view of changes to the model beans.

google. com/p/gwtx/), which adds to the core Java classes provided by GWT. Listing 4.1 shows the `User` object instrumented with the `PropertyChangeSupport` class.

Listing 4.1 Using the `PropertyChangeSupport` class in the `User` object

```
public class User implements IsSerializable {          <-- Include IsSerializable marker (1)

    private String username;
    private String firstName;
    private String lastName;
    private Address billingAddress = new Address();
    private Address shippingAddress = new Address();
    private String password;
    private String notes;
    private transient PropertyChangeSupport changes =     <-- Construct Property-ChangeSupport (2)
        new PropertyChangeSupport(this);

    public User() {
        super();
    }

    public String getFirstName() {
        return firstName;
    }

    public void setFirstName(String firstName) {         (3) Include PropertyChangeSupport to fire changes
        String old = this.firstName;
        this.firstName = firstName;
        changes.firePropertyChange(
"firstName", old, firstName);
    }

    public String getLastName() {
        return lastName;
    }

    public void setLastName(String lastName) {
        String old = lastName;
        this.lastName = lastName;
```

```
        changes.firePropertyChange("lastName", old, lastName );
    }

    public Address getBillingAddress() {
        return billingAddress;
    }

    public void setBillingAddress(Address billingAddress) {
        Address old = this.billingAddress;
        this.billingAddress = billingAddress;
        changes.firePropertyChange(
"billingAddress", old, billingAddress);
    }

     // The rest of the getters and setters are removed for brevity.

    public void addPropertyChangeListener(
PropertyChangeListener l) {
        changes.addPropertyChangeListener(l);            ❹ Add global change listener
    }

    public void addPropertyChangeListener(
        String propertyName,
PropertyChangeListener l) {                              ❺ Add property-specific listener
        changes.addPropertyChangeListener(
propertyName, l);
    }

    public void removePropertyChangeListener(PropertyChangeListener l) {
        changes.removePropertyChangeListener(l);
    }

    public void removePropertyChangeListener(
        String propertyName, PropertyChangeListener l) {
        changes.removePropertyChangeListener(propertyName, l);
    }

}
```

This gives us a model object capable of notifying the view of changes and exposing methods for attaching listeners.

DISCUSSION

This may be a lot more code than you are used to seeing in a model bean in a traditional web application, but it is mostly boilerplate. We first need to implement `IsSerializable` or `Serializable` ❶ (the GWT marker interfaces that tell the compiler this class should be made serializable), because we want this object to move back and forth between the client and the server. This time, though, we have a nonserializable property: the `PropertyChangeSupport` instance `changes` is marked transient ❷ and isn't part of the serialized version that will be sent back and forth. It is constructed each time with the object.

Once we have the `PropertyChangeSupport` class, we need to instrument the setter methods to fire change events. The sequence is repetitive, but very important. First you store the current value, then you set the new value, and only after the new value is set do you fire the change event ❸. It is critical that the change events only be fired after the instance value has been set, not at the top of the setter method. The reason for this is what happens inside the `PropertyChangeSupport` class.

`PropertyChangeSupport` (PCS) provides collections and fires change events much like the interfaces used in the previous calculator example. It also checks each call to `firePropertyChange()` to make sure the old and new values are different before firing the event. Figure 4.2 shows the execution sequence for a change event being fired and updating an element with a two-way bind.

If you called `firePropertyChange()` at the top of the setter method, when the last step in this sequence was reached, the current instance value on the model object would still be the same, and the whole event cycle would go into an infinite loop!

Finally, we need to provide methods on the model object for listeners to be added to the model. There are two kinds of listeners supported by the `PropertyChangeSupport` class. Global listeners ❹ will receive an event any time a change is fired. The listener would then look at the value returned by the call to `getPropertyName()` on the `PropertyChangeEvent` instance to decide what to do. The other type of listeners are property specific ❺. These will only be fired if the specified property changes, and they are generally the most useful listeners. However, if you have a complex model or one that requires a lot of translation between the model data and the data needed to properly render the view elements, it can be easier to just listen for any change and reset the entire view component.

Now we have built the model layer of our application, and we have given it the ability to notify listeners of changes, which can be used to bind data in the view layer. The

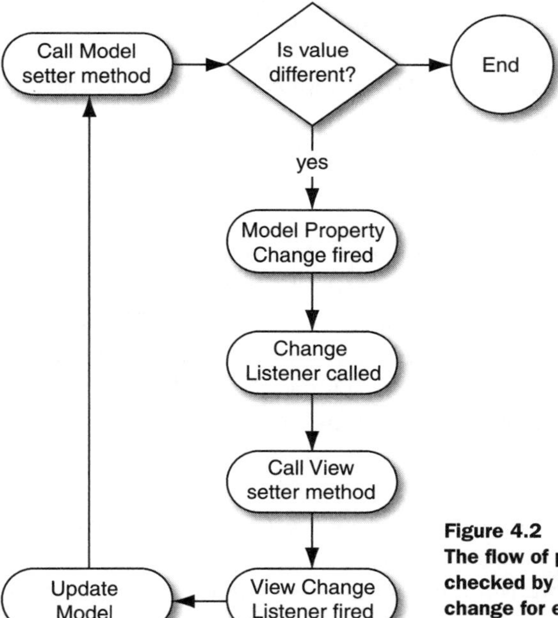

Figure 4.2
The flow of property change events firing will loop if not checked by the model. If the model doesn't check the change for equality, or if the change hasn't happened yet, an infinite loop is formed.

next part of the user registration application we need to build is the view layer itself. The view will both listen to changes coming from the model, and fire its own changes to update the model based on user input.

4.2 Building view components

Unlike page- or template-based technologies, the view layer of a GWT application is composed of Java classes. As a result, the best way to build your user interface is to build a component (or several) for each element of your view. Like building page templates for editing an object type when using a traditional system like Struts Tiles, components can be composed of several different types of view elements.

Most well-designed API libraries derive from a few core classes that encapsulate common functionality. GWT is no different. The `com.google.gwt.user.client.ui` package includes such foundational elements. These items are not typically instantiated directly but are the backbone of the API. The package starts with a root `UIObject` base class, and then fans out into the various component hierarchies that make up the remainder of the library. `UIObject`, as its name implies, is where you begin when building view components.

Figure 4.3 shows a simplified class diagram for the top portion of the API. You can see `UIObject`, `Widget`, and the other descendant elements that are used to create view components.

The API fans out from `UIObject` to three direct descendants: the further subclassed `Widget`, and two individual offshoots, `MenuItem` and `TreeItem`. The subclasses of `Widget` also fall into two distinct subsets: those that are not themselves further subclassed (at the lower left in figure 4.3), and those that are further subclassed (at the lower right in figure 4.3).

These are the core classes used to build GWT applications. When constructing a view layer, there are two general patterns for building UI elements: extending a base GWT widget, or constructing a composite. We will look at both of these methods in turn.

4.2.1 Extending widgets

Declaring your view class as extending a core widget is an easy way to start. You can then perform your setup in the constructor and add methods specific to your implementation, as we did in chapter 2's calculator. We will start with this same pattern here, by constructing a `Panel` that provides an edit view for an `Address` object.

PROBLEM

We need to construct a particular view for a model element, and this view will be used within our module.

SOLUTION

Extending a base GWT widget is certainly the easiest way to get started. We will use this technique to create an `AddressEdit` class. Figure 4.4 shows the address edit portion of a larger component we will complete in this chapter for editing user data, a `UserEdit` widget.

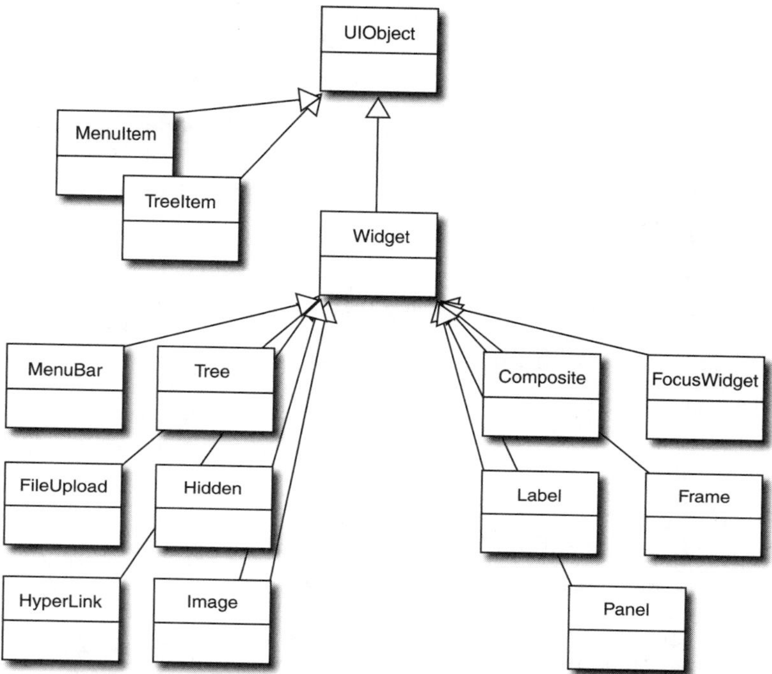

Figure 4.3 The top-level hierarchy of classes in the `client.ui` API. Notice that almost everything is a `Widget`, except for `MenuItem` and `TreeItem`, which are for limited use inside other widgets.

Figure 4.4 The `AddressEdit` widget showing editing of the `billingAddress` property nested in a `StackPanel`. The `StackPanel` shows the other elements of the larger `UserEdit` component.

Here the AddressEdit class simply extends the FlexTable widget, allowing us to lay out a fairly standard address entry form. Listing 4.2 shows how we build this form in the constructor of AddressEdit.

Listing 4.2 AddressEdit.java

```
public class AddressEdit extends FlexTable {

    private Address address;                          ❶ Include model reference
    private TextBox street1 = new TextBox();
    private TextBox street2 = new TextBox();          ❷ Construct component widgets for Address
    private TextBox city = new TextBox();
    private ListBox state = new ListBox();
    private TextBox postalCode = new TextBox();

    public AddressEdit(final Address address) {
        super();

        state.addItem("...");
        state.addItem("AL");
        state.addItem("AK");
        // rest omitted.

        this.setStyleName("user-AddressEdit");
        this.address = address;
        this.setWidget(0,0, new Label("Street"));
        this.setWidget(0,1, street1);                 ❸ Lay out grid
        this.setWidget(1,0, new Label("Street"));
        this.setWidget(1,1, street2);
        this.setWidget(2,0, new Label("City, State"));
        HorizontalPanel hp = new HorizontalPanel();
        hp.add(city);
        hp.add(new Label(","));                       ❹ Create subpanel where needed
        hp.add(state);
        this.setWidget(2,1, hp);

        this.setWidget(3,0, new Label("PostalCode"));
        this.setWidget(3,1, postalCode);
    }
}
```

AddressEdit extends a simple widget, FlexTable, and lays out the elements we need to edit an Address object.

DISCUSSION

Extending FlexTable ❶ makes laying out the widgets in the constructor method very easy. We simply create the elements we need ❷ and add them. FlexTable works much like a standard HTML table element, dynamically reconfiguring itself as elements are added to grid positions ❸.

FlexTable and Grid are both subclasses of HTMLTable and, as such, use the same methods for inserting elements into a table structure at a specified row and column. The difference is that FlexTable adds methods that enable you to insert new cells dynamically, while Grid does not. Grid does allow for the entire table to be resized, rows or columns, but does not allow on-the-fly expansion like FlexTable does. This is because Grid, by definition, must maintain its rectangular nature, and FlexTable is, how shall we put this, flexible.

Inside our widget we are using a HorizontalPanel to format city and state in the traditional sequence. Along with VerticalPanel, it is the most basic of container Widgets. This panel simply lays out the widgets added to it horizontally in the order they are added; in this case, a TextBox, a Label, and a ListBox are added ❹.

Extending a base GWT widget is problematic for widgets you want to expose as part of an API. Since the AddressEdit widget extends FlexTable, it is possible for external code to call the setWidget() method outside of the constructor and alter the composition of the widget. We don't want people doing this, since AddressEdit is really only intended to be used inside the scope of editing a user. To get around this problem, GWT provides the Composite widget.

4.2.2 Extending composite

In this chapter's AddressEdit example, and in chapter 2's calculator, we created a widget by combining provided panels and input components in a custom manner. We wanted to reuse all of the Widget features provided by the toolkit, so we extended a Panel, such as VerticalPanel. While this approach does work and is simple (which is why we have used it so far), it is not the preferred way to create custom GWT components. Instead of naively subclassing panel elements, it is much better to create a GWT Composite class.

Composite is a class that exposes only the getElement() method, as required by UIObject, and provides several protected methods for use by widgets that subclass the component. These methods are getWidget(), setWidget(), and initWidget(). Composite objects contain only a single base widget, which for obvious reasons will usually be a container of some kind. These widgets are constructed inside the local constructor of a Composite child, and then are added to the composite with initWidget(). The call to initWidget() must always be made before a Composite can be added to a container, and should therefore be the last call in your constructor.

In this section, to demonstrate the Composite concept, we will create the UserEdit class as a composite element.

PROBLEM

We need to create a widget, but we do not wish to expose the public methods of a basic GWT widget.

SOLUTION

Start by extending Composite, and expose only the methods you want, or none at all. Listing 4.3 shows the UserEdit class and the construction of a Composite widget.

Listing 4.3 Building a Composite UserEdit class

```
public class UserEdit extends Composite {
    private User user;
    private StackPanel stack = new StackPanel();
    private TextBox username = new TextBox();
```

❶ Create model layer object for widget

```
    private PasswordTextBox password = new PasswordTextBox();
    private PasswordTextBox passwordConfirm = new PasswordTextBox();
    private TextBox firstName = new TextBox();
    private TextBox lastName = new TextBox();
    private TextArea notes = new TextArea();
    private AddressEdit billingAddress;
    private AddressEdit shippingAddress;

    public UserEdit(final UserCreateListener controller, final User user) {
        super();
        this.user = user;
        stack.setHeight("350px");
        VerticalPanel basePanel = new VerticalPanel();
        Button save = new Button("Save");
        basePanel.add(save);
        basePanel.add(stack);
        FlexTable ft = new FlexTable();                          <-- Create FlexTable to lay out basic elements
        ft.setWidget(0,0, new Label("Username"));
        ft.setWidget(0,1, username);
        ft.setWidget(1,0, new Label("Password"));
        ft.setWidget(1,1, password);
        ft.setWidget(2,0, new Label("Confirm"));
        ft.setWidget(2,1, passwordConfirm );

        ft.setWidget(3,0, new Label("First Name"));
        ft.setWidget(3,1, firstName);
        ft.setWidget(4,0, new Label("Last Name"));
        ft.setWidget(4,1, lastName);

        stack.add(ft, "User Information" );
        billingAddress = new AddressEdit(
            user.getBillingAddress());
        stack.add(billingAddress, "Billing Address");            | Create AddressEdit
        shippingAddress = new AddressEdit(                       | classes for
          user.getShippingAddress());                            | addresses
        stack.add(shippingAddress, "Shipping Address");
        notes.setWidth("100%");
        notes.setHeight("250px");
        stack.add(notes, "Notes");

      this.initWidget(basePanel);
    }
}
```

In this example, we are using our `UserEdit` class as a component in a larger edit view of the `User` model object. While the object graph contains other structured objects (the `Address` classes), the `UserEdit` class brings these together with the editors for the other portions of our model that we created individually. It also provides direct edit widgets for simple values directly on the `User` class. At first blush, this looks very similar to the process we used in constructing the `AddressEdit` class, but it is actually a bit different.

DISCUSSION

Listing 4.3 creates our model layer object ❶ and a bunch of widgets relating to the fields on the model. The outer container is simply a `VerticalPanel`, and then we use a `StackPanel` to separate out different aspects of the `User` object. A `StackPanel` is a special kind of container that provides an expanding and collapsing stack of widgets with a label that toggles between them (much like the sidebar in Microsoft Outlook).

The use of the `StackPanel` is in keeping with one of the new principles you should note if you are coming from traditional web development: Build interface components, not navigation. In a traditional web application, each element of the stack might be a separate page, and it would be necessary to use a `Session` construct on the server to store the intermediate states of the `User` object. Here we can simply build the entire `User` object's construction process into one component that lets the user move through them. This means less resource use on the server, because we are spared a request-response cycle when we move between the different sections; we no longer have to maintain state information for each user accessing the application.

Once we have constructed the `UserEdit` object, it has no exposed methods other than `getElement()`, and it is public rather than package-scoped like `AddressEdit`. These aren't completed classes, however. We still need to enable them to interact with the model layer. This means handling user input via events and making changes to the model to update the data.

4.2.3 Binding to the model with events

We discussed in section 4.1 why we need events on the model layer, and how to provide that functionality. Now, in the view layer, we need to build the binding logic into our widgets. GWT includes a number of basic event types.

In fact, many of the GWT widgets provide much of the event notification you will ever need. In our `UserEdit` example thus far, we made use of `Button`, which extends `FocusWidget`, which in turn implements `SourcesClickEvents` and `SourcesFocusEvents` to raise events for our `ClickListener` implementation. Likewise, we used `TextBox`, which itself implements `SourcesKeyboardEvents`, `SourcesChangeEvents`, and `SourcesClickEvents`. In the GWT API, event types are specified by these `Sources` interfaces, which tell developers what events a widget supports. We can use these, along with the `PropertyChangeEvents` from our model layer to provide a two-way binding with the view.

PROBLEM

We need to bind the data from a widget or a view component to a property on a model object.

SOLUTION

We will revisit the `UserEdit` composite class to demonstrate data binding. Listing 4.4 shows the changes we will make to the constructor, and the new methods we will add to support this concept.

Listing 4.4 UserEdit.java, modified to include `PropertyChangeSupport`

```
public class UserEdit extends Composite{
     // Previously shown attributes omitted
    private PropertyChangeListener[] listeners =
        new PropertyChangeListener[5];
```

Create Array to hold PropertyChangeListeners

```
public UserEdit(final UserCreateListener controller, final User user) {
     super();
 // Previously shown widget building omitted.
 listeners[0] = new PropertyChangeListenerProxy(
    "street1",
    new PropertyChangeListener() {
        public void propertyChange(
    PropertyChangeEvent propertyChangeEvent) {
        street1.setText(
        (String) propertyChangeEvent.getNewValue());
            }
         });
 address.addPropertyChangeListener(listeners[0]);
 street1.addChangeListener(
     new ChangeListener() {
         public void onChange(Widget sender) {
             address.setStreet1(street1.getText());
         }
     });

     // Repeating pattern for each of the elements

     save.addClickListener( new ClickListener() {
         public void onClick(Widget sender) {
             if(!password.getText().equals(
                     passwordConfirm.getText())) {
                 Window.alert("Passwords do not match!");
                 return;
             }
             controller.createUser(user);
         }
     });

     this.initWidget(basePanel);

 }
 public void cleanup(){
     for (int i=0; i < listeners.length; i++) {
         user.removePropertyChangeListener(listeners[i]);
     }
   billingAddress.cleanup();
     shippingAddress.cleanup();
 }
```

Annotations:
1. Create PropertyChangeListener for model
- Add PropertyChangeListener to model object
2. Repeat for each property
3. Create change listener for view
- Update model
4. Check passwordConfirm before updating
5. Call controller
6. Clean up model listener
7. Clean up child view elements

Now we have the basics of data binding and housekeeping in the `UserEdit` class.

DISCUSSION

Providing two-way data binding, unfortunately, requires a good deal of repetitive code ❷. In Swing it is possible to simplify a lot of this boilerplate code with reflection-based utility classes, but since the Reflection API isn't available in GWT code, we must repeat this code for each of our properties. First, we create a `PropertyChangeListener` ❶ that watches the model and will update the view if the model changes. We wrap it in a `PropertyChangeListenerProxy` that will filter the events to just those we want to watch. While not critical here, it is a very good practice to provide this binding in your widgets. This ensures that if another part of the application updates the model, the view will reflect it immediately and you will not have a confused state between different components that are looking at the same objects.

NOTE While the `PropertyChangeSupport` class will let you add `PropertyChangeListeners` specifying a property name, it will wrap these in the `PropertyChangeListenerProxy` class internally. When it does this, you lose the ability to call `removePropertyChangeListener()` without specifying a property name. Since we just want to loop over all of these listeners in our `cleanup()` method, we wrap them as we construct them so the cleanup will run as expected.

Next, we create a `ChangeListener` and attach it to the widget responsible for the property ❸. With each change to the widget, the model will be updated. In this case, we are using `TextBoxes`, so we call the `getText()` method to determine their value. If you have done Ajax/DHTML programming before, you know that the common pattern for the `<input type="text">` element is that the `onChange` closure only fires when the value has changed and the element loses focus. Sometimes this is important to keep in mind, but since we know that the element will lose focus as the user clicks the Save button, we don't have to worry about it here. If you need that kind of detail about changes, you could use a `KeyboardListener` on the `TextBoxes`, which will fire on each keystroke while the box is focused.

For some widgets, you might have to provide a bit of logical conversion code to populate the model. The following is a small section from the `AddressEdit` class, where we update the state property on the `Address` object:

```
listeners[4] = new PropertyChangeListener() {
    public void propertyChange(
        PropertyChangeEvent propertyChangeEvent) {
        for(int i=0; i < state.getItemCount(); i++) {
            if(state.getItemText(i).equals(
                propertyChangeEvent.getNewValue())) {
                state.setSelectedIndex(i);
                break;
            }
        }
    }
};
address.addPropertyChangeListener("state", listeners[4]);
state.addChangeListener(new ChangeListener() {
    public void onChange(Widget sender) {
        String value = state.getItemText(state.getSelectedIndex());
        if(!"...".equals(value)) {
            address.setState(value);
        }
    }
});
```

This looks much like the repeating patterns with the `TextBoxes`, but in both listeners we must determine the value in relation to the `SelectedIndex` property of the state `ListBox`.

When the user clicks the Save button, we need to make the call back to the controller layer to store the user data ❺. You will notice that we are doing one small bit of data validation here: we are checking that the `password` and `passwordConfirm` values are the same ❹. The `passwordConfirm` isn't actually part of our model; it is simply a UI nicety. Where you do data validation can be an interesting discussion on its own. In some situations, you might know the valid values and simply put the checks in the setters of the model and catch exceptions in the `ChangeListeners` of the view. This can provide a lot of instant feedback to users while they are filling out forms. For larger things like either-or relationships, or things that require server checks, providing validation in the controller is the best option. Of course, since GWT is Java-based, you can use the same validation logic on the server and the client, saving on the effort you might have expended in more traditional Ajax development.

The final important thing to notice here is the `cleanup()` ❻ method. This simply cycles through the `PropertyChangeListeners` we added to the model class and removes them. This is important because once the application is done with the `UserEdit` widget, it needs a means to clean up the widget. If we didn't remove these listeners from the longer-lived `User` object, the `UserEdit` reference could never be garbage-collected, and would continue to participate in the event execution, needlessly taking up processor cycles. Of course, since the `AddressEdit` widget is doing this as well, we also need to clean up those listeners ❼.

Why do we clean up the `PropertyChangeListeners` and not the `ChangeListeners` and `ClickListeners` we used on the child widgets? Those change listeners will fall out of scope and be garbage-collected at the same time as our `UserEdit` class. Since they are private members, and the `UserEdit Composite` masks any other operations into itself, classes outside of the scope of `UserEdit` can't maintain references to them.

Now that we have the model and the view, and we have established the relationship between them, we need to set up the controller and send the user registration information back to the server.

4.3 The controller and service

You may have noticed that we passed a `UserCreateListener` instance into the `UserEdit` constructor. It is important in the design of your application that your custom widgets externalize any business logic. If you want to promote reuse of your view code, it shouldn't needlessly be tied to a particular set of business logic. In this example, though, our controller logic is pretty simple.

In this section, we will build the controller and the service servlet that will store our user in the database, pointing out places where you can extend the design with other functionality.

4.3.1 Creating a simple controller

The overall job of the controller is to provide access to business logic and provide a control system for the state of the view. Think, for a moment, about the controller level of an `Action` in a Struts application. Suppose it is triggered based on a user event, a form submission. It then validates the data and passes it into some kind of business logic (though many Struts applications, unfortunately, put the business logic right in the `Action` bean) and directs the view to update to a new state—redirecting to some other page. You should think of the controller in a GWT application as filling this role, but in a very different manner.

We will now take a look at a simple controller in the form of a `UserCreateListener`.

PROBLEM

We need to create a controller to manage the action events and state for our view class. This will trigger the use-case actions of our application.

SOLUTION

We will start by creating a simple implementation of the `UserCreateListener` interface, as presented in listing 4.5.

Listing 4.5 `UserCreateListenerImpl`—the controller for the `UserEdit` widget

```
package com.manning.gwtip.user.client;

import com.google.gwt.core.client.GWT;
import com.google.gwt.user.client.Window;
import com.google.gwt.user.client.rpc.AsyncCallback;
import com.google.gwt.user.client.rpc.ServiceDefTarget;
public class UserCreateListenerImpl implements UserCreateListener {
    private UserServiceAsync service =
        (UserServiceAsync) GWT.create(UserService.class);          <-- ❶ Create a service

    public UserCreateListenerImpl() {
        super();
        ServiceDefTarget endpoint = (ServiceDefTarget) service;
        endpoint.setServiceEntryPoint
            (GWT.getModuleBaseURL()+"UserService");              <-- ❷ Bind the server address
    }

    public void createUser(User user){
        if ("root"
              .equals(
                user.getUsername())) {                          <-- Validate the data
            Window.alert("You can't be root!");
          return;
        }
        service.createUser(user, new AsyncCallback() {
            public void onSuccess(Object result) {
                Window.alert("User created.");
                // here we would change the view to a new state.
            }

            public void onFailure(Throwable caught) {           <-- Alert user
                Window.alert(caught.getMessage());
```

```
                }
            });
        }
    }
```

Now we have a controller class for our `UserEdit` widget. This controller will make calls back to the remote service, completing the front end of the application.

DISCUSSION

This is a simple and somewhat trivial example, but it does demonstrate the logical flow you should see in your application. First, we get the service ❶ and bind it ❷, as you saw in chapter 3. Next, we implement the required method, `createUser()`. The method starts with a simple bit of data validation, and this could certainly be more advanced.

A good case would be to create a `UserValidator` object that could perform any basic validation we need. This simple example just shows where this would happen. Once the validation is done, we make the call to the remote service and handle the results. If this were part of a larger application, the `onSuccess()` method might call back out to another class to remove the `UserEdit` panel from the screen and present the user with another panel, like the forward on a Struts action controller.

Another validation case would be to present the user with an error notification if something "borked" on the call to the server. This might indicate an error, or data that failed validation on the server. For example, duplicate usernames can't easily be checked on the client. We have to check this at the point where we insert the user into the database.

All of which brings us to accessing the database in the service. For this, we will use the Java Persistence API.

4.3.2 JPA-enabling the model

One of the most common questions in GWT development is, "How do I get to the database?" You saw the basics of the Tomcat Lite configuration in chapter 3, but most people want to use something fancier than raw JDBC with their database. While JDBC works well, it is more cumbersome to work with than object-oriented persistence APIs. Today, that usually means some JPA provider like Hibernate, Kodo, OpenJPA, or TopLink Essentials.

There are two general patterns for using JPA in a GWT environment. The first is to JPA-enable a model shared between the client and the server. The second is to create a set of DTOs that are suitable for use on the client, and convert them in the service to something suitable for use on the server. Figure 4.5 shows the difference between these approaches in systems.

There are trade-offs to be made with either of these patterns. If you JPA-enable a shared model, your model classes are then limited to what the GWT JRE emulation classes can support, and to the general restrictions for being GWT-translatable (no argument constructor, no Java 5 language constructs currently, and so on). Using the DTO approach and converting between many transfer objects adds complexity and

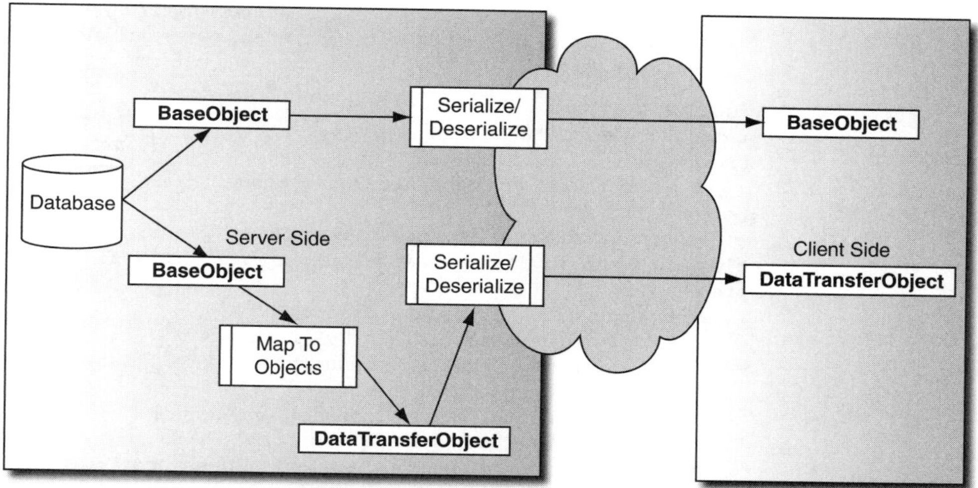

Figure 4.5 Flow from the server to the client with and without `DataTransferObjects`. Note that an additional mapping step is needed if DTOs are used.

potentially a lot of lines of code to your application, but it also provides you with finer-grained control over the actual model your GWT client uses.

Due to the restrictions in the direct JPA entity approach, and due to other advantages that a DTO layer can provide, it is common to use the DTO approach to communicate between GWT and a server-side model. We will take a look at this pattern, using transfer objects and all of the aspects it entails, in detail in chapter 9, where we will consider a larger Spring-managed application. In this chapter, we will look at JPA-enabling our GWT beans, which is the easiest method for simple standalone applications.

PROBLEM

We want to enable our model beans for use with JPA providers to persist them to a database.

SOLUTION

If you have been using JPA in the past, and you recall that GWT client components are bound to a Java 1.4 syntactical structure, you are likely thinking to yourself, "you can't add annotations to those beans!" Good eye—you would be thinking correctly. However, there is another way to describe JPA beans that doesn't normally get much attention but is designed for just such a scenario: using an orm.xml metadata mapping file. You, of course, also need a persistence.xml file to declare the persistence unit. Listing 4.6 shows the persistence unit definition.

Listing 4.6 Persistence.xml for the user

```
<?xml version="1.0" encoding="UTF-8"?>
<persistence xmlns="http://java.sun.com/xml/ns/persistence"
             xmlns:xsi="http://www.w3.org/2001/XMLSchema-instance"
```

```
            xsi:schemaLocation="http://java.sun.com/xml/ns/persistence
            http://java.sun.com/xml/ns/persistence/persistence_1_0.xsd"
            version="1.0">

    <persistence-unit name="user-service"
        transaction-type="RESOURCE_LOCAL">
        <provider>
            org.hibernate.ejb.HibernatePersistence     <-- Specify using Hibernate
        </provider>
        <class>com.manning.gwtip.user.client.User</class>
        <class>com.manning.gwtip.user.client.Address</class>
        <properties>
            <property name="hibernate.dialect"
            value="org.hibernate.dialect.MySQLDialect"/>     <-- Specify using MySQL
            <property name="hibernate.connection.driver_class"
             value="com.mysql.jdbc.Driver"/>
            <property name="hibernate.connection.username"
                value="userdb"/>
            <property name="hibernate.connection.password"
                value="userdb"/>
            <property name="hibernate.connection.url"
             value="jdbc:mysql://localhost/userdb"/>
            <property name="hibernate.hbm2ddl.auto"
            value="create-drop"/>     <-- Drop and create the DB each time
        </properties>
    </persistence-unit>
</persistence>
```

If you have used JPA before, this will look pretty standard. We aren't using a DataSource here, just making direct connections to the database. We are also using Hibernate. Even though we have experience using both Hibernate and TopLink Essentials as JPA providers, we chose Hibernate for this example because although Hibernate requires more dependencies, it is actually easier to demonstrate in the GWT shell. TopLink works in the shell also, but it requires additional steps beyond dependencies, such as an endorsed mechanism override of the embedded Tomcat version of Xerces, and the inclusion of the TopLink agent (we will use TopLink in several other examples later in the book).

Next, we need an orm.xml file to specify the metadata we would normally specify in annotations. Listing 4.7 shows the mapping file for our user objects.

Listing 4.7 The orm.xml file

```
<?xml version="1.0" encoding="UTF-8"?>
<entity-mappings xmlns="http://java.sun.com/xml/ns/persistence/orm"
        xmlns:xsi="http://www.w3.org/2001/XMLSchema-instance"
        xsi:schemaLocation="http://java.sun.com/xml/ns/persistence/orm
                http://java.sun.com/xml/ns/persistence/orm_1_0.xsd"
                version="1.0">

    <package>com.manning.gwtip.user.client</package>
    <entity class="User"
       metadata-complete="true" access="PROPERTY">     <-- 1 Save steps with metadata-complete
        <table name="USER"/>
```

```
        <named-query name="User.findUserByUsernameAndPassword">
            <query>select u from User u
                where u.username = :username
                       and u.password = :password</query>
        </named-query>
        <attributes>
            <id name="username" />
            <one-to-one name="shippingAddress" >          <-- Cascade to
                <cascade>                                      Address objects
                    <cascade-all />
                </cascade>
            </one-to-one>
            <one-to-one name="billingAddress" >
                <cascade>
                    <cascade-all />
                </cascade>
            </one-to-one>
        </attributes>
    </entity>
    <entity class="Address" metadata-complete="true" access="PROPERTY">
        <table name="ADDRESS"/>
        <attributes>
            <id name="id">
                <generated-value strategy="IDENTITY"/>      <-- Autoincrement
            </id>                                              ID field
        </attributes>
    </entity>
</entity-mappings>
```

This looks a lot like the annotations you might provide in the Java files themselves. Indeed, the orm.xml file maps pretty much one to one with the annotations. The important thing to pay attention to is the `metadata-complete` attribute on the `<entity>` element ❶. This tells the entity manager to use its default behavior for any properties on the object that aren't explicitly laid out in the file.

DISCUSSION

For the `id` property on the `Address` object, we are using an `IDENTITY` strategy that will use MySQL's autoincrementing field type. This is another area where Hibernate and TopLink differ in use. TopLink doesn't support the `IDENTITY` scheme with its MySQL4 dialect. You must use a virtual sequence. In this case, the address `<entity>` element would look like this:

```
<entity class="Address" metadata-complete="true" access="PROPERTY">
     <table name="ADDRESS"/>
     <sequence-generator
         name="addressId" sequence-name="ADDRESS_ID_SEQUENCE" />
     <attributes>
         <id name="id">
             <generated-value strategy="SEQUENCE" generator="addressId"/>
         </id>
     </attributes>
</entity>
```

MySQL doesn't support sequences as a database structure, but TopLink will create a table to maintain the sequence value. Hibernate balks at this configuration, because it knows that MySQL doesn't support sequences. In short, don't expect these configuration files to be write-once-run-anywhere. Everything from the JPA provider used, right down to the database used, is coupled in your application. Hopefully as the EJB 3/JPA implementations mature, these issues will go away.

The orm.xml file is not well documented. We have found the best documentation to be simply looking at the schema file itself (http://java.sun.com/xml/ns/persistence/orm_1_0.xsd) and using a validating XML editor. Another option is to use the OpenJPA reverse-engineering tool (http://incubator.apache.org/openjpa/), which has the ability to create an orm.xml file for you from an existing database schema.

Now we have our JPA mappings, enabling us to store the objects from the model we created in the first step to the database. The last step is to create the service component that will bridge the gap between the client-side controller we created in section 4.3.1 and the database.

4.3.3 Creating a JPA-enabled service

We mentioned in chapter 3 that it is generally a best practice to create a separate local service and have your `RemoteServiceServlet` proxy calls into it. While we will be looking at that pattern in detail in chapter 9, we will simply create our service code in the servlet here. Since we are JPA-enabling our model, the fact that our service is dependent on the GWT libraries doesn't have any negative ramifications.

PROBLEM

We need to create a JPA-enabled service servlet for our application to take model objects sent from the controller layer of the client and store them in a database.

SOLUTION

Listing 4.8 shows the `RemoteServiceServlet` that will take the model objects and persist them to the database.

Listing 4.8 `UserServiceServlet` with JPA calls

```
public class UserServiceServlet extends RemoteServiceServlet
    implements UserService {
    private EntityManagerFactory factory;      <-- (1) Cannot use @PersistenceUnit annotation

    public UserServiceServlet() {
        super();
        try{
             factory =
               Persistence.createEntityManagerFactory(   <-- (2) Create the EntityManagerFactory
           "user-service");
        } catch(Exception e){
           e.printStackTrace();
        }

    }
```

```
    public void createUser(User user) throws UserServiceException {
        if("root".equals(user.getUsername())) {
            throw new UserServiceException(
                "You can't be root!");              <-- ❸ Remember, never trust the client
        }
        try{
            EntityManager mgr = factory.createEntityManager();
            mgr.getTransaction().begin();
            mgr.persist(user);
            mgr.getTransaction().commit();          Catch persistence exceptions
        } catch(RollbackException e) {              <--
            throw new UserServiceException(
            "That username is taken. Try another!");
        } catch(PersistenceException p) {
            throw new UserServiceException(
            "An unexpected error occurred: "+p.toString());
        }
    }
}
```

This likely looks familiar to anyone who has done JPA work, but there are some important things to cover concerning how we are interacting with JPA here.

DISCUSSION

This is a pretty simple class, but there are some important things to note about it. First, we aren't using the `@PersistenceUnit` annotation to get our `EntityManagerFactory` ❶. This would be the "regular" way to get `EntityManagerFactory` in Java EE 5. The Tomcat in GWTShell—or Tomcat in general, for that matter—doesn't support Java EE 5 dependency injection. You can use Spring for this in regular Tomcat, but since all the servlets in the GWT shell are created by the shell proxy service, we can't easily do this in hosted mode. So, we simply create the factory on our own in the constructor ❷.

The next thing of note is that we revalidate the user data ❸. Remember, you should always check the data on both sides. Checking it on the client side improves the user experience; checking it on the server improves application robustness.

Finally, we check for the `RollBackException`, which is thrown if the username is already in the database. This is a broken part of Hibernate. If we were using TopLink, we would catch the "correct" exception, `javax.persistence.EntityExistsException`. These types of differences are another example of the current challenges of using the present generation of JPA providers.

Now we have all the necessary components of a basic web application. We have a model layer that notifies listeners of changes, a view layer that binds to the model and provides updates, and a controller layer that captures our use cases and passes requests to the service. Last, we have a service that takes our model layer and persists it to a database. While these are the same components that a Struts or JSF developer might be used to building, they manifest differently in code and bring with them a new set of design issues for the web developer to consider.

4.4 Summary

In this chapter, we introduced the standard patterns that make up a GWT application. While the typical MVC approach certainly still applies, the way we go about using it is very different from the server-side MVC you might have used in traditional web frameworks in the past. First, the model object on the client is much more intelligent than a simple value object. Data binding is done on an eventing basis, and calls to the server are more service-oriented, representing a use case for your application, not necessarily a "screen."

Some of these things you already know how to do, yet the ways you expect to do them might not work at first in the GWT shell environment. Here, we explored one way to integrate JPA with a GWT application. In chapter 9, we will look at another pattern that integrates Spring, JPA, and DTOs. Chapter 9's approach can be used to make your application integrate more cleanly with existing JEE systems. The direct JPA- and GWT-enabled model pattern we used here is better for simple, standalone applications.

Until now we have focused on building GWT applications using the standard RPC approach for communicating with servers. In addition to the RPC and servlet method, you can also communicate with other server backends, including those that are not servlet based. In the next chapter, we will cover additional means of talking to servers, including basic HTTP and more advanced XML, SOAP, REST, Flash, and Comet. Along the way, we will also deal with the key related concepts of client/server object serialization with Java and JavaScript, and of security.

5 Other Techniques for Talking to Servers

This chapter covers

- Security issues for communications
- Using GWT's HTTP classes
- Using Flash as a communication proxy
- Using Java applets as communication proxies
- The Comet technique for event-based communications

When I am working on a problem, I never think about beauty. I think only of how to solve the problem. But when I have finished, if the solution is not beautiful, I know it is wrong.

—Buckminster Fuller

While GWT's RPC mechanism, which we introduced in chapter 3, is great for greenfield development and can be used to proxy to other service implementations, sometimes it's more valuable to have your application talk directly to an external service. For instance, if you have existing SOAP-based services that are not colocated with your web application, a two-stage proxy from the web application server can hinder performance and drive up bandwidth costs. Other times you might want to talk to public web services from Amazon, Google, Yahoo, or others. In this chapter we'll address issues surrounding talking to servers. We'll start with the security concerns and then look at several technologies—GWT and non-GWT—that enable data transmission and server communication.

Regarding data transmission, we'll take a deeper look at GWT's Java-to-JavaScript mapping, highlighting issues developers should be aware of, and taking a look at the JavaDoc-style of annotation GWT uses (`typeArgs`), which supports serialization. Then we'll look at two means of working with foreign data: GWT's bundled support for the JSON data-serialization format, and the direct GWT XML Parser API.

Once we have a handle on how to deal with data, we'll look at several techniques for sending and receiving data. The first will be XML over HTTP using GWT's `HTTPRequest` class—a technique similar to Representational State Transfer (REST). Following that, we'll take a look at using Flash and Java applets to extend the capabilities of a stock web browser and, therefore, GWT. Finally, we'll look at Comet, a technique for sending streaming data to clients outside of the traditional client-request server-response cycle.

5.1 Web development methods and security

For traditional Java server developers, GWT may be a first step into the world of Ajax development. If this is true for you, this section will be an essential primer. If it's not, feel free to jump ahead to the next section where we'll dive deep into Java-to-JavaScript mapping. Go ahead. We won't be offended.

If you're still here, what we'll discuss in this chapter will affect your life as a GWT developer, but it isn't exclusive to GWT. JavaScript has been a blessing and a curse for Ajax developers since way back when they were called DHTML developers. When Netscape introduced JavaScript, it pushed the boundaries of what could be done with a browser, and it introduced a whole new series of concerns about security on the Internet and scripting access across websites. These concerns still exist and carry over into Ajax applications with the use of the `XMLHttpRequest` object, as well as synchronicity issues in applications. We'll take a look at each of these, starting with security.

Following our theme of using a variety of development tools to showcase the various GWT options, we'll use NetBeans for our example projects in this chapter. NetBeans is a capable and popular IDE, and it includes an available GWT project template to boot. We'll set up NetBeans at the end of this section.

5.1.1 Dealing with browser security

Many of the security issues dealt with in JavaScript environments fall into the category of XSS vulnerabilities in browsers. Before browsers implemented strict security measures, any web page could open an `<iframe>` to another web page and then reach into the structure of that site to inspect or potentially manipulate "secure" data (if both sites were opened in the same browser). This was quickly recognized as a problem, and today there are security measures in place to restrict such access. Though related issues still crop up from time to time in the major browsers, these are mostly relics. Today there are clear rules among the browsers about execution permissions between scripts and servers.

The best rule of thumb to remember is what the Mozilla Foundation calls the *same-origin policy.* Jesse Ruderman describes it as follows (http://www.mozilla.org/projects/security/components/same-origin.html):

> *The same origin policy prevents documents or scripts loaded from one origin from getting or setting properties of a document from a different origin. The policy dates from Netscape Navigator 2.0.*
>
> *Mozilla considers two pages to have the same origin if the protocol, port (if given), and host are the same for both pages.*

This basically means that a script from somedomain.com can't access scripts or pages from someotherdomain.com. The exception to this rule is the page that invokes the script. For example, when you include the Google Maps API in your HTML page using the following code, your originating host page has access to the script, and the script has access to your host page, as though they were on the same server:

```
<script src="http://maps.google.com/maps?file=api&amp;v=2"
            type="text/javascript"></script>
```

While this Google-provided script has access to the DOM from your page, and your page has access to the script, the script cannot access other domains or reach up and access your script information. Code within the script can communicate only within the maps.google.com domain, not up and out to your.domain.com. Table 5.1 illustrates several scenarios where the same-origin policy is applied to a hypothetical HTML page, with the result and reasoning.

The same-origin policy applies to most elements on the page by default, including most browser plugins such as Flash and Java. However, these plugins do often provide methods to get around this limitation, and we'll address this later in the chapter. The same-origin policy also extends to the `XMLHttpRequest` object.

Table 5.1 Same-origin policy enforcement from htttp://your.company.com/page.html

URL	Result	Reason
http://your.company.com/otherpage.html	Succeeds	
http://your.company.com/otherpath/otherpage.html	Succeeds	
https://your.company.com/otherpage.html	Fails	Different protocols
http://your.company.com:8080/servlet	Fails	Different ports
http://server.company.com/service	Fails	Different hosts

5.1.2 Understanding XMLHttpRequest

At the core of the Ajax technology is the `XMLHttpRequest` object, sometimes simply referred to as XHR. All communication from the JavaScript environment to other servers takes place through this object, and, as mentioned previously, it carries restrictions. A script can (ideally) only communicate with the server from which the script was served. If it's an inline script in an HTML page, it can only communicate with the originating host of the page. If the script was specified with the `src` attribute on an HTML page, it may then interact only with the host from which the included script was served.

For instance, when you use the Google Maps JavaScript API, you include the script files from the Google web server. If you copy the script files to your own web server, you'll find they no longer work reliably. The security policy will not allow the script to communicate with the Google server for things like image tilesets and location service calls.

The `XMLHttpRequest` object also carries these same implied limitations. It can, as a rule, only use `GET` and `POST` methods for HTTP requests. While the W3C specification doesn't limit this, it is not supported in all browsers. Browser vendors are expanding this to include the `PUT` and `DELETE` methods, but they are not supported universally. This means the GWT `HTTPRequest` object, which we'll look at a bit later, cannot offer complete HTTP functionality including `PUT` and `DELETE` and still maintain the cross-browser compatibility that GWT promises.

Each request made by the `XMLHttpRequest` object is also executed asynchronously from the JavaScript runtime, a property that carries its own set of considerations.

5.1.3 Coding asynchronously

As you saw in chapter 3, calls to servers are always handled asynchronously. This carries both curses and blessings for developers.

The curses generally stem from developers being used to the very procedural request-response cycle of traditional web programming. Making a call to the server is not like calling a method on an EJB or other Remote Method Invocation (RMI) exposed object, where the method returns a value and the code continues to execute procedurally. All calls are handled by callbacks. In JavaScript, this is done by attaching closures to the XHR object at runtime. In the Java world of GWT, these callbacks are handled by classes that implement the appropriate interface for receiving the event. While the GWT nomenclature can be a bit mismatched (`AsyncCallback` for RPC services, or `ResponseTextHandler` for the `HTTPRequest` object), all the related constructs follow a traditional Observer design pattern. You implement the observer to the API's observable.

The blessings of this asynchronicity are twofold. First, and most significant, when code is written this way, issues of runtime concurrency melt away. Second, when your thoughts shift away from the direct request-response terms of a standard web application, asynchronous calls help enforce better practices in overall application structure.

JavaScript in the browser environment executes in a single thread. In the case of Firefox, this is the same thread that the user interface renderer runs in, because JavaScript may want to immediately render changes to the interface. While this can result in negative user experiences if a client-side script does a lot of processing or runs wildly out of control, it's advantageous when dealing with server calls. Executing in a single thread means that no two returns from asynchronous calls ever execute at the same time, so the programmer doesn't have to deal with any issues of concurrent access to objects or methods in the code.

While perhaps inspiring rebellious thoughts, this aspect of Ajax (and GWT development) reflects an Orwellian attitude: "Right thinking will be rewarded, wrong thinking punished." In the ideal MVC application, calls to external services should be reflected in changes to the model layer, which in turn notifies the view layer to alter the display the user sees. While this pattern is somewhat flexible, thinking of your GWT application in these terms is a good habit. The fact that the browser gives you few other options is actually helpful in forcing you to come to terms with the pattern. Developing good habits early is better than trying to break bad habits later.

Now that you have some understanding of the coding and security issues revolving around calling server-side code, we need to set up our NetBeans IDE.

5.1.4 Developing GWT applications in NetBeans

In the examples in this chapter, we'll be using the NetBeans IDE, NetBeans Enterprise Pack, and GWT4NB plugin (https://gwt4nb.dev.java.net). The core IDE and the Enterprise Pack can be downloaded from NetBeans.org.

Once you have installed NetBeans and the Enterprise Pack using the installers provided, you need to install the GWT4NB plugin by selecting Tools > Plugins and selecting the Available Plugins tab. Figure 5.1 shows this selection. Select GWT4NB

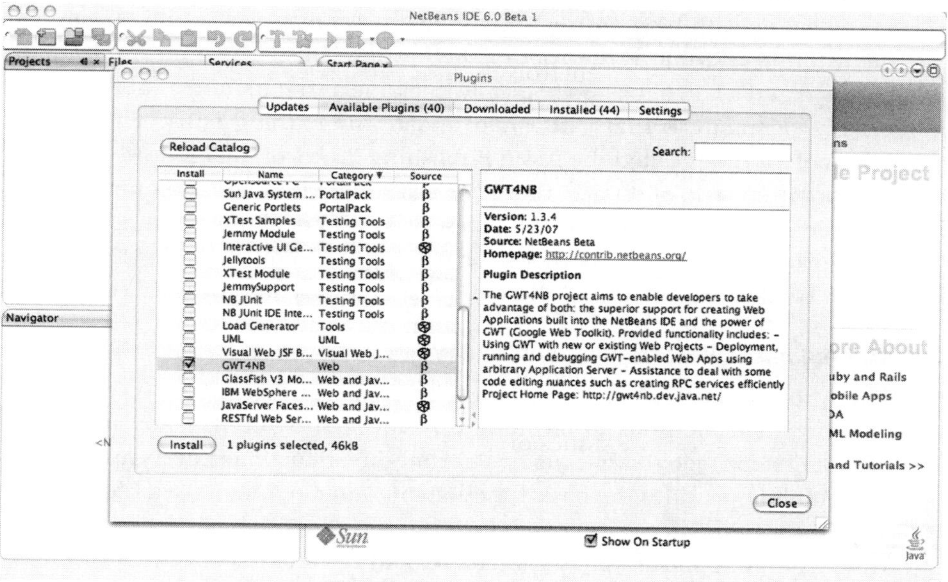

Figure 5.1 Selecting the GWT4NB module from the NetBeans Update Center

and click Install. It will take you through several more steps, which you can just click Next through.

The first time you create a GWT application project using NetBeans, you'll be prompted for the installation folder for GWT (the equivalent of GWT_HOME for the IDE). Once configured, NetBeans provides basic scaffolding for your GWT application and includes the appropriate .jar files in the library path. The code examples provided for this chapter (available at the Manning website) also each include a NetBeans project so that you can simply load and run things from there if you choose.

And speaking of code, let's get to it, starting with basic HTTP operations using the GWT APIs.

5.2 Enabling REST and POX communications

Though GWT provides its own Java-based RPC service, as we saw in chapter 3, you may want to directly access XML resources within your applications instead. Such resources usually come in two forms:

- POX (plain old XML over HTTP)
- REST (Representational State Transfer)

POX usually just involves an application interface exposed as XML with data transferred over HTTP. REST (http://www.ics.uci.edu/~fielding/pubs/dissertation/top.htm) is a little more descriptive. It deals with XML (or other format) representations of objects handled by actions represented by the four standard HTTP request methods: `PUT`, `GET`, `POST`, and `DELETE`. These map to the CRUD (Create Read Update Delete) operations most people use to describe basic data-centric applications. For instance, suppose you were dealing with blog entries. To create a new entry, you would `PUT` an `<entry>` element to the URI that is the root of the entries. This `PUT` would result in an ID being assigned and a URI allocated, typically the same as the ID, and a subsequent `POST` of an `<entry>` element to that URI would update the existing entry. There is a REST-style protocol for blogs called the Atom Publishing Protocol, that follows this exact pattern.

For either style of service, there are two simple functional requirements on the client side: making a request to the web service, and dealing with the XML data content. GWT provides two basic methods for making the request: basic HTTP and advanced HTTP. We'll examine both of these request methods and the XML content itself.

5.2.1 Making basic HTTP requests with GWT

The whole point of Ajax is enabling clients to send requests to servers. Of the two GWT-provided methods to facilitate this, the first is the `HTTPRequest` object. This is part of the `com.google.gwt.user.User` module that almost every application inherits. This module provides the basic functionality you need to make a request to the server.

PROBLEM

We need our application to send data to, and retrieve data from, the server.

SOLUTION

We will use the aptly named GWT `HTTPRequest` object to make basic HTTP requests.

Using `HTTPRequest` is very easy. It has four simple static methods to make `GET` and `POST` requests. For example, let's start with a simple XML `Person` representation file, as follows:

```
<?xml version="1.0" encoding="UTF-8"?>
<person>
    <firstName>Jane</firstName>
    <lastName>Doe</lastName>
</person>
```

We want to retrieve that file within GWT and, for now, simply echo the XML content to an alert box, as shown in figure 5.2.

Performing this file retrieval with GWT is very straightforward, as shown in listing 5.1.

Listing 5.1 Retrieving the person.xml file

```
HTTPRequest.asyncGet(GWT.getModuleBaseURL()+
    "/person.xml",
    new ResponseTextHandler(){
        public void onCompletion(String responseText) {
            Window.alert(responseText);
        }
    });
```

❶ Create HTTPRequest using asyncGet

Here we use the `HTTPRequest` object, simply passing in a URL and a `ResponseTextHandler`, to which the `String` containing the value returned by the server will be passed ❶. The other possible variations on this style of request include an additional `asyncGet()` version that takes a username and password for authentication, and two analogous `asyncPost()` methods that also each take a `String` value for `POST` data.

DISCUSSION

The advantage of the `HTTPRequest` object is that it's easy, and in many contexts it simply gets the job done. For most applications that utilize POX, this is all you need.

However, there are situations where such simplicity can be limiting. For instance, this approach obviously only supports half of the HTTP request methods; the other half are needed to support REST. Google provides the `com.google.gwt.http.HTTP` module, with its basic `RequestBuilder` class, to support REST.

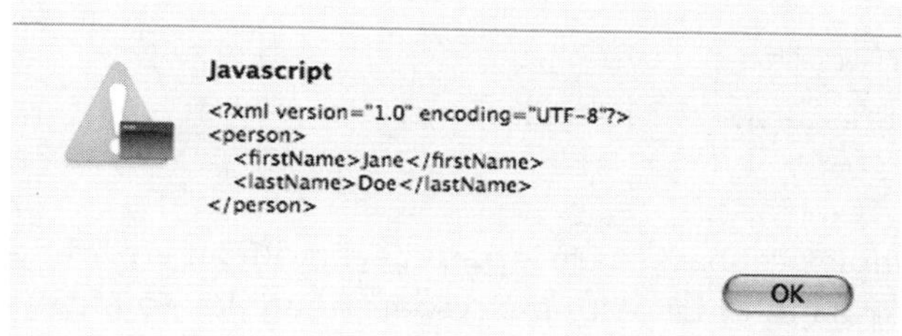

Figure 5.2 Echoing XML content in a JavaScript alert

5.2.2 Making advanced HTTP requests with GWT

If you are interacting with REST-based services, you need more methods and more options than `HTTPRequest` offers. The `com.google.gwt.http.HTTP` module provides these.

But before we look at this module, the bad news: doing pure REST isn't really possible. While XHR in many browsers supports `PUT` and `DELETE` requests, Safari notably does not. There are two ways to address this: use an HTTP tunnel and extract the actual method from an HTTP header, or ignore KHTML/WebKit-derived browsers. We'll take a quick look at each of these approaches.

PROBLEM

Our application needs advanced HTTP support not provided by `HTTPRequest`.

SOLUTION

When your needs exceed `HTTPRequest`'s capabilities, you can use the `RequestBuilder` object to perform actions with more HTTP methods and manipulate HTTP headers.

By inheriting the `com.google.gwt.http.HTTP` module in the gwt.xml file, we gain access to a much more full-featured HTTP client API. The basic class in this API is the `RequestBuilder`, which lets you manipulate headers, cope with status codes, and (if you desire) override the built-in HTTP methods to support `PUT` and `DELETE`.

With a few more lines of code than we used in listing 5.1, we can retrieve the same XML `Person` file using `RequestBuilder`. This is shown in listing 5.2.

Listing 5.2 Retrieving the person.xml file with `RequestBuilder`

```
RequestBuilder builder =
    new RequestBuilder(RequestBuilder.GET,          <-- (1) Create RequestBuilder
        GWT.getModuleBaseURL()+"/person.xml");

try {                                               (2) Manipulate request
  builder.addHeader("X-MyHeader", "somevalue");  <--    header state
  Request request = builder.sendRequest(null,
    new RequestCallback() {                                              <--
      public void onError(Request request, Throwable exception) {
            Window.alert("There was an error! "+
              exception.getMessage());
    }                                               Use RequestCallback (3)

    public void onResponseReceived(Request request,
      Response response) {
        Window.alert(response.getText());
      }
    });
} catch (RequestException e) {
   Window.alert("Unable to build the request.");
}
```

DISCUSSION

Here we have a more complex callback, `RequestCallback`, with an error handler and a more advanced response handler (3). With the response handler, you have access to the headers returned from the server, and by using the `RequestBuilder` you can also manipulate the headers sent to the server (2). If you were implementing a REST application with a tunnel to remap the action based on an HTTP header, you could set X-HTTP-Method-Override to PUT or DELETE and deal with the changes in the server implementation. Or, you could proxy the request with the appropriate method to that actual REST application.

You'll also notice that the method type comes from public, static, final values on the RequestBuilder object ❶. This would seem to limit you to the same GET and POST types available with HTTPRequest. Nevertheless, if you're willing to sacrifice browser compatibility, especially with older versions of Safari, you can get around this limitation by extending RequestBuilder. For example, if you wanted to build a DELETE request, you could implement something like what is shown in listing 5.3.

Listing 5.3 DELETE method RequestBuilder

```
public class DeleteRequestBuilder extends RequestBuilder {

    public DeleteRequestBuilder(String url) {
     super("DELETE", url);                          <-- Pass DELETE method to
   }                                                    parent constructor
}
```

Once you pass in the simple string value of the method you want to use, the RequestBuilder can be used as it would be for GET or POST requests.

Of course, now that we have the functionality, we also need to deal with the XML data. GWT provides for this as well.

5.2.3 Working with XML

Now that we've looked at how to send and receive XML data via HTTP, we need a way to deal with the XML itself. GWT includes this functionality in the com.google.gwt.xml.XML module. Once we have added the appropriate <inherits> element to the gwt.xml file, it becomes available to our code.

PROBLEM

We need to create and parse XML documents within our GWT application.

SOLUTION

GWT provides an XML module that includes an XMLParser and a Document, which we can use to parse and manipulate XML data. This XML parser is based on the XML models provided by the web browsers. The XMLParser object is used to both parse text and create Document instances.

As a simple example, let's parse the XML information from the person.xml file used in the previous examples. This is shown in listing 5.4.

Listing 5.4 Parsing XML

```
HTTPRequest.asyncGet(GWT.getModuleBaseURL()+"/person.xml",
          new ResponseTextHandler() {
      public void onCompletion(String responseText) {
          Document doc =                             ❶ Parse response text
              XMLParser.parse(responseText);     <--   to a document
```

```
            Element root = (Element) doc.getFirstChild();
            String firstName = root
                    .getElementsByTagName("firstName")     ❷ Get first firstName element
                    .item(0)
                    .getFirstChild()     ❸ Get TEXT node within firstName
                    .getNodeValue();
            String lastName = root                         ❹ Get String value of TEXT node
                    .getElementsByTagName("lastName")
                    .item(0)
                    .getFirstChild()
                    .getNodeValue();
            Window.alert("Hello "+ firstName + " "+ lastName);
        }
    });
```

If you have ever done any DOM-based XML programming, this example probably looks remarkably familiar. The parser is invoked by simply passing a string to the static `parse()` method, and a `Document` is returned.

DISCUSSION

It's important to remember that the `Document` object returned by the `XMLParser.parse()` method is of type `com.google.gwt.xml.client.Document` and not of type `org.w3c.dom.Document` ❶. These are *not* interchangeable. It's also important to remember that the `XMLParser` and all of the GWT DOM-style classes are implemented using calls to the browser's native XML functionality, and are not usable on the server side or outside of GWT at all.

These limitations aside, parsing XML is pretty easy. The `getElementsByTagName()` method can be used to get a collection of elements, and then a specific item can be obtained by index location ❷. Then the children ❸ and node values can be obtained ❹.

But what about serializing XML? It, quite literally, couldn't be easier. Simply call `toString()` on a `Document` or any `Element` object, and GWT serializes it to XML for you.

Now that we have covered the basics of XML, we're going to look at some finer points of Java and JavaScript interaction, both with the RPC mechanism and with JSON.

5.3 Understanding Java-to-JavaScript interaction

You have already seen the basics of how GWT handles Java-to-JavaScript mapping in previous examples. Now we'll explore this mapping further to better understand the nature of JavaScript serialization for server communications. We'll also discuss in more detail how Java and JavaScript objects are dealt with in your compiled code.

To begin with, serializing Java Collections with GWT requires giving the GWTCompiler a bit more information, because it does not yet support generics or Java 5 style annotations as of this writing.

5.3.1 Using GWT JavaDoc annotations to serialize collections

The GWT compiler is very aggressive about minimizing the code in the final JavaScript files. It examines the call tree and prunes unused methods from classes. It also traverses the graph of objects that are used for RPC calls—those that implement the `IsSerializable` or `Serializable` interfaces—and only serializes and deserializes for classes that are actually used in the application.

As you already know, GWT uses Java 1.4 language syntax in the Java source of your application. This precludes the use of generics to type the collection structures from the `java.util` package. But these structures need to be serializable to pass them back and forth from the client to RPC services, so how does the compiler know what it needs to provide handlers for?

PROBLEM

Serialization of collections does not provide typing via generics, and serializers don't get created for contained classes with Java 1.4 language structures.

SOLUTION

Using the `gwt.typeArgs` JavaDoc style annotation, you can declare property types, return types, and method parameters when dealing with collections. Doing so alerts the GWT compiler of your intentions and allows collections to be serialized.

The `gwt.typeArgs` annotation allows the GWT compiler and serialization mechanism to recognize and optimize types with collections. This is actually a JavaDoc style annotation that is inspected by the Java-to-JavaScript compiler when the application is built to determine what the top-level point of serialization for a particular property, argument, or return type should be. Let's look at a simple example that uses each of these.

First, for a property, we'll look at three classes in listing 5.5. A `Fleet`, which contains vessels, and two `Vessel` types: a `StarShip` and a `TugBoat`.

Listing 5.5 GWT JavaDoc `typeArgs` annotations with properties

```
public class Fleet implements IsSerializable{

   /**
  * @gwt.typeArgs <com.manning.gwtip.servercom.Vessel>      ❶ Specify typed collection elements
  */
  public ArrayList vessels;

  public Fleet() {
     super();
  }
//---

public class Vessel implements IsSerializable {      ❷ Specify IsSerializable type
    public String name;
    public String registry;
    public String captain;

    public Vessel() {
        super();
    }
}

//---
```

```
public class TugBoat extends Vessel {        <-- 3 Include GWT serialization handlers
    public int towCapacity;
    public TugBoat() {
        super();
    }
}

//---

public class StarShip extends Vessel{
    public int photonTorpedoCount;
    public StarShip() {
        super();
    }
}
```

In the `Fleet` class, we're specifying the type of the collection of `Vessel` objects by using the `typeArgs` JavaDoc annotation ❶. The types specified in this manner must themselves be of type `IsSerializable` or `Serializable` ❷. Inheritance is also supported when using GWT's serialization methods ❸.

It's important to remember that for both service calls and `typeArgs` references you want to be as specific as possible. The GWT compiler can't know which of these you might be passing between the server and the client. Even if you never cast a `Vessel` to a `StarShip` in the client, that data needs to be there if it goes back to the server. This means the compiler cannot omit the unused data from `StarShip`.

The `typeArgs` annotation can also be used to specify arguments and return types for service methods. Listing 5.6 shows a hypothetical service interface that demonstrates this.

Listing 5.6 `RemoteService` using `typeArgs`

```
public interface FleetRemoteService extends RemoteService {

    /**                                                        1 Provide typeArgs
     * @gwt.typeArgs fleets                                      for an argument
     *      <com.manning.gwtip.servercom.client.Fleet>      <--
     */
    public void setFleetsForOwner(String owner, Set fleets);

    /**
     * @gwt.typeArgs
     * <java.lang.String,[...]servercom.client.Fleet>        <-- Provide typeArgs
     */                                                          for a return type;
    public HashMap getAllFleets();                               package
}                                                              2 abbreviated
```

In this manner, the GWT `typeArgs` JavaDoc style annotation can alert the GWT compiler what types are used in a collection, either as input parameters or return values.

DISCUSSION

As listing 5.6 demonstrates, immediately following a `typeArgs` annotation on a method declaration, you can specify a particular argument being described, such as the `Set` named `fleets` ❶. You can also use `typeArgs` to specify a return type for a method. In the case of the `HashMap`, which has two object types, you can specify the key and the value ❷.

While a service is being demonstrated here, you can also use this same technique for getters and setters on Java beans. It's also worth noting that, unlike JDK 1.5's generics, you cannot implement your own classes that take `typeArgs` modifiers unless they simply extend one of the already supported types.

Of course, `typeArgs` only helps you make sure your objects are properly typed for standard GWT RPC use. You might also need to communicate with JavaScript libraries, or other non-RPC or non-XML services. For these situations, GWT provides support for JSON.

5.3.2 Using JSON

JavaScript Object Notation (JSON) is a notation for encoding structured data, not unlike XML, but it also carries with it a particular advantage: it is executable JavaScript on its own. Basic object structures can be created using JavaScript's short-form constructor notation, within the limitations of JavaScript's basic typing. Because of its utility as a thin messaging system with Ajax clients, and its direct interpretation into JavaScript, JSON has become a popular format for web services that communicate with browser-based clients.

You can find JSON implementations for many languages, including Java, at http://json.org. If you want to consume these services with your GWT client, Google provides a library for doing so.

PROBLEM

We need our GWT application to communicate with server-side resources that provide JSON-encoded object return types.

SOLUTION

GWT includes `JSONObject` and `JSONParser`, which, when coupled with HTTP communication, can integrate with JSON-based server resources.

Using the same HTTP access methods we explored earlier, we can get a response from an HTTP server and parse the value to a `JSONObject` instance by using the `JSONParser`. For our request example, we'll use a simple JSON file, once again a `Person` representation, as shown in listing 5.7.

Listing 5.7 JSON `Person` file

```
{
    "firstName" : "Carl",
    "lastName" : "Sagan"
}
```

There is nothing fancy in this approach. This is an object notation. By using `[]` instead of `{}`, you can define an array or associative array with the same `key:value` notation. In this case, our object has two attributes: `firstName` and `lastName`.

Now we need to get them from the server and parse them. Listing 5.8 demonstrates how to do this using the GWT JSON support.

Listing 5.8 Retrieving and parsing JSON

```
RequestBuilder builder = new RequestBuilder(
         RequestBuilder.GET,
         GWT.getModuleBaseURL()+"/person.js");

 try {
     Request response = builder.sendRequest(null,
       new RequestCallback() {
         public void onError(Request request,
                   Throwable exception) {
             Window.alert( "There was an error! "+
                   exception.getMessage());
         }

         public void onResponseReceived(Request request,
           Response response) {
             JSONObject person =                          Parse
                (JSONObject) JSONParser.parse(            JSONObject
                                 response.getText());     from request
             String message = "Found person: "+
              ((JSONString)person.get("firstName")).stringValue() +
              " "+
              ((JSONString)person.get("lastName"))
                                 .stringValue();      <-  Extract values
             Window.alert(message);                       as Strings
         }
     });
 } catch (RequestException e) {
     Window.alert("Unable to build the request.");
 }
```

Each method in the JSON API returns a `JSONValue`. If you're not completely sure what type you might be getting back, methods like `isArray()`, `isBoolean()`, `isNumber()`, and `isString()` are provided to help you determine what the result is.

DISCUSSION

Since we know that the values for `firstName` and `lastName` are `String` types, we cast them to `JSONString` objects and then call `stringValue()` to get the value as a `java.lang.String` object.

Also, as with other modules, you need to import the JSON module into your source to enable JSON support. This just means adding the following to your .gwt.xml file:

```
<inherits name="com.google.gwt.json.JSON"/>
```

While JSON is fairly popular with the Web 2.0 set, you may not have any of your services exposed as JSON if you're working in an enterprise environment. The more likely candidate there is SOAP, since it forms the basis of the WS-* specifications that are all the rage within the enterprise computing community. To that end, we'll look at options for accessing SOAP from GWT in the next two sections, and at the advantages and disadvantages of various approaches.

5.4 Creating a cross-domain SOAP client with Flash

Service-oriented architecture (SOA)—if you work in a fairly large enterprise, you no doubt hear people referring to it all the time. SOA is the buzzword of the year. In most real-world cases, this typically means building your infrastructure using some SOAP-related framework.

As an example, imagine that you had a SOAP web service that processed new orders for your company's widgets. You could, of course, use GWT's RPC service, and proxy RPC calls to that SOAP service from the server side. If this service was located in a different data center from your web application, though, that could be a very high-latency operation. You might well feel that it was better to make the SOAP call directly from the client. However, you have two problems here: simply making the call to the SOAP service, and making a call to a server that is not on your web apps server.

Unfortunately, web browsers still don't have a consistent API for using SOAP from JavaScript (and thus GWT). Flash, however, is nearly universally installed in web browsers (though it's not native), and it has an API for using SOAP. While this may raise a few eyebrows, Flash can be used for function over form.

Flash has a similar security model to the same-origin policy outlined earlier in this chapter. But unlike browsers, Flash additionally gives you the opportunity to work around the restrictions. Where it gets interesting is that you can use an empty Flash element as a direct SOAP client in your GWT application.

5.4.1 Using Flash as a SOAP client

Newer versions of Flash provide some pretty great functionality. With Flash MX 2004, basic SOAP support was added. Flash 8 added a nice feature called `ExternalInterface`, which provides a standard API for communicating between Flash and JavaScript, beyond the simple variable-passing available previously. If you couple these together, along with a little GWT JSNI magic, you can have a SOAP client for your GWT application.

PROBLEM

GWT and web browsers do not inherently provide consistent access to SOAP services.

SOLUTION

We can extend browser capabilities using the fairly ubiquitous Flash client to support SOAP access directly within a GWT client application.

To start building a SOAP client with Flash, we first need a Flash movie. Flash is coded in ActionScript, which is simply another implementation of ECMAScript, the specification for JavaScript that all browsers implement (with slight differences). For this example, you'll need Flash 8 Professional, which is available from Adobe.com in a free 30-day trial version.

If you haven't used Flash before, don't worry. We aren't going to get into the nitty gritty of it. To create a SOAP client movie, simply create a new FLA file, click on the big white background, and select Window > Actions. This brings up the code editor for the base movie file.

The movie we'll implement has a three-stage lifecycle, as far as external code is concerned. The first stage of this lifecycle calls a JavaScript method called `flashSOAPClientReadyNotify()` to let JavaScript know that the movie is fully loaded and ready for calls. In the next stage, the client can register a SOAP service by passing in an alias (a simple string) and a URL to a Web Services Description Language (WSDL) file. The movie then fires a callback to let the client know whether or not the WSDL import was successful. In the third stage, the client can pass in a request identifier, an alias, a method name, and an array of arguments to the service method, and the SOAP call is made. A callback method passes back the result or fault object to the host page script.

The entire ActionScript example is shown in listing 5.9.

Listing 5.9 `ActionScript` for a simple SOAP client

```
import flash.external.*;
import mx.services.*;
function WebServiceHandle(wsdlUrl){
    this.wsdlUrl = wsdlUrl;                          | Hold WSDL and
    this.webService = new WebService(wsdlUrl);       | WebService
}
var webServiceRegistry = new Array();
function registerWebService(alias, wsdlUrl) {
    var webServiceHandle = new WebServiceHandle(wsdlUrl);
    webServiceHandle.webService.onFault = function(fault) {
        ExternalInterface.call("callbackOnFault",
                               fault);               ❶ Invoke browser callback
    };
    webServiceHandle.webService.onLoad = function(wsdlDocument) {
        webServiceRegistry[alias] = webServiceHandle;
        ExternalInterface.call("callbackOnLoad");
    };
}
function callWebServiceMethod(id, alias, methodName, args) {
    var handle = webServiceRegistry[alias];
    var command = "handle.webService."+methodName;   Make
    var argsCount = 0;                               service call
    for (key in args) {
        argsCount++;
    }
    pendingCall = null;
    if (argsCount == 0) {
        pendingCall =  eval(command)();
    }                                                ❷ Count
    if (argsCount == 1) {                              arguments
        pendingCall =  eval(command)(args[0]);
    }
    if (argsCount == 2) {
        pendingCall =  eval(command)(args[0], args[1]);
    }
    if (argsCount == 3) {
        pendingCall =  eval(command)(args[0], args[1], args[2]);
    }
    if (argsCount == 4) {
```

```
        pendingCall =  eval(command)(args[0], args[1], args[2], args[3]);
    }
    // it goes on like this up to 10 arguments

    pendingCall.onFault = function(fault) {
        ExternalInterface.call("callbackOnFail",
            id, fault);
    };
    pendingCall.onResult = function(resultValue) {
        ExternalInterface.call("callbackOnSuccess",
            id, resultValue);
    };
}
ExternalInterface.addCallback("registerWebService",
    this, registerWebService);
ExternalInterface.addCallback("callWebServiceMethod",
    this, callWebServiceMethod);
ExternalInterface.call("flashSOAPClientReadyNotify");
```

❸ Callback results with request ID

❹ Expose to browser

This isn't too complicated. You don't have to be conducting master classes in Flash programming to understand the concepts involved in using a blank Flash movie to invoke a SOAP service in this manner.

DISCUSSION

`ExternalInterface` has two primary methods: `call(methodName, args...)` ❶ and `addCallback(externalMethodName, object, methodImplementation)` ❹. With them, you can pass data objects back and forth between JavaScript and Flash.

There are some caveats. The big one that stands out here is that JavaScript arrays come in as simple objects in ActionScript. This means you lose the array class's operators and properties, though the elements appear in the final object. To get around this, we count the elements on the object with a `for` loop and use the counter to figure out how many arguments there are.

The other thing that stands out is the large block of `if` statements where we invoke the actual service call ❷. You might wonder why this isn't taken care of with the `eval()` statement. The answer is that ActionScript will only let you return references with `eval()`, not execute methods. Therefore, we use `eval()` to get the reference to the appropriate method, and then we brute force the proper number of arguments ❷. This movie will only support a SOAP call with a maximum of 10 arguments, but that is generally enough for most purposes.

This invocation doesn't return a value, but instead returns a `PendingCall` object. This is a callback handler for asynchronous calls to the web service, to which we attach `onFault` and `onResult` closures that call back into the JavaScript environment ❸. At the end, we call `flashSOAPClientReadyNotify` via the `ExternalInterface` to inform the browser that the movie is ready for calls.

Once it's ready, we need to get to it from GWT. We do that with the `SOAPClient-Flash` class, shown in listing 5.10. Note that we've replaced some package names with `[...]` so the lines will fit on the page.

Listing 5.10 GWT SOAP client class

```
public class SOAPClientFlash {
    private static final String MOVIE = GWT.getModuleBaseURL() +
            "/flash/SOAPClient.swf";
    private static SOAPClientFlash INSTANCE = null;
    private Element flashObject;
    private Element flashEmbed;
    private Element flashObjectReference;

    public static SOAPClientFlash getInstance() {
        INSTANCE = INSTANCE == null ? new SOAPClientFlash() : INSTANCE;
        return INSTANCE;
    }

    private SOAPClientFlash() {
        this.flashObject = DOM.createElement("object");        // Use Object tag for IE
        DOM.setAttribute(
                this.flashObject, "classid",
                "clsid:d27cdb6e-ae6d-11cf-96b8-444553540000"
                );
        DOM.setAttribute(
                this.flashObject, "codebase",
                "http://fpdownload.macromedia.com/pub/shockwave/" +
                "cabs/flash/swflash.cab#version=8,0,0,0"
                );
        DOM.setAttribute(this.flashObject, "id", "SOAPClientFlash");
        DOM.setAttribute(this.flashObject, "width", "1px");
        DOM.setAttribute(this.flashObject, "height", "1px");
        Element param = DOM.createElement("param");
        DOM.setAttribute(param, "name", "allowScriptAccess");
        DOM.setAttribute(param, "value", "always");
        DOM.appendChild(this.flashObject, param);

        param = DOM.createElement("param");
        DOM.setAttribute(param, "name", "movie");
        DOM.setAttribute(param, "value", SOAPClientFlash.MOVIE);
        DOM.appendChild(this.flashObject, param);

        param = DOM.createElement("param");
        DOM.setAttribute(param, "name", "quality");
        DOM.setAttribute(param, "value", "high");
        DOM.appendChild(this.flashObject, param);

        param = DOM.createElement("param");
        DOM.setAttribute(param, "name", "bgcolor");
        DOM.setAttribute(param, "value", "#ffffff");
        DOM.appendChild(this.flashObject, param);

        this.flashEmbed = DOM.createElement("embed");      // Embed tag for other browsers
        DOM.setAttribute(this.flashEmbed, "src", SOAPClientFlash.MOVIE);
        DOM.setAttribute(this.flashEmbed, "quality", "high");
        DOM.setAttribute(this.flashEmbed, "bgcolor", "#ffffff");
        DOM.setAttribute(this.flashEmbed, "width", "0px");
        DOM.setAttribute(this.flashEmbed, "height", "0px");
        DOM.setAttribute(this.flashEmbed, "name", "SOAPClientFlash");
        DOM.setAttribute(this.flashEmbed, "allowScriptAccess", "always");
```

```
        DOM.setAttribute(this.flashEmbed, "type",
                "application/x-shockwave-flash");
        DOM.setAttribute(
                this.flashEmbed, "pluginspage",
                "http://www.macromedia.com/go/getflashplayer"
                );
        DOM.setAttribute(this.flashEmbed, "swLiveConnect", "true");

        DOM.appendChild(this.flashObject, this.flashEmbed);

        DOM.appendChild(RootPanel.getBodyElement(), this.flashObject);
    }

    public static void initialize( ReadyCallback callback ) {
        SOAPClientFlash.getInstance();
        INSTANCE.initializeJavaScript(callback);        <-- Initialize JavaScript callbacks with JSNI
    }

    private native Element initializeJavaScript(
        ReadyCallback callback)/*-{
        $wnd.flashSOAPClientReadyNotify = function(){
callback.@[...]SOAPClientFlash
                .ReadyCallback::onReady()();
        }
        $wnd.soapAsyncCallbacks = new Array();        <-- Create registry of callback handlers
        $wnd.callbackOnSuccess = function(id, result) {        <-- Create success callback handler
            asyncCallback = $wnd.soapAsyncCallbacks[id];
         asyncCallback.
@[...] AsyncCallback::onSuccess(Ljava/lang/Object;)
              (result);
            $wnd.soapAsyncCallbacks[id] = null;
        }
        $wnd.callbackOnFail = function(id, fault) {        <-- Create fault callback handler
            asyncCallback = $wnd.soapAsyncCallbacks[id];
            asyncCallback.
@[...]AsyncCallback::onFailure(Ljava/lang/Throwable;)
                (
                @[...]SOAPClientFlash::createSOAPFault(
                    Ljava/lang/String;Ljava/lang/String;)(
                     fault.faultString, fault.detail)
              );
            $wnd.soapAsyncCallbacks[id] = null;
        };
        $wnd.callbackOnLoad = function() {        <-- Create service registration callback handlers
               callback.@[...]SOAPClientFlash
                   .RegisterCallback::onLoad()();
        };
        $wnd.callbackOnFault = function(fault) {
                callback.@[...]SOAPClientFlash
                  .RegisterCallback::onFault
               (Lcom/google/gwt/core/client/JavaScriptObject;)
               (fault);
      };
    }-*/;

    public void registerWebService(
        String alias, String wsdlUrl, RegisterCallback callback){
```

```
        this.registerWebService(
            System.currentTimeMillis(),
            alias, wsdlUrl, callback);
    }

    private native void registerWebService(
            long id, String alias, String wsdlUrl,
            RegisterCallback callback
            )/*-{
       $wnd.document.SOAPClientFlash.registerWebService( alias, wsdlUrl );
    }-*/;

    public void callMethod(
        String alias, String methodName,
        JavaScriptObject args, AsyncCallback callback) {
        this.callMethod( System.currentTimeMillis(),
                alias, methodName, args, callback);
    }

    private native void callMethod(long id,
            String alias, String methodName, JavaScriptObject args,
            AsyncCallback callback)/*-{
        $wnd.soapAsyncCallbacks[id] = callback;
        $wnd.document.SOAPClientFlash.callWebServiceMethod(id, alias,
            methodName, args, 'callbackOnSuccess', 'callbackOnFail');
    }-*/;

    private static void callSuccess(AsyncCallback callback,
        JavaScriptObject object) {
        callback.onSuccess(object);
    }

    private static SOAPFault createSOAPFault(
        String message, String detail) {
        return new SOAPFault(message, detail);
    }

    public static interface ReadyCallback{
        public void onReady();
    }

    public static interface RegisterCallback {

         public void onLoad();

         public void onFault(JavaScriptObject fault);
    }
}
```

Reuse AsyncCallback

Get applicable AsyncCallback

Create SOAPFault

Define interfaces for startup and register callbacks

There is a good bit of JSNI code in this class. We introduced JSNI in chapter 1, and we'll explore it more completely in the next chapter, but we're simply using it here to pass JavaScript objects in and out of the SOAP client and back to the GWT classes. We have reused the `AsyncCallback` that GWT's RPC mechanism uses because it suits our needs and it helps clarify the usage pattern.

You'll notice at the top we're creating the same movie in two tags, `<object>` and `<embed>`, to handle browser differences concerning Flash. As we discussed in chapter 1, we could handle these differences with deferred binding, by creating separate browser-specific implementations in GWT, but we're avoiding that here for brevity.

There are a couple of extra things to note concerning the differences here. First is the `allowScriptAccess` property. This needs to be set so scripts can talk to the movie. Internet Explorer accesses the methods exposed via the ActiveX API in IE. In the Safari and Mozilla browsers, the Netscape Plugin API is used. This is used by more modern browsers as a replacement for the LiveConnect functionality from Netscape 4.x. Though the name has changed, the Netscape Plugin API still honors the `swLiveConnect` attribute on `<embed>` tags, so we have to make sure it is there.

Now that we have a functioning GWT SOAP client, we can use it to make calls into a SOAP service. We'll do this right out of the entry point, with a fairly hackish example. Although we have a three-stage lifecycle, our sample client code simply inlines it. If this were a real application, you might want to have the `ReadyCallback` register your WSDL aliases with the Flash movie and your register callback(s) remove a "loading" block from the page when all of them are ready to use. This would entail a fair bit more code than we want for the purposes of this example, so we're just going to nest the callbacks inside each other to call a "Hello" service. Our quick and dirty GWT SOAP `EntryPoint` is shown in listing 5.11. (Again, for production use you might want to expand this into a SOAP client `Widget` to enable reuse, rather than coding directly in an `EntryPoint`).

Listing 5.11 Entry point and client calls

```
public class Main implements EntryPoint {

    public Main() {
    }                                               Register WSDL ❶

    public void onModuleLoad() {
        SOAPClientFlash.initialize(new SOAPClientFlash.ReadyCallback() {

            public void onReady(){
                RootPanel.get().add(new Label("Getting WebService."));
                SOAPClientFlash client = SOAPClientFlash.getInstance();
                client.registerWebService("hello",
  "http://localhost:8080/gwtipXfire/services/HelloService?wsdl",
                    new SOAPClientFlash.RegisterCallback() {
                public void onFault(JavaScriptObject fault) {
                    Window.alert("Register Fault:"+fault.toString());

   }                                         Create Person ❷
                                             JavaScript
                public void onLoad() {       object
                 RootPanel.get().add(
                      new Label("Got WebService.") );
                 JavaScriptObjectDecorator person =
                   new JavaScriptObjectDecorator();
                 person.setStringProperty("firstName", "John");
                 person.setStringProperty("lastName", "Doe");
```

```
                    JavaScriptObjectDecorator args =           Create array of
                         new JavaScriptObjectDecorator(         arguments,
                            JavaScriptObjectDecorator        ❸  using Person
                                  .newArray()
                    );
                    args.setJavaScriptObjectProperty(
                         "0",                               ❹  Pass argument to
                         person.getObject());                   JavaScript as String
                    SOAPClientFlash client =
                              SOAPClientFlash.getInstance();

                    client.callMethod( "hello", "sayHello",
                         args.getObject(), new AsyncCallback() {
                        public void onSuccess(Object result) {
                            Window.alert(
                                  result.toString()
                               );                                     Show
                        }                                        ❺  response

                        public void onFailure(Throwable caught) {
                            Window.alert(caught.getMessage());
                        }

                    });
                }

            });
        }
    });
  }
}
```

With the GWT client making use of our Flash movie, we now have a fully functioning SOAP call. We first use our `SOAPFlashClient` to register a web service using a remote WSDL ❶. You'll notice we use JavaScript objects to deal with the calls and values. We create a `Person` object ❷ and pass it in to the service call as one of the arguments ❸. When we pass it, we're actually passing it as a `String`, but JavaScript does not care because it is not typed ❹. The return value from our service is just a simple `String` value, so we can use it directly from Java and display it as an alert with GWT ❺.

You will also notice that we're using the GWT `JavaScriptObject` extensively. This is the opaque GWT handle for referencing native JavaScript objects in Java. For the more complex objects, we're using a utility class called `JavaScriptObjectDecorator`. This is a simple wrapper around `JavaScriptObject` with JSNI calls to make getting and setting native properties easy. A portion of `JavaScriptObjectDecorator` is shown in listing 5.12.

Listing 5.12 A snippet of `JavaScriptObjectDecorator`

```
public int getIntProperty(String name){
      return this.getIntProperty(this.getObject(), name);     ❶  Get and
  }                                                                 set int

  private native int getIntProperty(
```

```
    JavaScriptObject object, String name) /*-{
     return object[name];
}-*/;

public void setIntProperty(
    String name, int value) {
     this.setIntProperty(
         this.getObject(), name, value);
}

private native void setIntProperty(
    JavaScriptObject object,
    String name, int value)/*-{
    object[name] = value;
}-*/;
```

❶ **Get and set int**

`JavaScriptObjectDecorator` gets and sets properties for various data types, both in Java and JavaScript ❶. The code for the full class continues on in the same vein as listing 5.12. In short, it lets you access JavaScript data objects in your Java code. You could, alternatively, use JSON to step back and forth between the two, but that seems rather inefficient just to pass data between the layers of the same application.

The complete GWT direct SOAP via Flash client application is displayed in figure 5.3.

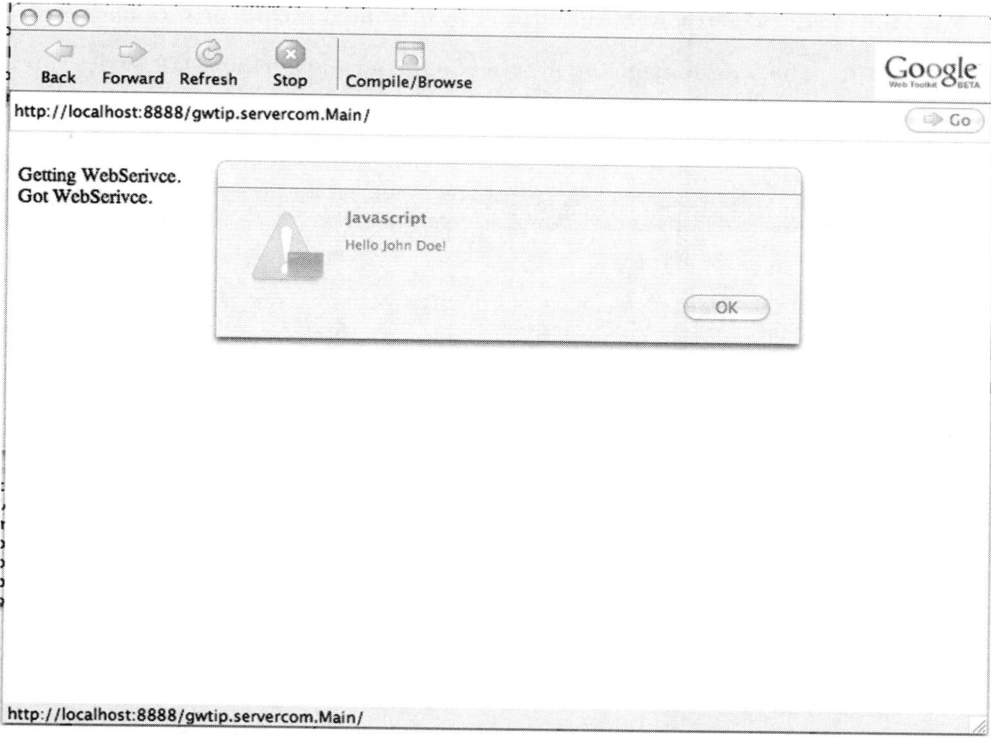

Figure 5.3 Calling back from a SOAP service

While this figure looks impressive, you'll likely get an error if you try it! That's because the SOAP service running on port 8080 is in a different domain than the GWT shell running on 8888. We're back to the issue of origin.

5.4.2 Setting a Flash security context

To complete our Flash SOAP example, we have to set the Flash security context. It all comes back to the same-origin policy. Just like using the XHR object from JavaScript, Flash honors the same-origin policy. Unlike REST, however, Flash gives you an option to get around it, with the clever use of XML files.

PROBLEM

The Flash SOAP client won't talk to the server because they are of different origins.

SOLUTION

You can address Flash client security restrictions related to the same-origin policy by specifying explicit permissions in the crossdomain.xml file on the server.

This is a pretty easy problem to solve if you have control over the SOAP server—or you can influence its configuration. On any host that you want to allow Flash to call, you need to add a crossdomain.xml file off the root directory of the server. If your SOAP service is at https://ws.mycompany.com/ServletContext/services/MySOAP, the file needs to be resolvable at https://ws.mycompany.com/crossdomain.xml.

NOTE The crossdomain.xml file goes on the server with the SOAP service you wish to call, *not* on the web server with your Flash movie or GWT application.

A sample crossdomain.xml file is shown in listing 5.13.

Listing 5.13 Cross-domain configuration file for Flash

```
<?xml version="1.0"?>

<!DOCTYPE cross-domain-policy SYSTEM "http://www.macromedia.com/xml/dtds/
  cross-domain-policy.dtd">
<cross-domain-policy>

   <allow-access-from domain="mycompany.com" />
   <allow-access-from domain="www.mycompany.com" />
   <allow-access-from domain="*.partner.com" />

</cross-domain-policy>
```

❶ Include all hostnames used

❷ Use asterisks as wildcards

Once you have your cross-domain permissions file set up with the applicable host names ❶ and wildcards ❷, you need to place it in the root directory of your web server. If you're using Tomcat, this would be the [CATALINA_HOME]/webapps/ROOT folder. If you're using Glassfish, as the sample SOAP service included in the code for this chapter does, the file goes in your [SERVER_HOME]/domains/domain1 folder.

DISCUSSION

It's worth noting that you can use Flash as an `XMLHttpRequest` replacement, as well, if you need access to JSON or REST services elsewhere in your enterprise, as long as you can establish the crossdomain.xml file. A good sample API for doing this is Fjax, available at http://fjax.net. However, this still will not allow you to call Amazon's SOAP API at will.

5.4.3 Drawbacks and caveats

Obviously, getting around the same-origin policy limitation of SOAP doesn't mean you can access any SOAP server on the Internet. You can only access servers that have a crossdomain.xml file defined that allows your host.

There are some other drawbacks as well. The big one is that the Flash SOAP implementation is fairly fragile. If your SOAP services are robust and are already known to work across multiple platforms (say, .NET, Axis, XFire, and PHP), then you'll likely not run into any problems. However, the Flash SOAP support is not very good at dealing with complex namespaces, and creating a SOAP service with the Glassfish JSR-181/JAX-WS implementation, for example, yields a service that you can't successfully call with Flash. (This is why the sample service included with the downloadable code for this chapter is built with XFire.)

You should also be aware that the `ExternalInterface` class is only available with Flash 8. This means it will not work with older Flash versions, including the production version for Linux right now, though there is a beta of a newer Flash for Linux available. As a workaround, you can use the `ExternalInterface` implementation available with the Dojo Ajax library. This implementation allows you to bundle a Flash 6 and Flash 8 movie with your application, and switch between them depending on which version of Flash is available on the client. More information on this is available at http://manual.dojotoolkit.org/WikiHome/DojoDotBook/Book50.

Wouldn't it be nice if you could access anything on the web from your application and have a SOAP client you knew was good, without a great deal of pain? Fortunately, there is another option in the series of workarounds to this problem: replacing the Flash layer with an applet.

5.5 Incorporating applets with GWT

The Java applet has been around for over a decade, and although it has never seen the adoption that some hoped for, it is still one of the most powerful web-embeddable frameworks around. One of the features that makes this so is the applet security model.

While the default behavior for an applet is not unlike the same-origin policy, it provides additional options through the signed applet policy. Once an applet has been signed with a certificate from a trusted authority, it can access all the features of Java, including talking to the local filesystem and communicating with any server. We'll look at building a GWT-accessible SOAP client with an applet, using the JAX-WS reference implementation from Sun and making a call to the Hello service from listing 5.11.

5.5.1 Using Java as a SOAP client

We're once again addressing the problem of getting access to SOAP services from a GWT client, but this time we'll be using a Java applet. Applets have some advantages and disadvantages. In the plus column, they are much more powerful than Flash, you can ensure that the SOAP client will work with any server out there much more easily, and, perhaps most importantly, you can actually make synchronous calls to the SOAP service via the LiveConnect/NPAPI implementation.

The main drawbacks include the general fragility of the Java applet plugin, the out-of-browser execution, and the lack of penetration among the general installed browser user base. Of course, if your application is part of an internal enterprise environment, this latter point is less important.

PROBLEM

Our client needs to access SOAP services, but GWT and web browsers do not inherently provide consistent access.

SOLUTION

You can create a robust SOAP client that can be used directly within a GWT client application by wiring together the communications through a Java applet.

We'll start by creating our applet. Because we're using NetBeans for this project, creating the web service client is remarkably easy. The first step is to create a web service reference in the NetBeans project. This is done by selecting File > New from the menus, and selecting Web Services > Web Service Client from the New File dialog box, as shown in figure 5.4.

In the New Web Service Client dialog box in NetBeans, shown in Figure 5.5, you're prompted to enter additional information. Enter the URL for your deployed HelloService WSDL file and specify a package name for the generated client classes to be placed into.

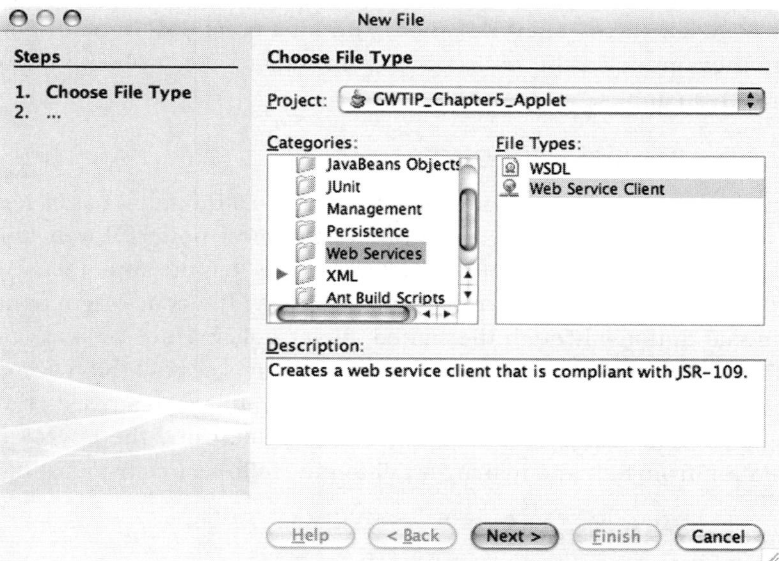

Figure 5.4 Creating a new web service client in NetBeans

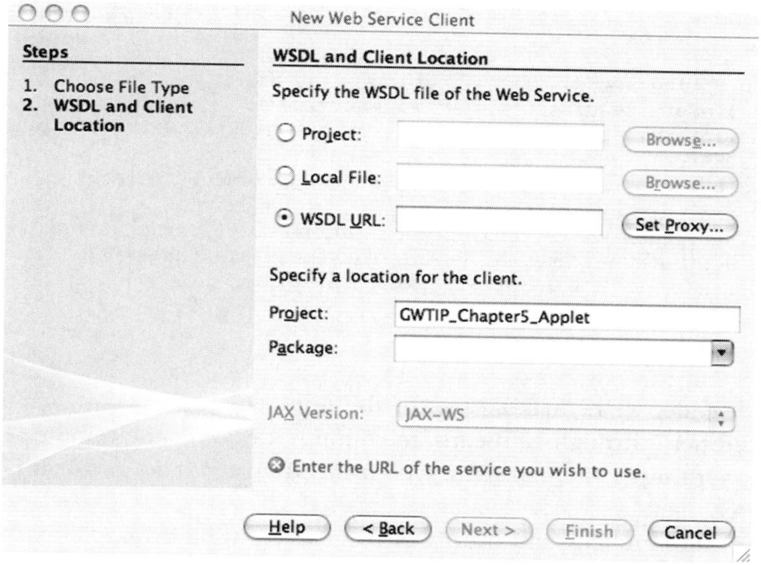

Figure 5.5 Setting WSDL and client configuration information for the client

After you have the web service reference added to your project, do an initial build. This will cause the Ant script of the project to generate the appropriate classes and place them in the build/generated folder of your project, making them available to your editor's autocomplete features.

Next we need to build the applet that will use the web service client we have established. This will be a remarkably simple class, but there are a few things worth noting. First, we're going to be using the `netscape.javascript.*` package. Despite the name, this is generally well supported in most browsers, including IE and Safari. However, you do need to add the JAR file to the build path of your project. It can be found in your [JAVA_HOME]/jre/lib/ folder as plugin.jar. Listing 5.14 shows our applet.

Listing 5.14 SOAP client applet

```
package com.manning.gwtip.servercom.applet;
import com.manning.gwtip.servercom.soap.HelloService;
import com.manning.gwtip.servercom.soap
        .HelloServicePortType;
import com.manning.gwtip.servercom.soap.Person;
import java.applet.Applet;
import netscape.javascript.JSObject;
public class SOAPApplet extends Applet {

    public SOAPApplet() {
        super();
    }
    public void start() {
        JSObject window = JSObject.getWindow(this);
```

❶ Import auto-generated classes from JAX-WS

❷ Import JSObject from plugin.jar

```
        window.eval("appletSOAPClientReadyNotify();");
    }
    public String sayHello() {
        HelloService client = new HelloService();
        HelloServicePortType service = client.getHelloServiceHttpPort();
        JSObject window = JSObject.getWindow(this);
        JSObject person = (JSObject) window.getMember("person");
        Person p = new Person();
        p.setFirstName((String) person.getMember("firstName"));
        p.setLastName((String) person.getMember("lastName"));
        String result = service.sayHello(p);
        return result;
    }
}
```

❸ Define sayHello() method using JSObject

In our applet code, we're making use of the autogenerated JAX-WS client-related classes, created here through NetBeans, to communicate with the remote service ❶. In addition, we're using the `JSObject` type from `plugin.jar` to perform JavaScript-related tasks ❷.

In spite of the simplicity and brevity of this class, you have likely already noticed that this is not nearly as generic an implementation as the Flash example. Since Java is a static language, we can't as easily create a "universal" client that doesn't involve complex building of each individual SOAP call. You'll also notice that the `sayHello()` method doesn't take any arguments, but rather fetches the value from a member on the `Window` object ❸. Unfortunately, the Java plugin doesn't like taking arguments to externally exposed methods, even those taking `JSObject`. To get around this, we'll have to make our calls by setting attributes on the `Window` object.

We'll copy the built applet into the `public.applet` package of our GWT project, along with its dependencies. Now we need to create our GWT class that will talk to the applet. As shown in listing 5.15, this is much simpler than the Flash version, but less generic.

Listing 5.15 GWT class to talk to the applet

```
public class SOAPClientApplet {

    private static final String
        JAX_WS_JARS="activation.jar,...
    private static SOAPClientApplet INSTANCE;
    private Element appletObject;

    public static SOAPClientApplet getInstance() {
        INSTANCE = INSTANCE == null ? new SOAPClientApplet() : INSTANCE;
        return INSTANCE;
    }

    private SOAPClientApplet() {

        this.appletObject = DOM.createElement("applet");
        DOM.setAttribute(this.appletObject, "id", "SOAPClientApplet");
        DOM.setAttribute(this.appletObject, "MAYSCRIPT", "true");
        DOM.setAttribute(this.appletObject, "code",
```

Truncated for line length

```
                "com.manning.gwtip.servercom.applet.SOAPApplet");
        DOM.setAttribute(this.appletObject, "type",
                "application/x-java-applet;version=1.5.0");
        DOM.setAttribute(this.appletObject,
            "pluginspage",
                "http://java.sun.com/j2se/1.5.0/download.html");
        DOM.setAttribute(this.appletObject, "archive",
                JAX_WS_JARS+",GWTIP_Chapter5_Applet.jar");
        DOM.setAttribute(this.appletObject,
            "cache_archive",                          <-1 Set cache_archive
                JAX_WS_JARS );
        DOM.setAttribute(this.appletObject, "width", "0px");
        DOM.setAttribute(this.appletObject, "height", "0px" );
        DOM.setAttribute(this.appletObject, "codebase",
                GWT.getModuleBaseURL()+"/applet/");
    }

    public static void initialize(ReadyCallback callback) {
        SOAPClientApplet.getInstance();
        INSTANCE.intializeJavaScript(callback);
    }

    private native Element intializeJavaScript(ReadyCallback callback)/*-{
        $wnd.appletSOAPClientReadyNotify = function(){
           callback.
     @[...]SOAPClientApplet.ReadyCallback::onReady()();   <-- Package name
        }                                                     replaced
     }-*/;                                                    with [...]

    public static interface ReadyCallback {
        public void onReady();
    }

    public native String sayHello(                 2 Define service
        JavaScriptObject person)/*-{             <-  method
        $wnd.person = person;
       return $wnd.document.getElementById("SOAPClientApplet").sayHello();
    }-*/;
}
```

Here we're recycling a number of concepts from the Flash version of our SOAP client.

Discussion

The `ReadyCallback` works the same way it did in the Flash example, this time invoked from the applet's `start()` method. We use an `<applet>` tag to instantiate the applet, and the `cache_archive` attribute to keep users from having to download the entire JAX-WS distribution every time they visit the page ❶.

TIP The deprecated `<applet>` tag is used in listing 5.15. While it's recommended that you use an `<object><embed></object>` construction for Java applets, as was used in the Flash example in listing 5.10, we have found that using LiveConnect in this configuration can be problematic.

The big difference between the applet and Flash methods is the hand-coded service method in this example ❷. While we're just returning a simple string here, you could return a `JavaScriptObject` and use the `JavaScriptObjectDecorator` to access it.

We now have a SOAP client, but once again have the same-origin policy security issue to deal with.

5.5.2 Signing JARs for security bypass

The Java security model allows for trusted applets to have access to the full features of the JRE inside a browser. Applets that are not trusted are subject to the same-origin policy and other security constraints.

Trusted applets are signed with a certificate from a trusted certificate authority. For publicly deployed applications, you should acquire a certificate from a public service such as Thawte or VeriSign. For internal use or examples, such as this book, you can create your own self-signed certificate.

PROBLEM

The applet SOAP client won't talk to the server because they are of different origins.

SOLUTION

By creating a trusted applet (using a trusted security certificate), we can enable communications with any SOAP resource, regardless of its origin.

We'll create a trusted applet by using a certificate. For the purposes of this example, we'll simply create a self-signed certificate. Listing 5.16 shows a shell session demonstrating how to use `keytool` and `jarsigner` to self-sign the applet's JAR.

Listing 5.16 Using `keytool` and `jarsigner`

```
$ keytool -genkey -alias gwtip -keyalg rsa
Enter keystore password:  googlewebtoolkit
What is your first and last name?
  [Unknown]:  GWT
What is the name of your organizational unit?
  [Unknown]:  Manning
What is the name of your organization?
  [Unknown]:  Manning
What is the name of your City or Locality?
  [Unknown]:  Atlanta
What is the name of your State or Province?
  [Unknown]:  Georgia
What is the two-letter country code for this unit?
  [Unknown]:  US
Is CN=GWT, OU=Manning, O=Manning, L=Atlanta, ST=Georgia, C=US correct?
  [no]:  yes

Enter key password for <gwtip>
        (RETURN if same as keystore password):

$ keytool -selfcert -alias gwtip
Enter keystore password:  googlewebtoolkit

$ jarsigner GWTIP_Chapter5_Applet.jar gwtip      <-- (1)
Enter Passphrase for keystore: googlewebtoolkit

Warning: The signer certificate will expire within six months.
```

(1) **Repeat this step with all dependency JARs**

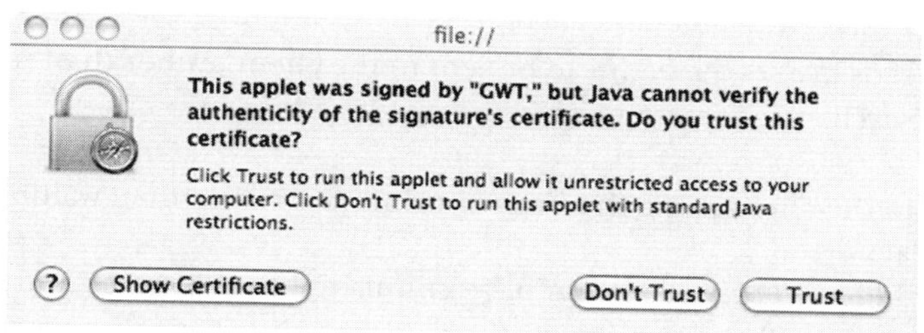

Figure 5.6 A prompt to trust the signed applet

Notice that you need to repeat the last step, using `jarsigner`, for each of the dependencies ❶. Each JAR will have its own security context, and if one of them isn't signed and attempts a security-restricted operation, such as talking to a non-origin server, you'll get a security exception.

Once you have successfully deployed the signed applet, its invocation causes Java to prompt the user to trust the applet's signatory within the JRE, as shown in figure 5.6.

DISCUSSION

Once the applet has been approved, it can call foreign servers. You can also use this technique to access files on the user's filesystem for local persistent storage.

The applet, as a client, does provide for synchronous calls like the other remote services we have looked at so far. However, it is a request-response type of communication with the server. There are other ways to provide streaming data from the server, and while they can also be done with an applet provider, we'll move on to a pure JavaScript technique called Comet.

5.6 Streaming to the browser with Comet

Ajax ... Comet ... get it? Well, OK, it's a moderately cute name at best. However, as a means of providing low-latency event type data to an application, such as Meebo.com's browser-based instant messaging client, Comet is pretty cool.

Comet takes advantage of how modern web browsers load pages: inline JavaScript is executed as it's parsed by the browser, rather than once the whole page has loaded. This behavior can confuse new DHTML developers, because calling an object declared farther down the page from the current script execution may result in JavaScript errors being thrown. However, it provides a way to send small executable messages to the client because the TCP stream serving the page never completely closes.

If you're old enough in web terms, you might remember the old technique of server-push animation. In this technique, a stream serving an image file was never closed, and updated images were incrementally pushed to the browser. Each new image would clobber the previous image, and it would appear as though the browser were slowly downloading an animated GIF file or playing a movie. Comet uses a very similar concept.

PROBLEM

Our application needs live server events to be sent to the client, rather than relying on a request-response cycle.

SOLUTION

We will push data to the client using the Comet technique, rather than waiting for the client to request data.

By keeping a hidden `<iframe>` on the page connected to the server and continuously loading, you can send messages from the server to the client in near-real time. While Comet is a technique, more than a library, we'll be looking at a specific implementation for GWT created by Luca Masini and available for download at http://jroller.com/masini/entry/updated_comet_implementation_for_gwt. We'll cover the basics of this concept in this chapter, and in chapter 11 we'll build an enhanced version of this implementation to support some additional features.

There are three parts to this Comet implementation that we'll focus on here: the client-side GWT message receiver, the server-side servlet that brokers messages to the Comet stream, and the regular GWT RPC service for sending messages. This last part is a regular GWT RPC service with some additional code to create the streaming connection frame and register a callback method (using JSNI) to handle messages from that frame.

Listing 5.17 shows the code for the first part—the client message receiver.

Listing 5.17 Streaming message receiver class

```
public class StreamingServiceGWTClientImpl implements StreamingService
{
    private int watchDogTimerTime = 100000;

    Map callbacks = new HashMap();

        private boolean keepAlive = false;
        private final String streamingServicePath =
           GWT.getModuleBaseURL()+ "streamingServlet";
        private static StreamingService instance = null;
        private final StreamingServiceInternalGWTAsync service =
         (StreamingServiceInternalGWTAsync)GWT.create(
             StreamingServiceInternalGWT.class);
        private final Map waitingSubscriber = new HashMap();

    private final static AsyncCallback voidCallback =
          new AsyncCallback() {
        public void onFailure(Throwable caught) {}
        public void onSuccess(Object result) {}
    };

    private final AsyncCallback restartStreamingCallback =
         new AsyncCallback() {
        public void onFailure(Throwable caught) {}
        public void onSuccess(Object result) {
            restartStreamingFromIFrame();
            callback("restartStreaming", (String)result);
        }
    };
```

```
    private final AsyncCallback internalKeepAliveCallback =
        new AsyncCallback() {
    public void onFailure(Throwable caught) {}
    public void onSuccess(Object result) {

        alert("keepAlive");
        keepAlive = true;
        watchDogTimerTime = 10*Integer.parseInt(result.toString());

        for(Iterator iter =
              waitingSubscriber.entrySet().iterator();iter.hasNext();)
        {
            Entry callback = (Entry)iter.next();
            subScribeToEvent((String)callback.getKey(),
                  (AsyncCallback)callback.getValue());

            iter.remove();
        }

        callback("keepAlive","");
    }
};

public static StreamingService getInstance() {
      if(instance == null) {
        instance = new StreamingServiceGWTClientImpl();
      }
    return instance;
}
    private StreamingServiceGWTClientImpl() {                  ❶

    callbacks.put("keepAliveInternal", internalKeepAliveCallback);
    callbacks.put("restartStreamingInternal",
                restartStreamingCallback);

    ((ServiceDefTarget) service).setServiceEntryPoint(
                    GWT.getModuleBaseURL()+ "streamingService");

    setUpNativeCode(this);

    restartStreamingFromIFrame();

    createWatchDogTimer();
}

    private void callback(
       String topicName, String data) {                         ❷

    keepAlive = true;

    if(callbacks.containsKey(topicName))
    {
        AsyncCallback callback =
             (AsyncCallback)callbacks.get(topicName);

        try {
            Object dataToSend = data;

            if(data.startsWith("$JSONSTART$") &&
                         data.endsWith("$JSONEND$")) {
```

❶ **Define constructor with callbacks**

❷ **Pass message to user's callback**

```
                    dataToSend = JSONParser.parse(
                                 data.substring(
                                  "$JSONSTART$".length(),
                                   data.length()-"$JSONEND$".length()));
                }
                callback.onSuccess(dataToSend);
            } catch (JSONException e) {
                callback.onFailure(e);
            }
        }
    }

    private native void setUpNativeCode(
        StreamingService thisInstance)
     /*-{
        $wnd.callback = function(topicName, data)
        {
          thisInstance.
           @org.gwtcomet.client.StreamingServiceGWTClientImpl
           ::callback
           (Ljava/lang/String;Ljava/lang/String;)
           (topicName,data);
        }
    }-*/;

    private void createWatchDogTimer() {
        Timer t = new Timer() {
            public void run() {
                if(!keepAlive) {
                    restartStreamingFromIFrame();
                }

                keepAlive = false;
            }
        };
        t.scheduleRepeating(watchDogTimerTime);
    }

    private void restartStreamingFromIFrame() {
        Element iframe = DOM.getElementById("__gwt_streamingFrame");

        if(iframe!=null) {
            DOM.removeChild(RootPanel.getBodyElement(), iframe);
        }

        iframe = DOM.createIFrame();
            DOM.setAttribute(iframe, "id", "__gwt_streamingFrame");
          DOM.setStyleAttribute(iframe, "width", "0");
          DOM.setStyleAttribute(iframe, "height", "0");
          DOM.setStyleAttribute(iframe, "border", "0");
          DOM.appendChild(RootPanel.getBodyElement(), iframe);

          DOM.setAttribute(iframe, "src", streamingServicePath);
    }

    public void sendMessage(String topicName, String data) {
        service.sendMessage(topicName, data, voidCallback);
    }
```

❸ Create native callbacks to call GWT class

```
    public void sendMessage(String topicName, JSONValue object) {
        sendMessage(topicName,
                     "$JSONSTART$"+object.toString()+"$JSONEND$");
    }

    public void subScribeToEvent(String topicName,
      AsyncCallback callback) {
        if (keepAlive) {
            service.subscribeToTopic(topicName, voidCallback);
            callbacks.put(topicName, callback);
        }
        else {
            alert("Streaming is not alive, subscriber '"+
                   topicName+
                   "' is cached with callback "+
                   callback+" until online");

            waitingSubscriber.put(topicName, callback);
        }
    }

    private final TextArea textArea = new TextArea();
}
```

There is a good bit of code here, but the operating principle is very simple. When the Comet client is set up, it registers a JavaScript method on the window object ❶, ❸, and then calls back into the local `callback()` method ❷ on the GWT Java class. This method then takes the message and passes it to the user's `AsyncCallback` implementation where it's processed by the rest of the application. Native callbacks are also used to pass data back into the GWT application ❸.

The callback is fired by `<script>` tags served incrementally by the server. These scripts invoke the JavaScript callback method on the `window` object. The messages themselves come from a servlet using an observable to notify clients. Our example servlet for this task is shown in listing 5.18.

Listing 5.18 `StreamingServlet` class

```
public class StreamingServlet extends RemoteServiceServlet {

    private final static long serialVersionUID = 1;
    private final static byte[] PAYLOADCONTENT = "//payload\n".getBytes();

    private long keepAliveTimeout = 10000;
    private long numberOfIteration = 20;
    private int payload = 500%PAYLOADCONTENT.length;
    private int counter = 0;

    public StreamingServlet() {
    }

    private void writeToStream(OutputStream out, String contents)
    throws IOException {

        out.write(contents.getBytes());

        for (int i = 0; i < payload; i++) {
```

```
            out.write(PAYLOADCONTENT);
        }

        out.flush();
    }

    private void sendKeepAlive(OutputStream out)        ❶ Send keep-alive message
       throws IOException {

        writeToStream(out,
            writeCallback(
                new StringBuffer(),
                "keepAliveInternal",
                Integer.toString(counter++)));
    }

    private StringBuffer writeCallback(StringBuffer stream,
        String topicName,
        String data) throws UnsupportedEncodingException {
        stream.append(
            " <script type='text/javascript'>\n");
          stream.append("\twindow.parent.callback('"+      ❷ Write message as a <script>
        topicName+
        "',unescape('"+
            URLEncoder.encode(data, "iso-8859-1")
            .replaceAll("\\x2B","%20")+"'));\n");
        stream.append("</script>\n");

        return stream;
    }

    public void init() throws ServletException {        ❸ Read initialization parameters

        String keepAliveTimeoutString =
            getServletConfig()
            .getInitParameter("keepAliveTimeout");
        if (keepAliveTimeoutString != null) {
            keepAliveTimeout =
                  Long.parseLong(keepAliveTimeoutString);
        }

        String payloadString =
                  getServletConfig().getInitParameter("payload");
        if (payloadString != null) {
            payload =
                  Integer.parseInt(payloadString)/PAYLOADCONTENT.length;
        }

        String numberOfIterationString = getServletConfig()
             .getInitParameter("numberOfIteration");
        if (numberOfIterationString != null) {
            numberOfIteration =
                   Long.parseLong(numberOfIterationString);
        }
    }

    protected void doGet(HttpServletRequest request,     ❹ Begin stream cycle
        HttpServletResponse response)
        throws ServletException, IOException {
```

```
final HttpSession session = request.getSession();
final ConcurrentLinkedQueue<StreamingServiceBusiness.Event>
    eventList = new
    ConcurrentLinkedQueue<StreamingServiceBusiness.Event>();

getServletContext().log("thread "+
Thread.currentThread().getName()+
" starting streaming for client "+session.getId());

Observer updatesObserver = new Observer() {            ❺ Create observer to watch events
    public void update(Observable o, Object arg) {

        StreamingServiceBusiness.Event event =
             (StreamingServiceBusiness.Event)arg;

        if(StreamingServiceImpl.getStreamingServiceBusiness()
         .isClientSubscribedToQueue(
           event.queueName, session.getId()))
        {
            eventList.add(event);
        }
    }
};

StreamingServiceImpl
.getStreamingServiceBusiness()
    .addObserver(updatesObserver);

response.setContentType("text/html;charset=ISO-8859-1");
OutputStream out = response.getOutputStream();

try {
    for (int i = 0;                                    ❻ Loop for fixed number of iterations
          i < numberOfIteration; i++) {
        if (eventList.size() > 0) {
            StringBuffer stream = new StringBuffer();
            for (Iterator<StreamingServiceBusiness.Event> iter =
        eventList.iterator();
        iter.hasNext();) {
                StreamingServiceBusiness.Event event =
                          iter.next();

                if((System.currentTimeMillis()-event.eventTime)
            <
            (keepAliveTimeout*10)) {
                    writeCallback(stream, e
            vent.queueName,
                        event.message);

                    getServletContext().log("streamed "+event);
                }

                  iter.remove();

            }
            writeToStream(out, stream.toString());
        }
        else {
             sendKeepAlive(out);
        }
```

```
                StreamingServiceImpl
                .getStreamingServiceBusiness()
                .waitForEvents(keepAliveTimeout);
            }
        }
        finally {
            StreamingServiceImpl
            .getStreamingServiceBusiness()
            .deleteObserver(updatesObserver);

            writeToStream(out,
            writeCallback(new StringBuffer(),
            "restartStreamingInternal", "").toString());

            getServletContext().log("thread "+
            Thread.currentThread().getName()+
            " finished streaming for client "+session.getId());

            out.close();
        }

    }
}
```

❼ Block thread execution waiting for events

❽ Tell client to restart stream

To get a feel for the flow of this class, let's talk about the lifecycle of the servlet ❹. First, the servlet reads in initialization parameters with `init()` ❸. Once a request comes in, the servlet creates an `Observer`, registers it with the service implementation ❺, and begins a loop of a fixed number of iterations ❻. Each of these represents a burst of messages sent to the client as script elements ❷. The servlet then sends any pending messages, or, if there are none, it sends a keep-alive event to keep the socket open ❶. Once the messages are flushed, the servlet calls `waitForEvents()` on the service, which blocks the thread's execution until there are more events needing to be sent ❼. Finally, once the number of iterations has been reached, the servlet sends the client a message to restart the stream connection ❽.

This last step, restarting the connection, is important for a number of reasons. First, remember that all of this is being written to an `<iframe>` in the client browser, which means it's a document held in memory. This is true even if the events fired by the callback are transient in the GWT application. This means that a communication frame is expanding in your browser's memory, and it should be cleaned up from time to time. Such housekeeping also helps with browsers that get irritable on long socket reads. Some browsers timeout a socket read if the page rendering starts taking too long; resetting it from time to time prevents this.

You'll also notice the use of `URLEncoder` and `unescape()` paired with each event sent. This ensures that special characters that might otherwise break the JavaScript string are properly handled, without a complex replacement at call time. The final value is then passed to the `window.parent.callback()` method, which was created in the previous listing, and which takes the data and passes it through to the GWT code.

Now that we have seen it referenced a few times, it's time to look at the business service, which is shown in listing 5.19.

Listing 5.19 Business service class

```
public class StreamingServiceBusiness {

    private final static long serialVersionUID = 1;

    private final ConcurrentMap<String,
                    ConcurrentHashMap<String, Boolean>>
      queues
=
        new ConcurrentHashMap<String,
                    ConcurrentHashMap<String, Boolean>>();
    private final Observable observable = new EventObservable();

    public StreamingServiceBusiness() {
        super();
    }

    public static class EventObservable extends Observable {
        public synchronized void notifyObservers(Object arg) {
            setChanged();
            super.notifyObservers(arg);
            notifyAll();
        }
    }

    public void subscribeToTopic(String topicName,
        String clientName) {                                  ❶
        if (!queues.containsKey(topicName)) {
            queues.put(topicName,
            new ConcurrentHashMap<String, Boolean>());
        }

        queues.get(topicName).putIfAbsent(clientName, Boolean.TRUE);
    }

    public void unsubscribeFromTopic(String topicName,
      String clientName) {                                    ❷
        if (queues.containsKey(topicName)
        && queues.get(topicName).containsKey(clientName)) {
            queues.get(topicName).remove(clientName);
        }
    }

    public boolean isClientSubscribedToQueue(
        String topicName, String clientName) {
        return queues.containsKey(topicName)
    && queues.get(topicName).containsKey(clientName);
    }

    public static class Event {
        public final String queueName;
        public final String message;
        public final long eventTime = System.currentTimeMillis();

        public Event(String queueName, String message) {
            this.queueName = queueName;
            this.message = message;
        }
```

❶ Subscribe client to event queue

❷ Unsubscribe client from queue

```
        public String toString() {
            return "Event("+queueName+","+message+","+eventTime+")";
        }
    }

    public void addObserver(Observer observer) {
        observable.addObserver(observer);
    }

    public void deleteObserver(Observer observer) {
        observable.deleteObserver(observer);
    }

    public void waitForEvents(long keepAliveTimeout) {
        try {
            synchronized(observable)
            {
                observable.wait(keepAliveTimeout);        ❸ Block thread
            }
        } catch (InterruptedException e) {
        }
    }

    public void sendMessage(String queueName, String message) {

        synchronized(observable) {
            observable.notifyObservers(new Event(queueName,message));
        }
    }
}
```

Here, Luca is keeping a set of `ConcurrentHashMap` objects to store the subscription state of a user to a particular queue. Once a message comes in, it's sent to the observable and the servlet determines whether a client should receive it. The servlet can determine this, of course, based on which clients have subscribed ❶ (and clients may also unsubscribe ❷). The clients can then block their loop ❸ as you saw in the servlet (listing 5.18) on the `waitForEvents()` method. If the keep-alive timeout is reached before a message is received, the servlet's thread will resume and it will send the keep-alive message.

DISCUSSION

Once it's all rolled up, the service can be used through the service class that encapsulates all of these:

```
StreamingService streamingService =
        StreamingServiceGWTClientImpl.getInstance();
streamingService.subScribeToEvent("SomeEventQueue", new MyCallback());
```

The callback can then be used like any other service event notification you have seen previously in this chapter. This time, however, the events do not have to be initiated by the client, but are pushed to the client by the server.

5.7 Summary

We have given you a fairly exhaustive tour of the various ways to communicate with servers from GWT. While you're unlikely to use all of the techniques in every application, this discussion has presented several browser technologies and techniques available for use with GWT.

We examined the security issues surrounding browser-server communications, as well as several techniques for communicating with servers and working around related limitations. We either discussed or demonstrated the use of POX, REST, and SOAP for communication, and we looked at using Flash and Java applets to enhance or enable certain aspects of the process. Table 5.2 summarizes the server communications technologies we discussed, and the related capabilities and methods involved with using each.

Table 5.2 Capabilities of server communication methods

Method	Origin server	Other servers	Methods
GWT HTTP and XML support	Yes	No	POX/REST
Flash	Yes	Yes, if controlled	POX/SOAP
Java	Yes	Yes, if signed	Any

Related to our more general discussion of server communications, we also covered the Comet technique for sending stream/event type data to the client from the server. We'll take a deeper look at this technique in chapter 11, as it forms the basis of the large practical application presented there.

In addition to all of these concepts and technologies, we took a brief look at one of the options for developing GWT applications in the NetBeans IDE (highlighting another tool available to developers). So far in this book, we have used the Google `ApplicationCreator` and `ProjectCreator` utilities, the Eclipse IDE, and the NetBeans IDE.

In the next chapter, we'll explore IntelliJ IDEA IDE support for GWT while we take a closer look at JSNI. While many of the examples presented in this chapter made some use of it, we'll take a look at the full functionality of JSNI and at some JavaScript libraries that might be useful to integrate with your GWT applications.

6 Integrating Legacy and Third-Party Ajax Libraries

This chapter covers

- Working with the JavaScript Native Interface
- Creating JSNI Wrappers
- Dealing with JavaScript eventing models
- Working with the JSIO project

Before software can be reusable it first has to be usable.

—Ralph Johnson

Although we believe GWT represents a superior environment for developing Ajax applications, sometimes the functionality you want to reuse is in existing JavaScript libraries. These might be your own legacy code or third-party libraries. Additionally, there may be times when you want to directly tweak aspects of your GWT application with JavaScript. To perform either of these tasks, you need to use JSNI.

We introduced JSNI in chapter 1 and used it in several other examples in this book, so you should already have a handle on the basics. Though JSNI is very powerful, it can also be confusing and problematic. When working with JSNI, you have to keep in mind that you're on your own, and your own feet are in range of your shotgun. Methods that you implement as native JavaScript, or that you wrap and inherit, are typically less portable across different browsers, are more prone to memory leaks, and are less performant than JavaScript optimized and emitted by the GWT compiler. For this reason, though it's possible to use JSNI for more than integration, we recommend that you stick to integrating existing well-tested JavaScript code when using JSNI. That will be our focus here.

In this chapter, we'll take a closer look at the specifics of JSNI usage and at some common gotchas you may encounter. Knowing a few key things can lessen the confusion and reduce the possibility for errors. Then we'll look at a couple of larger examples where we take two popular JavaScript libraries, Script.aculo.us and Moo.fx, and integrate them with GWT by creating a wrapper module for each.

As we present these examples, you'll see common tasks and patterns for working with JavaScript from GWT, including packaging JavaScript files, dealing with typing compatibility, and handling events. We'll begin with a recap of JSNI basics and then move into more involved examples.

6.1 A closer look at JSNI

JSNI is required any time you want to call into native JavaScript from Java, or vice-versa, so you need to understand it when working with any existing JavaScript or when tweaking display parameters beyond the exposure of the GWT browser abstraction. The GWT documentation notes that JSNI can be thought of as the "web equivalent of inline assembly code." This goes back to the browser-as-virtual-machine idea that GWT embraces.

Before we dive into some involved GWT "assembly" code, we'll revisit the JSNI basics, cover some common pitfalls, and get our working environment for this chapter's examples in order.

6.1.1 JSNI basics revisited

There are two sides to the JSNI coin: Java and JavaScript.

You can write native JavaScript methods directly in Java by using the `native` keyword and the special `/*- -*/` comment syntax. This syntax gives you the opportunity to write JavaScript code that will be run in the browser, as is. Here's an example:

```
/*-{
    alert( message );
}-*/;
```

You can also access Java fields and methods from within JavaScript by using another special syntax that indicates classes with the `@` symbol and method or field names with `::` (two colons). Examples of each of these follow (where `instance-expr` is optional and represents either an instance if present or a static reference if absent):

```
[instance-expr.]@class-name::field-name

[instance-expr.]@class-name::method-name(param-signature)(arguments)
```

Along with having a unique syntax, JSNI also has a specific type mapping. Like JNI does with platform-specific code, GWT uses a set of character tokens to indicate the type information for the method you're calling. Understanding this is important, because type conversion will determine what parameters are being passed and *which* method will be called in the case of overloaded methods. Table 6.1 lists the tokens for each of the standard Java types and how they're mapped using JSNI tokens.

For example, if you had a Java method with a signature like the following,

```
public String figureSomething(String[] string, int startPoint, boolean
  flag);
```

you would invoke it from JSNI with a statement such as this:

```
x.@com.my.ClassName:: figureSomething([Ljava/lang/String;IZ)(array, 2,
  false);
```

Notice that there is no separation between the tokens in the JSNI arguments portion.

Another important basic component in JSNI code is the `JavaScriptObject` class. We used this magical class in our examples in chapter 5 as the return type of our native methods. That's the basic job of `JavaScriptObject`. It provides an opaque representation of a JavaScript result to Java.

While the JSNI rules seem simple, troubleshooting can sometimes be problematic. When incorporating legacy JavaScript, it's critical that you understand the potential pitfalls of using the JSNI libraries.

Table 6.1 Mappings of Java types to JSNI type signature tokens

Java type	JSNI signature token
`boolean`	`Z`
`byte`	`B`
`char`	`C`
`short`	`S`
`int`	`I`
`long`	`J`
`float`	`F`
`double`	`D`
Any Java class	`L(fully-qualified class path);` example: `Ljava/lang/String;`
Arrays	`[` followed by the JSNI token for the contained type

6.1.2 Potential JSNI pitfalls

The dual nature of JSNI makes things a bit more complicated than traditional coding. You have to be aware of not only the logic and usage of one language, but also of the syntax, interaction, type conversions, and boundaries with another. Several potentially problematic issues are often encountered.

It's important to remember that arrays of primitives or `JavaScriptObjects` passed into a native method will be completely opaque and can only be passed back via JSNI or returned. Additionally, a JavaScript array of string values can't be passed as `Ljava/lang/String;`. You'll see an example of how to get around this in section 6.3.4.

As you saw in chapter 5, `JavaScriptObject` modifies the native object as it's passed into Java code. `JavaScriptObject` is instrumented with functions like `equals()` and `hashCode()` to make it easier to work with in Java. If you're using a security-restricted object, like a DOM element representing a plugin or ActiveX control, this will cause security exceptions. Also, `JavaScriptObjects` denoting the same native reference will not evaluate to `true` with the `==` operator. You must use the `equals()` method.

Another important thing to keep in mind when you're working with JSNI code is the behavior of the `JavaScriptObject`. You should never return the JavaScript special value `undefined` to your Java code, as it can lead to all kinds of unexpected results. If you do, your compiled Java code will continue to pass this around until there is a call to a utility method, or something that evaluates one of the GWT-added values, and strange `HostedModeExceptions` will start to be thrown. If you do this, you can get lost for hours trying to figure out where things went wrong.

While including JavaScript in your Java code is very easy with JSNI, sometimes you just want to include a JavaScript file. For instance, if you have a third-party JavaScript library, or if you're using your own legacy JavaScript, you need to make those files available to your JSNI code inside your GWT application. The easiest way to do this is to use a `<script>` tag in your module's gwt.xml file. While you can link scripts directly from host pages, doing so can be problematic—modules cannot be easily distributed and reused if they need an external JavaScript file.

As we discussed in chapter 2, the `<script>` tag in your module definition takes care of this by allowing a module definition to include a JavaScript file in the public package of the module, and it tells the gwt.js file to load that script before the rest of the module starts executing. Since the public directory will be included in any modules that inherit from the original, the loading of the script is automatic. Listing 6.1 shows a sample.

Listing 6.1 A simple use of the `<script>` tag

```
<module>
    <script src="myscript.js"><![CDATA[
        if( $wnd.MyClass ) {
            return true;
        } else {
```

```
            return false;
        }
    ]]></script>
</module>
```

The `src` attribute is almost self-explanatory. This is the location of the JavaScript file relative to the public package of the module. Inside the `<script>` tag is a block of code that can be executed, returning `true` or `false`, to determine whether the script has been successfully loaded. This is JavaScript written in JSNI notation, and it is usually contained in a `CDATA` section because, well, because entity-escaped code is ugly. You'll also notice the use of the `$wnd` global variable. We'll get to that in a bit.

Why do we need this block of code? Although including a script in the HTML harness page is easy, the script has to work within the confines of the single-threaded JavaScript interpreter for GWT to load it. Even a script that's being included dynamically has to be executed on the same thread as the GWT application.

Let's say you wanted to write a method to load a script file. You might write something like this:

```
private void addScriptTag(String source) {
    Element script = DOM.createElement("script");
    DOM.setAttribute(script, "src", source);
    DOM.appendChild(RootPanel.getBodyElement(), script);
}
```

Using this technique, you would find out very quickly that your application behaves erratically. Why? Because that script will not execute at the moment `DOM.appendChild()` is called. It will queue up and wait for your GWT application to go into event-wait before execution, like Glick's metaphorical bees waiting to visit the queen. Therefore, any method you called in the same execution run as `addScriptTag()` would never see the script. You could, of course, create an event callback to let you know when the script is loaded—and if you wanted to use a JSON service dynamically within JSNI from a non-same-origin server, this might be a good idea. For most uses, though, this is a lot of code to write when what you really want is for the script to be available when your GWT module begins executing.

Going back to listing 6.1, the `$wnd` global variable is one of two special tokens GWT supports inside JSNI code, the other being `$doc`. The entirety of your monolithic GWT application runs in an isolated context, so the usual JavaScript global variables, `window` and `document`, will not give you access to the HTML host page's window and document values. To access them, you need to use `$wnd` and `$doc` directly. Scripts that are loaded with a `<script>` tag are in the host page's execution context. This means that if you want to call methods or use objects defined in your external scripts, you need to prefix these calls with `$wnd` to make sure that GWT calls the top level and not the GWT scope.

Now that we have covered the specifics of talking to JavaScript and including JavaScript in your GWT application and we've addressed some common issues, we'll look at some examples where we wrap third-party JavaScript for use in GWT. First, though, we need to set up IntelliJ IDEA, our spotlight tool in this chapter, for use with GWT.

6.1.3 Configuring IntelliJ IDEA

It's not coincidental that this chapter on integrating JavaScript using JSNI is the one in which we're introducing IntelliJ IDEA as the spotlight tool. Of all the IDEs, IDEA's core GWT support is exceptionally good. While it's not a free option like Eclipse or NetBeans, it's a fantastic development environment. For GWT applications, it includes a lot of shortcuts for creating modules, enhanced highlighting, and more.

To get started with IDEA, you must first configure the GWT home location, as you do for the NetBeans module. This is done by selecting the Settings option (the wrench icon on the toolbar) and selecting the GWT icon, as shown in figure 6.1.

Clicking this icon brings up a dialog box prompting you for the location of the GWT home directory. At we write this, IDEA doesn't know about GWT for the Macintosh, but that will likely change soon. You can sidestep the error message on the Mac by simply copying and renaming the gwt-dev-mac.jar file in the home folder to gwt-dev-linux.jar.

What makes IDEA's support special? Well, two things stand out as great features. First, it restricts your project's classpath scanning to modules declared as `<inherits>`

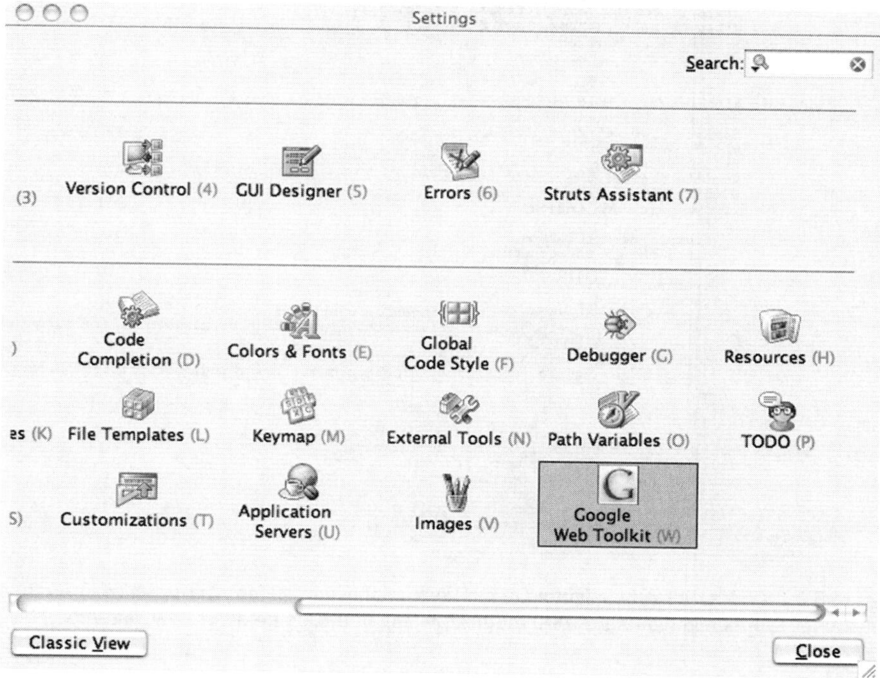

Figure 6.1 The Google Web Toolkit settings option in the IntelliJ IDEA settings panel. This setting can be used to specify your GWT Home folder.

in your module's gwt.xml file. This is an incredibly useful feature if you're dealing with multiple dependencies for packaged JSNI scripts, which we'll look at in this chapter. The second feature is the syntax highlighting, which is smart enough to skip into `/*-{ }-*/` blocks, giving you the advantages of JavaScript highlighting and formatting in your native methods, as pictured in figure 6.2. (Don't worry if the code in the figure seems a bit alien right now—we'll expand on this in section 6.3.)

The syntax highlighting feature alone makes IDEA a worthy candidate for your GWT development needs. Even better, if you're a well-established open source project, you can apply for a free license. Even at $250 for a personal edition, though, it's not out of reach for the average developer working on closed source projects, and a free thirty-day evaluation is available at http://www.jetbrains.com/.

Now that we have a development environment set up, it's time to get started. Our first task is to create a GWT module that encapsulates a JavaScript library. We'll start by wrapping the Moo.fx animation framework in a GWT module and build a small sample module that uses it. This will demonstrate the basics of working with JSNI, and it should better acquaint you with reading JSNI code.

```
DragAndDrop.java | Scriptaculous.gwt.xml

        JavaScriptObject array, JavaScriptObject object)/*-{
    if( array == null ) array = new Array();
    array.push( object );
}-*/;
private static native JavaScriptObject addToArray(
        JavaScriptObject array, String object)/*-{
    if( array == null ) array = new Array();
    array.push( object );
}-*/;


private static native void setDroppable( Element target,
        JavaScriptObject acceptClasses,
        JavaScriptObject containment,
        String hoverClass,
        String overlap,
        boolean greedy,
        UIObject uiObject )/*-{
    $wnd.Droppables.add( target,
        {
            accept: acceptClasses,
            containment: containment,
            hoverclass: hoverClass,
            overlap: overlap,
            greedy: greedy,
            onDrop: function(draggable, droppable, overlap){
                    @gwtip.javascript.scriptaculous.client.DragAndDrop::fireOnDrop(Lcom/go
            },
            onHover: function(draggable, droppable){
                    @gwtip.javascript.scriptaculous.client.DragAndDrop::fireOnHover(Lcom/g
            },
        });
}-*/;

public static void unsetDroppable(UIObject target){
    if( droppables.contains( target) ){
        unsetDroppable( target.getElement());
        dropListeners.remove( target );
        if( draggables.get( target ) != null ){
            elementsToUIObjects.remove( target );
```

Figure 6.2 IDEA's syntax highlighting of the JavaScript inside the `setDroppable()` method. The JavaScript syntax highlighting of JSNI methods is one of IDEA's greatest GWT features.

6.2 Wrapping JavaScript libraries

In the next two sections we're going to take a look at common patterns for integrating JavaScript and Ajax, and arm you with the tools and a general idea as to the process of using non-Java libraries with GWT. To this end, we'll generate wrappers for two JavaScript libraries so they can be used with GWT: Moo.fx and Script.aculo.us.

Moo.fx (http://moofx.mad4milk.net/) is one of our favorite JavaScript libraries. It's very small, and while it's limited in functionality, it can make a web application feel a lot more polished (maybe more polished than it actually is). The core Moo.fx library includes just three basic visual effects: width, height, and opacity. These let you change the respective attributes of a DOM object or toggle the presence of any object on screen. Also provided are several different transition types, including the sinoidal transition, which is a very natural and appealing looking transition that many applications you know and love, such as the Apple iLife suite, are already using.

We're going to use Moo.fx with a simple application that takes a photograph and alters its appearance. The example application, with no effects applied, is shown in figure 6.3.

The first step in creating our simple photo-effect application is to get the Moo.fx script ready for use in GWT. Because this is something we might want to reuse in other applications, we'll package the JSNI Moo.fx support as its own GWT module.

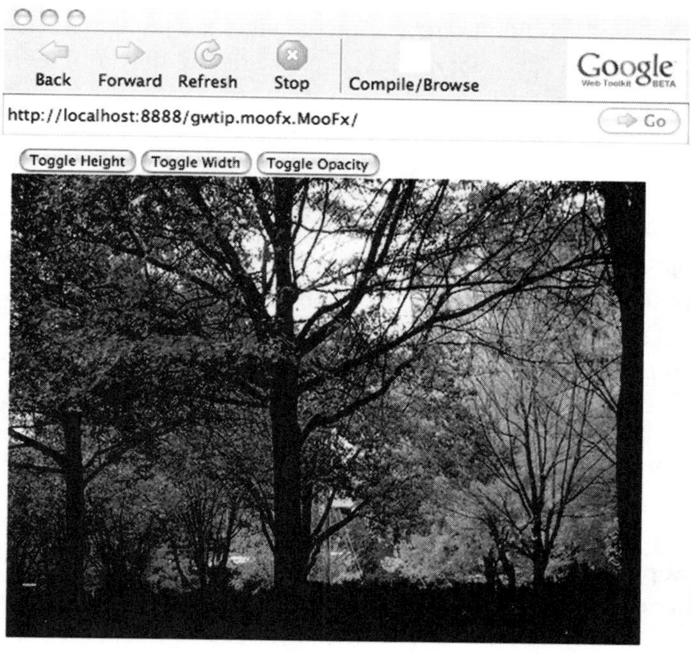

Figure 6.3 The sample Moo.fx application in hosted mode. We'll use Moo.fx to apply the three animated effects represented by the buttons above the photograph.

6.2.1 Creating a JavaScript module

As you saw earlier, the `<script>` tag makes directly including a JavaScript file in a module relatively simple. For this project, we're going to take the Moo.fx library and make it a GWT module that can be used with any GWT project. We'll start by creating the module descriptor, as shown in listing 6.2.

Listing 6.2 MooFx.gwt.xml module descriptor

```
<module>
    <script src="prototype.lite.js"><![CDATA[
        // Confirm that prototype is loaded
        if ($wnd.Class) {
            return true;
        } else {
            return false;
        }]]></script>
    <script src="moo.fx.js"><![CDATA[
        // Confirm that prototype is loaded
        if ($wnd.fx) {
            return true;
        } else {
            return false;
        }]]></script>
</module>
```

Include Prototype Lite for Moo.fx

Defined by Prototype Lite

Include Moo.fx script

Check for fx object

Once the module descriptor is filled out, we need to copy the JavaScript files into the `com.manning.gwtip.javascript.moofx.public` package, so they will be included with the compiled application.

Now that we know the script will load, we can use the object referenced by `fx` in our Java code to animate the image. To do that, we'll write a series of wrapper classes.

6.2.2 Creating wrapper classes

Each of Moo.fx's effect classes take two arguments as a constructor: the DOM element you wish to modify; and an associative array of options including how much time the effect should take to execute, a `Transition` object that determines the step value, and a callback that's notified when the effect is complete. For our JavaScript wrapper classes, we'll invoke the constructor and hold onto the created effect at the instance level, replicating the way Moo.fx is used in a pure JavaScript environment.

PROBLEM

We want to wrap a hierarchy of JavaScript classes from within Java.

SOLUTION

The best way to wrap a hierarchy of JavaScript classes from within Java is to replicate the exposure you need from JavaScript in a matching Java hierarchy. Moo.fx has several types of `Effect`, so in Java we'll create an `Effect` class and subclass it appropriately. We'll start with the `Effect` parent class, as shown in listing 6.3.

Listing 6.3 The `Effect` parent class

```
public class Effect {

    protected JavaScriptObject nativeEffect;
    protected EffectListener handler;
    protected UIObject uiObject;
    protected long duration;
    protected JavaScriptObject transition;

    protected Effect(UIObject uiObject, EffectListener handler,
            long duration , JavaScriptObject transition) {
        super();
        this.uiObject = uiObject;
        this.handler = handler;
        this.duration = duration;
        this.transition = transition;
    }

    public void toggle() {
        toggle(this.nativeEffect);
    }

    private native void toggle(
        JavaScriptObject effect)/*-{
        effect.toggle();
    }-*/;

    public void hide() {
        hide(this.nativeEffect);
    }

    private native void hide(
        JavaScriptObject effect) /*-{
        effect.hide();
    }-*/;

    public void clearTimer() {
        clearTimer(this.nativeEffect);
    }

    private native void clearTimer(
        JavaScriptObject effect) /*-{
        effect.clearTimer();
    }-*/;

    public void custom(int start, int end) {
        custom(this.nativeEffect, start, end);
    }

    private native void custom(JavaScriptObject nativeEffect,
         int start, int end) /*-{
        nativeEffect.custom(start, end);
    }-*/;
}
```

1 Hold native implementation in JavaScriptObject

Define callback interface for Java

Specify Transition to use

Wrap native methods

Define JSNI methods to invoke native code

Listing 6.4 shows where the `nativeEffect` comes from by presenting the `Height` class as a representative sample.

Listing 6.4 The Height Effect

```
public class Height extends Effect {

    public Height(UIObject uiObject, EffectListener handler,
            long duration, JavaScriptObject transition) {
        super(uiObject, handler, duration, transition);        ❷ Call Effect constructor
        this.nativeEffect =
             getEffectClass(uiObject.getElement(),            Create fx.Height object
                duration,
                handler,
            transition);
    }

    private native JavaScriptObject getEffectClass(
            JavaScriptObject element,
            long time,                                          Closure
            EffectListener handler,                             that wraps
            JavaScriptObject transitionFunction ) /*-{          EffectListener
        var complete = function(){                              callback
            if( handler != null ){
                handler.@gwtip.javascript.moofx.client.EffectListener::
                onComplete()();
            }
        };                                                      Construct fx.Height
        return new $wnd.fx.Height(element,                      and return it
    { duration: time, transition: transitionFunction, onComplete::
                complete });
    }-*/;
}
```

Now we have an Effect parent class and a Height child. This structure replicates the relationship the JavaScript objects have with each other.

DISCUSSION

The Effect class is mostly just a data structure, but it does contain the methods that invoke the JavaScript to perform an action. The native implementation in listing 6.3 ❶ will be set by the individual effect subclasses, such as the Height class. Mostly we're just capturing the UIObject that you want to perform the effect on and the other values that Moo.fx needs in that constructor.

The Height effect is a pretty simple class that simply passes the constructor arguments back up to Effect (❶ in listing 6.3) and then sets the nativeEffect with the proper implementation (❷ in listing 6.4). Here we're also extracting the DOM element enclosed by GWT's UIObject and passing it to the native object. Obviously, Moo.fx doesn't know anything about a GWT UIObject, but it does understand DOM elements. The getElement() method will become your friend when you're mixing GWT widgets and third-party JavaScript. Since the callback is handled by the EffectListener Java interface, we need to create a simple closure around it for the native effect to call when the transition is completed.

Speaking of transitions, Moo.fx includes four basic transition types that are stored as closures on the object referenced by the fx global variable. We'll expose these to

Java so they can be passed into the `Effect` subclasses using the `Transition` class, which is shown in listing 6.5. This class would be a standard example of a Java class holding constant values, except that we must have the native methods to retrieve the object references.

Listing 6.5 The `Transition` class

```
public class Transition {
    public static final JavaScriptObject SINOIDAL = getSinoidal();
    public static final JavaScriptObject LINEAR = getLinear();
    public static final JavaScriptObject CUBIC = getCubic();
    public static final JavaScriptObject CIRC = getCirc();

    private static native JavaScriptObject getSinoidal()
    /*-{return $wnd.fx.sinoidal;}-*/;
    private static native JavaScriptObject getLinear()
    /*-{return $wnd.fx.linear;}-*/;
    private static native JavaScriptObject getCubic()
    /*-{return $wnd.fx.cubic;}-*/;
    private static native JavaScriptObject getCirc()
    /*-{return $wnd.fx.circ;}-*/;
}
```

Our Moo.fx GWT wrapper is now ready to be compiled and packaged as a module for use in another GWT application.

6.2.3 Using the wrapped packages

To use the JSNI-wrapped module we have just created, we need to start by inheriting it in a different GWT application. This is old hat by now, but let's look at the module descriptor.

PROBLEM

We need to inherit a GWT JSNI-wrapped module in your GWT application.

SOLUTION

To use the JSNI wrapper module in the code, we need to inherit the module in the `gwt.xml` file as we would a Java module.

```
<module>
    <!-- Inherit the core Web Toolkit stuff. -->
    <inherits name='com.google.gwt.user.User'/>
      <inherits name='com.manning.gwtip.javascript.moofx.MooFx'/>
    <!-- Specify the app entry point class. -->
    <entry-point class='gwtip.moofx.client.MyEntryPoint'/>
</module>
```

Once the `<inherits>` elements are processed, GWT will extract the `moofx.public` package into the web application and will process the `<script>` elements from that module as they are encountered. We have packaged Prototype Lite with our Moo.fx module here, but it might also be wise to separate it out. If we were mixing several different JSNI modules that needed Prototype, or Prototype Lite, we wouldn't want the scripts to fight over which version was running at a particular time.

Next, we'll create a simple EntryPoint implementation to demonstrate each of the effects in listing 6.6.

Listing 6.6 An EntryPoint using the effects

```
public class MyEntryPoint implements EntryPoint {
    Image img = new Image(GWT.getModuleBaseURL()+"/fireworks.jpg");

    Height height = null;
    Width width = null;
    Opacity opacity = null;
    EffectListener listener = new EffectListener() {
        public void onComplete() {
            Window.alert("complete");
        }
    };
    public MyEntryPoint() {
        super();
    }

    public void onModuleLoad() {
        Button b = new Button("Toggle Height", new ClickListener() {

            public void onClick(Widget widget) {
                height = (height == null) ?
                    new Height(img,
                        listener,
                        500,
                        Transition.SINOIDAL
                        ) : height;
                height.toggle();
            }
        });
        RootPanel.get().add(b);

        b = new Button("Toggle Width", new ClickListener() {

            public void onClick(Widget widget) {
                width = (width == null) ? new Width(img,
                        listener,
                        500,
                        Transition.LINEAR
                        ) : width;
                width.toggle();
            }
        });
        RootPanel.get().add(b);
        b = new Button("Toggle Opacity", new ClickListener() {

            public void onClick(Widget widget) {
                opacity = (opacity == null) ?  new Opacity(img,
                        listener,
                        500,
                        Transition.CIRC
                        ) : opacity;
                opacity.toggle();
            }
```

❶ Hold effects at class level

Create simple EffectListener

Create effect if it doesn't exist

```
        });
        RootPanel.get().add(b);

        RootPanel.get().add(img);    <-- Add image to panel
    }
}
```

The `EntryPoint` example in listing 6.6 makes use of the wrapper classes we created for Moo.fx to animate a photograph with the three `Effect` types and binds three buttons to toggle each of them.

DISCUSSION

Most of this is fairly standard code for creating a basic set of widgets. The big thing you'll notice is that the `Effect` objects are held at the class level ❶, not created inside the `ClickListeners` for the buttons. This is because the `toggle()` method stores the original state of the DOM element in the native instance, so if you want `toggle()` to work, you need to keep the `Effect` reference around to restore the element to its original state. In your applications, you might think about creating your own `UIObject` subclasses that contain the appropriate effect and expose the `toggle()` or `clearTimer()` methods as needed. Finally, we simply call the toggle methods to make our image dance and sing, or maybe just dance. Figure 6.4 shows the application during an `Opacity` transition.

So far, you have seen Moo.fx used to load a JavaScript dependency into a GWT module, and you saw the basics of wrapping classes and using the GWT-created DOM

Figure 6.4 The image partially faded with the `Opacity` effect from Moo.fx. After you click the Toggle Opacity button, the image will fade out of existence.

elements in the JavaScript libraries. In the next section, we'll look in more detail at maintaining interactions between GWT components and JavaScript libraries. This is a pattern you'll find useful to repeat when building JSNI wrappers for many JavaScript libraries.

6.3 Managing GWT-JavaScript interaction

Script.aculo.us (http://script.aculo.us) is a more general-purpose UI library than Moo.fx. It includes an effects library very similar to the one provided by Moo.fx, and on top of that it has a `Slider` widget, an `Autocompleter` widget, an animation framework, a set of DOM utilities, and a testing framework. In the GWT world, a lot of this is uninteresting. Script.aculo.us's drag-and-drop functionality, on the other hand, is very interesting. While a native drag-and-drop system is on the drawing board for GWT, none is included right now, and this stands out as a major shortcoming when compared to other RIA toolkits.

In this sample project we're going to wrap the Script.aculo.us dragdrop.js support to enable our GWT application to use this feature. Note that we need to add prototype.js, effects.js, and dragdrop.js to the module definition, as these are requirements for Script.aculo.us.

Let's get to the meaningful classes. We'll start by implementing basic drag support.

6.3.1 Maintaining lookups

The core of Script.aculo.us's dragdrop.js is the `Draggable` class. This is a wrapper class that combines a standard DOM element with the code to enable dragging. Once the `Draggable` is created, the element can be dragged until the `destroy()` method is called. We want to make this as easy as possible on the developer, so we'll make instrumentation with the drag code available as a single static method call, and keep the static references around for calls to `destroy()` within the API code.

We'll start by building a simple application that lets us drag our image around the window, as seen in figure 6.5.

We'll be building a `DragAndDrop` class over the course of this section, so these early code samples will not have the complete code in them that you'll see in the samples from the Manning website. Our code will end up in the same completed state, but we'll be adding to the samples as we go.

Our Script.aculo.us support will look very much like the wrapper classes we created for the Moo.fx library, but it's important to note the maintenance of lookups in the Java code to coordinate between Java and JavaScript. To move back and forth between DOM element references and GWT classes, you will need to maintain lookup structures. As mentioned in the previous section, this is a pattern you'll find useful in any JSNI wrapper you're creating.

PROBLEM

Our JavaScript library is DOM `Element`-based, but your GWT code depends on `UIObject`.

Figure 6.5 Dragging the image around in the window creates a ghost image as a placeholder. When the image is dragged, a partially transparent copy will follow the mouse.

SOLUTION

We'll start by creating the `setDraggable()` and `unsetDraggable()` methods and their supporting code, as shown in listing 6.7. This supporting code maintains lookups between `Elements` and `UIObjects`.

Listing 6.7 The first portion of the `DragAndDrop` class

```
public class DragAndDrop {

    public static final String
        CONSTRAINT_VERTICAL="vertical";
    public static final String
        CONSTRAINT_HORIZONTAL="horizontal";

    private static Map draggables = new HashMap();

    public static void setDraggable(UIObject source,
            UIObject handle,
            boolean revert,
            int zIndex,
            String constraint,
            boolean ghosting
```

Annotations: Set fixed values for constraint; ❶ Map UIObject to JavaScriptObject (Draggable); ❷ Set options for Draggable

```
        ) {
    if (draggables.get(source) != null) {                Unset current
        unsetDraggable(source);                      <-- drag profile
    }
    JavaScriptObject draggable = setDraggable(source.getElement(),
            ((handle == null) ? null : handle.getElement()),
            revert,
            zIndex,
            constraint,
            ghosting);                                   Save JavaScriptObject
    draggables.put(source, draggable);               <-- to map
}

private static native JavaScriptObject setDraggable(
        JavaScriptObject element,
        JavaScriptObject handle,
        boolean revert,
        int zIndex,
        String constraint,
        boolean ghosting
        )/*-{
    return new $wnd.Draggable(
            element,
            {
            handle : handle,
            revert : revert,
            zindex : zIndex,
            constraint: constraint,
            ghosting: ghosting
            });
}-*/;

public static void unsetDraggable(                      3 Remove drag profile
    UIObject source) {                               <-- from UIObject
    if (draggables.get(source) != null) {
        JavaScriptObject draggable =
                (JavaScriptObject) draggables.remove(source);
        destroyDraggable(draggable);
    }
}

private static native void destroyDraggable(
    JavaScriptObject draggable)
/*-{ draggable.destroy(); }-*/;
}
```

This class exposes several static methods to provide `UIObjects` with drag support and to keep track of the `JavaScriptObjects` created by Script.aculo.us.

DISCUSSION

It may seem that there are a lot of arguments in the methods at the beginning of the `DragAndDrop` class in listing 6.7 ❷, but they're mostly straightforward. Passing a `UIObject` to `setDraggable()` makes the `UIObject` draggable. Passing it to `unsetDraggable()` disables dragging. Each of the arguments is explained in table 6.2.

Table 6.2 Arguments for `setDraggable()`. These are part of the associative array in JavaScript but are fixed arguments in the Java methods.

Argument	Description
`source`	Specifies the `UIObject` we want to drag.
`handle`	Specifies the `UIObject` we want to be a handle, or the clickable part, for the draggable object. Think of the title bar on a window as a handle.
`revert`	Specifies whether the object should revert to its original position after the drag is completed.
`zIndex`	Specifies the CSS `z-index` property used to bring the draggable to the front.
`constraint`	Limits the dragging to one axis. Used with the static final `String` values, or `null`.
`ghosting`	Causes the dragging to use a partial transparency while leaving a duplicate of the element in place.

When we create a draggable, we store the resulting native object in the `draggables` lookup map ❶ so we can get back to it to call the `destroy()` method when necessary ❸. This is an important pattern to remember when integrating with JavaScript libraries: you should maintain the associations between GWT objects and the JavaScript objects on your own. This puts more of the onus on your code, sometimes even duplicating state that might exist in JavaScript. In the end, though, this will minimize unexpected errors caused by JavaScript incompatibilities or bugs.

In listing 6.8 we create a simple `EntryPoint` for our draggable application using `DragAndDrop`.

Listing 6.8 An `EntryPoint` using the `DragAndDrop` class

```
public class MyEntryPoint implements EntryPoint {
    Image img = new Image(GWT.getModuleBaseURL()+"/fireworks.jpg");
    VerticalPanel panel = new VerticalPanel();

    public MyEntryPoint() {
        super();
    }

    public void onModuleLoad() {
        Button b = new Button("Make Draggable", new ClickListener() {
            public void onClick(Widget widget) {
                DragAndDrop.setDraggable(img,                    | Set up
                        null, false, 1000, null, true);          | options
            }
        });
        panel.add(b);

        panel.add(img);
        RootPanel.get().add(panel);
    }
}
```

In listing 6.8 we make the image draggable with no handle, no reverting to the original position, a z-index of 1000, no constraints, and ghosting enabled. You've already seen the results of this in the ghosted image of the trees (figure 6.5).

This approach is pretty easy, and it works well, but right now it's simply browser candy. If we want to make dragging useful, we need to know when it happens. We need to add some event listeners.

6.3.2 Daisy-chaining Java listeners into JavaScript closures

In its native operation, Script.aculo.us supports capturing events in two ways, and each of these is handled using different metaphors. First, there is a `change()` closure that can be attached to the `Draggable` object. This is fired whenever something happens to the drag-enabled DOM element. The other is through an Observer pattern object, much like a standard Java event listener. These listeners implement `onStart()`, `onDrag()`, and `onEnd()`, receiving an event name and the `Draggable` object that fired the event as arguments. These are a bit limiting, so we'll wrap them in something that's a little more robust. We will look at each of these methods in turn.

PROBLEM

JavaScript provides a simple closure for event notifications, but our Java code needs an Observer pattern to receive events.

SOLUTION

First, we need the `DragListener` interface as shown in listing 6.9.

Listing 6.9 DragListener

```
public interface DragListener {
    void onChange(UIObject source);
}
```

There is not much to the `DragListener` interface. To get from the JavaScript event to the `UIObject`, we custom-generate the closure that gets called, and store the `UIObject` in the local scope.

Next we want to track the listeners in the `DragAndDrop` class. In listing 6.10 we continue to add on to the `DragAndDrop` class to add this support.

Listing 6.10 Changing DragAndDrop to support DragListener

```
private static Map dragListeners = new HashMap();      <-- Lookup of UIObject to DragListeners

public static void addDragListener(UIObject source,
        DragListener listener) {
    JavaScriptObject draggable =
          (JavaScriptObject) draggables.get(source);
    if (draggable == null) {                           <-- Validate passed draggable object
        throw new RuntimeException("That is not a draggable object.");
    }
    List listeners = (List) dragListeners.get(source);
    if (listeners == null) {
        listeners = new ArrayList();
```

```
            dragListeners.put(source, listeners);
        }
        listeners.add(listener);                          <-❶ Add listener to List
        unsetChange(draggable);                               Remove current options.change closure
        for (Iterator it = listeners.iterator(); it.hasNext();) {
            appendListener(source, draggable,
                (DragListener) it.next() );                   New Listener calls into options.change closure
        }
    }

    private static native void unsetChange(JavaScriptObject draggable)
    /*-{draggable.options.change = null;}-*/;

    private static native void appendListener(
            UIObject source, JavaScriptObject draggable,
            DragListener listener )/*-{
        var oldChange = draggable.options.change;
        var newChange = function(element) {                   ❷ Daisy-chain closures
            if (oldChange) oldChange(element);
            listener.@gwtip.javascript.scriptaculous.client.DragListener::
            onChange(Lcom/google/gwt/user/client/ui/UIObject;)(source);
        }
        draggable.options.change = newChange;                 ❸ Set new closure
    }-*/;

    public static void remoteDragListener(
        UIObject source, DragListener listener) {
        JavaScriptObject draggable =
            (JavaScriptObject) draggables.get(source);
        if (draggable == null) {
            throw new RuntimeException("That is not a draggable object.");
        }
        List listeners = (List) dragListeners.get(source);
        if (listeners != null) {
            listeners.remove(listener);                       <-❹ Remove listener and rebuild
            unsetChange(draggable);
            for (Iterator it = listeners.iterator(); it.hasNext();) {
                appendListener(source, draggable, (DragListener) it.next());
            }
        }
    }
```

Here we keep a list of Java listeners around and rebuild a chain of JavaScript closures to fire them as part of the single closure the Script.aculo.us library provides for event notification.

Discussion

Listing 6.10 might, at first glance, seem very complicated, but it's actually not that bad. First, we keep an `ArrayList` of listeners keyed to `UIObjects`. When it comes time to add or remove a listener, we modify the `ArrayList` as needed ❶ ❹. Then we cycle through the listeners and add them to a daisy chain of closures on the `options.change` property of the `draggable` element ❷ ❸.

This daisy-chaining ❷ might seem odd if you have not done Ajax work in the past, but this technique allows a single closure object to support multiple methods. This is a common idiom for letting scripts overload the <body> element's `onload` event. Each time we want to add a closure, we take the current one and hold it. Then, in the next closure method, we first call the original, if needed, and execute the current event. When the final closure is called, we climb up to the top of the chain and execute each closure in turn. In this case, each of them fires the `onChange` event of the listener they were created to handle.

Now that we're supporting `DragListeners`, we can modify the `EntryPoint` class to show that they are working. Listing 6.11 shows the new listeners added to our draggable.

Listing 6.11 `MyEntryPoint.onModuleLoad` handling listeners

```
public void onModuleLoad() {
    Button b = new Button("Make Draggable", new ClickListener(){

        public void onClick(Widget widget) {
            DragAndDrop.setDraggable(img, null, false, 1000, null, true);
            DragAndDrop.addDragListener(img, new DragListener() {
                public void onChange(UIObject source) {
                    panel.add(new Label("Listener 1 event."));
                }
            });
            DragAndDrop.addDragListener(img, new DragListener() {
                public void onChange(UIObject source){
                    panel.add(new Label("Listener 2 event."));
                }
            });
        }
    });
    panel.add(b);
    panel.add(img);
    RootPanel.get().add(panel);
}
```

Now when we drag the image around the window, we'll see `Labels` that indicate events filling up the bottom of the screen, as shown in figure 6.6.

Because our daisy-chained closures call the previous closure first, they execute in the order they were added. If, for instance, we wanted to allow one listener to consume the event and stop processing, we could have the `DragListener` interface return a boolean indicating whether processing should continue. If any closure gets a `false` returned from its predecessor, it simply returns `false` and exits.

This is pretty useful functionality, but we might want to do more with it than we currently are. Most importantly, these events don't tell us what kind of event fired them, meaning we don't know the difference between picking up, moving, and dropping. What we're lacking is the global `Observer` support.

6.3.3 *Maintaining listeners in Java*

The `DragObserver` is both powerful and complex to implement. We have already discussed the three methods Script.aculo.us supports—`onStart()`, `onDrag()`, and `onEnd()`—so let's just start with the interface.

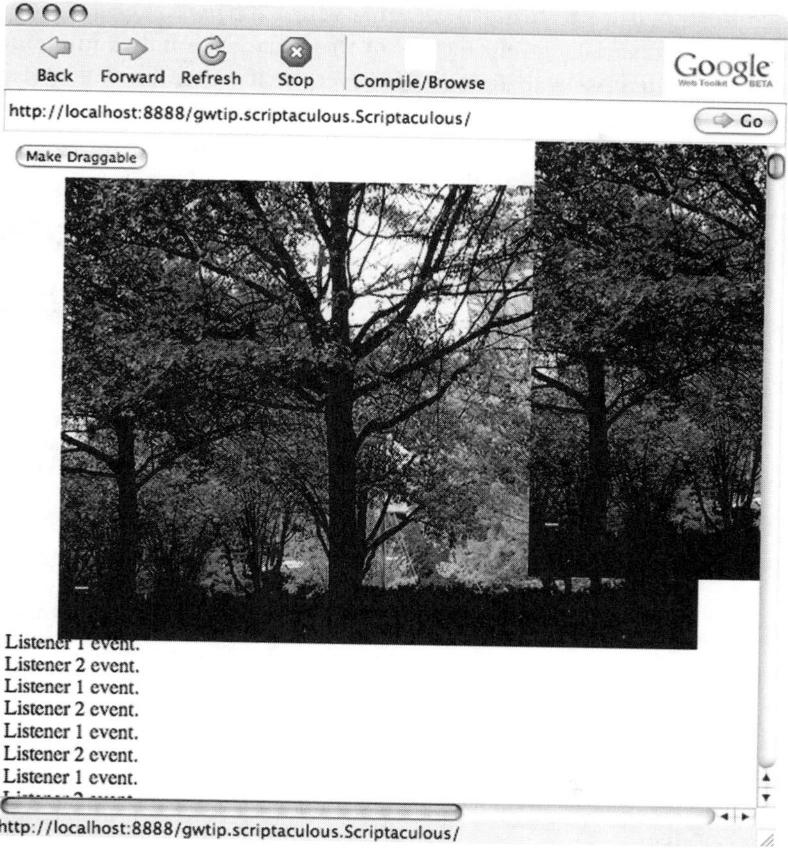

Figure 6.6 `DragListener` **events rendering to the screen as the image is dragged. The text at the bottom of the page shows the drag events firing as the image is dragged off to the right.**

PROBLEM

The JavaScript Observer pattern is not addressable from our GWT Java code.

SOLUTION

To proxy between JavaScript and Java observers, we must start by defining the interface we will use to capture events, as shown in listing 6.12.

Listing 6.12 The `DragObserver` Interface

```
public interface DragObserver {
    void onStart(String eventName, UIObject source);
    void onDrag(String eventName, UIObject source);
    void onEnd(String eventName, UIObject source);
}
```

You'll notice here that we're firing the events with `UIObject`. The JavaScript native `Draggables` object is actually going to pass in the `Draggable` native implementation, which we're storing in a `HashMap` already. However, we'll create a new `HashMap` of `Elements` to `UIObjects` to make this lookup easier to use when we get into drop targets. Let's look at how we can wire up the `DragAndDrop` class to support the drop observers. Listing 6.13 represents additions to the class.

Listing 6.13 Changes to the `DragAndDrop` class to support drop observers

```
private static Map elementsToUIObjects = new HashMap();      ❶ Create data
private static List dragObservers = new ArrayList();            structures

static{
    initDragObservers();
}                                                             ❷ Fire listeners
                                                                from a single
private static native void initDragObservers()/*-{              observer
    var observer = {
            onStart: function(name, draggable, event) {
                @gwtip.javascript.scriptaculous.client.DragAndDrop::
fireOnStart(Ljava/lang/String;Lcom/google/gwt/user/client/Element;)(
                    name, draggable.element);                 Pass element,
            },                                                not draggable
            onEnd: function(name, draggable, event) {
                @gwtip.javascript.scriptaculous.client.DragAndDrop::
fireOnEnd(Ljava/lang/String;Lcom/google/gwt/user/client/Element;)(
                    name, draggable.element);
            },
            onDrag: function(name, draggable, event) {
                @gwtip.javascript.scriptaculous.client.DragAndDrop::
                fireOnDrag
      (Ljava/lang/String;Lcom/google/gwt/user/client/Element;)
      (name, draggable.element);
            }
    };                                                        Add observer
                                                              to Draggables
    $wnd.Draggables.addObserver(observer);
}-*/;
                                                              Look up UIObject
private static void fireOnStart(String name,                  by element
    Element element) {
    for (Iterator it = dragObservers.iterator();
        it.hasNext();
       ) {
        ((DragObserver) it.next())
                .onStart(                                     ❸ Fire events
                    name,                                       to registered
                    (UIObject) elementsToUIObjects              observers
                        .get(element)
                );
    }
}
private static void fireOnDrag(String name, Element element) {
    for (Iterator it = dragObservers.iterator(); it.hasNext();) {
```

```
            ((DragObserver) it.next())
                    .onDrag(
                        name,
                        (UIObject) elementsToUIObjects.get(element)
                    );
        }
    }
    private static void fireOnEnd(String name, Element element) {
        for (Iterator it = dragObservers.iterator(); it.hasNext();) {
            ((DragObserver) it.next())
                    .onEnd(
                        name,
                        (UIObject) elementsToUIObjects.get(element)
                    );
        }
    }

    public static void addDragObserver(DragObserver observer) {
        dragObservers.add(observer);
    }
    public static void removeDragObserver(DragObserver observer) {
        dragObservers.remove(observer);
    }
```

Look up UIObject by element

Now we have the Java interface for `DragObserver` and methods for adding observers to and removing them from the `DragAndDrop` class.

DISCUSSION

What we're actually doing in listing 6.13 is creating the list of `Observers` in Java ❶, registering a single JavaScript `Observer` that calls back into our Java ❷, and then firing the Observers as appropriate ❸.

An astute reader might notice something missing here. For brevity, we omitted adding the `elementsToUIObjects.remove()` call in the `unsetDraggable()` method and the `elementsToUIObjects.put()` call in the `setDraggable()` method. These, however, need to be there to make sure the lookup is populated. Next we simply add a few lines to the entry point so we can see these events firing:

```
DragAndDrop.addDragObserver(new DragObserver(){
    public void onStart(String eventName, UIObject source) {
        panel.add(new Label(
            eventName +" "+ ((Image) source).getUrl()));
    }

    public void onEnd(String eventName, UIObject source) {
        panel.add(new Label(
            eventName +" "+ ((Image) source).getUrl()));
    }

    public void onDrag(String eventName, UIObject source) {
        panel.add(new Label(
           eventName +" "+ ((Image) source).getUrl()));
    }

});
```

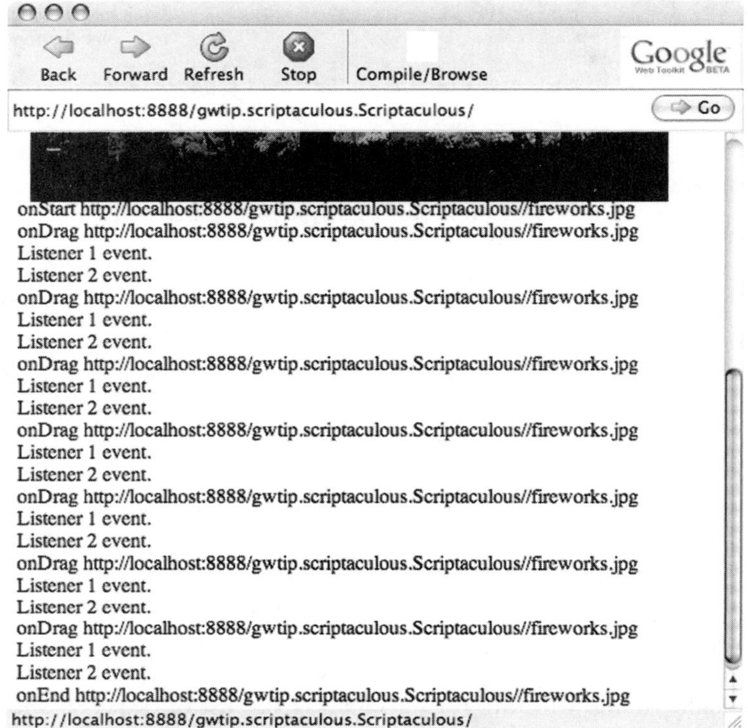

Figure 6.7 `DragListeners` and `DragObservers` fired through a drag. Here we see the `DragObserver` events firing, followed by the `DragEvents` we saw in the previous section. Notice that the observers see `onStart()` and `onDrag()`, and not just the basic event.

Now when we run the sample app, as shown in figure 6.7, we can see the order in which the events are fired during a short drag operation.

In these last two sections, you have seen two different techniques for translating JavaScript events into Java. The *right* way varies by situation and the code you're working with. Sometimes it's easier to work with the JavaScript listeners or to daisy-chain closures on an object. Sometimes it's easier to simply move the event-firing logic into Java and work from there. The big, and rather blindingly obvious, lesson here is to look at your JavaScript and think about what you need, then get into Java and select the best approach from there.

We aren't quite done yet, though. We still need drop support, and that means a whole new set of Java to JavaScript communications.

6.3.4 Conversion between Java and JavaScript

Drop targets are created in Script.aculo.us by calling `Droppables.add()`. We're going to wrap this in a Java method, and then we're going to support `DropListeners` within

Figure 6.8 Removing one of three file icons by dragging it to the trash and dropping it. Notice the hover events followed by the drop event as a file icon is dragged and dropped onto the trash can. (Icons courtesy of kellishaver.com.)

the `DragAndDrop` class. Finally, we'll create a simple `EntryPoint` to show the drop operations. In the end, we'll be able to drag and drop elements in the GWT context, as shown in figure 6.8.

You have seen two different methods for dealing with events and keeping track of lookups to smooth interactions between Java and JavaScript. In this section we'll combine these two to handle drop events. We'll also elaborate on an important and common troublesome task in working with JSNI—dealing with arrays.

PROBLEM

We need to deal with complex data conversions between Java and JavaScript, such as array conversions.

SOLUTION

First let's look at the code we need to add to the `DragAndDrop` class to register a droppable object. The `setDroppable()` method takes the arguments outlined in table 6.3.

You'll notice that `acceptClasses` and `containment` are both arrays. You'll recall from the first part of this chapter that arrays are completely opaque to your JavaScript code, so we'll have to convert between Java arrays and JavaScript arrays. Listing 6.14 shows this and the other modifications needed for our `DragAndDrop` support class to handle drop targets.

Table 6.3 Arguments for `setDroppable()`. As with `setDraggable()`, many of these are encapsulated in the JavaScript associative array. In Java we use named arguments.

Argument	Description
`target`	The `UIObject` to enable as a drop target.
`acceptClasses`	A `String` array of `Style` class values specifying what can be dropped on the target.
`containment`	A `UIObject` array of which dropped items must be children.
`hoverClass`	A `Style` class that will be applied to the target when something is hovering over it but not dropped.
`overlap`	One of `OVERLAP_VERTICAL`, `OVERLAP_HORIZONTAL`, or `null`. If set, the drop target will only react to a dragged item if it's overlapping by more than 50% on the given axis.
`greedy`	A flag indicating that the drop target should end calls to targets that may be beneath it once its own events have fired.

Listing 6.14 `DragAndDrop` additions to handle drop targets

```
public static final String OVERLAP_VERTICAL="vertical";
public static final String OVERLAP_HORIZONTAL="horizontal";

private static Set droppables = new HashSet();          Hold droppables
private static Map dropListeners = new HashMap();       and listeners

public static void setDroppable(UIObject target,        Pass arguments
        String[] acceptClasses,                         from table 6.3
        UIObject[] containment,
        String hoverClass,
        String overlap,
        boolean greedy
        ){
    JavaScriptObject acceptNative =                     Convert
        javaArrayToJavaScriptArray( acceptClasses);     arrays
    JavaScriptObject containmentNative = null;
    if (containment != null) {
        Element[] containElements = new Element[containment.length];
        for (int i = 0; i < containment.length; i++){
            containElements[i] = containment[i].getElement();
        }
        containmentNative = javaArrayToJavaScriptArray(containElements);
    }
    droppables.add(target);
    setDroppable(target.getElement(),
            acceptNative,
            containmentNative,
            hoverClass,
            overlap,
            greedy,
            target);
}
```

```
private static JavaScriptObject
    javaArrayToJavaScriptArray(Object[] array) {
    JavaScriptObject jsArray = null;
    for (int i = 0; array != null && i < array.length; i++) {
        if (array[i] instanceof String) {                          <-- Switch on object type
            jsArray = addToArray(jsArray, (String) array[i]);
        } else {
            jsArray = addToArray(jsArray, (JavaScriptObject) array[i]);
        }
    }
    return jsArray;
}

private static native JavaScriptObject addToArray(
    JavaScriptObject array, JavaScriptObject object)
/*-{
    if (array == null) array = new Array();
    array.push(object);
}-*/;
private static native JavaScriptObject addToArray(
        JavaScriptObject array, String object)/*-{
    if (array == null) array = new Array();
    array.push(object);
}-*/;
                                           Create arrays and push each element

private static native void setDroppable(Element target,
        JavaScriptObject acceptClasses,
        JavaScriptObject containment,
        String hoverClass,
        String overlap,
        boolean greedy,
        UIObject uiObject)/*-{
    $wnd.Droppables.add(target,
        {
           accept: acceptClasses,
           containment: containment,
           hoverclass: hoverClass,
           overlap: overlap,
           greedy: greedy,
           onDrop: function(draggable,
                        droppable, overlap) {              <-- Create onDrop event closure
              @gwtip.javascript.scriptaculous.client.DragAndDrop::
              fireOnDrop
             (Lcom/google/gwt/user/client/ui/UIObject;
              Lcom/google/gwt/user/client/Element;)
             (uiObject, draggable );
                 },
           onHover: function(draggable, droppable) {       <-- Create onHover event closure
              @gwtip.javascript.scriptaculous.client.DragAndDrop::
              fireOnHover
             (Lcom/google/gwt/user/client/ui/UIObject;
              Lcom/google/gwt/user/client/Element;)
             (uiObject, draggable );
                 },
        });
}-*/;
```

We have added the methods to create drop targets and added utility methods to convert between the Java and JavaScript array types.

DISCUSSION

The code we used in listing 6.14 to add drop support should be looking familiar to you at this point. The big change here is that we have to convert the Java arrays into JavaScript arrays, enclosed by `JavaScriptObjects`, to pass them around. This convoluted structure is necessary because you can't add to the JavaScript array from Java, nor can you read from a Java array within JavaScript.

The final portion of the `DragAndDrop` class, shown in listing 6.15, involves setting up the event registry and removing droppables. This is not unlike the `DragObserver` support we added earlier.

Listing 6.15 Finishing up the `DragAndDrop` class

```
public static void unsetDroppable(UIObject target) {
    if (droppables.contains(target)) {
        unsetDroppable(target.getElement());
        dropListeners.remove(target);                    <-- Clean up listeners
        if (draggables.get(target) != null) {            <-- Ensure drag features don't collide
            elementsToUIObjects.remove(target);
        }
    }
}

private static native void unsetDroppable(Element element)
/*-{ $wnd.Droppables.remove(element ); }-*/;

private static void fireOnHover(
  UIObject source, Element hovered) {
    UIObject hoveredUIObject =
        (UIObject) elementsToUIObjects.get(hovered);     <-- Convert back to UIObject
    List listeners = (List) dropListeners.get(source);
    for (int i = 0; listeners != null && i < listeners.size(); i++) {
        ((DropListener) listeners.get(i))
              .onHover(source, hoveredUIObject);
    }
}

private static void fireOnDrop(
   UIObject source, Element dropped) {
    UIObject droppedUIObject =
        (UIObject) elementsToUIObjects.get(dropped);
    List listeners = (List) dropListeners.get(source);
    for (int i = 0; listeners != null && i < listeners.size(); i++) {
        ((DropListener) listeners.get(i))
              .onDrop(source, droppedUIObject);
    }

}
public static void addDropListener(
  UIObject target, DropListener listener) {
    ArrayList listeners = (ArrayList) dropListeners.get(target);
    if (listeners == null) {
```

```
            listeners = new ArrayList();
            dropListeners.put(target, listeners);
        }
        listeners.add(listener);
    }
```

You'll notice in listing 6.15 that we're checking the draggables before we remove them from the `elementsToUIObjects` lookup hash. You need to add this to the `unsetDraggable()` method to prevent collisions. Now we have a fully functional `DragAndDrop` class.

NOTE If you're using this library in your own application, remember that you *must* remove droppables before taking them off the screen. If you don't, the entire Script.aculo.us dragdrop library will break down.

The final step in bringing our little example to fruition is writing the entry point. This is shown in listing 6.16, and it demonstrates how a drag-and-drop system that instruments classes in place, rather than requiring the developer to implement special drag-and-drop enabled classes, is easy to use. If you have worked with a very complex DnD system like Java Swing, the simplicity of using this kind of system is obvious.

Listing 6.16 `EntryPoint` for `DragAndDrop`

```
public class MyEntryPoint implements EntryPoint {
    VerticalPanel panel = new VerticalPanel();
    HorizontalPanel hpanel = new HorizontalPanel();
    VerticalPanel output = new VerticalPanel();       <-- Create Panel for Event output

    public MyEntryPoint() {
        super();
    }

    public void onModuleLoad() {
        Image trash = new Image("trash.png");
        String[] accept = {"file"};
        DragAndDrop.setDroppable(trash, accept, null, null, null, true);
        DragAndDrop.addDropListener(trash, new DropListener() {
            public void onHover(UIObject source, UIObject hovered) {
                output.add(new Label("Hover "+((File) hovered).name));
            }

            public void onDrop(UIObject source, UIObject dropped) {
                output.add(new Label("Drop file "+
                  ((File) dropped).name));
                panel.remove((File) dropped);
            }
        });

        hpanel.add(panel);
        hpanel.add(trash);
        File f = new File("foo", "webpage.png");      <-- Specify name and image for Files
        f.setStyleName("file");                            Create three files as draggable
        panel.add(f);
        DragAndDrop.setDraggable(f, null, true, 1000, null, true);
```

```
        f = new File("bar", "webpage.png");        <-- Create three files
        f.setStyleName("file");                        as draggable
        panel.add(f);
        DragAndDrop.setDraggable(f, null, true, 1000, null, true);

        f = new File("baz", "webpage.png");        <-- Create three files
        f.setStyleName("file");                        as draggable
        panel.add(f);
        DragAndDrop.setDraggable(f, null, true, 1000, null, true);

        RootPanel.get().add(hpanel);
        RootPanel.get().add(output);
    }
}
```

With listing 6.16 we have completed our basic example. Keep in mind that while we have demonstrated the key concepts, you would be better served moving the setup for your drag-and-drop operations out into your UI classes, and to manage events from your Controller level rather than in an entry point. However, this simple example keeps things concise and demonstrates the lifecycle of drop targets.

As you can see, there are lots of design issues to keep in mind when you're creating your JSNI wrappers. There is an easier way, for those who feel adventurous.

6.4 Wrapping JavaScript with GWT-API-Interop

While wrapping JavaScript APIs with GWT code is still the only officially sanctioned way to create JSNI modules, it can be slow going. Fortunately, there is an easier way. The GWT-API-Interop project (http://code.google.com/p/gwt-api-interop) provides a compile-time linking between GWT interfaces and JavaScript libraries.

We say that wrapping manually is the only *sanctioned* method because of this library's readme notes: "This project should be considered experimental, AS-IS, and generally unsupported at this time." While not officially supported, it's the basis of other code that the Google team has shipped for GWT. Your mileage may vary. We'll take a quick look at how to use this very handy module, in spite of this warning.

PROBLEM

Wrapping a large JavaScript library by hand is tedious.

SOLUTION

Using the GWT-API-Interop package can greatly simplify the process of wrapping a JavaScript library. This module uses a set of annotations on GWT-style Java interfaces to generate wrappers for JavaScript libraries at compile time.

The first step in the process is to import the JSIO module into your project. This will bring in the appropriate code generators:

```
<inherits name="com.google.gwt.jsio.JSIO"/>
```

Next, you need to create Java interfaces that map to your JavaScript library and extend `com.google.gwt.jsio.client.JSWrapper`. These will then be annotated with meta information about how they should be mapped. Listing 6.17 shows a simple interface mapped to a hypothetical JavaScript type.

Listing 6.17 Defining a JSIO-wrapped JavaScript object

```
/**
 *
 * @gwt.constructor $wnd.MyJavaScriptObject        ❶ Specify constructor
 */
public interface MyJavaScriptObject extends JSWrapper {

    /**                                 ❷ Specify method field
     * @gwt.fieldName doMethod
     */
    void doMethod(String string, int integer);
                                                   ❸ Get simple attribute
    int intAttribute();
}
```

DISCUSSION

Here we're creating a `JSWrapper` interface and specifying two annotations. First, we define the constructor function from the JavaScript API ❶. This will be called when the interface is instantiated using `GWT.create()`. Next, we define a method and use the `fieldName` annotation to associate it with the JavaScript field containing the function that implements the method ❷. For simple value attributes, we can simply name a method based on the attribute of the JavaScript object we want to return ❸.

Wow, that's easy! There are some caveats here, though. First, we still have to deal with issues of arrays. For this, the JSIO module includes the `JSList` interface. This is an implementation of `java.util.List` that you can use as a wrapper for JavaScript `Array` return or argument types. Note that you must annotate uses of `JSList` with the `gwt.typeArgs` annotation the same way you would with RPC calls or `IsSerializable` objects.

Another issue we spent a good deal of time on earlier was dealing with callbacks and events from JavaScript libraries. The JSIO module includes a means of handling this as well. The `JSFunction` abstract class allows you to create callbacks and pass them in with method calls. Listing 6.18 shows a brief example of this.

Listing 6.18 Creating a callback class for a JSFunction

```
/**                                        ❶ Specify JavaScript
 * @gwt.exported onMyEvent                   function to be called
 */
public abstract class MyCallback extends JSFunction {
                                                       ❷ Specify method
    void onMyEvent(String callbackArgument);              to call
}
```

Here we specify the method signature we want invoked in our GWT Java code ❷. To specify the callback from this method, we use the `exported` annotation ❶. This tells the code generator that the `onMyEvent()` Java method should be exposed, name intact, to JavaScript callers, and we're declaring this with a single function. You could, however, use the `exported` annotation on multiple methods if there are multiple possible states, such as `onSuccess` and `onFailure`. This will convert these methods into JavaScript closures that can be applied to asynchronous method calls, which works for simple calls where you might pass in a callback to the method call. You can also use the exported annotation on a mixed abstract class and use one of the techniques discussed in the previous section to handle Observer pattern listeners, such as using the exported annotation at the method level on an abstract class that extends JSWrapper.

The JSIO module includes a number of other annotations. Table 6.4 provides a complete list.

Table 6.4 A complete list of JSIO-supported annotations

Annotation	Location	Description
gwt.beanProperties	Class, method	This annotation indicates that methods that look like bean-style property setters should be generated so as to read and write object properties rather than import functions. This is most useful with JSON-style objects. The setting may be applied on a per-method basis in an imported class and may be overridden on a per-method basis by gwt.imported. If the backing object does not contain data for a property accessor, null, 0, ' ', false, or an empty com.google.gwt.jsio.client.JSList will be returned.
gwt.constructor	Class, method	The annotation gwt.constructor may be applied to a class to specify a JavaScript function to execute when constructing a JSWrapper to use as the initial backing object. A JavaScript Date object could be created by using the value $wnd.Date. If the gwt.constructor annotation is applied to a method within a JSWrapper and the method is invoked, the parameters of the method will be passed to the named global function, and the resulting JavaScript object will be used as the backing object.
gwt.exported	Method	Individual Java functions may be exported to JavaScript callers by declaring a gwt.exported annotation on a concrete Java method within a JSWrapper. The Java method will be bound to a property on the backing object per the class's NamePolicy or a gwt.fieldName annotation on the method. When applied at the class level to a com.google.gwt.jsio.client.JSFunction, it specifies which of the methods declared within to export as a JavaScript Function object.
gwt.fieldName	Method	When implementing a bean property accessor, the default NamePolicy will be used unless a gwt.fieldName annotation appears on the property's getter or setter. This is also used with imported and exported functions to specify the object property to attach to.
gwt.global	Class	The annotation gwt.global is similar to gwt.constructor, however it may be applied only at the class level and the value is interpreted as a globally accessible object name rather than as a function.

Table 6.4 A complete list of JSIO-supported annotations *(continued)*

Annotation	Location	Description
`gwt.imported`	Method	This is an override for methods within classes annotated with `gwt.beanProperties`.
`gwt.namePolicy`	Class	This annotation specifies the default transformation to use when converting bean property accessor function names to fields on the underlying `JavaScriptObject`. The valid values for the `namePolicy` are the field names on the `com.google.gwt.jsio.rebind.NamePolicy` class, or the name of a class that implements `NamePolicy`.
`gwt.noIdentity`	Class	This annotation suppresses the addition of the `__gwtObject` property on the underlying `JavaScriptObject`. The object identity of the `JSWrapper` will no longer maintain a one-to-one correspondence with the underlying `JavaScriptObject`. Additionally, `com.google.gwt.jsio.client.JSWrapper#setJavaScriptObject` will no longer throw `com.google.gwt.jsio.client.MultipleWrapperException`.
`gwt.readOnly`	Class	This annotation prevents the generated `JSWrapper` implementation from containing any code that will modify the underlying `JavaScriptObject`. This implies `gwt.noIdentity`. Invoking a bean-style getter when the underlying `JavaScriptObject` does not contain a value for the property will result in undefined behavior.

While it's important to remember that the GWT-API-Interop/JSIO module is unsupported and experimental, it can save you a great deal of hand-coding if you wish to use legacy or third-party JavaScript. We have only taken a brief look at its use here, but you can find more documentation at the project website (http://code.google.com/p/gwt-api-interop).

6.5 Summary

The JSNI component is both the most powerful and the most fraught with danger in the Google Web Toolkit. While you can use it to add nearly unheard-of ease of use to your Java classes, as the drag-and-drop example demonstrates, moving data successfully between the two environments can be an exercise in frustration. Mysterious errors crop up, and unlike GWT's compiled Java, in JavaScript you have to deal with cross-browser compatibility on your own.

In this chapter you have seen most of the issues involved with JSNI integration and picked up a couple of useful GWT modules to boot. One of the great advantages of mixed-mode development with GWT is that you can maintain the structure and common typing of Java and—only when you need to—break down to the lower-level flexibility of JavaScript to manipulate the browser.

Packaging JSNI libraries as easily reusable GWT modules is a great way to ease the development of your application. But once you start using these techniques, you need to be well versed at packaging and deploying your GWT applications. While we have seen simple examples running in the GWT development environment thus far, we'll take a closer look at building and deploying GWT applications for production in the next chapter.

7 Building, Packaging, and Deploying

This chapter covers

- Building and packaging GWT modules
- Building and deploying GWT applications
- Managing and automating the build process

I learned very early the difference between knowing the name of something and knowing something.

—Richard Feynman

After you start working with GWT, there will come a point when you need to step out of development mode and into the realm of building, packaging, and deploying your projects.

GWT applications can be broken up into multiple logical modules, and modules can be used as libraries or general components. Modules offer a lot of versatility beyond the configuration and inheritance they enable, which we first covered in chapter 1. In this chapter, we're going to once again discuss modules, but this time in the context of building and packaging.

Packaging happens both on the micro level, with modules, and on the larger macro level with entire applications. GWT components are packaged into modules, which are shared and reused as Java Archive (JAR) files. Applications, which are made up of multiple modules, and other JAR files and configuration elements are then typically packaged into larger Web Application Archive (WAR) files. Once all of the required artifacts are bundled up into an application, they are then typically deployed to a servlet container to be made available to the world.

Building and packaging GWT projects, depending on the scope, can be daunting. There are many configuration issues to keep in mind, and many different destinations: hosted mode, web mode, JEE servlet containers, other server-side resources, and more. In this chapter we'll expose the machinery involved to help you get a better understanding of the overall process, and then we'll try to help you manage that process with build tools. First, we'll focus on packaging GWT modules, then we'll move on to larger application level builds and deployment, and along the way we'll incorporate tools such as Ant and Maven.

7.1 Packaging GWT modules

One of the most significant aspects of GWT development is the reusable nature of components, all the way from code to the interface level. For example, in chapter 6 we used GWT modules that were created by using JSNI to wrap the Script.aculo.us and Moo.fx libraries. Also, earlier in the book we used other third-party modules and modules included with GWT itself, such as `User`. Recall that modules are inherited by using the `<inherits>` element within the module descriptor.

Creating your own modules to share with your team, or with the world, is an important advantage GWT offers. You can provide others with the latest version of your module, and they can use it by importing it. And although this functionality is very powerful, the process of turning your project into a module is fairly simple, thanks in large part to the design of GWT and automated build tools such as Ant.

7.1.1 Building and packaging modules

In order to divide up projects at logical junctures, create libraries, and otherwise share resources in GWT fashion, you need to understand what is required, and then know how to build and package resources as modules.

Just about every Java developer is familiar with the popular Apache Ant Java build tool (http://ant.apache.org/). Ant uses XML configuration files to control and automate the build process. Ant code and extensions direct the build: what gets compiled where, what is copied where, what tokens are replaced, and so on. GWT itself is built with Ant.

In addition to using Ant internally, GWT also provides a tool to help you generate an Ant build file that's capable of packaging your project as a module. By using this Ant build file and examining the components, you can get a good handle on what is required to build and package GWT modules.

PROBLEM

We need to create a GWT module JAR artifact based on a project.

SOLUTION

The GWT utility `ProjectCreator`, which we first introduced in chapter 3, includes the Ant-related command-line parameter `-ant`. Using `ProjectCreator` with `-ant`, you can create a default build XML file for your project that's capable of turning your GWT project into a module saved as a single JAR file. Here is an example:

```
[GWT_HOME]\projectCreator -ant com.manning.gwtip.antmaven.SimpleApp
```

The build file produced by this command, com.manning.gwtip.antmaven.SimpleApp.ant.xml, is shown in listing 7.1.

Listing 7.1 Default Ant build file created by `ProjectCreator`

```
<?xml version="1.0" encoding="utf-8" ?>
<project name="com.manning.gwtip.antmaven.SimpleApp"
     default="compile" basedir=".">
  <description>
    com.manning.gwtip.antmaven.SimpleApp build file.
     This is used to package up your project as a jar,
    if you want to distribute it. This isn't needed for normal operation.
  </description>

  <path id="project.class.path">                        ❶ Set up classpath
    <pathelement path="${java.class.path}/"/>
    <pathelement path="[GWT_HOME]/gwt-user.jar"/>
    <!-- Additional dependencies (such as junit) go here -->
  </path>

  <target name="compile"                                ❷ Compile project
     description="Compile src to bin">
    <mkdir dir="bin"/>
    <javac srcdir="src:test" destdir="bin"
      includes="**" debug="on"
      debuglevel="lines,vars,source" source="1.4">
      <classpath refid="project.class.path"/>
    </javac>
  </target>

  <target name="package" depends="compile"              ❸ Package project as a JAR
     description="Package up the project as a jar">
    <jar destfile="com.manning.gwtip.antmaven.SimpleApp.jar">
      <fileset dir="bin">
        <include name="**/*.class"/>
      </fileset>
      <!-- Get everything; source, modules, html files -->
      <fileset dir="src">                                ❹ Include source
        <include name="**"/>
      </fileset>
      <fileset dir="test">
        <include name="**"/>
      </fileset>
    </jar>
  </target>

  <target name="clean">
```

```
    <!-- Delete the bin directory tree -->
    <delete file="com.manning.gwtip.antmaven.SimpleApp.jar"/>
    <delete>
      <fileset dir="bin" includes="**/*.class"/>
    </delete>
  </target>

  <target name="all" depends="package"/>

</project>
```

The generated Ant build file is very basic, but it achieves the stated goal of allowing you to build a reusable GWT module using Ant with only a few minor twists, which we will discuss next.

DISCUSSION

A basic `ProjectCreator`-supplied build file does several key things: it sets up the classpath ❶, provides a compile target for the project ❷, and provides a package target that can package the entire thing into a JAR resource ❸.

You should note that when the compile target executes, the javac compiler is at work, not the GWT compiler. The GWT compiler is not involved here. This is because when you package a GWT module, you include the client *source* so that those inheriting your module have it. Then the inheriting project must use `GWTCompiler`, with its code and your inherited code, to create a resulting application. For this reason, the source code must be included in the module JAR ❹.

Ant can get much more involved than the default build file suggests. We'll expand this build file in section 7.3.1 to include the GWT compiler and build a WAR file.

The key to building and packaging GWT modules, as the default build file demonstrates, is that you need to include the source. Typically a module will include any required public resources (images, external JavaScript, CSS, and so on), the module descriptor file, and the source and compiled code for all of the client elements (Java). Once you create a JAR module, you can then import it into or distribute it to other GWT projects.

7.1.2 Sharing modules

Modules and reuse are baked into the toolkit. The concept of inheritance is central to GWT, and both creating and using modules are easily accomplished. Once you create a module and include the source for your code in a JAR archive, other projects can inherit that module.

There are a few key points to remember concerning sharing. First, you may not need an entry point in a pure module (that is, a project intended to be inherited, a library). In fact, including an entry point can be, let's say, interesting. Second, you should include documentation for your module that lets potential users know what dependencies are required, if any, including details on server-side resources.

For example, if your library is a logging utility that makes calls back to the server side to record client-side activity, users who inherit your module will need to know about, and how to properly configure, the server-side service servlets and dependencies.

This can be a good reason to use an automated build tool that can automatically set up dependencies and server-side resources (at least in hosted mode).

Though there are a few things to be aware of, sharing GWT libraries via modules is quite simple for the most part. Through inheritance and the configuration information provided by modules, GWT provides a clear path for expansion of the toolkit. GWT really is a foundation, and anyone can contribute libraries or modules that add functionality to the base set included with the distribution. In appendix A, we're including a list of current third-party GWT related projects and modules that we find useful or promising.

Once you're familiar with creating basic modules, you'll have the background to create more involved GWT applications. A typical GWT project will use functionality or support from multiple modules. When you've got your GWT application packaged, you'll then need to deploy it.

7.2 Building and deploying applications

Once you combined your code and modules into an application, you then need to deploy your project to an external web server (and your server-side components in a JEE container if you're using GWT RPC). This is where all the advantages of GWT's web-based delivery model come into play.

There are many ways to accomplish the various tasks involved in deploying web applications, and everyone seems to have a preferred approach. We cannot cover all the possibilities here, but we'll outline the overall process, and then we'll demonstrate several methods that we think work well with GWT.

There are two obvious types of GWT application components: client-side and server-side components. This somewhat obvious distinction is an important one to make, because even in a single application you can choose to build and deploy these portions independently, each as its own module. These component types are outlined in table 7.1.

Table 7.1 Two GWT application component types, showing how applications can be separated into constituent parts

Component type	Components
Client side	HTML, JavaScript, images, CSS, Flash, and so on (no RPC code involved)
Server side	GWT RPC code, `RemoteServiceServlet`, and related code

We'll deal with building and deploying GWT applications using either client- or server-side code or both. We'll begin with the simplest configuration, including client-side code only, and then progress to more involved scenarios.

7.2.1 The client side

You've already encountered simple client-side code, such as the examples provided with the toolkit (Hello World and Kitchen Sink) and our calculator in chapter 2. In these cases, no servlets or GWT RPC are involved. All of the processing with client-side components, once deployed, is local to the client browser. In terms of the application, this means that the code base is made up of HTML, JavaScript, and CSS.

Of course, your client code may also talk to servers if you're using JSON or POX/REST to communicate directly from the client with non-GWT resources. In those cases, though, you're still not using any server-side Java in the application.

PROBLEM

We need to deploy GWT client-side code with no server-side resources.

SOLUTION

We simply need to compile the GWT code with the GWT compiler, and then copy the output HTML, JavaScript, and other client public assets to a web server.

DISCUSSION

In cases where you're dealing with pure client-side code, the code can run on any web server. No JEE container is required. When you take client-side GWT code and compile it, either manually or via the Compile/Browse button of the shell, you're invoking the GWT compiler.

As we have previously discussed, the compiler will generate a set of HTML and XML files that comprise your application, and it will package up graphics, stylesheets, and other assets from the public directories of your module. All of the code processed by the compile step, whether from the source path or public path, will end up in a designated output directory in the resulting application—the default output directory is www. This type of code is very easy to work with. It runs in the hosted mode, and you can deploy it by simply copying the output directory to any web server.

The fact that any HTTP server can serve the client-side portion of a GWT application seems obvious, but it's sometimes overlooked. Again, there is no JEE servlet container, no WAR file, no configuration. Compile it, move it to a web-hosted location, and you're done. Because this is so simple and is handled so well by GWT and the shell, this can be a great way to divide even more complicated applications that do require server-side resources into separate pieces.

We'll cover building and deploying the server side of GWT applications next. Keep in mind that separating a large project into two smaller ones—the client side and the server side—can often simplify the process.

7.2.2 The server side

If you're using GWT's RPC functionality to communicate with server-side service servlet resources, there is another aspect to building and deploying that you'll have to cope with: dealing with the servlet container.

GWT automatically deploys and configures service servlets when running in hosted mode. As we have seen in previous examples, `GWTShellServlet` is a special servlet that runs your service servlets in hosted mode based on the `<servlet>` elements in your module file. The complication comes in when you have an application that uses GWT RPC and you're ready to click the Compile/Browse button. What happens then?

When you compile a GWT application that has RPC resources, nothing changes in terms of the compiled scripts. The compiler will still use your source path and your public path, it will create the cache.html files, and it will output the result as expected. Server-side code, in any path other than client or public (typically the `.server` package), is not handled in any special manner by the compiler. Getting that code deployed is left up to you.

7.2.3 Manually building a WAR file

Fortunately, GWT service servlets are nothing special in terms of JEE standards. These are ultimately `HttpServlet` elements that must be defined in a servlet container. The most common, and simple, way to build and deploy a GWT application that includes RPC resources is to simply wrap the whole project up as a single WAR file. A GWT WAR file is nothing more than a standard WAR file, which itself is a zipped-up version of your application in a specific format. If you're already familiar with JEE concepts, this will be nothing new.

PROBLEM

We need to create a WAR file to deploy a GWT application that includes server-side assets.

SOLUTION

The Java servlet specification defines the format for WAR files. We need to know this format and create the structure and contents from the GWT application. Creating WAR files manually is not something you're likely to do very often because the process can be automated, as we'll see in section 7.3. Nevertheless, it's good practice to do it once by hand, or at least to have a working knowledge of what is involved.

To manually create a WAR file from your project, you need to perform the following steps:

1. Ensure that the project runs as expected in hosted mode.
2. Compile the server-side resources of the project with `javac`. This is often done automatically with an IDE or build script (if you use `ProjectCreator` and Eclipse, for example, the default output directory for compiled Java will be bin).
3. Create the standard WAR directory structure, as shown in figure 7.1. (Create a new WAR directory, place the GWT compiler's output www contents into your WAR directory, and create a WEB-INF subdirectory inside your WAR directory.)
4. Copy the entire contents of the compiled Java output (again, usually bin, which should contain your service servlets) to the WEB-INF/classes directory.
5. Copy the GWT provided gwt-servlet.jar file to the WEB-INF/lib directory.
6. Create a deployment descriptor, web.xml (refer to the samples in listings 7.4-7.7), with `<servlet>` and `<servlet-mapping>` entries for each service servlet in

your GWT module file. Place the `web.xml` deployment descriptor in the WEB-INF directory.

7 Package it all up with the `jar` utility and name it with a .war extension.

Figure 7.1 shows the complete hierarchy of the basic GWT WAR file that results from the preceding steps. Included are the module directory (output of the GWT compiler, renamed from www to the module name, containing the cache.html files, the gwt.js JavaScript file, and the application HTML host page), the WEB-INF subdirectory and the included web.xml file, the WEB-INF/classes subdirectory, and the WEB-INF/lib subdirectory with dependency-related JAR files.

After you have the required resources for a WAR file, and you have the structure, you can zip up the entire lot and deploy it to a servlet container.

DISCUSSION

If you're not already familiar with WAR files, you may wonder where this specific structure comes from and why it's necessary. The specifications for everything JEE-related, including the servlet specification that determines the WAR file structure, come out of the Java Community Process (JCP). This process is how the Java community works together (*cough*) and produces Java specifications. Such specifications define standards, among other things, so that various assets can run on a variety of containers (and so what you end up building is not vendor-specific). The knowledge you can gain

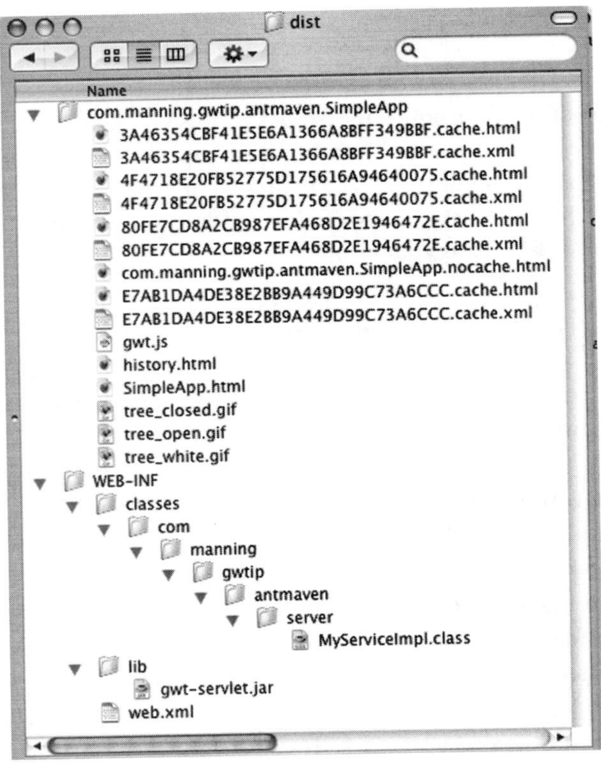

Figure 7.1 The structure of a WAR file based on a GWT project, demonstrating the required elements and their locations

from reading a specification can be very valuable—you may find yourself saying, "ah, that's why they did that." Table 7.2 outlines the most recent servlet specifications, where documentation for each can be found, and some example containers for each.

Table 7.2 Recent servlet specifications covering WAR file structure and contents

Specification	JSR	Location	Example container implementations
Servlet 2.5	JSR 154 (maintenance release)	http://jcp.org/aboutJava/communityprocess/mrel/jsr154/	Tomcat 6.x Jetty 7.x Resin 3.1
Servlet 2.4	JSR 154	http://jcp.org/aboutJava/communityprocess/final/jsr154/	Tomcat 5.x Jetty 7.x Resin 3.0
Servlet 2.3	JSR 053	http://jcp.org/aboutJava/communityprocess/first/jsr053/	Tomcat 4.x Jetty 4.x Resin 2.1

Overall, even though it may seem a bit formal, the structure and process surrounding WAR files is a good thing. What you create in the development shell (using Tomcat 5.x) should work on other servlet containers that implement the 2.4 spec.

Obviously, manually creating WAR files, as we did here, is not the most convenient thing in the world. We went through the exercise by hand because we wanted to explicitly go over the structure. Now that you have a grasp of the process, you'll probably want to avoid doing things this way and instead use an automated build that can recreate the WAR structure and contents from your project assets in one step. Such automation is possible with many IDE plugins, and with build tools like Ant and Maven.

7.3 Automating the build

As we saw in section 7.1, automated build tools can be a big help in building and packaging modules. The standard build-related tasks, such as compiling and running projects, can be automated, as can the packaging of artifacts, including deployable WAR files.

Ant and Maven are two of the more popular Java build tools. They are both very powerful build solutions, but they take different approaches. We'll look at each of them in turn.

7.3.1 Extending the Ant build

Although the GWT-generated Ant build file (which we saw in section 7.1) is intended to create JAR files for module sharing, it can be extended to create deployable WAR files as well.

PROBLEM

We want to automate the process of building a GWT project as a WAR file using Ant.

SOLUTION

To automate the process of creating WAR files using Ant we need to expand upon the Ant build file that GWT provides. We need to add targets for compiling, copying, and compressing our project assets into the correct structure for a WAR file.

Ant is very flexible, and it offers many ways to build a WAR file. Listing 7.2 shows one of these ways. The build file we're using here is intentionally verbose in order to demonstrate each step; this could be shortened some with the Ant war task, for example.

Listing 7.2 Ant build file with additional targets for generating a WAR file

```
<?xml version="1.0" encoding="utf-8" ?>
<project name="com.manning.gwtip.antmaven.SimpleApp"
     default="compile" basedir=".">
    <description>GWT Ant Build File Example</description>

    <property name="project.dir" value="." />
    <property name="gwt.module"
  value="com.manning.gwtip.antmaven.SimpleApp" />
    <property name="source.path"
  value="src/main/java" />
    <property name="test.path"
  value="src/main/test" />                         ❶ Declare properties
    <property name="resource.path"
  value="src/main/resources" />
    <property name="webapp.path"
  value="src/main/webapp" />

    <property environment="env" />
    <property name="build" location="build" />
    <property name="dist" location="dist" />

    <target name="init">                          ❷ Initialize build directories
        <tstamp />
        <mkdir dir="${build}" />
        <mkdir dir="${build}/bin" />
        <mkdir dir="${build}/www" />
        <mkdir dir="${dist}" />
        <mkdir dir="${dist}/WEB-INF/classes" />
        <mkdir dir="${dist}/WEB-INF/lib" />
    </target>
                                                  ❸ Establish javac classpath
    <path id="project.class.path">
        <pathelement path="${java.class.path}/" />
        <pathelement path="${env.GWT_HOME}/gwt-user.jar" />
    </path>
                                                  ❹ Establish GWT classpath
    <path id="gwt.classpath">
        <pathelement location="${project.dir}/${source.path}" />
            <pathelement location="${project.dir}/${test.path}" />
        <pathelement location="${project.dir}/${resource.path}" />
        <pathelement location="${env.GWT_HOME}/gwt-user.jar" />
```

```
    <pathelement location="${env.GWT_HOME}/gwt-dev-mac.jar" />
    <pathelement location="${env.GWT_HOME}/gwt-dev-linux.jar" />
    <pathelement location="${env.GWT_HOME}/gwt-dev-windows.jar" />
</path>

<target name="copyserver" depends="init, compile"
   description="Copy javac output to \
   dist/WEB-INF/classes">
    <copy todir="${dist}/WEB-INF/classes">
        <fileset dir="${build}/bin" />
    </copy>
</target>

<target name="copyclient" depends="init, gwtcompile"
   description="Copy GWT generated \
   files to root of dist">
    <copy todir="${dist}">
        <fileset dir="${build}/www/${gwt.module}/" />
    </copy>
</target>

<target name="copylib" depends="init"
   description="Copy required libs \
  to dist/WEB-INF/lib">
    <copy todir="${dist}/WEB-INF/lib">
        <fileset dir="${env.GWT_HOME}">
            <include name="gwt-servlet.jar" />
        </fileset>
    </copy>
</target>

<target name="copyweb" depends="init"
   description="Copy source webapp \
   contents to dist">
    <copy todir="${dist}">
        <fileset dir="${webapp.path}" />
    </copy>
</target>

<target name="distwar" depends="init,
   copyserver, copyclient, copylib, copyweb"
   description="Perform steps to create
   dist directory for war">
</target>

<target name="gwtcompile"
  description="Invoke the GWTCompiler
  against GWT Java source files">
    <echo>env.GWT_HOME=${env.GWT_HOME}</echo>
    <java classname="com.google.gwt.dev.GWTCompiler" fork="true">
        <arg line="-out ${build}/www" />
        <arg value="${gwt.module}" />
        <classpath refid="gwt.classpath" />
    </java>
</target>

<target name="compile" depends="init"
  description="Compile src and test to build/bin">
```

5 Include series of copy targets

6 Include web.xml

7 Perform GWT compilation

```
        <javac srcdir="${source.path}:${test.path}"
          destdir="${build}/bin" includes="**" debug="on"
          debuglevel="lines,vars,source" source="1.4">
            <classpath refid="project.class.path" />
        </javac>
    </target>

    <target name="war" depends="distwar"
      description="Package up the dist
      directory as a war - using module name">       ❽ Package WAR
        <jar destfile="${gwt.module}.war" basedir="${dist}" />
    </target>

    <target name="jar" depends="init, compile"
      description="Package up the project as a jar -
      for use as distributed module">                  ❾ Package JAR
        <jar destfile="${gwt.module}.jar">
            <fileset dir="${build}/bin">
                <include name="**/*.class" />
            </fileset>
            <fileset dir="${source.path}">
                <include name="**" />
            </fileset>
            <fileset dir="${test.path}">
                <include name="**" />
            </fileset>
        </jar>
    </target>

    <target name="clean">
        <delete file="${gwt.module}.jar" />
        <delete file="${gwt.module}.war" />
        <delete dir="${build}" />
        <delete dir="${dist}" />
    </target>
</project>
```

Our updated Ant build file can package assets into either a JAR file, for use as a shared module, or a WAR file, for deployment in a servlet container. New configuration elements and steps are now present, as are goals for including the GWT compile step.

DISCUSSION

Our expanded Ant build file in listing 7.2 demonstrates several important points. Initially we set up a few Ant properties ❶, including the module name, the path structure for our project, and the *build* and *dist* values. Build and dist are important concepts here, because they are used to specify where all the code should be built and then placed for distribution. Dist is basically the expanded directory for any artifact we later want to package up (be it a JAR or a WAR file). With the properties set up, an init target creates our initial directories ❷. Next we have classpath reference items for both the standard javac compiler ❸ and GWT compiler, including versions of gwt-dev for all platforms ❹. (What is not present will be ignored, so this will work for Mac, Linux, or Windows.)

After the initial setup, the build file then contains a series of copy targets ❺. Each of these targets copies a specific type of resource into the destination distribution directory. The `copyweb` target, for example, takes care of moving the source web.xml file to the destination location ❻. Next is the `gwtcompile` target—one of the most significant portions of the updated build file ❼. In order to build a WAR file, we'll have to compile our server-side code with javac, and our client-side code with the GWT compiler.

Once things are aligned in the proper dist directory and compiled, we finally have simple targets that depend on the other steps to create either a WAR file ❽ or a JAR file ❾.

With this build file in place, we can create a WAR file for our project by issuing the Ant command `ant -buildfile [buildfile.ant.xml] war`. This will create the build and dist directories in preparation for a WAR file, and then package up dist as ModuleName.war.

As this process demonstrates, Ant can be very useful and can be customized to just about any degree you desire. If you plan to use Ant on a regular basis, you'll likely want to add targets for testing, reporting, analysis, and so on. Though the customization of Ant for those tasks is beyond our scope here, you can poke around for online Ant resources or grab a book on the topic, such as Manning's *Java Development with Ant*. The basics though, including building and packaging your project into a module JAR or a deployable WAR, are handled by what we have already covered.

Another automated build-management tool that can be used with GWT-related projects is Maven. Maven has its roots in Ant and still uses many Ant tasks under the hood. Maven can be used to create WAR files for GWT projects, and for a few other related things as well.

7.3.2 Using Maven

Maven, like Ant, is an open source build-management tool under the aegis of the Apache Software Foundation (http://maven.apache.org/). Maven calls itself a "software project management and comprehension tool." While that description is a bit nebulous, we do find Maven, and the build process it provides through a series of plugins, to be useful.

Maven provides centralized dependencies, a standardized directory structure across projects, a somewhat standardized build lifecycle based on phases, and some common ground in the build landscape. This differs from Ant, which is very powerful but leaves the commonality and discipline up to you. Although useful in these regards, Maven does have a few downsides. For example, you may find it frustrating at times when you want to do something outside of the norm. Sometimes the standards Maven attempts to achieve, or the way those standards are implemented, limit the customization possibilities. To make a long story short, Maven is not perfect, but it's good overall.

The plugin nature of Maven allows you to customize settings for integrating a new component into the build. We'll focus on integrating GWT and Maven in order to manage the GWT build and deployment process.

PROBLEM

We need to automate the process of building GWT applications and creating deployable artifacts.

SOLUTION

By using Maven and the GWT-Maven plugin, we can easily manage many aspects of the GWT build process, including the generation of WAR files for deployment.

DISCUSSION

While it's our goal to present a broad view of GWT tools and points of integration through the course of this book, the GWT Maven plugin, called GWT-Maven, bears a special place because it's a project initiated by the authors of this book. We developed this Maven plugin to help us get around what seemed like the somewhat confining GWT project structure and to eliminate some of the complexity of debugging, testing, building, and deploying GWT applications in an automated fashion.

GWT-Maven (http://code.google.com/p/gwt-maven/) includes both Maven 1 and Maven 2 versions of the plugin. For most of the examples in this book, including the one in this section, we'll use Maven 2, because it's the most up-to-date and popular version. (For downloadable code samples, we're including configuration files for both versions.)

> **Maven 1 versus Maven 2**
>
> Maven 1 and Maven 2 differ in terms of implementation, names, and locations, but the concepts are similar. We have chosen to use Maven 2 for the bulk of the book's examples, but the Maven 1 version of the GWT-Maven plugin is actively supported. If you want to find out more about Maven 1 GWT support, see the GWT-Maven site.

In addition to the building, compiling, and creating artifacts (such as JAR and WAR files), GWT-Maven also includes special *goals*:

- merging a web.xml file with a module descriptor (for hosted and web modes)
- running the GWT shell
- running the JUnit shell for `GWTTestCase`-based tests
- generating translatable GWT model beans

When using GWT-Maven, invoking the GWT shell and the GWT compiler becomes a simple matter of executing the commands `mvn gwt:gwt` and `mvn gwt:compile`, respectively. While this is not a difficult task outside of Maven, the significance here is that you can manage your dependencies and classpath with Maven. If you make changes, the shell or compiler set up using the plugin will automatically be aware of the modifications. Also, creating a deployable WAR file with GWT-Maven becomes a matter of executing the command `mvn clean install` (when the packaging for the project is set to `war`). Table 7.3 provides a complete list of the goals supported by the GWT-Maven plugin.

Table 7.3 Goals provided by GWT-Maven

Goal name	Description
`gwt:gwt`	Starts the GWT shell for the configured project.
`gwt:debug`	Starts the GWT shell with remote debugging activated. You can attach to the debugger on the same port the GWT shell runs on, and the shell will block startup until the remote debugger connects.
`gwt:testGwt`	Runs `GWTTestCase`-based tests through the JUnit shell in a separate process (to get around difficulties with the standard Maven Surefire plugin and GWT).
`gwt:compile`	Invokes the compiler to output the compiled JavaScript files for deployment.
`gwt:war`	Used in Maven 1. In Maven 2, the packaging type and the install goal are used. In either case, it calls `gwt:compile`, `gwt:mergewebxml`, and generates a deployable WAR file.
`gwt:mergewebxml`	Examines the module descriptor and included GWT servlets in the web.xml deployment descriptor, and merges the differences in either direction. This is used internally as part of other goals and is not normally invoked manually.
`gwt:generateClientBeans`	Creates client-side DTOs in your source directory.

To get started with Maven, you need to download it from the Apache Maven site (http://maven.apache.org/download.html), unpack it, and follow the very simple installation instructions for your platform. Basically, you just need to add the Maven bin directory to your path, and ensure that you have the environment variable `JAVA_HOME` configured. (Complete instructions are on the download page and are included with the distribution.)

For GWT-Maven, itself, there is no downloadable package. You simply include the plugin details in your build configuration Project Object Model (POM) file, and Maven grabs the needed files when it's invoked. This will download and install GWT-Maven locally. Listing 7.3 shows a sample POM file for a GWT project using GWT-Maven (Maven 2.x version). We'll use this file as a starting point to further explore the properties and goals of GWT-Maven.

Listing 7.3 A sample Maven 2.x style project.xml POM file using the GWT-Maven plugin

```
<?xml version="1.0" encoding="UTF-8"?>
<project xmlns="http://maven.apache.org/POM/4.0.0"
    xmlns:xsi="http://www.w3.org/2001/XMLSchema-instance"
    xsi:schemaLocation="http://maven.apache.org/POM/4.0.0
 http://maven.apache.org/maven-v4_0_0.xsd">
    <modelVersion>4.0.0</modelVersion>
```

```
<groupId>com.manning.gwtip</groupId>
<artifactId>com.manning.gwtip.antmaven</artifactId>
<packaging>war</packaging>
<version>1.0</version>
<name>GWT Ant/Maven example</name>
<url>http://maven.apache.org</url>
<repositories>
    <repository>
        <id>gwt-maven</id>
        <url>
            http://gwt-maven.googlecode.com/svn/trunk/mavenrepo/
        </url>
    </repository>
</repositories>
<pluginRepositories>
    <pluginRepository>
        <id>gwt-maven</id>
        <url>
            http://gwt-maven.googlecode.com/svn/trunk/mavenrepo/
        </url>
    </pluginRepository>
</pluginRepositories>
<dependencies>
    <dependency>
        <groupId>junit</groupId>
        <artifactId>junit</artifactId>
        <version>4.1</version>
        <scope>test</scope>
    </dependency>
    <dependency>
        <groupId>com.googlecode.gwtx</groupId>
        <artifactId>GWTx</artifactId>
        <version>20070605</version>
    </dependency>
    <dependency>
        <groupId>com.google.gwt</groupId>
        <artifactId>gwt-user</artifactId>
        <version>1.4.60</version>
        <scope>provided</scope>
    </dependency>
    <dependency>
        <groupId>com.google.gwt</groupId>
        <artifactId>gwt-servlet</artifactId>
        <version>1.4.60</version>
        <scope>runtime</scope>
    </dependency>
</dependencies>
<build>
    <finalName>testme</finalName>
    <plugins>
        <plugin>
            <groupId>org.apache.maven.plugins</groupId>
            <artifactId>maven-war-plugin</artifactId>
            <version>2.0</version>
            <configuration>
```

❶ **Include Maven project properties**

❷ **Define dependency repositories**

❸ **Define plugin dependency repositories**

❹ **Include project dependencies**

❺ **Define dependency scope**

```
                <webXml>target/web.xml</webXml>          ◁┐  Define web.xml
            </configuration>                          ❻  target location
        </plugin>
        <plugin>
            <groupId>com.totsp.gwt</groupId>
            <artifactId>                            ❼ Include settings
              maven-googlewebtoolkit2-plugin       ◁┘ for GWT-Maven
            </artifactId>
            <version>2.0</version>
            <configuration>                          ❽ Specify runTarget
                    <style>PRETTY</style>               that GWTShell
              <logLevel>INFO</logLevel>                 invokes
                <runTarget>                          ◁┘
                   com.manning.gwtip.antmaven.SimpleApp/index.html
                </runTarget>
                <compileTargets>               ◁─❾ Specify compileTarget(s)
                <param>                              that GWTCompiler builds
                  com.manning.gwtip.antmaven.SimpleApp
                </param>
                </compileTargets>
            </configuration>                        ❿ Define plugin
            <executions>                               goals run during
                <execution>                            build phases
                    <goals>                         ◁┘
                        <goal>mergewebxml</goal>
                        <goal>compile</goal>
                        <goal>testGwt</goal>
                    </goals>
                </execution>
            </executions>
        </plugin>
    </plugins>
  </build>
</project>
```

In the POM sample in listing 7.3, we start out with standard basic project properties, such as the name and identification of the project, and what type of artifact packaging the default result should be ❶. From there, we define which repositories should be used to locate standard ❷ and plugin dependencies ❸. Maven uses a set of sensible defaults for most properties, including the remote locations (*repositories*) from which it attempts to retrieve dependencies such as JAR files. If you're using files that are not in the standard set of default Maven repositories, such as GWT JAR files, or plugins that are not part of the standard distribution, such as GWT-Maven, you will need to configure the locations where these items can be found. Once dependencies are downloaded, they are stored in a local repository on the machine where Maven is running (the default local repository location is in your user home directory, ~/.m2/repository). This means that other projects will not have to obtain dependencies that are already present, and it allows you to build and work on local versions of projects.

Dependencies themselves are identified by group, artifact, and version ❹. Along with their identification, dependencies can also optionally be scoped so that they are involved with a particular phase of the build, and the resulting artifact, or not ❺. The gwt-user.jar file contains a lot of things that are simply build-time dependencies, so it is not required in a WAR artifact, while the gwt-servlet.jar file contains the `RemoteServiceServlet` implementation and will be needed on the server at runtime. There are a number of reasons you might include dependencies that are not part of a WAR file. For instance, if you wish to use Tomcat-managed `DataSource` classes, you need to include Jakarta Commons-DBCP, Commons-Pool, and Commons-Collections as dependencies. These will then appear on the classpath when the GWT shell runs, and they'll enable the embedded Tomcat to create the `DataSource` resources. In a production environment, these are not necessary because a full Tomcat (or other servlet container) will often already have them.

The next part of the POM file involves configuration for the plugins. Just about everything Maven does in every phase of the build is based on a plugin. Only plugins that are not part of the default set that Maven uses, or those that you need to tweak (default or not) need to be present in the `<plugins>` section of the POM. In listing 7.3, we're configuring the Maven WAR plugin to specify the location of the output web.xml file ❻. We need this because we'll be merging this file during the build, something we'll discuss in more detail in section 7.4. We're also including GWT-Maven and defining all the configuration elements it requires ❼. Among these settings are the `<runTarget>` ❽ and `<compileTarget>` elements ❾, which define the application the GWT shell will launch when it's invoked via the plugin, and what module the plugin will build for, respectively. Lastly, we're define a set of `<goals>` that we want run ❿. These goals are a subset of what the plugin offers, and by specifying them here we're telling the plugin to use these during the build lifecycle phase (each goal knows which phase it applies to).

Another thing to keep in mind concerning this process is that if you're packaging a GWT module JAR file for use in other applications, as we did earlier in this chapter with Ant, you need to make sure the source files for your classes are included in the final JAR result. This can be done by modifying the POM file's `<build>` element with the following lines:

```
<resources>
    <resource>
        <directory>src/main/resources</directory>
    </resource>
    <resource>
        <directory>src/main/java</directory>
    </resource>
</resources>
```

Specifying resources such as source brings us to another important aspect regarding using Maven in general—the standard directory structure. If you have never used Maven before, the process might seem a little odd, but Maven is a build tool that fosters the Convention over Configuration concept. If you use a standard project structure, Maven simply knows what steps to take to configure an artifact or build target.

For a GWT project or any JEE web project, the standard Maven layout is as follows:

- project home
  - `src/main`
    - `java` (contains Java source files)
    - `resources` (contains non-Java assets for the classpath, such as properties files)
    - `webapp` (contains the document root for a web project)
      - `WEB-INF` (contains the deployment descriptor—web.xml)
      - `META-INF` (contains the Tomcat-specific context descriptor, if using Tomcat)
    - `target` (the folder where the project will be built)
    - `docs` (XDOC documentation for the project)
    - `pom.xml` (build configuration file; in the root of the project)
    - `settings.xml` (properties that are global; in the root of project or in user's home directory)
  - `src/test`
    - `java` (contains Java test source files)
    - `resources` (contains non-Java assets for the classpath, for testing purposes)

Though this is the default setup, and quite a reasonable one, these paths are not set in stone and can be overridden if necessary. As we have already demonstrated, the pom.xml file located in the project root directory is the heart of any Maven project. Having looked at the POM and the structure it assumes, it's time to look at the global settings.

Maven supports a general settings file, settings.xml, which is used for additional configuration elements that are not project-specific. GWT-Maven requires a few such global settings, which are shown in listing 7.4.

Listing 7.4 A sample Maven 2.x style settings.xml file with GWT-Maven extrajvmargs

```
<?xml version="1.0" encoding="UTF-8"?>
<settings>
    <profiles>            <-❶ Define different profiles
        <profile>
            <id>gwt-1.3.3</id>
            <properties>
                <google.webtoolkit.home>
                   /Users/cooper/gwt-mac-1.3.3
                </google.webtoolkit.home>
                <!-- you only need XstartOnFirstThread on a mac -->
                <google.webtoolkit.extrajvmargs>
                     -Xmx256m -Xms256m -XstartOnFirstThread
                </google.webtoolkit.extrajvmargs>

            </properties>
        </profile>
```

```
        <profile>
            <id>gwt-1.4.60</id>
            <properties>
                <google.webtoolkit.home>      <-- 2 Specify google.webtoolkit.home as required
                   /Users/cooper/gwt-mac-1.4.60
                </google.webtoolkit.home>
                <!-- you only need XstartOnFirstThread on a mac -->
                <google.webtoolkit.extrajvmargs>      <-- 3 Include extra arguments for JVM
                    -Xmx256m -Xms256m -XstartOnFirstThread
                </google.webtoolkit.extrajvmargs>

            </properties>
        </profile>
    </profiles>
    <activeProfiles>      <-- 4 Specify active profile
        <activeProfile>gwt-1.4.60</activeProfile>
    </activeProfiles>
</settings>
```

Your settings.xml file can be placed in the project root directory or in the home directory of the user you plan to run Maven as (~/.m2/settings.xml). Also, elements in settings.xml can be placed directly in a POM file. Settings are meant to be machine wide, not project-specific. Where you put configuration elements leads to a hierarchy of properties, and a frequent question—which version wins. The home directory settings.xml file takes precedence over all other settings found anywhere else. This is the royal flush of Maven settings. It wins, and it's the recommended place to put global configuration properties.

In the settings.xml configuration in listing 7.4, there are multiple `<profile>` elements that define where different versions of GWT are installed on the machine ❶. Within each profile, we can also define some GWT-Maven properties. These include `google.webtoolkit.home`, which is required, and which GWT-Maven uses to locate native GWT resources ❷, and `google.webtoolkit.extrajvmargs`, an optional parameter used to pass extra arguments and system properties to forked JVM instances ❸. Finally, we also specify which profile is active at any given time ❹.

Table 7.4 gives a complete list of properties available for the GWT-Maven plugin and identifies which are optional (or not) and the default value for each. Any property not specifically defined in a POM or in a settings.xml file assumes the default value.

Table 7.4 GWT-Maven properties

Property name	Optional?	Default	Description
`home`	No	`${basedir}/../gwt-amiga-1.7.58` (make sure to change this, please)	Specifies the location where GWT is installed.
`extrajvmargs`	Yes	None	Specifies extra arguments that are passed to the JVM that executes the GWT shell.

Table 7.4 GWT-Maven properties *(continued)*

Property name	Optional?	Default	Description
`runtarget`	No	`MyModule/MyModule.html`	Specifies the relative URL (GWT module and host page) the hosted mode browser should open when launched.
`compiletarget`	No	`MyModule`	Specifies the GWT module the GWT compiler will build.
`style`	Yes	`OBF`	Specifies the style of the GWT compiler's JavaScript output (`PRETTY`, `DETAILED`, `OBF`).
`logLevel`	Yes	`INFO`	Specifies the logging level the GWT shell console will display.
`noServer`	Yes	`false`	Starts the GWT shell with the `-noserver` flag, or not.
`port`	Yes	`8888`	Specifies the port where the development mode server will run.
`debugPort`	Yes	`8000`	Specifies the port where the JPDA debugger process will run.
`debugSuspend`	Yes	`true`	Specifies whether or not to delay shell startup until a debugger connects.
`sourcesOnPath`	Yes	`true`	Toggles whether src/main/* will be in the classpath for runtime.
`webXml`	Yes	`/src/main/webapp/WEB-INF/web.xml`	Specifies the location of your source, web.xml.
`contextXml`	Yes	`src/main/webapp/META-INF/context.xml`	Specifies a source, context.xml.
`tomcat`	Yes	`${project.build.directory}/tomcat`	Specifies the location where the Tomcat directory will be created.
`generatorRootClasses`	Yes	None	Defines where existing model beans to generate translatable beans from are located.
`generatorDestinationPackage`	Yes	None	Destination package for generated beans.

Table 7.4 GWT-Maven properties *(continued)*

Property name	Optional?	Default	Description
`generateGettersAndSetters`	Yes	`false`	Includes getters and setters, or not, on generated beans.
`generatePropertyChangeSupport`	Yes	`false`	Automatically generates `PropertyChangeSupport` on generated beans.
`overwriteGeneratedClasses`	Yes	`false`	Overwrites existing generated bean classes, or not.
`gen`	Yes	`${project.build.directory}/.generated`	Specifies the `-gen` flag to the GWT shell (temporary output files location).

Once you have Maven configured, you're set to execute the goals we saw in table 7.3 to build and run your project. To use Maven in general, you type `mvn [goalname]` at the command line. For example, running the GWT shell, with a project configured to use the sample POM file in listing 7.3, via `mvn clean gwt:gwt` results in a lot of command-line output (Maven details at each phase of the lifecycle) and the shell running, as shown in figure 7.2.

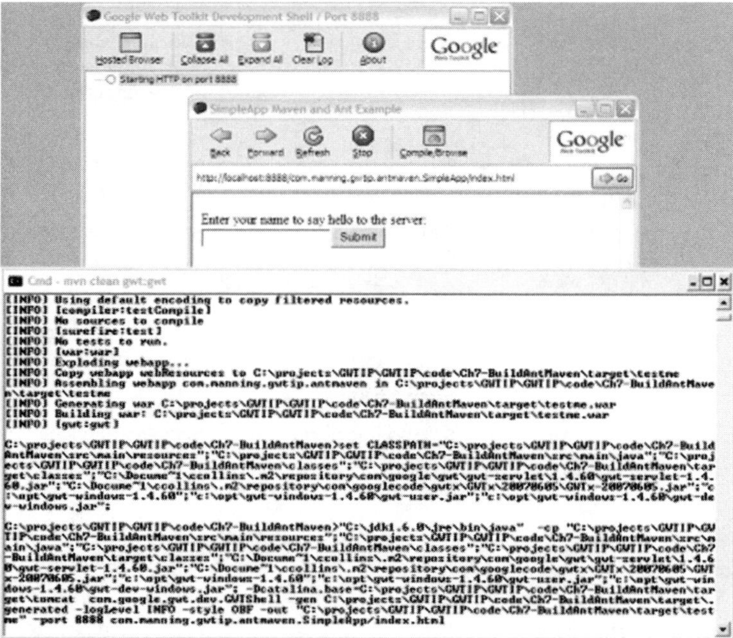

Figure 7.2 Sample application running the GWT shell through the use of Maven with the GWT-Maven plugin

In addition to the convenience that running the shell from a standard build provides, you also have all of the power of Maven at your disposal. The `mvn clean install` command will compile and bundle your project into a WAR artifact that can be deployed to any JEE servlet container. You can also package your project into a module by simply issuing the command `mvn clean jar:jar` (presuming you have included the source in the POM as discussed). You can run tests, including those based on `GwtTestCase` (which we'll cover in detail in the next chapter) by using `mvn clean test`.

The behavior of most of the GWT-Maven goals should be fairly obvious. The benefit of Maven, and these goals, is that once you have a configuration in place, you can use, change, and share your build easily and get consistent results. Another reason for using the GWT-Maven plugin, beyond the general convenience for GWT tasks it provides, is the way it helps to manage and merge the WAR file deployment descriptor, web.xml. This file is used in hosted mode with the embedded Tomcat server GWT includes, and in web mode when you deploy your application as a WAR file. Because of this dual use, there are a few configuration overlap points and divergences that have to be dealt with.

7.4 Managing Tomcat Lite from the build

We first discussed Tomcat Lite, the embedded Apache Tomcat instance included in GWT, in chapter 3. There we discussed the issues surrounding the maintenance of multiple configuration files—one for the hosted mode and one for the web mode—and how to manage those configuration files so that your projects can make use of service-side features provided by the JEE container.

Tomcat Lite maintains its own set of context.xml (ROOT.xml in GWT terms) and web.xml configuration files. Obviously, the ideal deployment process would need to work both in hosted mode terms *and* in terms of creating a WAR file. This means what we really need is a context.xml file and a web.xml file, which are local source files for our project, and which get copied into and deployed with our WAR files and also are used in hosted mode.

Creating an automated build process that allows the inclusion of project-local configuration files (context.xml and web.xml) that are used both for creating WAR files *and* for automatically configuring Tomcat Lite has several advantages. First, you can maintain configuration information in one place, rather than in several. Second, you can use common JEE container-managed resources, such as servlet filters, security realms, and data sources in hosted mode. Third, if you import any module that includes servlet declarations, they are automatically available to your module without your having to just know about them and manually configure them. (This third point, and the fact that GWT testing, something we will discuss in the next chapter, needs the embedded Tomcat, are the main reasons not to abandon the embedded instance altogether.)

TIP You may recall from chapter 3 that you do not have to use the embedded Tomcat instance supplied with GWT. Instead, you can use the `-noserver` option and configure an external JEE container instance on your own. If you use `-noserver`, and you plan to share your module with others, you need to include instructions for any server-side resources required.

To automate the process of handling this configuration, you have to be aware of the various files involved, and you need to have a process in place that automatically configures resources based on the context—whether hosted mode or WAR.

PROBLEM

We need server-side resources, GWT service servlets, and other resources to automatically be available both for hosted mode use and when deployed as a WAR file.

SOLUTION

It's standard practice to include JEE configuration files, such as the web.xml deployment descriptor, as source resources in your project. Then, at build time, these resources are normally copied into the proper distributable locations, such as WEB-INF. This is exactly what we did in section 7.2.4 when we used an Ant build to create a WAR file. Using this approach, the web.xml file can be specific to the project, managed by source control, and modified with each build without affecting other builds. The key is that the configuration file is part of the *source*, and is copied into the distribution at build time.

You can extend this concept to manipulate the Tomcat Lite configuration files based on the same project-local configuration data. That is to say, you can use the manipulation and copying of files that a build process provides not only to create a distribution artifact (such as copying web.xml to where it belongs for a WAR file), but also to configure the embedded GWT Tomcat instance.

DISCUSSION

In order to manage the Tomcat configuration for both the GWT-embedded Tomcat instance and for a deployable WAR file, we'll need to manipulate and merge several source files. We'll use the deployment descriptor web.xml file, the Tomcat-specific configuration context.xml file, and the GWT module file.

Listing 7.5 shows a sample MyProject web.xml file—this is meant to represent the web.xml local to your application. This file contains no references to GWT service servlets (because we're going to inject those based on information from the module), but it may certainly contain other resources such as servlet filters, non-GWT servlets, database references, and so on.

Listing 7.5 A sample web.xml project deployment descriptor

```
<?xml version="1.0" encoding="UTF-8"?>
<!DOCTYPE web-app PUBLIC
  "-//Sun Microsystems, Inc.//DTD Web Application 2.3//EN"
  "http://java.sun.com/dtd/web-app_2_3.dtd">
<web-app>
    <display-name>MyProject</display-name>
    <filter>                                          <- Include servlet filter
       <filter-name>MyFilter</filter-name>
        <description>This is a filter that does something
```

```
                interesting, like log requests</description>
        <filterclass>
          com.manning.gwtip.myproject.server.MyServletFilter
        </filter-class>
    </filter>
    <filter-mapping>
        <filter-name>MyFilter</filter-name>
        <url-pattern>/*</url-pattern>
    </filter-mapping>
    <distributable />
    <session-config>
        <session-timeout>30</session-timeout>
    </session-config>
    <welcome-file-list>
        <welcome-file>index.jsp</welcome-file>
        <welcome-file>index.html</welcome-file>
    </welcome-file-list>
</web-app>
```

Listing 7.5 shows a fairly standard web.xml file, and that's good. That's what we want in terms of the source file. Next, listing 7.6 shows the embedded GWT Tomcat included ROOT/WEB-INF/web.xml file.

Listing 7.6 The base GWT web.xml in tomcat/webapps/ROOT/WEB-INF

```
<?xml version="1.0" encoding="UTF-8"?>
<web-app>
  <servlet>
    <servlet-name>shell</servlet-name>
    <servlet-class>
      com.google.gwt.dev.shell.GWTShellServlet
    </servlet-class>                            <-- ❶ Include GWTShellServlet
  </servlet>
  <servlet-mapping>
    <servlet-name>shell</servlet-name>
    <url-pattern>/*</url-pattern>
  </servlet-mapping>
</web-app>
```

The only notable thing about the standard Tomcat Lite web.xml file, shown in listing 7.6, is that it has a servlet entry for `GWTShellServlet` ❶. In order to use something like our own filter from listing 7.5 within hosted mode, we basically need a combination of these files, as is shown in listing 7.7.

Listing 7.7 The merged GWT hosted mode

```
<?xml version="1.0" encoding="UTF-8"?>
<!DOCTYPE web-app PUBLIC "-//Sun Microsystems, Inc.
//DTD Web Application 2.3//EN"
"http://java.sun.com/dtd/web-app_2_3.dtd">

<web-app>
  <display-name>Sample Server</display-name>
  <filter>
```

```
    <filter-name>MyFilter</filter-name>                      <-❶ Include ServletFilter
    <description>This is a filter that does something
      interesting, like log requests</description>
   <filter-class>gwtip.module.sample.server.MyServletFilter</filter-class>
  </filter>
  <filter-mapping>
    <filter-name>MyFilter</filter-name>
    <url-pattern>/*</url-pattern>
  </filter-mapping>
  <!--inserted by GWT-Maven-->
  <servlet>
    <servlet-name>shell</servlet-name>
    <servlet-class>
       com.google.gwt.dev.shell.GWTShellServlet
    </servlet-class>                          <-┐ Include
  </servlet>                                    ❷ GWTShellServlet
  <!--inserted by GWT-Maven-->
  <servlet-mapping>
    <servlet-name>shell</servlet-name>
    <url-pattern>/*</url-pattern>
  </servlet-mapping>
</web-app>
```

The combination of the project-specific web.xml file and the default GWT hosted mode web.xml file, as seen in listing 7.7, gives us a new file for use in hosted mode that enables our `ServletFilter` to be present ❶ and the `GWTShellServlet` also to remain ❷. This will ensure that our filter is there when our application runs in the shell.

This combination provides our hosted mode support and enables us to maintain our own configuration in that environment. But, that's the only environment where this file will work; it won't work in web mode. So, we have one more web.xml resource we need to deal with. We need a deployment-specific web.xml file for our WAR file that includes all of our GWT service servlet entries. Listing 7.8 displays this final web.xml incarnation—the one that needs to go in our WAR file for deployment.

Listing 7.8 A deployable web.xml file

```
<?xml version="1.0" encoding="UTF-8"?>
<!DOCTYPE web-app PUBLIC
  "-//Sun Microsystems, Inc.//DTD Web Application 2.3//EN"
  "http://java.sun.com/dtd/web-app_2_3.dtd">
<web-app>
  <display-name>Sample Server</display-name>        ❶ Include ServletFilter
  <filter>                                             again
    <filter-name>MyFilter</filter-name>           <-┘
    <description>This is a filter that does something
         interesting, like log requests</description>
    <filter-class>
      gwtip.module.sample.server.MyServletFilter
    </filter-class>
  </filter>
  <filter-mapping>
    <filter-name>MyFilter</filter-name>
```

```
      <url-pattern>/*</url-pattern>
    </filter-mapping>
    <!--inserted by GWT-Maven-->
    <servlet>
      <servlet-name>
      gwtip.module.sample.server.MyServiceServlet/MyService
      </servlet-name>
      <servlet-class>
        gwtip.module.sample.server.MyServiceServlet
      </servlet-class>
    </servlet>
    <!--inserted by GWT-Maven-->
    <servlet-mapping>
      <servlet-name>
       gwtip.module.sample.server.MyServiceServlet/MyService
      </servlet-name>
      <url-pattern>
       /gwtip.module.sample.server.MyServiceServlet/MyService
      </url-pattern>
    </servlet-mapping>
</web-app>
```

❷ Notice that <servlet> element is generated

In our final web.xml the `ServletFilter` element from our original source project-specific file is still present ❶, and we additionally have an explicit `<servlet>` element referring to a GWT service servlet ❷. Remember, we cannot use the `GWTShellServlet` in a deployed WAR file; rather, we must have these explicit servlet entries. We can get the servlet entries for the deployment-time web.xml file by inspecting our GWT module file (and all of those in the `<inherits>` chain) and including `<servlet>` and `<servlet-mapping>` entries for each servlet defined there.

At this point, we're dealing with four web.xml files, which is admittedly not an ideal situation. Additionally, if we wanted to configure something outside of the standard web.xml, such as a context-managed `DataSource` reference for use in hosted mode, we would have to include our own application-local context.xml file as well. Then we would need to apply that file to Tomcat Lite, too. This *source* file would be placed in our application at src/main/webapp/META-INF/context.xml (in similar fashion to an src/main/webapp/WEB-INF/web.xml file). Then, before the embedded Tomcat instance is invoked, we would need to replace the GWT Tomcat Lite file, tomcat/conf/gwt/localhost/ROOT.xml, with our own (renamed to ROOT.xml).

You can manage this process manually by maintaining multiple web.xml files (one for hosted mode, one for deployment) and a context.xml file, and then overwriting the Tomcat Lite configuration as needed, but this is not very convenient. Or you can elect to go the `-noserver` path and not even try to configure the Tomcat Lite instance. This approach is very powerful and helpful, but it really just shifts the configuration problem rather than solving it. What we have chosen to do is to automate the management of this process through the GWT-Maven plugin. This is what the mergewebxml goal mentioned in table 7.3 does.

Using GWT-Maven, you maintain only two files. These are the same two files you maintain for any standard JEE servlet-based application using Tomcat, a project-local web.xml file and a project-local context.xml file. The plugin does the merge for you. The GWT-Maven plugin can configure Tomcat Lite for hosted mode, can manage the required hosted mode classpath, and will also configure the correct web.xml for deployment. If you do not wish to use Maven, you could use the same approach with other build tools as well. The main point is that source files can be used to both configure the embedded GWT Tomcat instance and create what is needed for a deployable WAR file—and all of this can be automated.

This is admittedly an involved process, but once it's automated it's a huge help. With an automated build that manages the process, you can control the configuration in the source, just as with standard non-GWT Java projects. Also, you can share GWT projects that involve not only RPC but other server-side resources and concepts, such as filters and data sources, without requiring others to manually set up the required configuration for hosted mode.

7.5 Summary

Configuring a GWT project for build and deployment can be confusing at first, but things on the inside are really not much different from a combined standard web application and a JEE servlet-based application. The compounding factor is that you basically have two environments to build for: hosted mode and web mode. Even though you aren't deploying things for hosted mode, you still have to get the configuration correct so that the development shell is productive. And when deployment time does arrive, you need the same configuration to work in an external setting.

In this chapter we addressed building and packaging GWT modules, and building and deploying GWT-based applications. Along the way, we also brought the Ant and Maven automated build tools into the fold. These tools can be used to manage configuration elements and direct the build process, even down to the configuration of the GWT-embedded Tomcat instance. In the next chapter, we'll extend the concepts behind the automated build to include testing and benchmarking. Then we'll bring all of those components together, again with Maven, to build and test a GWT project using a continuous integration server.

8 Testing and Continuous Integration

This chapter covers

- Understanding and implementing GWT tests
- Exploring advanced testing techniques, remote and benchmark
- Obtaining code coverage information with GWT tests
- Using continuous integration with GWT projects

A test that reveals a bug has succeeded, not failed.

—Boris Beizer

Completing your code and turning out a quality application are not often synonymous nor simultaneous. Beyond the syntax, the compiler, and the resulting bits, a quality application is usually the result of careful design, adequate testing, and proper component integration. These fundamental concepts can be applied to all software projects, but putting them to work with GWT is a bit different than in other environments.

In this chapter, we're going to follow up on some of the tasks related to building, packaging, and deploying that we addressed in the last chapter, with a focus on testing and automating builds. Along with testing, we'll also touch on benchmarking in a GWT context. Once we have all the pieces in place, we'll work through a sample project that utilizes Maven and a continuous integration (CI) server, in order to take full advantage of the complete process. All of these concepts go hand in hand because testing and metrics should ideally be part of an automated build process that's CI managed.

The concepts of testing, benchmarking, and continuous integration are fairly well accepted tenets in any good software development practice, regardless of language or technology. Even though we cannot hope to cover these broad subjects comprehensively in a single chapter, we'll go into some detail on the general principles, and we'll focus on getting these things working with a GWT project.

8.1 GWT testing

To make testing possible, GWT provides several testing tools and related supporting classes, which allow you to run tests against Java bytecode in hosted mode or against JavaScript in web mode. These are the same concepts that apply during development when using the GWT shell. When using web mode testing, a special JavaScript translatable JUnit support layer is automatically invoked by the toolkit.

Before we begin looking at GWT testing, we first need to narrow down what the testing support is intended to address and what it is not. We'll also look at some of the common issues concerning testing and touch on the testing process. Once we have that background, we'll work through several `GWTTestCase`-derived tests to hash out the details. After we have looked at testing GWT client-side code, we'll also briefly cover testing server-side code, and entire applications, outside of the toolkit.

Knowing the what, how, and where of testing will enable you to create better tests, which in turn will help you better understand your code and the toolkit, which will result in better applications.

8.1.1 Knowing what to test

The testing support provided by GWT is intended for testing your GWT client-side code, but not your UI. This may sound contradictory, and possibly even controversial, but it's important to understand it nonetheless. Non-UI client-side code includes your client-side model (logic and data) and any client-side controller you may be using, but not the view. In GWT unit testing, you should test asynchronous application-related event handling, client model beans, client-side logic, and the client side of GWT RPC. You should not worry about testing browser-based events (button clicks, mouse movements, and the like) or panel layout.

You can, with some special test and event-related helper code, test UI concepts within GWT unit tests, but you should not be very concerned about doing so. When you click on a GWT `Button`, the `ClickListener` that responds is part of the toolkit itself, not your code. If that `ClickListener` contains non-UI logic, in the `onClick()` method for example, you might be tempted to try to test the button in order to exercise your code. Yet, an often cleaner and easier practice is to move the logic from the UI widget into a client-side model, and invoke it through a client-side controller. (We discussed these concepts in chapters 2 and 4, and have used them in the examples throughout the book; we'll do the same with the code later in this chapter.)

In other words, design your application so that you can test logic and events through a controller method, rather than through the GWT UI. With such a design, you can test the controller directly without needing to worry about a `Button`. There are many benefits to the separation of responsibilities MVC provides, and making unit testing easier and more focused, especially in the context of a UI toolkit, is a significant one.

We also need to stress that we're referring to GWT unit tests in this chapter. You should still test the overall UI in integration or acceptance testing with tools outside of GWT. Also, when testing non-GWT specific code, such as server-side code, you do not need GWT support. In those cases, you should use standard JUnit or similar testing mechanisms. We'll come back to this in section 8.1.5 when we cover testing from outside the GWT perspective. GWT tests have a specific scope, translatable client-side logic and data, and RPC marshaling and interaction. Other testing mechanisms can pick up where these tests leave off.

Deciding what to test using the GWT testing support involves being familiar with all the moving parts. Knowing a bit about what is happening behind the scenes will help you utilize and troubleshoot GWT tests.

8.1.2 How GWT testing works

`GWTTestCase` is where it all begins. When you write a test case in GWT, you extend `GWTTestCase`, which itself extends the standard JUnit `TestCase`. `GWTTestCase` requires you to tell the test what module it will be using via the `getModuleName()` method and includes several other very simple methods that allow the adding and removing of *checkpoints* (these are used to simulate something resembling a stack trace in web mode, which otherwise would not be possible). `GWTTestCase` also invokes the JUnit shell, the all-around traffic cop of the GWT testing system.

The JUnit shell is an extension of the standard GWT shell, with test-specific capabilities. It is basically a harness that controls all the GWT magic for tests. One special aspect of the JUnit shell is that it's invoked automatically for you, so you can't pass arguments directly to it the way you'd do with the standard GWT shell. The JUnit shell supports many of the same options as the GWT shell, but you need to use the `-Dgwt.args` system property when invoking a test runner to route arguments to it. We'll see how to use this technique in several examples later in this chapter. The JUnit shell also forces the inheritance of a special GWT JUnit module into each test module that passes through it, and it caches module definitions.

The GWT JUnit module does several important things. First, when the module definition loader encounters classes that are of `GWTTestCase` type, it defines the generator used to create JUnit test case *stubs*, as follows:

```
<generate-with
  class="com.google.gwt.junit.rebind.JUnitTestCaseStubGenerator">
  <when-type-assignable class="com.google.gwt.junit.client.GWTTestCase"/>
</generate-with>
```

Generators, as we learned in chapter 1, are used in GWT in conjunction with deferred binding to create source files for later use in the compilation process on the fly. Each stub test class uses a few conventions to provide information about the test to the JUnit system.

The second thing the JUnit module does is to set the servlet path in the module definition to the special `JUnitHost` class. This class acts as the server-side endpoint for GWT JUnit tests.

All the moving parts—`GWTTestCase`, `JUnitShell`, the GWT JUnit module, and `JUnitHost`—operate in a loop with a message queue, as outlined in figure 8.1. For this reason, tests are not inline, and `TimeoutExceptions` can sometimes occur. In these cases, the testing harness may not always know exactly why your test didn't complete. We'll elaborate more on this in the next section, when we cover common testing issues.

Although there are several components involved in GWT testing, and having an overall understanding of the process helps, don't worry if it seems daunting at first. You don't have to dig into the details in most cases, because the toolkit handles the complexity and translation for you. With a few guidelines in mind, you can simply concentrate on writing `GWTTestCase`-derived tests.

However, it is helpful to be aware of some common pitfalls.

8.1.3 Testing gotchas

GWT testing throws a few curves at the traditional Java developer. These differences from more familiar testing practices are not difficult or cumbersome to deal with once

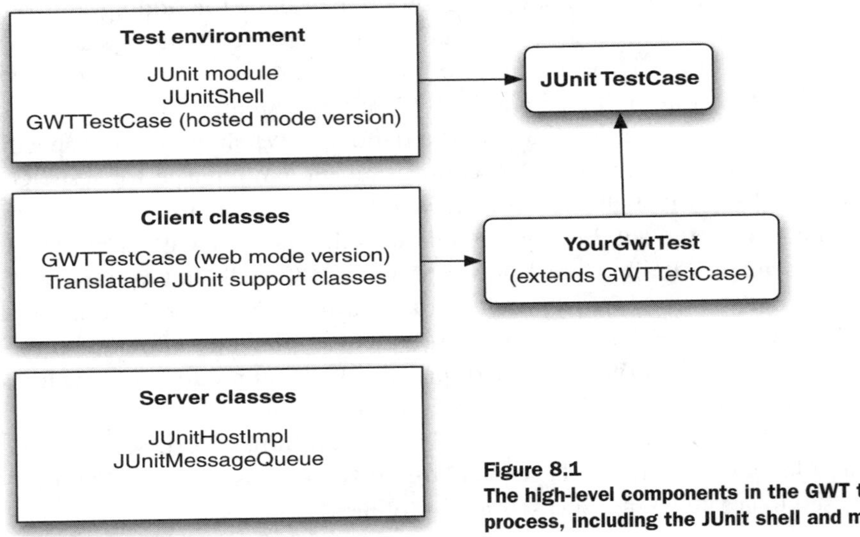

Figure 8.1 The high-level components in the GWT testing process, including the JUnit shell and module

you understand them, but they are sometimes tricky to remember—especially if you have years of non-GWT testing habits. The most common GWT testing issues that are apt to trip up traditional developers fall into three main areas: paths, `TimeoutException`, and test class initialization.

First, when dealing with paths, remember that *GWT requires the source on the classpath for its compilation step*, and this applies to testing and test sources, too. This issue comes into play for everything that passes through the GWT compiler. A common error in GWT testing is to forget to add the test source itself to the classpath.

You have to remember this step for every tool or testing process and add the source to the classpath. If you're using Eclipse 3.x, for example, you can add the source to the User Entries section of the run configuration by clicking the Advanced button on the Classpath tab of the Run configuration window, as shown in figure 8.2. You have to do this manually. Eclipse, like most other Java tools, does not include the source in the run configuration by default.

Along with the sources on the classpath, you also have to remember to include all translatable code in the GWT source path. This includes test cases themselves. The

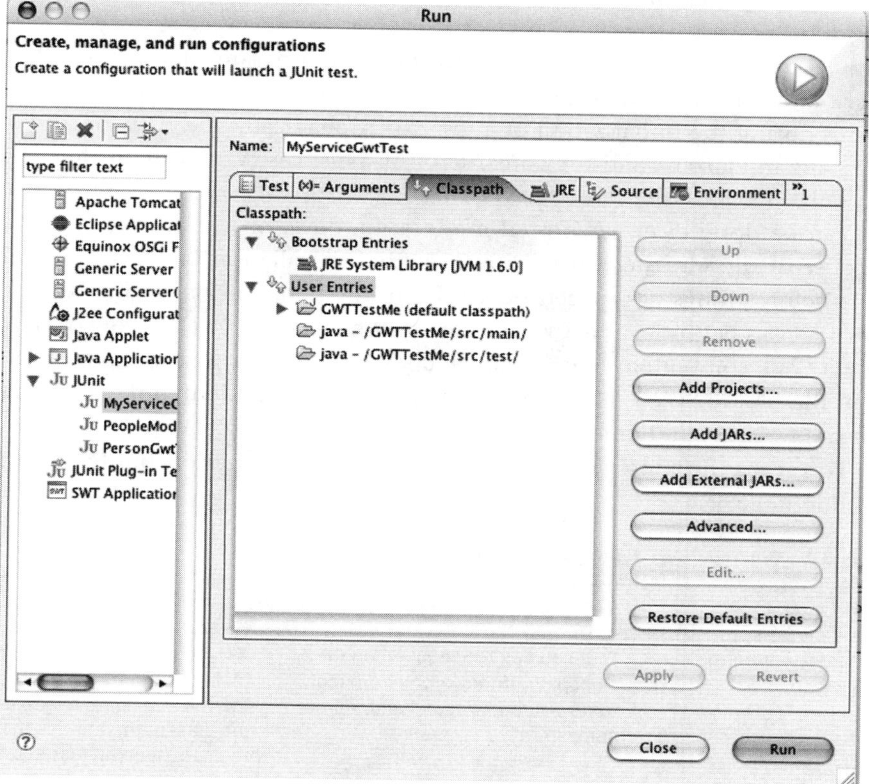

Figure 8.2 Adding src and test source paths to the User Entries portion of the classpath, as required for GWT

source path, as discussed in chapter 2, is defined in your module's gwt.xml file and tells the GWT compiler where the sources are located. If your test case is not in the default client source path package, you need to add the package it's in (whatever you name it) to the configuration. The GWT compiler performs a compilation step to translate your test classes into JavaScript, and if it cannot find your test classes, `GWTTestCase` will throw a `TimeoutException`, which can be misleading.

The next common problem area is the `TimeoutException` in general. The current generation of GWT testing support is, well, not speedy. This is more than just an inconvenience. The process is rather involved, and it can take a while if a lot of classes have to be translated or compiled by GWT, or both. This can cause problems, because the JUnit shell will also throw a `TimeoutException` if it hasn't seen a test method fire and contact the testing harness within 60 seconds. If you have a problem with slowness and have double-checked that your classpath and source path are correct, you may want to create a test-specific module. Such modules can reference fewer classes, leaving out the UI entirely, for example. This allows the compiler to prune and optimize things specifically for the tests, which speeds things up and may eliminate a `TimeoutException` problem (if the timeout is due to a large number of translatable classes being present).

In addition to being aware of the most common reasons that a `TimeoutException` might crop up, you should also be aware that you should not try to use GWT-related classes during the initialization of a test case. Specifically, the JUnit `setUp()` method, any static initializers, and the constructor of a test case are off limits for GWT-related instantiation. This is because the GWT testing process serves a dual purpose. GWT testing can be done in either hosted mode, using Java, or web mode, using JavaScript. Because of the way the JUnit `setUp()` method is called in `GWTTestCase`, which happens before things are passed off to the JUnit shell, you have to avoid doing GWT-specific tasks before your actual test case gets beyond `setUp()`. If you do try to instantiate a GWT component before the `setUp()` method completes, "badness ensues," as Scott Blum of the GWT team puts it. This can be inconvenient, but it is also something you can work around once you're aware of it.

To recap, the most common testing problems people encounter with GWT are listed in table 8.1.

Table 8.1 Common GWT testing issues and their solutions

Test gotcha	Description	Resolution
Sources not on the classpath	Test sources are required on the classpath. If they are not present, tests will not be found and will not compile.	As with non-test code, code that's going to be passed through the GWT compiler has to be on the classpath, and this includes tests. Include all test sources on the classpath.

Table 8.1 Common GWT testing issues and their solutions *(continued)*

Test gotcha	Description	Resolution
Test sources not in the source path	Test sources must be in the source path of your testing module. If they are not present, a `TimeoutException` will occur.	The default source path that GWT modules implicitly scan is client. If you create tests outside that package, such as in test, you must specify your source path in the module file. Include all test packages in the source path.
Tests throw `TimeoutException`	The JUnit shell will timeout if it takes more than 60 seconds (the timeout currently defined in the code) for the test browser to contact the test server. This can happen if you have a large code base and a lot of compilation is required before the test can run.	Create a test-specific module to cut down on involved classes, and create a simple initial test in your test case so that the first test completes quickly (without needing RPC).
GWT-specific code outside of test methods in test case classes	If you use the JUnit `setUp()` method, a static initializer block, or a constructor to create GWT-specific components you'll run into problems.	Keep your GWT-specific code in your test methods. Do not use the `setUp()` method, static initializers, or constructors for GWT code-related `GWTTestCase` purposes.

We've now covered the background and outlined some common problems, so let's get to some actual tests.

8.1.4 Basic GWT tests

We'll start looking at the simplest GWT tests and focus on getting dependencies and commands in order. We'll start small to prove the infrastructure is in place, and then move on. If GWT testing is new to you, this is the place to stay focused. Even though these are basic tests, GWT testing is a bit different from any other form of unit testing you may have previously done.

If you have already done some GWT testing and are familiar with the basics, you may want to skip ahead to the next section, where we'll look at more advanced concepts.

USING JUNITCREATOR

GWT provides many useful utilities for developers. Tools like `ApplicationCreator`, and `ProjectCreator`, which we covered in chapters 2 and 3, get a basic project outline in place and enable you to create IDE- or Ant-related files respectively. Along those same lines, GWT includes `JUnitCreator` for wiring up some initial GWT testing.

PROBLEM

We want to get a basic `GWTTestCase` test in place and running quickly, so we can familiarize ourselves with the concepts involved.

SOLUTION

The most basic test scenario in GWT is a new Hello World project with a test that extends GWTTestCase. Fortunately, GWT gives you both of these things right out of the box, through the ApplicationCreator tool we have used previously and JUnitCreator, which is a similar tool for testing.

We'll create a new project using ApplicationCreator, and then create a test using JUnitCreator. This can be done as follows:

```
mkdir [PROJECT_HOME]/test
cd [PROJECT_HOME]/test
[GWT_HOME]/applicationCreator com.manning.gwtip.client.MyProject
```

Using ApplicationCreator in this manner will create a new GWT project, MyProject, and the associated command-line scripts to start the project in the shell and compile it. Once we have a project, we can then use JUnitCreator to stub out a test case class as shown:

```
[GWT_HOME]/junitCreator -junit [PATH_TO_JUNIT] -module \
com.manning.gwtip.MyProject \
com.manning.gwtip.client.MyProjectTest
```

Using JUnitCreator this way will create a MyProjectTest class in the project, and several command-line scripts for invoking the test. These command-line scripts, MyProjectTest-hosted and MyProjectTest-web, will start JUnit with the correct classpath dependencies and options for hosted or web mode respectively.

DISCUSSION

We placed the test in the client package when using JUnitCreator. This was intentional. If you use a different package, such as test, you need to add that package to the source path in the module's gwt.xml file (remember, client is the default, and it's required when using ApplicationCreator).

If you take a look at the test class JUnitCreator produces, you'll see that it's a barebones class. The only interesting thing about it is the fact that it extends GWTTestCase. The command-line scripts ProjectCreator produces are where the real details are. These scripts include the required dependencies in the classpath (including JUnit and GWT themselves, and the source and compiled classes for the project), and they pass the test to JUnitRunner. For example, on the Mac platform, MyProjectTest-hosted, as generated by JUnitCreator, looks like this:

```
#!/bin/sh
APPDIR=`dirname $0`;
java -XstartOnFirstThread -Dgwt.args="-out www-test" \
-cp "$APPDIR/src:$APPDIR/test:$APPDIR/bin:\
[JUNIT_JAR]:[GWT_HOME]/gwt-user.jar:\
[GWT_HOME]/gwt-dev-mac.jar" junit.textui.TestRunner\
com.manning.gwtip.client.MyProjectTest "$@";
```

One last step is needed before the command-line script can be used and the test can be run. The test class has to be compiled with javac. This can seem counterintuitive, but the test scripts will look for the compiled class in the bin directory by default, and will expect you to have taken care of the compilation step on your own (it's not done for you). Normally you'd automatically get the bin output with an IDE, but you can also just compile things manually for this quick example as follows:

```
javac -d bin -cp "[JUNIT_JAR]:\
[GWT_HOME]/gwt-user.jar" \
test/com/manning/gwtip/client/*.java
```

With the structure and files in place, as provided by `ApplicationCreator` and `JUnitCreator`, you should now be able to run a simple `GWTTestCase`-derived test with the `MyProjectTest-Hosted` script. Keep in mind that when it runs, it invokes the GWT shell through the JUnit shell extension, so it may take a moment to complete. When the test finishes, the results will report something like this:

```
Time: 6.683
OK (1 test)
```

You'll probably quickly outgrow `JUnitCreator` and graduate to creating your own tests and running them via a build tool, such as Maven (which we'll use later in this chapter). Nevertheless, `JUnitCreator` can be a big initial help in terms of understanding the components involved.

To further exercise our GWT testing muscles, we're now going to step into a sample project that involves passing a model bean across the wire, and we'll work on some related tests. As we proceed, we'll look more closely at several aspects of `GWTTestCase`-derived classes, and we'll investigate asynchronous testing of an RPC service.

TESTING A MODEL BEAN

In this section, and the next few, we'll be using a sample project named GWTTestMe. This is a very simple project that includes a model bean class for `Person`, a controller that invokes a single RPC service, and a simple GWT `Widget` for the view. The project allows for `Person` objects to be added to, or removed from, a list, and the current version of the list is displayed to the user. We can put this small GWT project through some testing, while remaining focused on the tests themselves. We'll only look at the relevant sections of the project code in the text, but the complete source for this project is available at the Manning website.

The `Person` bean we'll be using is a translatable client-side model object that we'll serialize and send across the wire to the server using GWT RPC. The service interface is shown in listing 8.1.

Listing 8.1 The `MyService` service interface

```
public interface MyService extends RemoteService {

    public void addOrUpdatePerson(Person p);
    public void addOrUpdatePersonSlow(Person p);     <-- 1 Define special slow
    public void removePerson(Person p);                    service method

    /**
     * @gwt.typeArgs <com.manning.gwtip.testme.client.model.Person>
```

```
        */
        public List listPeople();
    }
```

The service interface in listing 8.1 performs some fairly common persistence tasks on a model object. We do have one unusual interface method definition though, the special addOrUpdatePersonSlow() method, which will be used later to purposely time out an asynchronous test ❶. What happens on the server side of these interface methods could be persistence via the JPA, a proxy call to a non-Java interface via SOAP, or any other type of mechanism to deal with the data.

To put the Person object and GWT object serialization to the test, so to speak, we need to implement a few GWTTestCase classes. The first of these is a simple test of the model object itself.

PROBLEM

We want to test a basic GWT model bean in the context of GWT JRE emulation.

SOLUTION

Listing 8.2 shows a basic GWTTestCase-derived test, in this case testing our Person model object.

Listing 8.2 Testing a Person model object with GWTTestCase

```
public class GwtTestPerson extends GWTTestCase {        ❶ Extend GWTTestCase

    public String getModuleName() {                     ❷ Specify module name
        return "com.manning.gwtip.testme.TestMe";
    }

    // ...

    public void testPersonEquals() {                    ❸ Perform equality test
        Person p1 = new Person("first1", "last1");
        Person p2 = new Person("first1", "last1");
        Person p3 = new Person("first1", null);
        Person p4 = new Person("first2", "last2");

        Assert.assertTrue(p1.equals(p2));
        Assert.assertFalse(p1.equals(p3));
        Assert.assertFalse(p1.equals(p4));
    }
}
```

Testing even basic client-side objects is important with GWT, because it ensures your classes work within the confines of the GWT environment.

DISCUSSION

GwtTestPerson, shown in listing 8.2, extends GWTTestCase ❶ which means it invokes all the GWT testing machinery when run. Before we cover the details of this specific test, it should be noted that even simple model beans such as this one can benefit from GWT testing.

You may say, "hey, I can test that without GWTTestCase," and you'd be correct, but such a test would have several shortcomings. Without GWTTestCase, you cannot test that your classes—even simple beans—operate as you expect in the limited JRE environment available to you with GWT. Also, you cannot test the GWT translation to JavaScript for web mode, which means you cannot test what really happens at runtime. Additionally, in order to work with GWT RPC, perform remote GWT testing across different browsers, or use GWT benchmarking, you need a `GWTTestCase`-derived test.

Within our test class, the `getModuleName()` method is *required* to inform the JUnit shell which module needs to be run ❷. Also, this test checks the equality of a `Person` object ❸. The `equals()` method we have implemented does not use the `getClass()` method, as it normally might, because that's not available in a GWT context. This means we have a test that works differently because of the ultimate JavaScript nature of this model object. A normal Java object—one that we didn't attempt to translate by using a `GWTTestCase`-derived test—would work fine with a `getClass()` call within it, but with GWT this reflection-based usage breaks down (`getClass()` is not allowed, as was explained in chapter 1). In this case, it's not actually the test that's different, but the fact that we're using `GWTTestCase` at all, which brings along the GWT environment, that makes the difference.

To run this test, we need to invoke a JUnit `TestRunner` and pass it our `GWTTestCase`-derived test with the required GWT and JUnit dependencies on the classpath, just as the `JUnitCreator` scripts we saw in the previous section do. There are many ways to get all these parts in order to run the test. You can do it with a shell script, just like `JUnitCreator`, or an IDE, but those can be difficult to manage and automate later. Or, you can use a build tool that can invoke tests and handle the configuration for you, such as Ant or Maven.

We recommend Maven and the GWT-Maven plugin, which we introduced in chapter 7, and we'll use it again in several sections later in this chapter when we discuss code coverage and continuous integration. GWT-Maven can automatically configure `GWTTestCase`-derived tests to run. The sample code for this chapter makes use of GWT-Maven and includes the files required to run the GWTTestMe project using Maven.

Testing GWT RPC

Now that you know what is required for a `GWTTestCase`-derived test, the basic approach for implementing such a test, and the purpose of using GWT test support, we'll move on to testing GWT RPC. This involves testing asynchronous operations.

Problem

We need to implement a test that can cope with the asynchronous nature of GWT RPC.

Solution

Testing asynchronous operations that involve callbacks, such as the service calls made with GWT RPC, requires a mechanism to *delay* and *finish* test case classes where appropriate. This is needed because tests would otherwise run to completion before any asynchronous events returned. The GWT testing support includes methods on the `GWTTestCase` class for just this purpose. These methods, `delayTestFinish()` and `finishTest()`, enable testing of asynchronous GWT RPC.

To demonstrate using the GWT's asynchronous testing support, we'll use a controller object to send a Person bean across the wire. The test shown in listing 8.3 performs this function.

Listing 8.3 GWT asynchronous testing support

```
public class GwtTestMyService extends GWTTestCase {          ❶ Extend GWTTestCase
    private static final int TEST_DELAY_1 = 500;
    private static final int TEST_DELAY_2 = 3050;

    public String getModuleName() {
        return "com.manning.gwtip.testme.TestMe";
    }

    public void setUp() throws Exception {          ❷ Remember, no GWT in setUp()
        super.setUp();
    }

    public void tearDown() throws Exception  {
        super.tearDown();
    }

    public void testAddOrUpdatePerson1() {
        Person person = new Person("Angus", "Young");
        PeopleModelData peopleData =
           new PeopleModelData();          ❸ Use client model and controller
        Controller controller =
           new Controller(peopleData);

        peopleData.addPropertyChangeListener(          ❹ Add PropertyChangeListener on model
           new PropertyChangeListener() {
            public void propertyChange(PropertyChangeEvent e)  {
                List newPeople = (List) e.getNewValue();
                Assert.assertEquals(1, newPeople.size());
                finishTest();          ❺ Call finishTest()
            }
        });

        delayTestFinish(TEST_DELAY_1);          Use delayTestFinish()
        controller.addOrUpdatePerson(person);          ❻ Invoke controller
    }

    public void testAddOrUpdatePerson2()  {
        Person person = new Person("Bon", "Scott");
        PeopleModelData peopleData = new PeopleModelData();
        Controller controller = new Controller(peopleData);

        peopleData.addPropertyChangeListener(
           new PropertyChangeListener() {
            public void propertyChange(PropertyChangeEvent e)  {
                List newPeople = (List) e.getNewValue();
                Assert.assertEquals(2, newPeople.size());
                finishTest();
            }
        });

        delayTestFinish(TEST_DELAY_2);
```

```
            controller.addOrUpdatePersonSlow(person);
        }
    }
```

❼ Invoke slow test method

In the test shown in listing 8.3, we're exercising GWT RPC and a client-side model and controller. This allows us to go through several important points in a `GWTTestCase`-based test.

DISCUSSION

In listing 8.3, we again extend `GWTTestCase` and use the convention of naming the test with a *GwtTest* prefix ❶. This allows us to easily filter tests and separate GWT tests from standard tests later. We use a prefix, rather than a suffix, in order to ensure that GWT tests are handled completely separately from the way JUnit expects to see tests by default. GWT tests need different dependencies and run in the JUnit shell, so we want to explicitly invoke GWT tests when we're ready for them, and not have them involved with standard JUnit testing.

Inside our test class, we're careful not to instantiate any GWT objects in a constructor, in a static initializer, or in our `setUp()` method because we know that can cause problems ❷. In our first test method, `testAddOrUpdatePerson1()`, we create an instance of our model, `PeopleModelData` (a bean that holds multiple `Person` objects), and of our `Controller` ❸. From there, we use a `PropertyChangeListener` on the model, where the view layer would typically connect ❹. This is important; by testing our controller and model directly, and the event handling involved, we can ensure that everything works right up to the point where it might be displayed in the view. With this approach, testing of the view beyond this point would only be checking that GWT components themselves work, and we don't really need to do that here.

Once we have that structure, we call the special GWT `finishTest()` method from the `propertyChange()` method. This tells the test case to complete successfully ❺. Next, we use the related `delayTestFinish()` method to allow the asynchronous RPC to take place before we invoke the RPC via the controller ❻. If we didn't do this in straight line code, the `finishTest()` method would never get called because the test would complete and exit before the RPC process itself completed.

To further demonstrate the use of `finishTest()` and `delayTestFinish()`, we have included another test method, `testAddOrUpdatePerson2()`. This method is identical to the first except that it calls the *slow* method on the controller, and the delay period it uses is longer ❼. The controller, in that case, delays the RPC call solely for the purposes of demonstrating the GWT testing facilities. To make this test fail, you can change the `DELAY_TEST_2` value to a lower threshold. Once it gets below the time it takes to complete the RPC call, the test will fail.

Testing using the JUnit shell and `GWTTestCase` is really the only way you can unit-test GWT translatable components. This includes testing client-side logic and data, testing in web mode, and testing the serialization that GWT RPC entails.

The testing framework that GWT provides is very valuable, but there are also other ways to test some portions of GWT applications.

8.1.5 Testing outside of GWT

Testing outside of GWT is often desirable because it's simpler and easier than testing inside of the toolkit. Testing components without using `GWTTestCase` can make sense in some scenarios and is straightforward, but you should also understand the limitations of this approach with regard to the client side of GWT applications. The server side, of course, is another matter. Server-side elements can and should be tested with standard testing practices that are not related to GWT. The best approach, all told, is usually a combination of testing client-side code with GWT testing support, testing server-side code outside of GWT, and running complete acceptance testing of the entire stack through the UI.

Each of these types of testing—internal GWT testing for client components, external standard Java testing for server components, and acceptance testing of the complete application—requires a different bit of knowledge and a different approach, but they are all essential to a complete testing regimen. Since we have already addressed internal GWT testing in the previous sections of this chapter, we're going to look at standard Java testing of the server side of a GWT application here, and provide a few pointers about broader acceptance testing.

PROBLEM

We want to test the server side of a GWT application when GWT RPC is involved.

SOLUTION

In keeping with standard programming practices, your communication layer should basically wrap another layer that performs logic and operations. With service servlets, this means you can extend `RemoteServiceServlet` and implement an interface for operations. We did this in chapter 3, with the `HelloServlet` (listing 3.5), and we'll use it again in listing 8.4.

With this type of design, you can test `HelloServiceImpl`, the implementation of the `HelloService` interface we introduced in chapter 3, using standard JUnit tests. This, of course, leaves GWT entirely out of the picture. Additionally, `HelloServiceImpl` is not bound by the JRE limitations of client-side GWT components, so any dependency or syntax typically available to you outside of GWT is allowed.

That handles your logic outside of GWT, but what about load testing or profiling for your service servlets themselves? This falls into the boundary between GWT and non-GWT testing, but you can also test service servlets by invoking them directly. To do this, you need to capture the RPC request before it's serialized and play it back for your tests.

You can submit HTTP data to servlets using a variety of tools capable of submitting HTTP requests, such as Apache JMeter (http://jakarta.apache.org/jmeter/). To get the data you need to send, you can use several methods. One is to use profiling tools, such as Firebug (http://www.getfirebug.com/) to inspect and capture virtually every aspect of any HTTP conversation. Another way, specifically for GWT, is to directly print and copy the RPC data by overriding the `onBeforeRequestDeserialized()` method of `RemoteServiceServlet`. Listing 8.4 provides an example of this technique using the `MyServiceServlet` that's part of the GWTTestMe sample project.

Listing 8.4 Override of `onBeforeRequestDeserialized()`

```
public class MyServiceServlet
    extends RemoteServiceServlet implements MyService {

    private MyService impl = new MyServiceImpl();

    public MyServiceServlet() {
    }
                                                        ❶ Override
    protected void onBeforeRequestDeserialized(          onBeforeRequestDeserialized
     String serializedRequest) {
        System.out.println("serializedRequest - " + serializedRequest);
    }

    public void addOrUpdatePerson(Person p) {
        impl.addOrUpdatePerson(p);
    }

    public void addOrUpdatePersonSlow(Person p) {
        impl.addOrUpdatePersonSlow(p);
    }

    public void removePerson(Person p) {
        impl.removePerson(p);
    }

    /**
     * @gwt.typeArgs <com.manning.gwtip.testme.client.model.Person>
     */
    public List listPeople() {
        return impl.listPeople();
    }
}
```

Once you override the `onBeforeRequestDeserialized()` method, you then have access to the RPC payload in `String` form before it's deserialized and processed. You can use that string to play back requests directly to service servlets and perform various types of testing directly on the GWT RPC server-side code.

DISCUSSION

If we run the GWTTestMe application with the `onBeforeRequestDeserialized()` override in place to capture the RPC call structure ❶, and pass several random names to represent `People` to our application, we'll see output such as what is shown in listing 8.5.

Listing 8.5 Capturing the RPC call structure

```
serializedRequest - 3?0?8?http://localhost:8888/
   com.manning.gwtip.testme.TestMe/?AC280ACA2779\
90CD7CF16A64E5A116D5?com.manning.gwtip.testme.client.MyService?addOrUpdat\
ePerson?com.manning.gwtip.testme.client.model.Person?com.manning.gwtip.te\
stme.client.model.Person/2995197803?Johnny?Clegg?1?2?3?4?1?5?6?7?8?

serializedRequest - 3?0?8?http://localhost:8888/
   com.manning.gwtip.testme.TestMe/?AC280ACA2779\
90CD7CF16A64E5A116D5?com.manning.gwtip.testme.client.MyService?addOrUpdat\
```

```
ePerson?com.manning.gwtip.testme.client.model.Person?com.manning.gwtip.te\
stme.client.model.Person/2995197803?Bob?Marley?1?2?3?4?1?5?6?7?8?

serializedRequest - 3?0?8?http://localhost:8888/
  com.manning.gwtip.testme.TestMe/?AC280ACA2779\
90CD7CF16A64E5A116D5?com.manning.gwtip.testme.client.MyService?addOrUpdat\
ePerson?com.manning.gwtip.testme.client.model.Person?com.manning.gwtip.te\
stme.client.model.Person/2995197803?Tish?Hinojosa?1?2?3?4?1?5?6?7?8?
```

Once you have the output RPC payload, as shown in listing 8.5, you can then construct test HTTP calls with standard HTTP testing utilities to invoke service servlet methods directly. This type of testing is useful for testing the amount of load the server can handle and what the bandwidth requirements of your application are.

The next logical step to take in terms of testing outside of the GWT testing mechanisms is to test directly from the UI, all the way through your application. This level of acceptance testing is important for all web applications, GWT or not, and is enabled by impressive tools such as Selenium (http://www.openqa.org/selenium/). These types of tools can run your tests just as the end user will use your application—through a browser—in an automated fashion.

Once you have unit tests in place for client and server, and you have done some load and integration testing for the server, you should also look into broader acceptance testing practices. The use of external acceptance testing tools is beyond our scope here, but we recommend that you research these tools on your own. Such tools can be very helpful with Ajax applications in general, including GWT.

Next we'll look at a collection of advanced testing topics relating to GWT: remote GWT unit testing, patching GWT (or using an extension JAR) to enable code-coverage data to be collected when running unit tests, and using the GWT `Benchmark` test extension.

8.2 Advanced testing concepts

One useful utility GWT provides is the `Benchmark` class. Benchmarks allow you to extend your tests to include a range of possible inputs and to capture and report on metrics. Benchmarks gain you access to metrics that would otherwise be very cumbersome to obtain. They are a convenience that extend the GWT testing process.

Another extension to that process is the toolkit's support for remote testing. While GWT does a great job at making sure your Java code is compiled into efficient, cross-browser JavaScript, testing on all the browsers is still a good idea. To that end, GWT provides an undocumented system for running your tests remotely, on different platforms, using different browsers.

After you have all of your testing in place, it's critical that you make sure your testing regimen is adequate, so code coverage is another metric you want to pay attention to. GWT does provide a means to instrument your code and obtain coverage data, but the process is not yet painless.

In the next few sections, we'll look at all of these advanced GWT testing topics, beginning with the `Benchmark` class.

8.2.1 Benchmarking

As a complement to tests, benchmark data can provide further insight into the capabilities of a code base. GWT includes support for a modified test, known as a `Benchmark` that includes built-in timing- and performance-reporting capabilities, and can be run with a range of parameters.

GWT benchmarking is intended to be used with client components. Benchmarking does not support asynchronous testing and is not really intended for general application testing. But if you need to test a client library, JRE emulation class, or a particular widget, you'll need a lot of iterations across multiple platforms with as many input variations as possible, and that's when you need benchmarking.

PROBLEM

We need to use a GWT benchmark to iterate and parameterize a client-side test.

SOLUTION

To demonstrate the important aspects of GWT benchmarking, we're intentionally going to use an existing example, `ArrayListAndVectorBenchmark`. This class is used in the GWT `Benchmark` documentation. Adding, removing, and retrieving elements from the client-side GWT implementations of `ArrayList` and `Vector` is a perfect example of where `Benchmark` is applicable and how it's applied. For this reason, although we have generally tried to avoid repeating any examples from the documentation, we will reuse this example here.

Listing 8.6 shows the relevant portions of `ArrayListAndVectorBenchmark` that demonstrate what a `Benchmark` is all about.

Listing 8.6 Portions of `ArrayListAndVectorBenchmark` showing `Benchmark` tests

```
public class ArrayListAndVectorBenchmark extends Benchmark {
...
final IntRange baseRange = new IntRange(512, Integer.MAX_VALUE,
        Operator.MULTIPLY, 2);                              <-- 1 Define baseRange using IntRange
        /**
     * Appends <code>size</code> items to an empty ArrayList.
     * @gwt.benchmark.param size -limit = baseRange      <-- 2 Annotate benchmark test method
     */
    public void testArrayListAdds(Integer size) {
      int num = size.intValue();
      for (int i = 0; i < num; i++) {
        list.add("hello");
      }
    }
                                                        3 Include method for JUnit
    // Required for JUnit                           <--
    public void testArrayListAdds() {
    }
...
  void beginArrayListAdds(Integer size) {           <-- 4 Use beginX idiom
    list = new ArrayList();
  }
```

Even though listing 8.6 is a relatively small sample, within it we see all of the more advanced Benchmark features in use.

DISCUSSION

ArrayListAndVectorBenchmark extends Benchmark and makes use of the GWT client IntRange object to define a range of integers ❶. The @gwt.benchmark.param JavaDoc style annotation then specifies that this range of integers should be used when the benchmarking method is run ❷. This specifies size as the name of the parameter to be replaced with the range, that a limit should be enforced, and that the variable baseRange is the range to be used. Notice that the method name testArrayListAdds must be repeated twice—once annotated and with parameters for the benchmarking support, and once without decoration or parameters for JUnit ❸. Additionally, this example makes use of the Benchmark-provided begin and end facilities ❹. A method named with the begin or end prefix will be executed before or after a test method of the same name, and will not be part of the timing results.

In this case, the testArrayListAdds method will be run with a starting value of 512 and multiplying that value by 2 until Integer.MAX_VALUE is reached or until the test times out due to the -limit switch.

As each benchmark test method runs, timing results will be collected and stored in an XML output file. The location of this file defaults to the current working directory, but it can be controlled using the com.google.gwt.junit.reportPath system property. Once you have run the test, you can take a look at the results with the benchmark report viewing tool GWT provides for this purpose.

Running ArrayListAndVectorBenchmark with GWTTestMe

If you have downloaded the GWTTestMe project code for this chapter, it includes ArrayListAndVectorBenchmark in a subdirectory named benchmark-example. This class is not in the same location or module as the other test examples, and is intentionally not named with the GwtTest prefix. If you wish to run this example, you'll need to do so manually. See the benchmark-example subdirectory of the project code for more information.

The GWT ReportViewer tool is itself a GWT module that runs a small web application and parses the benchmarking XML results for display. Running ReportViewer against the output of ArrayListAndVectorBenchmark presents the results shown in figure 8.3.

Once again, benchmarks can be very useful if you're writing a library. If you want to recreate a library or utility that's available in the standard Java world but is not available in the GWT JRE emulated world, such as a ToStringBuilder or Logger, benchmarks can help you quickly test, iterate, and record results. Additionally, if you want timing results recorded for your application components, or you want to troubleshoot some particularly annoying issue, benchmarks can often help.

The next step is moving beyond testing on a single local platform and testing remotely across different browser versions.

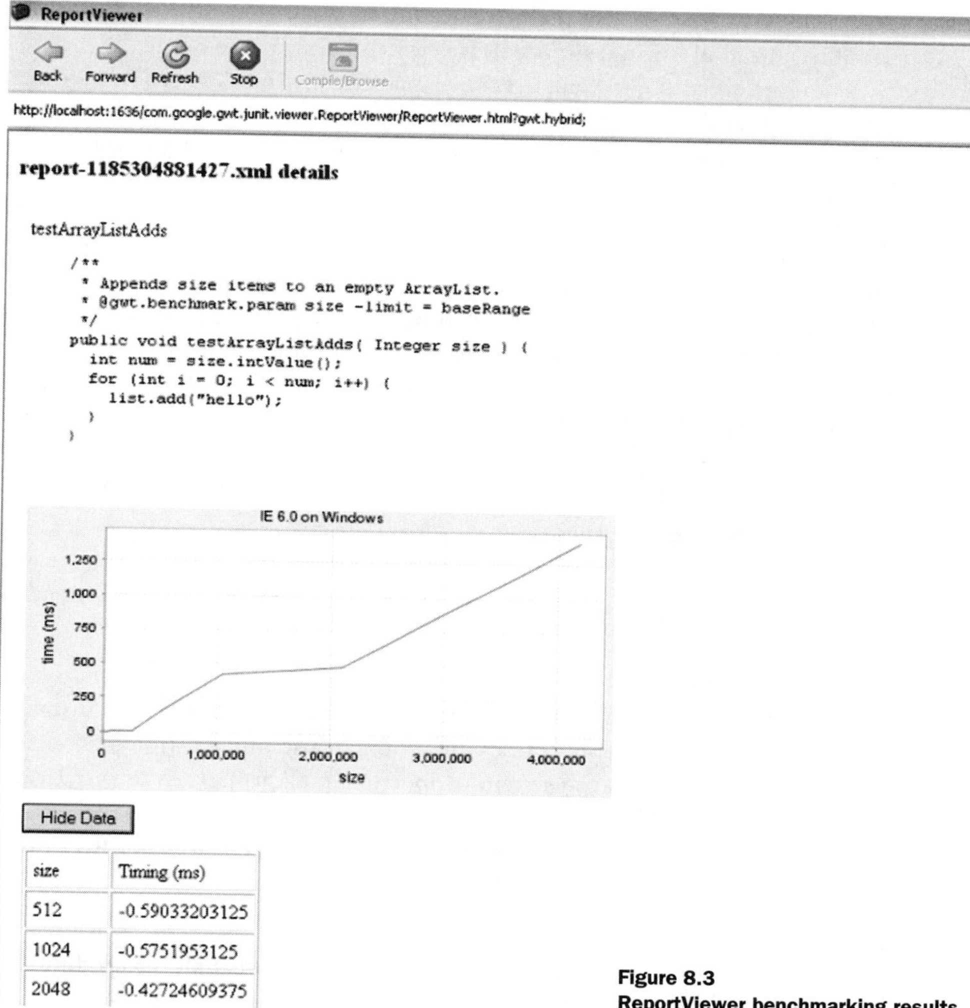

Figure 8.3
ReportViewer benchmarking results

8.2.2 *Remote testing*

Web developers are all too familiar with the dreaded differences in browsers. Because of these differences, testing on many platforms with a combination of browser versions is essential for all but the most trivial web applications.

PROBLEM

We need to run GWT tests across different browsers and platforms.

SOLUTION

GWT provides a RemoteWeb testing mechanism that allows you to run tests remotely. This enables you to make use of different platforms, and the different browsers on each platform. This support, per the code comments, is "undocumented, unsupported, and experimental." Even so, this feature is useful, so it's likely to remain in the toolkit (and possibly gain more formal support). It is worth being aware of.

The com.google.gwt.junit.remote package in the GWT User module provides the classes that make remote testing possible. To use the remote testing, a Java-based server RMI component must be started on each machine you plan to run tests against. Then, providing some further undocumented arguments to the JUnit shell allows GWTTestCase tests to be run as RMI clients.

GWT itself, and the RemoteBrowserManager class, must be present on each remote machine that has a browser you want to test on (for instance, a Windows XP machine running Internet Explorer 6). When you start the RemoteBrowserManager, you need to include pairs of arguments that specify an identifier name (used in the RMI registry) and the path to the browser executable you wish to run (multiple pairs can be specified to denote multiple entries). The following command (with the standard GWT libraries in the classpath) can be used to start the RemoteBrowserManager on Windows, register the name WinIE6, and define the path to the IE executable:

```
java com.google.gwt.junit.remote.BrowserManagerServer WinIE6 \
"C:\Program Files\Internet Explorer\IEXPLORE.EXE"
```

Once the command executes, you should see the following in the command shell:

```
RMI registry ready.
WinIE6 started and awaiting connections
```

After you have a server listening (running a RemoteBrowserManager instance), you're ready to connect to it from a test case. You can use any existing GWTTestCase-based test and use the -Dgwt.args system property to pass properties to the JUnit shell process that GWT will ultimately invoke. The -remoteweb argument is used to tell the test harness to call out to the remote server and run the test in web mode at that location:

```
... -Dgwt.args=-remoteweb rmi://hostname/identifier
```

DISCUSSION

The fact that GWT contains a remote testing mechanism at all is a credit to the toolkit. Nevertheless, using it's not for the faint of heart. It's undocumented and unsupported at present, by design. There are currently problems with limited Safari support and with launching Firefox remotely if it's already running in another instance on the same machine. This feature is currently most useful for remotely launching tests against IE or Firefox on an isolated machine (virtual or not) that's designated for such testing.

The alternative to using the built-in remote testing in the toolkit is to simply run your tests via a GWT installation on each target platform. This can be cumbersome, but it is possible. Using virtual machines can ease the burden of this task. With virtualization, you can install the toolkit and your project on each virtual machine and run the tests locally. Though this may seem like a large undertaking, it's a common practice in web development circles when it comes to integration testing anyway, so you may be able to leverage existing processes.

In conjunction with testing and benchmarking, many developers will be looking for code-coverage information, so we'll look at it next.

8.2.3 Code coverage

If you're a traditional tester, you're probably quite familiar with the concept of *code coverage* (and you deserve kudos). Coverage is a metric of how much of your code, line by line, method by method, is actually exercised by your tests. Using coverage information, you can gauge whether your application is adequately tested, and you can see which areas need attention.

Obtaining coverage information with GWT is not a walk in the park. You can obtain code-coverage data, but it requires a bit of special understanding and an extension to the toolkit. (The code that enables coverage support may be included as part of a future release, but for now it's a patch, which can also be included via an extension JAR file.) To qualify that a bit, server-side code, which runs as standard Java, is no different from any other Java code when using GWT. Client-side code is different. Client-side code is executed as Java bytecode in hosted mode, and this is where things get tricky in GWT coverage terms.

PROBLEM

We want to obtain code-coverage information for a `GWTTestCase`-derived test.

SOLUTION

To get code coverage working with GWT, you have two options: you can patch GWT yourself with a code-coverage patch, or you can include an extension JAR file that already includes the patch on your classpath. The easier route is to use the extension JAR, so that's what we'll focus on here. That said, patching the toolkit on your own is not that difficult, and having the knowledge to do it may come in handy in other situations as well. If you want to build and patch GWT on your own, see the "Making GWT Better" guide in the GWT documentation for full instructions (http://code.google.com/webtoolkit/makinggwtbetter.html#workingoncode).

The GWT code-coverage extension JAR file that we'll use is based on a coverage patch that the GWT team has provided (codecoverage-r676.patch). For details on the patch, see issue 779 in the GWT issue tracker (http://code.google.com/p/google-web-toolkit/issues/detail?id=779). We have also further modified the patch to allow the code-coverage process to filter out classes that you probably don't want to instrument—details on the modification are also in the aforementioned code-coverage issue.

The code-coverage patch, and our modification to allow for filtering which classes do and do not get instrumented is available in the form of a JAR file that you can add to your classpath. Including this coverage JAR (gwtcoverage-1.4.60.jar) in your classpath, in front of the GWT dev jar for your platform, overrides the necessary classes and gives you code-coverage capability.

Once you have the coverage JAR file in your classpath, you also need to include an EMMA library JAR file for coverage support. EMMA is a popular open source code-coverage tool that GWT's coverage support uses. You can obtain EMMA from the

EMMA project's website (http://emma.sourceforge.net/). With these prerequisites in place, you simply need to pass the special system property `gwt.coverage.enable=true` to the JVM when invoking GWT tests to get coverage data output.

With coverage support enabled, GWT will output EMMA coverage data files to the current working directory. Those files can then be processed with the reporting facilities of EMMA to generate a code-coverage report. Figure 8.4 shows the top-level page of such a report, obtained when running the tests from the GWTTestMe project we have used in this chapter.

DISCUSSION

It's obviously not ideal to have to build and patch the toolkit just to get code-coverage data. This is why we created and provided the coverage support JAR file, which should ease the process somewhat. Even though using this JAR is not entirely painless, and it would be better if GWT simply included more robust coverage support to begin with, at least this solution makes it possible to obtain coverage information. The good news is that the GWT team is aware of this shortcoming and plans to include the coverage patch, and possibly more testing and coverage-related enhancements, in a future release. For now, we think including the coverage JAR to get the coverage data is worth the effort.

There are several reasons why GWT's hosted mode coverage situation is complicated, which is what makes all of this necessary in the first place and negates more traditional code-coverage techniques. First, the JUnit support in GWT recompiles code from source. This means coverage tools that work offline, and instrument classes, are instrumenting classes that never get run by GWT. Second, the same JUnit support has

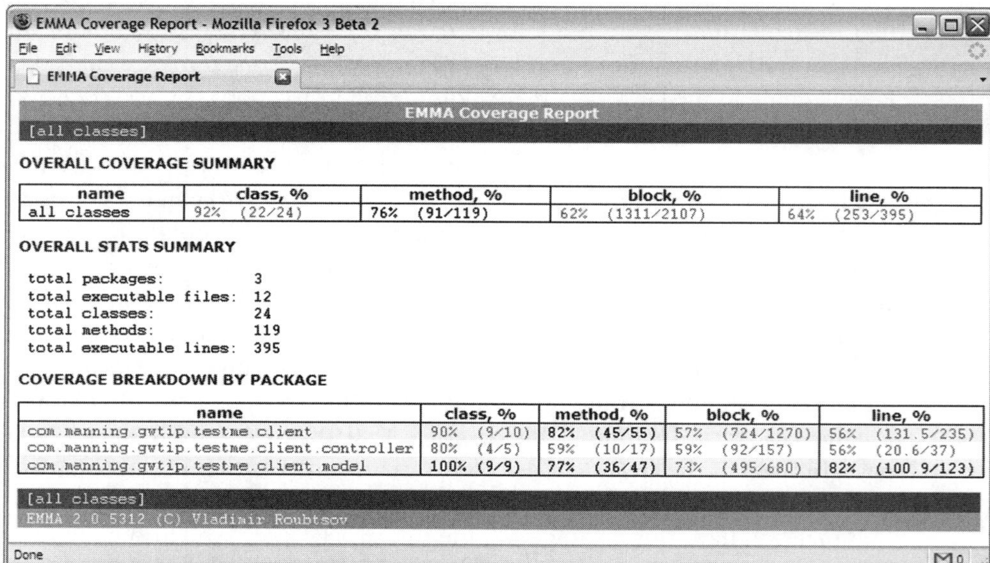

EMMA Coverage Report

[all classes]

OVERALL COVERAGE SUMMARY

name	class, %	method, %	block, %	line, %
all classes	92% (22/24)	76% (91/119)	62% (1311/2107)	64% (253/395)

OVERALL STATS SUMMARY

```
total packages:          3
total executable files:  12
total classes:           24
total methods:           119
total executable lines:  395
```

COVERAGE BREAKDOWN BY PACKAGE

name	class, %	method, %	block, %	line, %
com.manning.gwtip.testme.client	90% (9/10)	82% (45/55)	57% (724/1270)	56% (131.5/235)
com.manning.gwtip.testme.client.controller	80% (4/5)	59% (10/17)	59% (92/157)	56% (20.6/37)
com.manning.gwtip.testme.client.model	100% (9/9)	77% (36/47)	73% (495/680)	82% (100.9/123)

[all classes]

EMMA 2.0.5312 (C) Vladimir Roubtsov

Figure 8.4 The top-level page of an EMMA code-coverage report for the GWTTestMe project

its own CompilingClassLoader. This means that even on-the-fly instrumenting classloaders are knocked out of the picture (without some hacking of the toolkit). This is why there is special support in GWT for obtaining code-coverage data.

There are a few main points to take away from this discussion of GWT-enabled code coverage. The filtering of which classes are and are not instrumented is only available if you use the extension to the GWT patch that we have created. The standard GWT patch still works, but it instruments every class that passes through the GWT compiler, which means GWT classes, JUnit classes, test classes, and the like all end up in your coverage reports, rather than just the code you really care about—your own. Also, GWT is doing the instrumentation step for you, because of the gwt.coverage.enable system property. This means you do not need to manually run EMMA either on the command line or using a build tool as you might normally expect. All you need to do is run the tests with the system property set, and coverage data will be output to the current working directory.

Coverage data, in terms of EMMA, means two files: coverage.ec and coverage.em. For more on what exactly these files are, see the EMMA documentation (available on the EMMA website). To generate a coverage report manually, you need to run the EMMA report command against these coverage data files. This can be done from the command line as follows:

```
java -cp $GWT_TOOLS_HOME/lib/emma/emma-2.0.5312.jar \
emma report -in coverage.em,coverage.ec -r html
```

When you generate a report with EMMA using this command, it will output a series of HTML files in a subdirectory named coverage. Each of the packages shown in the EMMA coverage report, shown in figure 8.4, is navigable. Clicking on a package name will drill down into that package and show the individual classes. From there you can also go one step further and get a color-coded view of each class, showing exactly what code was executed and what was not. Figure 8.5 shows a detailed EMMA report of the Controller class within GWTTestMe.

In figure 8.5 you may notice that we failed to test the removePerson() method on our Controller class. There it is in red: 0% tested. Also, you might be wondering about the four other Controller$1-4 classes shown in the report. These are the anonymous instances of AsyncCallback that we used within Controller, and the report shows that we used several, but not all, of them during the test. This is exactly what code coverage is about. Until you have run tests and checked the coverage, you cannot really be sure you're covering all the bases.

Obtaining coverage information for your GWT tests is important, but having to run down all of these steps by hand each time you want to see your project's metrics is very inconvenient. Once you get things set up, and are satisfied that the coverage process is working, you may wish to use a build tool such as Maven or Ant to add some convenience. By using these tools, you can automatically run your tests, generate coverage data, and create reports.

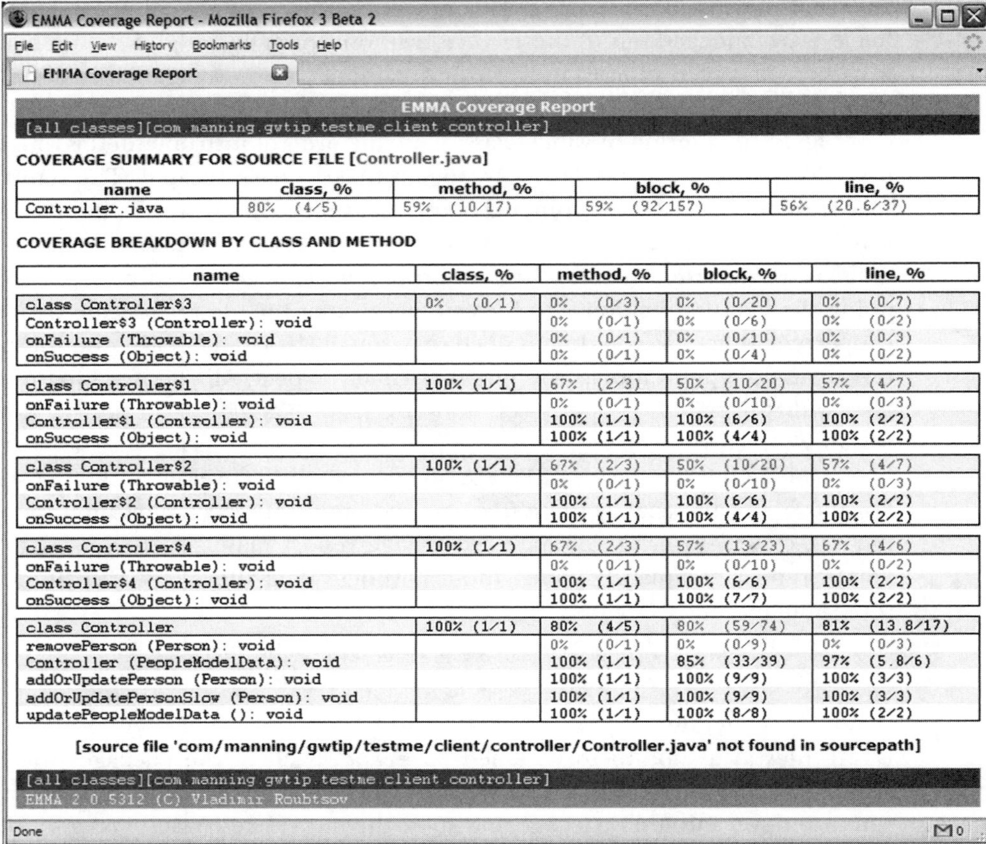

EMMA Coverage Report - Mozilla Firefox 3 Beta 2

EMMA Coverage Report

[all classes][com.manning.gwtip.testme.client.controller]

COVERAGE SUMMARY FOR SOURCE FILE [Controller.java]

name	class, %	method, %	block, %	line, %
Controller.java	80% (4/5)	59% (10/17)	59% (92/157)	56% (20.6/37)

COVERAGE BREAKDOWN BY CLASS AND METHOD

name	class, %	method, %	block, %	line, %
class Controller$3	0% (0/1)	0% (0/3)	0% (0/20)	0% (0/7)
Controller$3 (Controller): void		0% (0/1)	0% (0/6)	0% (0/2)
onFailure (Throwable): void		0% (0/1)	0% (0/10)	0% (0/3)
onSuccess (Object): void		0% (0/1)	0% (0/4)	0% (0/2)
class Controller$1	100% (1/1)	67% (2/3)	50% (10/20)	57% (4/7)
onFailure (Throwable): void		0% (0/1)	0% (0/10)	0% (0/3)
Controller$1 (Controller): void		100% (1/1)	100% (6/6)	100% (2/2)
onSuccess (Object): void		100% (1/1)	100% (4/4)	100% (2/2)
class Controller$2	100% (1/1)	67% (2/3)	50% (10/20)	57% (4/7)
onFailure (Throwable): void		0% (0/1)	0% (0/10)	0% (0/3)
Controller$2 (Controller): void		100% (1/1)	100% (6/6)	100% (2/2)
onSuccess (Object): void		100% (1/1)	100% (4/4)	100% (2/2)
class Controller$4	100% (1/1)	67% (2/3)	57% (13/23)	67% (4/6)
onFailure (Throwable): void		0% (0/1)	0% (0/10)	0% (0/2)
Controller$4 (Controller): void		100% (1/1)	100% (6/6)	100% (2/2)
onSuccess (Object): void		100% (1/1)	100% (7/7)	100% (2/2)
class Controller	100% (1/1)	80% (4/5)	80% (59/74)	81% (13.8/17)
removePerson (Person): void		0% (0/1)	0% (0/9)	0% (0/3)
Controller (PeopleModelData): void		100% (1/1)	85% (33/39)	97% (5.8/6)
addOrUpdatePerson (Person): void		100% (1/1)	100% (9/9)	100% (3/3)
addOrUpdatePersonSlow (Person): void		100% (1/1)	100% (9/9)	100% (3/3)
updatePeopleModelData (): void		100% (1/1)	100% (8/8)	100% (2/2)

[source file 'com/manning/gwtip/testme/client/controller/Controller.java' not found in sourcepath]

[all classes][com.manning.gwtip.testme.client.controller]

EMMA 2.0.5312 (C) Vladimir Roubtsov

Figure 8.5 The `Controller` class details of an EMMA coverage report for the GWTTestMe project

8.2.4 Coverage in an automated build

Armed with an understanding of what it takes to support and configure code coverage in GWT, the next step is to automate the process. An automated build that includes tests, coverage data, and reports is critical when it comes to continuous integration.

Continuous integration (CI) is something we'll tackle in section 8.3 of this chapter, but before we get there we need to be running a build process that will work in a CI environment. Most CI products support a variety of build tools, with Ant and Maven being the most widely used. For GWTTestMe, as we have done with other projects up to this point, we're going to use Maven 2 and the GWT-Maven plugin.

PROBLEM

We want to manage the process of testing, coverage, and reporting for GWT projects.

SOLUTION

Use Maven and the GWT-Maven plugin in conjunction with a coverage-enabled version of GWT.

Discussion

We first met the GWT-Maven plugin in chapter 7. By setting GWT-specific properties for the GWT-Maven plugin, and some additional EMMA properties to generate a report, we can achieve a completely automated build with testing, coverage, and reporting.

In standard Maven 2 usage, the Surefire plugin (the default testing plugin) is invoked during the test build phase, and standard tests are run. The Surefire plugin chokes on running the JUnit shell, though, so it cannot handle `GWTTestCase`-derived tests. The reasons why it doesn't work are complicated but basically boil down to classpath issues and the fact that you cannot pass JVM arguments. (System properties, such as `-Dgwt.args`, can be passed, but not arguments such as `-XstartOnFirstThread`.) Because of the problems with Surefire and GWT, GWT-Maven includes its own test goal, `testGwt`, which also gets run during the test phase.

The `testGwt` goal invokes the JUnit shell and runs any GwtTest* named tests with the needed classpath and dependencies. Notice that, as we discussed in section 8.1.4, GWT tests are named differently from standard tests in order to distinguish them. By default, GWT-Maven looks for tests with the prefix *GwtTest*, and Surefire looks for tests with the suffix *Test* or *TestCase*. This means that when using Maven, if you have both GWT tests and standard tests, they will both be run during the test phase of the build, but they will be run by different plugins. (Also, the output of Surefire tests is placed in the target/test-report directory, and the output of GWT-Maven tests is placed in the target/gwtTest directory.) The bottom line with a GWT project using GWT-Maven is that both types of testing are supported: standard tests and `GWTTestCase`-based tests.

Now that you know a bit about the background, we'll look at a Maven POM file that makes use of GWT-Maven and wires all the pieces together to automate testing and reporting for the GWTTestMe project. The first portion of the POM file is shown in listing 8.7.

Listing 8.7 Coverage dependencies and the `testGwt` goal in the GWTTestMe POM file

```
<dependencies>
    ...
    <dependency>                              ❶ Include coverage support
        <groupId>emma</groupId>                  JAR and EMMA
        <artifactId>emma</artifactId>
        <version>2.0.5312</version>
        <scope>test</scope>
    </dependency>
    <dependency>
        <groupId>com.google.gwt</groupId>
        <artifactId>gwtcoverage</artifactId>
        <version>1.4.61</version>
        <scope>provided</scope>
    </dependency>
    <dependency>
      ...
</dependencies>
<build>
    <plugins>
        <!-- other plugins omitted for brevity -->
```

```
        <plugin>
            <groupId>com.totsp.gwt</groupId>
            <artifactId>
                      maven-googlewebtoolkit2-plugin        <-- ❷ Set up GWT-
                   </artifactId>                                 Maven plugin
            <version>2.0-beta5</version>
            <configuration>
                <logLevel>INFO</logLevel>
                <runTarget>
                     com.manning.gwtip.testme.TestMe/TestMe.html
                </runTarget>
                <compileTargets>
                  <param>
                             com.manning.gwtip.testme.TestMe
                           </param>
                </compileTargets>
            </configuration>
            <executions>
                <execution>
                    <goals>
                      <goal>mergewebxml</goal>
                      <goal>compile</goal>
                      <goal>testGwt</goal>        <-- ❸ Include
                    </goals>                            testGwt goal
                </execution>
            </executions>
        </plugin>
        <!-- other plugins omitted for brevity -->
    </plugins>
</build>
```

After we have the dependencies to support code coverage ❶, and we're using GWT-Maven as a plugin ❷, we can include the `runTarget` and `compileTarget`, which we introduced in chapter 7, and we can include the special `testGwt` goal ❸. When Maven plugins define goals, they also define which phase of the build they are intended for—the goal knows when to run if it's included in the `<execution>`.

In addition to the POM file, we also need to include some machine-wide settings for Maven in the settings.xml file to complete the setup for GWTTestMe. As we discussed in the previous section, your GWT tests will automatically be instrumented by EMMA if you're using the GWT coverage JAR file and have coverage enabled. With Maven, you can enable and disable coverage using your settings.xml file (typically located in the m2 subdirectory within the home directory of the user you run Maven as, as we discussed in chapter 7). To use the patched version of GWT and enable coverage, you can update your settings file as shown in listing 8.8.

Listing 8.8 A Maven settings.xml profile for GWT that enables code coverage

```
<profile>
   <id>gwt-1.4.60</id>
      <google.webtoolkit.home>        ❶ Define
         /opt/gwt-mac-1.4.60      <--    google.webtoolkit.home
```

```
        </google.webtoolkit.home>
        <google.webtoolkit.extrajvmargs>
           -Dgwt.coverage.enable=true
        </google.webtoolkit.extrajvmargs>
    </properties>
</profile>
```

❷ Include google.webtoolkit.extrajvmargs

With Maven set up and configured to use GWT-Maven as we have shown, including specifying the google.webtoolkit.home ❶ and google.webtoolkit.extrajvmargs configuration elements ❷, you can run the tests using the following command:

```
mvn clean test
```

Running the Maven test phase will invoke the tests, fire the `gwtTest` goal, and produce test results and coverage data. The last thing you need for an automated build are reports. Using Maven you can obtain reports for dependencies, tests, static analysis metrics, and more—and all of these things can automatically be included in an HTML site that documents your project. This is made possible by the Maven Site plugin.

The POM we've included with the GWTTestMe project (available with the downloadable code for this chapter on the Manning website) does demonstrate a few of the standard Maven reports using the Maven Site plugin, but that's not our focus here because it's beyond our scope and is well covered in other articles and books. Automating the coverage report from the coverage data files EMMA produces from GWT tests is our focus. Because EMMA is not used in the typical fashion with GWT, we need a nonstandard way to use Maven to automatically include a coverage report in the output for the project's site. To do this, we'll use the Maven AntRun plugin to invoke the EMMA Ant report task on our GWT coverage data files. Listing 8.9 shows how this is done in the POM file.

Listing 8.9 The AntRun portion of the `GWTTestMe` POM file

```
<plugin>
  <artifactId>
    maven-antrun-plugin
  </artifactId>
    <executions>
      <execution>
        <id>emma-coverage-report</id>
        <phase>pre-site</phase>
        <configuration>
        <tasks>
          <taskdef resource="emma_ant.properties"
              classpathref="maven.plugin.classpath" />
            <emma enabled="true">
              <report>
              <infileset dir="${project.build.directory}"
         includes="*.em, *.ec" />
              <html   outfile="${project.build.directory}/coverage/\
coverage.html" depth="method" \
columns="name,class,method,block,line" />
```

❶ Set up AntRun plugin

❷ Include EMMA Ant support

❸ Run EMMA report task

❹ Create HTML report

```
            </report>
            </emma>
            <copy todir="${project.build.directory}/site/">
            <fileset
      dir="${project.build.directory}/coverage" />       <-- 5 Copy report to site
            </copy>
        </tasks>
        </configuration>
      <goals>
        <goal>run</goal>
      </goals>
      </execution>
    </executions>
    <!-- plugin dependencies omitted for brevity -->
</plugin>
```

With the AntRun plugin configured, we can include standard Ant tasks ❶. Once we have Ant support in our Maven POM, we can include the EMMA Ant tasks ❷. We use the EMMA Ant `<report>` task to create our report ❸, in HTML format ❹, based on the coverage data files created by coverage-enabled GWT tests.

This is a very vanilla use of the EMMA tasks, which works fine and creates the desired reports, but we still have a small problem. Because we're not using the standard Maven plugin report support, our coverage reports will not end up in the Maven site documentation by default. To address this, we use the Ant `<copy>` task to copy the coverage report into the Maven site directory ❺.

Once the coverage HTML report is in the site directory, we also need to include that report alongside other standard Maven reports in a site.xml file for our project. The Maven Site plugin uses the site.xml file to generate HTML. (For more about how, and why, Maven does this, see the Maven documentation online.) So, we need to use a site.xml file, as shown in listing 8.10, to incorporate our nonstandard coverage report in the final version of our site.

Listing 8.10 A Maven site.xml file that includes the EMMA coverage report in the site

```
<?xml version="1.0" encoding="UTF-8"?>
<project>
  <body>
    <menu name="Overview">
      <item name="Introduction" href="index.html"/>
      <item name="Coverage Report"
        href="coverage.html"/>          <-- 1 Include coverage.html report
      <item name="Dependency Report"
        href="dependencies.html"/>      <--
      <item name="Surefire Test Report"     2 Include standard Maven reports
        href="surefire-report.html"/>   <--
    </menu>
  </body>
</project>
```

Because the coverage.html file is copied to the site directory using AntRun, we can simply link to it in the site.xml file ❶. Along with the custom coverage report, we also

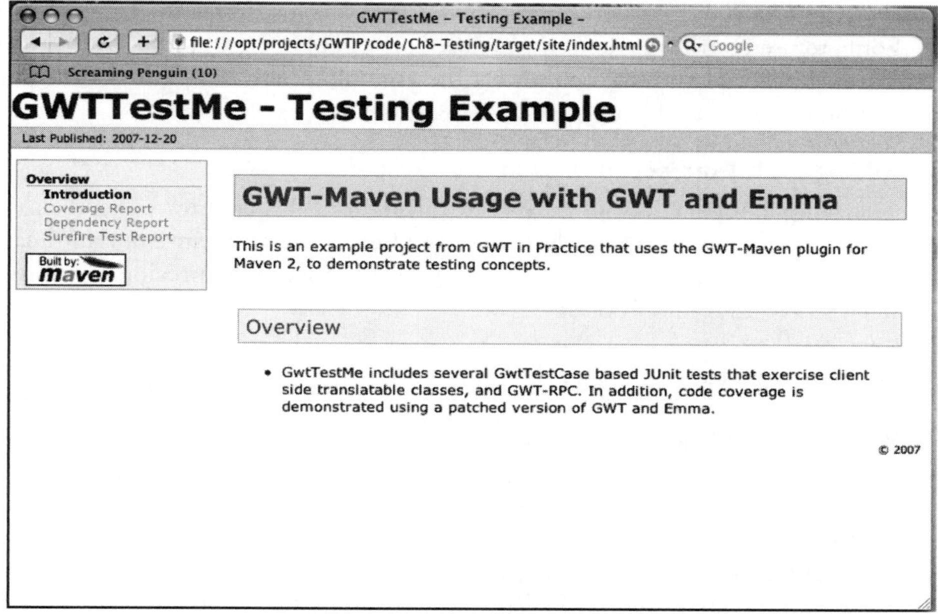

Figure 8.6 The Maven-generated site, including standard and additional reports, such as GWT code-coverage data

include some of the other standard Maven reports ❷. To run our project's tests with Maven and generate a site, we can issue the following command:

```
mvn clean test site
```

Using this technique, Maven will clean the target directory, compile the project, run the tests—standard and GWT—and finally generate a site. The final site will include several standard reports, such as dependencies and regular test results, and a link to our coverage report, as seen in figure 8.6.

With the toolkit patch and some configuration using Maven, we now have a means to obtain code-coverage data for GWT tests in an automated build process. Using the automated process is much more convenient than the manual mode we used in the previous section, and it becomes a requirement when you want to use continuous integration.

8.3 Continuous integration

Continuous integration (CI) has many benefits. Once you're engaged in the process, you always know the exact state of your application through a reporting Dashboard, and you know that all of your components integrate as they should and are thoroughly tested. This can improve your knowledge of your application and the overall quality of your software. Continuous integration is the final step in a well-oiled development process. It follows once you have a solid automated build with adequate tests and good reporting.

There are several good open source CI servers available. For this example, we're going to use Hudson to demonstrate the concept of using CI with a GWT project. Hudson is Java-based and runs either via the command line or within an existing servlet container (making it available on any platform that can run Java).

8.3.1 Adding a GWT project to Hudson

The sample application we have used throughout this chapter will serve as the basis for the project we want to include in our CI builds. We made sure our automated build was ready, including testing, coverage, and reporting, in the previous sections. Now we need to get this build into the CI fold.

PROBLEM

We want to add a GWT project to Hudson.

SOLUTION

You can obtain Hudson from the project website (https://hudson.dev.java.net/). The recommended approach is to get the WAR version, drop it in a servlet container, and then browse to the installation location (http://localhost:8080/hudson). Hudson is completely configurable from the web interface it provides.

With Hudson running, configuration is very straightforward. There is a main Manage Hudson section where you can configure all of the global options. From this page,

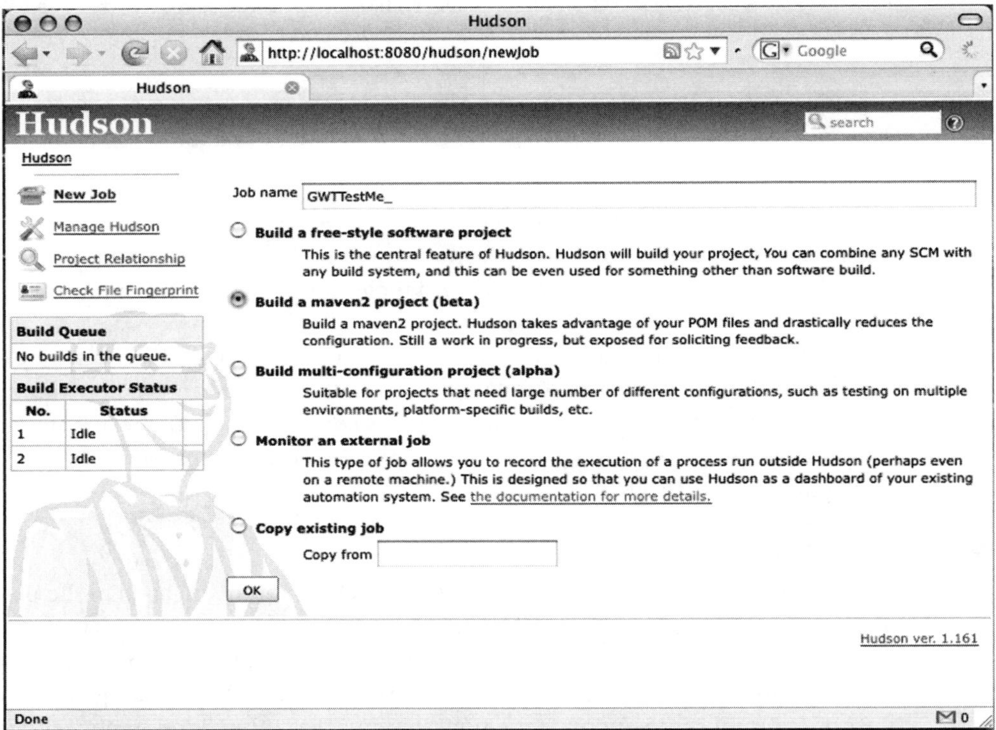

Figure 8.7 The Hudson New Job creation page

you tell Hudson what directory to run from and where key components are located. Hudson needs to know, for example, where your JDKs are, where Ant and Maven are, and some basic settings such as which mail server to use. You can use different combinations of Java versions and build tools across projects.

After you set up the main configuration, you will want to add a project to Hudson using the New Job link on the Manage Hudson page. Here you give the new project a name and select the type of build you want to use. With the Maven 2 setup we have in place for the GWTTestMe project, we'll use the Build a Maven 2 Project option, which can be seen in figure 8.7.

After you click OK to add the job, follow the bouncing ball to configure it. Even though the Maven 2 automatic support is a beta version in Hudson, it works well in most cases, and it is recommended if your build process is based on Maven 2. If you're not using Maven or you need more granular control, you can use the freestyle build type, which allows you to combine virtually any build process with any source control management (SCM) system. A CI server product generally needs to know, at a minimum, how to get the source code for the project and what command to run to build it. Figure 8.8 shows the top half of the GWTTestMe configuration page.

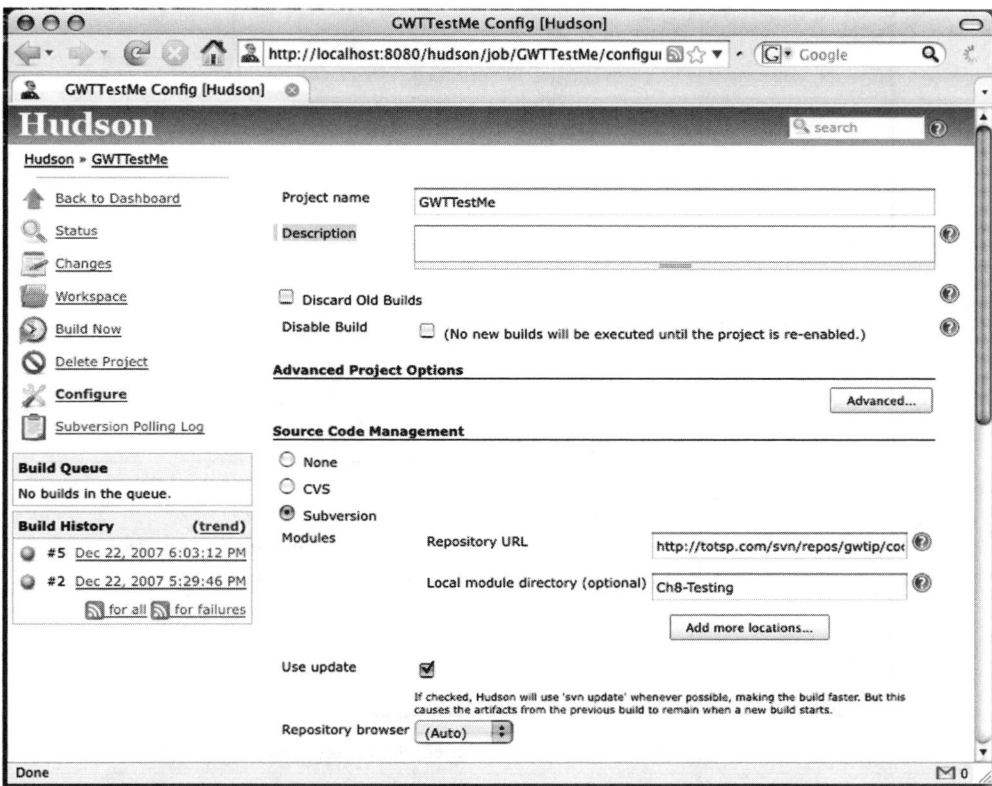

Figure 8.8 The top half of the Hudson job configuration page

In figure 8.8 we're using Subversion (SVN) for source control management, and we've provided the repository URL. Then, in the bottom half of the configuration page, shown in figure 8.9, we set up the remaining options.

In figure 8.9 we have set our CI server to poll our SCM system every five minutes past the hour. This means Hudson will use SVN to check out anything that has changed. If there are changes, then, as the Build information shows, a build will take place using Maven 2, executing the `clean test site` goals. After the build section, we also have set up the email configuration. Through email, we send a notification message to a mailing list that project developers can subscribe to, and we send a note specifically to the person who "broke the build." Using a CI system like this can help motivate developers to keep things in order, in addition to the other benefits it offers.

As you can see, no detailed explanation is required for setting up Hudson itself, or for adding projects, because it's beautifully simple. Once a project is in Hudson, you then use the Hudson Dashboard to view project information and build results.

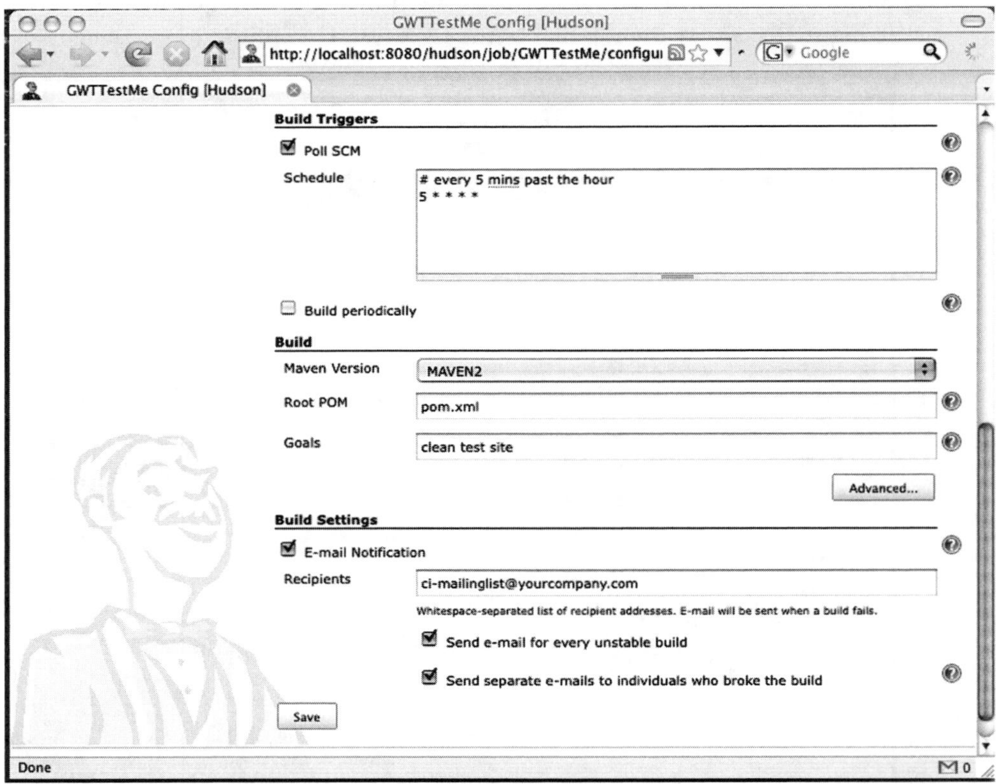

Figure 8.9 The bottom half of the Hudson job configuration page

DISCUSSION

Hudson is not only very easy to set up, it's also quite intuitive to use. From the main Dashboard page, shown in figure 8.10, you can see and select the main items. The build queue and current execution status are shown, as is each configured job or project.

From the Dashboard you can quickly get an idea of the status of all of the projects you have configured. The status of each project is displayed, along with an overall barometer that shows trends—stormy, cloudy, or sunny weather based on the ratio of successful to failed builds. If you click on a project, you can pull up the project details page, as shown in figure 8.11 on page 244.

From the Hudson project details page, you can access all sorts of project information, down to the level of console output as the build runs if you need it. Included here are project status, build history, configuration, change-log, a test results graph, RSS feed links, a Workspace, and more. The project workspace (which by default is the hudson subdirectory of the Hudson user's home directory), contains the files checked out to run the project, and any build artifacts. In the case of Maven, the target directory portion of the workspace, shown in figure 8.12 on page 245, is where the build output, including the site, is located.

With our CI-managed build for the GWTTestMe project, we can see that our process is working, running the tests—both standard and `GWTTestCase`-based—and it's producing metrics. The same reports and artifacts that we saw in section 8.2, when using Maven manually are present in our automated CI build. CI provides a lot of bang

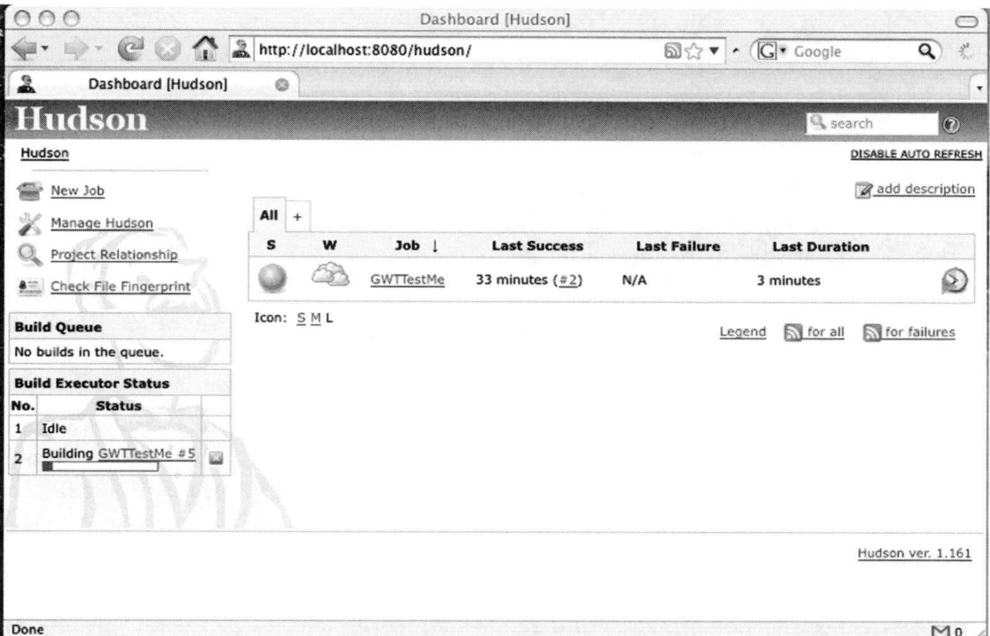

Figure 8.10 The Hudson Dashboard

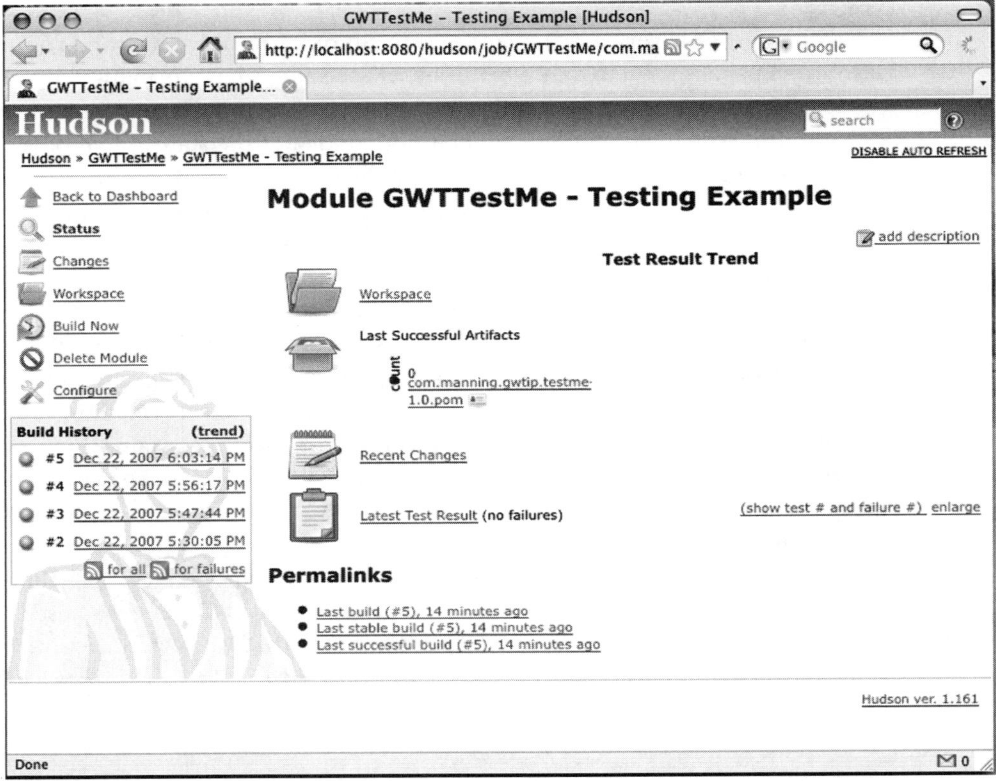

Figure 8.11 The Hudson project details page

for the buck through a seamless continuous process that will gauge the state of the project and alert developers automatically (and maybe more importantly, pester them repeatedly, if needed) when things get out of whack.

There are many more useful aspects of CI in general, and features in Hudson, than we have addressed here, but we have demonstrated the basics of using a CI server with a GWT project. Regardless of whether you use Hudson or other products, such as CruiseControl, Continuum, DamageControl, Bamboo, and the like, you're continually keeping up with changes to your application. Individual components are being integrated in the larger build, and metrics on testing, code coverage, and other aspects of your project are being automatically gathered. This process helps to reduce the effort needed to integrate components later, and it improves overall project quality by keeping the focus on a working, tested build.

8.4 Summary

CI, testing, benchmarks, and related concepts such as capturing project metrics, all revolve around building the best possible software. Testing provides concrete results of what the software does, and it helps you manage change when it inevitably occurs.

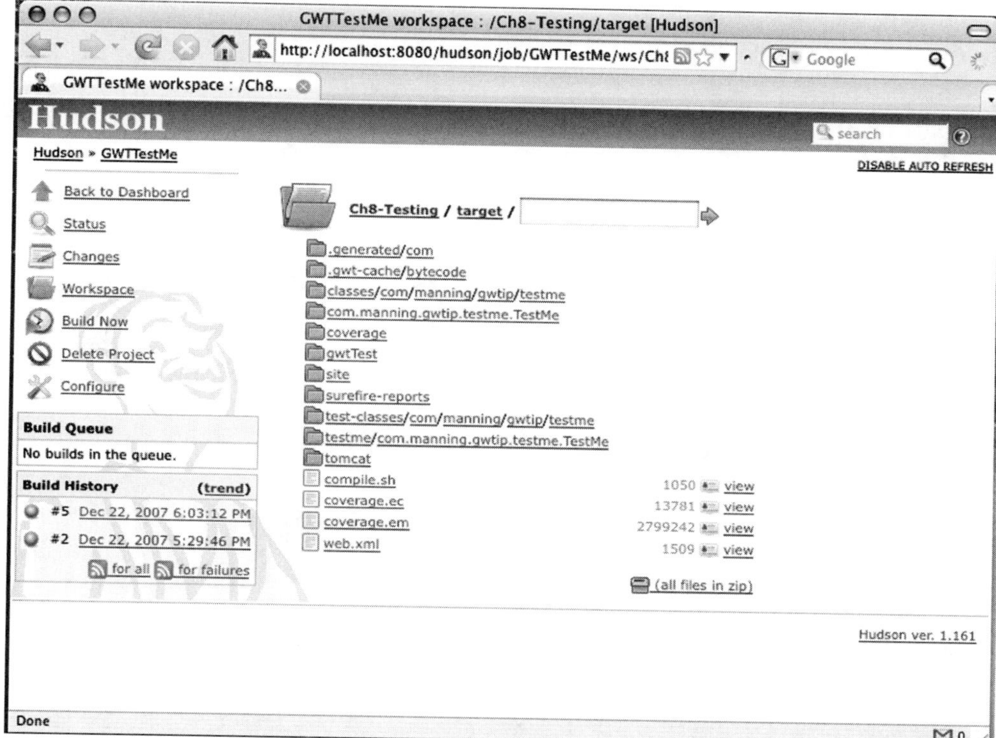

Figure 8.12 The Hudson project Workspace showing the Maven target directory

Benchmarking helps to capture detailed timing metrics across different scenarios. CI overcomes the hurdle of a separate integration phase and ensures that tests, reports, and other metrics such as those obtained with static analysis tools, are present all the time as a sort of thermostat for the overall health of an application. None of these concepts themselves are specific to GWT, but each requires some special treatment and understanding when used with the toolkit.

In this chapter, we have addressed what GWT tests are really meant to do and how they do it. We have covered basic and more involved tests. We have highlighted some undocumented testing aspects, such as how to obtain code-coverage information and how to perform remote testing. Additionally, we have covered how to benchmark a running GWT application. We also put all of these concepts together with an automated, continuously integrated build. In each of these areas, we highlighted where GWT specializations come into play, where GWT is strong, and where it has some failings.

Next, in part 3 of the book, we'll go into some in-depth, code-heavy samples and a larger running application. In this final part of the book, we'll tie together concepts we have already seen, address some common scenarios, and encounter some more advanced GWT concepts.

Part 3

Fully Formed Applications

And now for something completely different. If you are like us, sometimes technology books can seem narrow in focus and lacking in big picture application issues. In this final part, we plan to rectify this. Rather than small code examples, we are going to work with a couple of fully formed applications that will let you see a larger GWT application in practice. It is our intent that you read through these chapters with the project source code available on your computer. We aren't going to cover everything about these applications, but give you a tour of the moving parts so you can see how they fit together.

We aren't skimping on new information here, though. First we will look at a new pattern for working with JPA and using Data Transfer Objects (DTOs) to move from client to server. You will also get some tricks for making your GWT app work in Single Sign-on (SSO) environments, dealing with cookies when communicating with the server, and handling state all through your application.

9 Java Enterprise Reinvented

This chapter covers

- Working with annotation-based JPA models
- Using DTOs for RPC transfer
- Synchronizing between client models and JPA models
- Binding states for complex widgets
- Handling file uploads from the browser

The sciences do not try to explain, they hardly even try to interpret, they mainly make models. By a model is meant a mathematical construct which, with the addition of certain verbal interpretations, describes observed phenomena. The justification of such a mathematical construct is solely and precisely that it is expected to work.

—John von Neumann

To this point you have encountered the details of working with the GWT tools and have seen various techniques for solving engineering problems in your applications. In this final part of the book, we want to do something different. We're going to tour two larger GWT projects—a bookstore application and a screen-sharing application—and look at the techniques, tools, and decisions we made in building them so that you can see more clearly how GWT fits into a larger project scope. As we look at these projects using these applications we will to highlight the important aspects of working with GWT in a Java EE environment.

The first application we're going to create is a basic CRUD application for a bookstore. A screenshot of this application is shown in figure 9.1.

In some ways, this application revisits the concepts we saw in chapter 4, but in a more complete and robust form. If you recall, in chapter 4 we used Hibernate and JPA to insert data into a database. In that instance we were using the most basic configuration: our JPA beans were the same beans we were sending back and forth to the client. While that can be a workable solution in simple scenarios, it also has several drawbacks, which we'll come to in a moment.

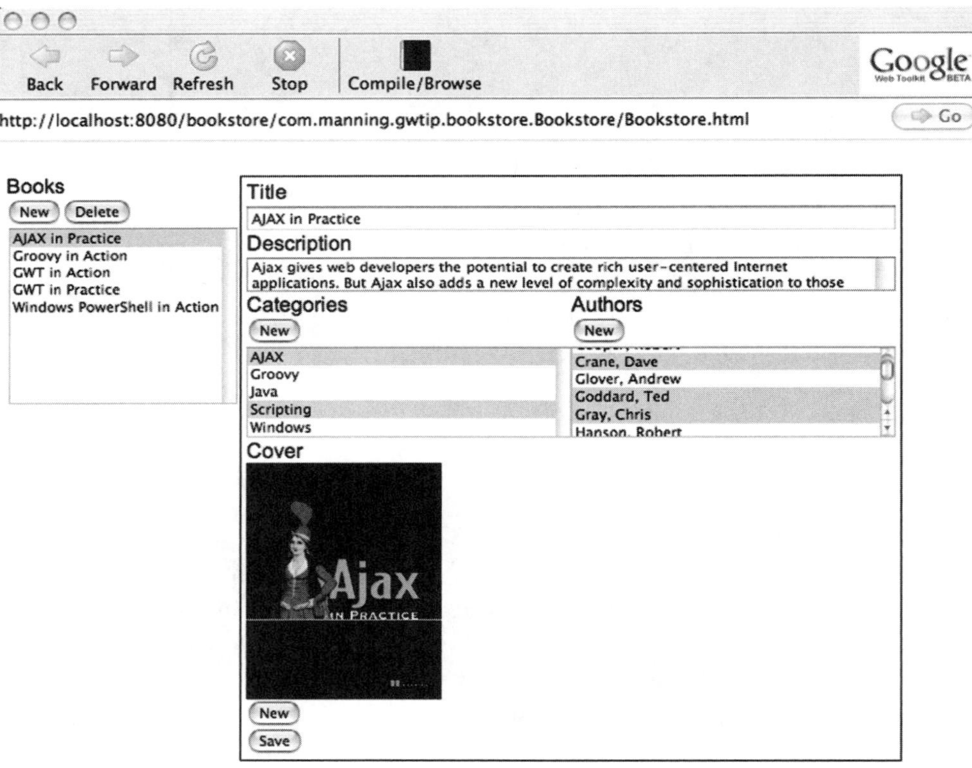

Figure 9.1 The Create-Read-Update-Delete application for our bookstore. Many-to-many relationships between the authors and categories are maintained with select boxes and options to create new entries.

In the next section, we'll extend the JPA and GWT approach we introduced in chapter 4 to include a DTO layer, and we'll use that technique to create our bookstore CRUD application. This, coupled with MVC and the `PropertyChangeSupport` class we saw in other examples is the pattern we have found to be most useful in building GWT applications.

9.1 Constructing two models

In order to directly use JPA entities with GWT, as we did in chapter 4, you have to maintain a potentially unwieldy XML configuration (orm.xml), because GWT does not yet support annotations. And even in the future, when GWT does support Java 5 syntax and annotations (which is the plan for GWT 1.5), JPA entities will still not always serialize. This is the killer: regardless of the metadata approach that is used, annotations or not, serialization of JPA entities to the GWT client will break down in some scenarios. Specifically, entities that have lazy loaded properties on objects, or lazy loaded collections, are often instrumented in one manner or another under the covers by the various ORM (Object-Relational Mapping) frameworks. You can't tell that these objects are not POJOs at build time, but when GWT inspects them at runtime and tries to serialize them, it gets ugly and does not work.

To address these issues, we'll construct an ordinary JPA-annotated model for our application, one that we'll use to store and retrieve information from the database. Then we'll mirror our JPA model with a DTO layer for use with GWT. Listing 9.1 shows our `Book` class with the appropriate annotations.

Listing 9.1 The `Book` server-side class with JPA annotations

```
@Entity
@NamedQueries( {
        @NamedQuery(
        name = "Book.findBookById",
        query = "SELECT b FROM Book b " +
                "WHERE " +
                "    b.id = :id"),
        @NamedQuery(
        name = "Book.findBooksByCategory",
        query = "SELECT b FROM Book b, IN(b.categories) c " +
                "WHERE " +
                "    c.name = :name"),
        @NamedQuery(
        name = "Book.findBooksByAuthor",
        query = "SELECT b FROM Book b, IN(b.authors) a " +
                "WHERE " +
                "    a.id = :id"),
        @NamedQuery(
        name = "Book.findAllBooks",
        query = "SELECT b FROM Book b ORDER BY b.title")
        })
public class Book extends AbstractModelBean {
```

❶ Define named queries to use in DAO

```
private Integer id;
private String title;
private List<Author> authors;
private String description;
private String image;
private List<Review> reviews;
private List<Category> categories;

public Book() {
    super();
}

@Id
@GeneratedValue(strategy=GenerationType.AUTO)
public Integer getId() {
    return id;
}

public void setId(Integer id) {
    this.id = id;
}

public String getTitle() {
    return title;
}

public void setTitle(String title) {
    this.title = title;
}

@ManyToMany(cascade=CascadeType.ALL)
public List<Author> getAuthors() {
    return authors;
}

public void setAuthors(List<Author> authors) {
    this.authors = authors;
}

@Lob
public String getDescription() {
    return description;
}

public void setDescription(String description) {
    this.description = description;
}

public String getImage() {
    return image;
}

public void setImage(String image) {
    this.image = image;
}

public List<Review> getReviews() {
    return reviews;
}
```

Use annotations this time!

```
    public void setReviews(List<Review> reviews) {
        this.reviews = reviews;
    }

    public float calculateRating() {      <-- Create business method
        float total = 0;
        for (Review r : this.getReviews()){
            total += (float) r.getRating();
        }
        return this.getReviews() == null ||
            this.getReviews().isEmpty() ? 0 :
            (float) Math.round(
                total * 10f / (float) this.getReviews().size() )
                / 10f;
    }

    @ManyToMany(cascade=CascadeType.ALL)
    public List<Category> getCategories() {
        return categories;
    }

    public void setCategories(List<Category> categories) {
        this.categories = categories;
    }
```

This is all pretty standard JPA stuff. We have all our JPA information in the beans, rather than in the mappings file we used in chapter 4. We're creating a set of `NamedQueries` for the common lookups we'll need for our beans ❶, and we're creating one smart method on our bean for calculating the rating. We won't worry about that right now. You'll see where it comes into play in the next chapter.

This bean obviously can't be used by the GWT service interface because it doesn't implement one of the GWT serialization interfaces and it uses annotations, which means it isn't compatible with the GWT serialization mechanism. Moreover, it doesn't support the `PropertyChangeEvents` we'll want to wire up to the user interface on the client side. So, we'll create a new bean that maps directly to the `Book` class in listing 9.1, but it will be GWT-enabled and will be copied into our client package structure. Listing 9.2 shows the client-side version of the `Book` class.

Listing 9.2 The client-side `Book` class with property-change support

```
public class Book implements IsSerializable {      <-- Make wire transferable
    /**
     * @gwt.typeArgs
     * <com.manning.gwtip.bookstore.client.model.Author>      <-- Provide typeArgs hints for serialization
     */
    private List authors;

    /**
     * @gwt.typeArgs <com.manning.gwtip.bookstore.client.model.Category>
     */
    private List categories;
    private String description = "";
    private Integer id;
```

```
private String image;

/**
 * @gwt.typeArgs <com.manning.gwtip.bookstore.client.model.Review>
 */
private List reviews;
private String title = "";
private transient PropertyChangeSupport changes =
    new
        PropertyChangeSupport(                         <-- Define transient
            this);                                         PropertyChangeSupport

/**
 * @gwt.typeArgs newValue
 *   <com.manning.gwtip.bookstore.client.model.Author>
 */
public void setAuthors(List newValue) {
    List oldValue = this.authors;
    this.authors = newValue;
    this.changes.firePropertyChange(
        "authors", oldValue, newValue);
}

/**
 * @gwt.typeArgs <com.manning.gwtip.bookstore.client.model.Author>
 */
public List getAuthors() {
    return this.authors;
}

/**
 * @gwt.typeArgs newValue
 *   <com.manning.gwtip.bookstore.client.model.Category>
 */
public void setCategories(java.util.List newValue) {
    List oldValue = this.categories;
    this.categories = newValue;
    this.changes.firePropertyChange(
        "categories", oldValue, newValue);
}

/**
 * @gwt.typeArgs <com.manning.gwtip.bookstore.client.model.Category>
 */
public List getCategories() {
    return this.categories;
}

public void setDescription(String newValue) {
    String oldValue = this.description;
    this.description = newValue;
    this.changes.firePropertyChange(
        "description", oldValue, newValue);
}

public String getDescription() {
    return this.description;
}
```

```
public void setId(Integer newValue) {
    Integer oldValue = this.id;
    this.id = newValue;
    this.changes.firePropertyChange("id", oldValue, newValue);
}

public Integer getId() {
    return this.id;
}

public void setImage(String newValue) {
    String oldValue = this.image;
    this.image = newValue;
    this.changes.firePropertyChange(
        "image", oldValue, newValue);
}

public String getImage() {
    return this.image;
}

public PropertyChangeListener[] allPropertyChangeListeners() {
    return changes.getPropertyChangeListeners();
}

/**
 * @gwt.typeArgs newValue
 *   <com.manning.gwtip.bookstore.client.model.Review>
 */
public void setReviews(List newValue) {
    List oldValue = this.reviews;
    this.reviews = newValue;
    this.changes.firePropertyChange(
        "reviews", oldValue, newValue);
}

/**
 * @gwt.typeArgs <com.manning.gwtip.bookstore.client.model.Review>
 */
public List getReviews() {
    return this.reviews;
}

public void setTitle(String newValue) {
    String oldValue = this.title;
    this.title = newValue;
    this.changes.firePropertyChange(
        "title", oldValue, newValue);
}

public String getTitle() {
    return this.title;
}

public void addPropertyChangeListener(
    PropertyChangeListener l) {
    changes.addPropertyChangeListener(l);
}
```

Create listener methods needed

```
        public void addPropertyChangeListener(
            String propertyName, PropertyChangeListener l) {
            changes.addPropertyChangeListener(propertyName, l);
        }
        public void removePropertyChangeListener(PropertyChangeListener l) {
            changes.removePropertyChangeListener(l);
        }
        public void removePropertyChangeListener(
            String propertyName, PropertyChangeListener l) {
            changes.removePropertyChangeListener(propertyName, l);
        }
    }
```

Now we have a set of JPA beans we can share with other projects, and a set of client DTO beans for use in our GWT application. But that's a lot of code to create, and a lot of places fat-finger errors can introduce bugs.

Is there a great solution to this? Well, not really. Yet one good solution is to generate the DTOs from a core set of beans, which is the approach we have taken for the applications we developed in our GWT work. The GWT-Maven plugin includes a goal that will generate your client-side beans for you using reflection to traverse a graph of beans. In either the Maven 1 or Maven 2 plugin, this can be invoked with the `gwt:generateClientBeans` goal. If you choose to generate GWT client beans using GWT-Maven, there are a set of options you need to configure, as shown in table 9.1.

Like in chapter 4, the use of `PropertyChangeSupport` requires a third-party implementation, such as that from GWTx (http://code.google.com/p/gwtx/). The Maven goals depend on two things. First, you're using Java 5 generics for collection mapping. These will be converted properly to `gwt.typeArgs` notation for child classes. Second, that there is a compiled version of the classes available in your project when you run. This means you should run `maven java:compile` or `mvn compile` before calling the `gwt:generateClientBeans` goal.

Table 9.1 Settings for `generateClientBeans` in Maven 1 and Maven 2. Analogs are supported in each version to control the code that's generated.

Maven 1 properties	Maven 2 plugin configuration	Description
`google.webtoolkit.generateGettersAndSetters`	`generateGetters-AndSetters`	Toggles generation of getters and setters.
`google.webtoolkit.generateProperty-ChangeSupport`	`generate-Property-ChangeSupport`	Adds `PropertyChange-Support` to the beans; implies `generateGettersAndSetters`.
`google.webtoolkit.generatorRootClasses`	`generator-RootClasses`	Specifies a comma-separated list of classes to begin graph examination.
`google.webtoolkit.generatorDestination-Package`	`generator-Destination-Package`	Specifies the destination package for the generated beans.

Why do all this? Well, here we're using JPA beans, but these beans might be generated classes from JAX-WS, JAX-RPC, or Axis for talking to backend web services. These could be shared objects from a larger server application that don't support change events or require constructs that are not supported by the GWT JRE emulation library. Also, it's often a fact of life that a persistence model does not map directly to what a client application needs. By using a DTO layer, you can control what is sent to the client. (Having different models can cut back on the usefulness of generating the DTO classes, but it's another option that allows you finer-grained control.)

In general, this approach provides a clean isolation between your GWT code and the backend code for your application. While it does bloat your code base, the generation of DTOs can generally be automated. Since the JPA model can only be used in the scope of the server, we'll need a way to map the DTO model objects to the JPA model. This can be automated as well.

9.2 Mapping to DTOs

The next class we need to examine is the RPC service itself. GWT RPC services should be old hat for you by now, but we're going to add a couple of new elements to the mix to support conversion between the local model and the remote DTO model.

First, we need to map between the beans our local service implementation knows and the client beans we use in the GWT application. This will allow us to send the information from the database to our client application. To handle this in the Bookstore application, we're using another custom class called `BeanMapping`, which is available from the GWT-Maven site (http://code.google.com/p/gwt-maven). This class is a simple recursive mapper that will map between similarly named properties or attributes on Java classes. Listing 9.3 shows its use in the `BookstoreServiceServlet` class.

Listing 9.3 `BookstoreServiceServlet` with server-side GWT-RPC communication

```
public class BookstoreServiceServlet
   extends RemoteServiceServlet
   implements com.manning.gwtip.bookstore.client.remote.BookstoreService {
    private BookstoreService service;
    private Properties mappingProperties = new Properties();

    public BookstoreServiceServlet() {
        super();
        mappingProperties.setProperty(
        "com.manning.gwtip.bookstore.model.*",
        "com.manning.gwtip.bookstore.client.model.*");
    }

    public void init(ServletConfig config) throws ServletException {
        super.init(config);

        BeanFactory factory =
               WebApplicationContextUtils.getWebApplicationContext(
                     config.getServletContext());
```

❶ Specify mappings between the model packages

Retrieve Spring application context

```
    this.service =
          (BookstoreService)
           factory.getBean("BookstoreService");
}

public void deleteBook(Book book) throws BookstoreRemoteException {
    try {
        service.deleteBook(
          (com.manning.gwtip.bookstore.model.Book)
              BeanMapping
              .convert(mappingProperties, book)
        );
    } catch(Exception e) {
        throw new BookstoreRemoteException(e.toString());
    }
}

public List findAllBooks() throws BookstoreRemoteException {
    try {
        List serverBooks = service.findAllBooks();
        List clientBooks = new ArrayList();

        for (Object o : serverBooks) {
            clientBooks.add(
                BeanMapping.convert(
                               mappingProperties,
                               o)
            );
        }

        return clientBooks;
    } catch(Exception e) {
        throw new BookstoreRemoteException(e.toString());
    }
}

public Book findBookById(int bookId)
    throws BookstoreRemoteException {
    try {
        return (Book)
           BeanMapping.convert(mappingProperties,
            service.findBookById(bookId)
           );
    } catch(Exception e) {
        throw new BookstoreRemoteException(e.toString());
    }
}

public List findBooksByCategory(String categoryName)
    throws BookstoreRemoteException {
    try {
        List serverBooks = service.findBooksByCategory(categoryName);
        List clientBooks = new ArrayList();

        for (Object o : serverBooks) {
            clientBooks.add(BeanMapping
               .convert(mappingProperties, o));
        }
```

Retrieve service implementation

Convert DTOs and JPA beans

Map between objects in collections

```
            return clientBooks;
        } catch(Exception e) {
            throw new BookstoreRemoteException(e.toString());
        }
    }

    public Book storeBook(Book book) throws BookstoreRemoteException {
        try {
            return (Book) BeanMapping.convert(mappingProperties,
                service.storeBook(
                    (com.manning.gwtip.bookstore.model.Book)
                    BeanMapping.convert(
                        mappingProperties, book)));
        } catch(Exception e) {
            e.printStackTrace();
            throw new BookstoreRemoteException(e.toString());
        }
    }

    /* Some methods omitted for brevity */
}
```

Compared to what you might have expected would be required to map between the two object packages, this isn't that bad. First, we create the mapping properties. Using the wildcard notation, this says "map all the classes in `com.manning.gwtip.bookstore.model` to the similarly named classes in `com.manning.gwtip.bookstore.client.model`" ❶. You could also specify individual classes if you wanted multiple representations or summary or short form representations of your classes mapped. The `BeanMapping` class won't complain about properties on one object that are not present on the other. If you want to specify an alternative mapping for a specific class, you can simply map the class explicitly, like this:

```
mappingProperties.setProperty(
            "com.manning.gwtip.bookstore.model.ClassA",
            "com.manning.gwtip.bookstore.client.model.ClassB");
```

We find that the simple `BeanMapping` class does the job 90 percent of the time. Nevertheless, if you need more advanced mapping—for instance, if you're using different nongenerated DTO classes for more control—one option is the Dozer library (http://dozer.sourceforge.net). Dozer provides a much more sophisticated bean-mapping system, but it also requires more setup to use. When using Dozer, you need to create an XML config file that explicitly maps each bean to its counterpart. Here's an example:

```
<?xml version="1.0" encoding="UTF-8"?>
  <!DOCTYPE mappings PUBLIC "-//DOZER//DTD MAPPINGS//EN"
    "http://dozer.sourceforge.net/dtd/dozerbeanmapping.dtd">
<mappings>
  <mapping wildcard="true">
    <class-a>com.manning.gwtip.bookstore.model.Book</class-a>
    <class-b>com.manning.gwtip.bookstore.model.client.Book</class-b>
  </mapping>
  <mapping wildcard="true">
    <class-a>com.manning.gwtip.bookstore.model.Category</class-a>
```

```
    <class-b>com.manning.gwtip.bookstore.model.client.Category</class-b>
  </mapping>
  <!-- ... -->
</mappings>
```

While this seems like a lot of work just to get going, Dozer's advantages stand out if you need to map a complex graph of objects to a more simple one. For instance, if you're flattening a complex internal model to simple DTO objects, you can use the dot notation to map deep properties to shallow ones:

```
<mapping>
  <class-a
   map-null="false">com.manning.gwtip.bookstore.model.Book</class-a>
  <class-b>com.manning.gwtip.bookstore.model.Book</class-b>
  <field>
    <a>author.name</a>
    <b>authorName</b>
  </field>
</mapping>
```

The dot notation specifying `<a>author.name</a>` will extract the `name` property of the `author` property of the root bean and map it to the `authorName` property on the secondary bean. Specifying `map-null="false"` simply causes the mapping to be skipped if the author property of `com.manning.gwtip.model.Book` is `null`.

Dozer has a great deal more functionality including, but not limited to, type mapping (between strings and dates, number types, and so on), customizable factory settings, XMLBeans and JAXB object support, and Spring integration. If you're working with a complex legacy API, it can be a great tool for keeping your GWT DTOs clean and minimalist.

Speaking of Spring integration, this is what we'll look at next.

9.3 Wiring applications with Spring

Spring is all the rage. While Java EE 5 is, in our opinion, also very capable on its own for most tasks, it's still a new kid on the block in terms of Java application frameworks. You may have a large investment in Spring technologies in your enterprise or application, so understanding how Spring relates to your GWT application is important. We'll backtrack a bit and start by looking at the DAO classes for our Bookstore model, then how they are wired into the local service implementation with Spring.

Listing 9.4 shows a sample from the `BookDAO` class. This is really a utility class that wraps the JPA calls and the named queries we added to the `Book` object in section 9.1.

Listing 9.4 The `BookDAO` class wraps JPA calls used for retrieving and persisting books

```
public class BookDAO extends AbstractDAO {

    public BookDAO() {
        super();
    }
```

```
public Book store(Book book){
    EntityManager em =
        this.getEntityManagerFactory()          ❶ Defined in
                            .createEntityManager();   AbstractDAO object
    try {
        em.getTransaction().begin();

        for (int i=0;
                book.getCategories() != null &&
            i < book.getCategories().size();
            i++) {
            try {
                book.getCategories().set(i,            ❷ Loop categories
                    em.merge(                            and merged
                        book.getCategories()             objects
                            .get(i))
                    );
            } catch (Exception e) {
                    e.printStackTrace();
                    em.persist(book.getCategories().get(i));
            }
        }

        if (book.getId() == null) {        Check whether creating
            em.persist( book );            or updating book
        } else {
            book = em.merge(book);
        }
        em.getTransaction().commit();
    } finally {
        if (em != null) {
            em.close();
        }
    }
    return book;
}

public Book findBookById(int bookId){
    EntityManager em = this.getEntityManagerFactory()
                            .createEntityManager();
    try {
        em.getTransaction().begin();
        Query q = em.createNamedQuery("Book.findBookById");
        q.setParameter("id", bookId);
        return (Book) q.getSingleResult();
    } catch (NoResultException e) {
        return null;
    } finally {
        if (em != null) {
            em.getTransaction().commit();
            em.close();
        }
    }
}

public List<Book> findAllBooks(){
    EntityManager em = this.getEntityManagerFactory()
```

```
                                  .createEntityManager();
        try {
            em.getTransaction().begin();
            Query q = em.createNamedQuery("Book.findAllBooks");
            return q.getResultList();

        } finally {
            if (em != null) {
                em.getTransaction().commit();
                em.close();
            }
        }
    }

    public List<Book> findBooksByCategory(String categoryName) {
        EntityManager em = this.getEntityManagerFactory()
                                  .createEntityManager();
        try {
            em.getTransaction().begin();
            Query q = em.createNamedQuery("Book.findBooksByCategory");
            q.setParameter("name", categoryName);
            return q.getResultList();

        } finally {
            if (em != null) {
                em.getTransaction().commit();
                em.close();
            }
        }
    }

    // Some methods omitted

    public void delete(Book book){
        EntityManager em = this.getEntityManagerFactory()
                                  .createEntityManager();
        try {
            em.getTransaction().begin();
            book.setCategories(null);     <-- Clear categories
            book = em.merge(book);        ❸ for deletion
            em.remove(book);

        } finally {
            if (em != null) {
                em.getTransaction().commit();
                em.close();
            }
        }
    }
}
```

This is a fairly standard DAO approach. The one special case we're dealing with is categories. Here we want cascading categories, but we don't want to remove the 1...n relationships or end up with duplicates. To ensure this, we look through them and merge or create categories during the store action ❷, and we remove the relationship but not the categories on deletion ❸. The calls to `getEntityManagerFactory()` are referencing the parent AbstractDAO class ❶. The EntityManagerFactory could be injected by Java EE 5, or Spring, to make the example code simpler, but we're getting it the old-fashioned way by referencing the persistence unit. The rest of the service infrastructure we'll wire up with Spring.

Now that we have our DAO layer for the server-side model, we need to create the service and inject the appropriate DAOs into it. Listing 9.5 shows the applicationContext.xml file we'll use.

Listing 9.5 The Spring configuration file wiring the DAOs to the service bean

```
<?xml version="1.0" encoding="UTF-8"?>
<beans xmlns="http://www.springframework.org/schema/beans"
  xmlns:xsi="http://www.w3.org/2001/XMLSchema-instance"
  xsi:schemaLocation="http://www.springframework.org/schema/beans
    http://www.springframework.org/schema/beans/spring-beans.xsd">
  <bean id="authorDAO"
        class="com.manning.gwtip.bookstore.model.dao.AuthorDAO"/>
  <bean id="bookDAO"
        class="com.manning.gwtip.bookstore.model.dao.BookDAO"/>
  <bean id="categoryDAO"
        class="com.manning.gwtip.bookstore.model.dao.CategoryDAO"/>
  <bean id="bookstoreService"
        class="com.manning.gwtip.bookstore.service.BookstoreServiceImpl">
     <constructor-arg>
       <ref bean="authorDAO" />
     </constructor-arg>
     <constructor-arg>
       <ref bean="bookDAO" />
     </constructor-arg>
     <constructor-arg>
       <ref bean="categoryDAO" />
     </constructor-arg>
   </bean>
</beans>
```

Inject DAOs into service bean

Once the service instance is wired up, we initialize the Spring context using the ContextListener declaration in the web.xml file in listing 9.6.

Listing 9.6 The web.xml file loads the Spring context

```
<?xml version="1.0" encoding="UTF-8"?>
<web-app xmlns="http://java.sun.com/xml/ns/j2ee"
         xmlns:xsi="http://www.w3.org/2001/XMLSchema-instance"
        version="2.4"
        xsi:schemaLocation="http://java.sun.com/xml/ns/j2ee
                  http://java.sun.com/xml/ns/j2ee/web-app_2_4.xsd">
    <description>GWTIP JPA Example</description>
    <display-name>GWT Bookstore</display-name>
    <distributable />
    <context-param>
        <param-name>contextConfigLocation</param-name>
        <param-value>
```

```
            /WEB-INF/applicationContext.xml        <-- Specify
        </param-value>                                 applicationContext.xml
    </context-param>                                   file (listing 9.5)

    <listener>
        <listener-class>
  org.springframework.web.context.ContextLoaderListener   <-- Register standard
            </listener-class>                                 Spring context
    </listener>                                               loader
</web-app>
```

There are several things you likely noticed here. First, we get the service reference into the `RemoteServiceServlet`. At the top of listing 9.3, we retrieve the Spring context factory manually from the `ServletContext` as the servlet is initialized. While it's possible to use Spring to configure your GWT servlet instances into the web context, you'll lose the implicit mapping and packaging advantages. Of course, the GWT `RemoteServiceServlet` is still not declared in the web.xml, which brings us to the second point.

We once again need to merge our configuration for a deployable WAR file. This can be done manually or, as was discussed in chapter 7, we can take advantage of GWT-Maven, which includes goals that can automatically merge the servlet declarations from the module descriptor into the web.xml file while the WAR deliverable is being built.

For the Spring purist, this might seem less than desirable: having a Spring and non-Spring portion of your application deployment. Another option is to use the GWT-SL Spring wrappers (available from http://gwt-widget.sourceforge.net). These provide two different options for wrapping GWT servlets. The first is the `GWTRPCServiceExporter`, an example of which is shown in listing 9.7.

Listing 9.7 `GWTRPCServiceExporter` in an applicationContext.xml file

```
<bean id="MyPOJO"
  class="org.gwtwidgets.server.spring.GWTRPCServiceExporter">
    <property name="service" ref="MyPOJO" />
    <property name="serviceInterfaces">           <-- (1) Use serviceInterfaces
        <value>                                           if it's a POJO
            com.me.my.service.MyInterface
        </value>
    </property>
</bean>
<bean
  class="org.springframework.web.servlet.handler.SimpleUrlHandlerMapping">
    <property name="mappings">
        <map>                                          (2) Map service
            <entry key="/MyService"                        to a URL
                value-ref="MyPOJOService" />      <--
        </map>
    </property>
</bean>
```

This will take your POJO and use CGLIB to generate a wrapper servlet for it (1). You can then use the Spring `SimpleUrlHandlerMapping` to map it to a URL (2).

You can, alternatively, use the `GWTHandler` to wrap and deploy your beans in a single step. Listing 9.8 demonstrates doing this in the applicationContext.xml file.

Listing 9.8 Using the `GWTHandler` to export services

```
<bean id="urlMapping" class="org.gwtwidgets.server.spring.GWTHandler">
    <property name="mappings">
        <map>
            <entry key="/MyService" value-ref="MyPOJO" />
        </map>
    </property>
</bean>
```

This simply does in a single step what we did in two in listing 9.7. This method comes with a caveat, however. Because of the wrapping in this step, all exceptions thrown will become `InvocationExceptions`. You'll lose your custom service exceptions.

It's important to remember that even when using this Spring-configured service, you still will want an internal and external service that maps between different object models, so this doesn't save you much time. Because, in the end, the RPC servlet is usually a thin veneer over a completely configured Spring service, we find simply using the integrated GWT-Maven deployment process to be easier in many cases. Figure 9.2 shows the relationship between the server-side model objects and service and the client-side model. Notice that there are almost two mirror-image groupings, which reflect this translation through the RPC servlet layer.

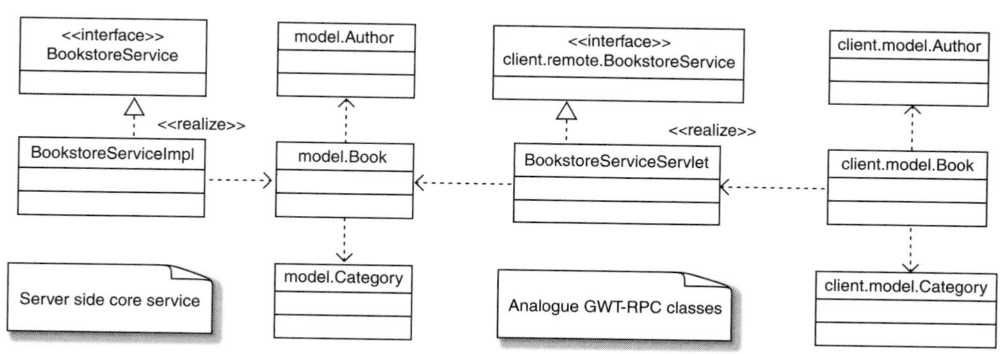

Figure 9.2 The local service and local model matches the remote model, with the `BookstoreServiceServlet` translating between the two using the `BeanMapping` class

Now we have toured the backend of our CRUD application: the two backend models, the service-exposure mapping between the two, and the Spring-configured service layer. We need a front end for all of this, which we'll look at next.

9.4 Constructing the client application

As we have demonstrated in earlier examples, the client application will represent its own MVC pattern. In the first section of this chapter, we constructed the DTOs that will make up the backbone of the model. In this section, we'll take a look at the classes that make up the rest of the application.

First we need to create our core model and the controller, which calls into the service.

9.4.1 The controller and global model

The controller and model likely seem pretty familiar to you by now, so we'll move through them quickly and look at some of the techniques we used for building the editor UI.

First we need a model that can hold the global level information. Since we have three major types that we want to keep track of independently, we'll make each of them an observable property on the `ModelState` singleton in listing 9.9.

Listing 9.9 The `ModelState` singleton class holds the global model object

```
public class ModelState {

    private PropertyChangeSupport changes =
       new PropertyChangeSupport(this);
    private List books;
    private List authors;
    private List categories;
    private static ModelState instance;

    private ModelState() {
        super();
    }

    public static ModelState getInstance() {
        return (instance == null) ?
           instance = new ModelState() : instance;
    }

    public void addPropertyChangeListener(PropertyChangeListener l) {
        changes.addPropertyChangeListener(l);
    }
    public void addPropertyChangeListener(String property,
        PropertyChangeListener l){
        changes.addPropertyChangeListener(property, l);
    }
    public void removePropertyChangeListener(PropertyChangeListener l) {
        changes.removePropertyChangeListener(l);
    }
    public void removePropertyChangeListener(String property,
        PropertyChangeListener l) {
        changes.removePropertyChangeListener(property, l);
    }

    public void clearPropertyChangeListeners() {
        PropertyChangeListener[] listeners =
            changes.getPropertyChangeListeners();
        for (int i=0; listeners != null && i < listeners.length; i++) {
            this.removePropertyChangeListener(listeners[i]);
```

```
            }
        }

        public List getCategories() {
            return categories;
        }

        public void setCategories(List categories) {
            this.categories =
                (categories == null)?
                    new ArrayList() :
                    categories;
            changes.firePropertyChange("categories",
                null, this.categories);
        }

        public void setBooks(List books) {
            this.books = (books == null) ? new ArrayList() : books;
            changes.firePropertyChange("books",
                null, this.books);
        }

        public List getAuthors() {
            return authors;
        }

        public List getBooks() {
            return books;
        }

        public void setAuthors(List authors) {
            this.authors = (authors == null) ? new ArrayList() : authors;
            changes.firePropertyChange("authors", null, this.authors);
        }
    }
```

Short circuit equality check on nulls

What is worth noting here is that we always pass in `null` to the `firePropertyChange` methods on the collection setters. Since we're not doing two-way binding on these, we don't need them, and this just lets us ensure the change events will fire when we want them to in the model.

Next we'll move on to the `Controller` class. This is, for the most part, a simple pass-through to the RPC services, with updates to the model. Listing 9.10 shows the `Controller` class and how it calls to the `BookstoreService`.

Listing 9.10 The `Controller` class updating the model as needed

```
public class Controller {

    private static Controller instance;
    private BookstoreServiceAsync service =
            (BookstoreServiceAsync) GWT.create(BookstoreService.class);
    private ModelState model =
        ModelState.getInstance();

    private Controller() {
        super();
```

Get service reference

Get model reference

```
        ServiceDefTarget endpoint = (ServiceDefTarget) service;
        endpoint.setServiceEntryPoint(GWT.getModuleBaseURL() +
                                       "/BookstoreService");
    }

    public static Controller getInstance() {
        return (instance == null) ?
            instance = new Controller() :
            instance;
    }

    public void updateCategories() {
        service.findAllCategories(new AsyncCallback() {
            public void onSuccess(Object result) {
                model.setCategories((List) result);
            }

            public void onFailure(Throwable caught) {
                Window.alert("There was an error " +
                             "retrieving the category list.");
                GWT.log("Exception from service", caught);
            }
        });
    }

    public void deleteBook(Book b) {
        service.deleteBook(b, new AsyncCallback() {
            public void onSuccess(Object object) {
                findAllBooks();
            }

            public void onFailure(Throwable throwable) {
                Window.alert("Failure");
                GWT.log("Exception from service", throwable);
            }
        });
    }

    public void storeBook(Book book){
        service.storeBook(book, new AsyncCallback() {
            public void onSuccess(Object result) {
                Window.alert("Success");
                findAllBooks();
            }

            public void onFailure(Throwable caught) {
                Window.alert("Failure");
                GWT.log("Exception from service", caught);
            }
        });
    }

    public void findAllAuthors() {
        service.findAllAuthors(new AsyncCallback() {
            public void onSuccess(Object object) {
                model.setAuthors((List) object);
            }
```

❶ **Refresh list on updates**

```
            public void onFailure(Throwable throwable) {
                GWT.log("Exception getting books", throwable);
                Window.alert("Failed to retrieve author list.");
            }
        });
    }

    public void findAllBooks() {
        service.findAllBooks(new AsyncCallback() {
            public void onSuccess(Object object) {
                model.setBooks((List) object);
            }

            public void onFailure(Throwable throwable) {
                GWT.log("Exception getting books", throwable);
                Window.alert("Failed to retrieve book list.");
            }
        });
    }
}
```

The error handling here is, admittedly, simplistic. The important thing to note is the flexibility we have with this design. Although we're using `findAllBooks()` as the default list strategy here because the model and view are sufficiently isolated, we could easily add result-chunking to the `findAllBooks()` method. Our view simply shows the books on the `ModelState` object in listing 9.9 and listens for changes. Also notice that on store and delete calls we're refreshing the book list ❶. This doesn't have to happen in real time because of the asynchronous nature of the application, but it keeps the user's list of books up to date after changes are made.

Now that this layer is in place, we'll shift to building the user interface. This involves several bound components and a couple of cautionary tales.

9.4.2 *The basic CRUD wrapper*

Your basic CRUD application has four functions. On the outer layer, your UI requirements consist of generating a list of records to view or edit, the ability to delete an existing record, and create a new record. You can see this outer-layer functionality in figure 9.3.

To enclose this basic functionality, we use the `AdminPanel` class shown in listing 9.11. It's a simple set of widgets with bindings to the model and controller where appropriate.

Listing 9.11 The `AdminPanel` class encapsulating the basic CRUD functionality

```
public class AdminPanel extends HorizontalPanel {
    private static final BookstoreConstants CONSTANTS =
       (BookstoreConstants) GWT.create(BookstoreConstants.class);   <- Get internationalization constants
    private Book book;
    private BookEdit edit;
    private Button deleteBook =
        new Button(CONSTANTS.delete());   <- Create widgets using constants
```

```
private Button newBook = new Button(CONSTANTS.create());
private HorizontalPanel buttons = new HorizontalPanel();
private ListBox select = new ListBox();
private ModelState model = ModelState.getInstance();
private PropertyChangeListener bookListener =
    new PropertyChangeListenerProxy("books",
      new PropertyChangeListener() {
        public void propertyChange(
               PropertyChangeEvent propertyChangeEvent) {
            List books = (List) propertyChangeEvent.getNewValue();
            select.clear();

            for (Iterator it = books.iterator(); it.hasNext();) {
                Book b = (Book) it.next();
                select.addItem(b.getTitle(), b.getId().toString());
            }
        }
    });

private VerticalPanel side = new VerticalPanel();

public AdminPanel() {
    this.setStyleName("adminPanel");
    side.add(new Label(CONSTANTS.books()));
    buttons.add(newBook);
    buttons.add(deleteBook);
    side.add(buttons);
    newBook.addClickListener(new ClickListener() {
            public void onClick(Widget widget) {
                if (edit != null) {
                    remove(edit);
                    edit.cleanup();
                }

                book = new Book();
                edit = new BookEdit(book);
                add(edit);
            }
        });
    deleteBook.addClickListener(new ClickListener() {
            public void onClick(Widget widget) {
                Controller.getInstance()
                    .deleteBook(book);

                if (edit != null) {
                    remove(edit);
                    edit.cleanup();
                }
            }
        });
    model.addPropertyChangeListener(bookListener);
    select.addChangeListener(new ChangeListener() {
            public void onChange(Widget widget) {
                if (edit != null) {
                    remove(edit);
                    edit.cleanup();
                }
```

1 Bind books to select box

Create new Book

Create BookEdit widget

2 Pass call to controller

Call cleanup to unbind listeners

```
                    If (select.getSelectedIndex() == -1) {
                        return;
                    }

                    book = (Book) model.getBooks()
                                .get(select.getSelectedIndex());
                    edit = new BookEdit(book);        <-- Create BookEdit widget
                    add(edit);
                }
            });
        select.setVisibleItemCount(10);
        side.add(select);
        Controller.getInstance().updateCategories();     | Initialize state
        Controller.getInstance().findAllBooks();         | for panel
        Controller.getInstance().findAllAuthors();       |
        this.add(side);
    }
}
```

This widget has a single bound element ❶, the `select ListBox` containing the list of books. It's keeping an internal model of the single `book` currently selected and making the call to the controller for delete operations where needed ❷.

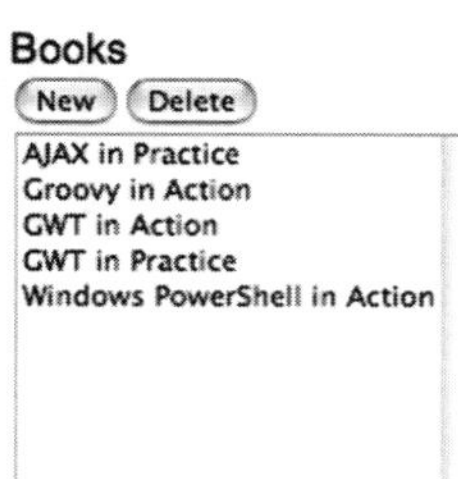

Figure 9.3 The wrapper for the CRUD application, represented by the `AdminPanel` class. You can click New to create a new record or select a book for editing or deletion.

Now we have our basic operations for deleting books. The call to the controller for saving a book to the database is handled inside the `BookEdit` class, which handles most of the other functionality for editing books. We'll examine this in the next section.

9.4.3 The BookEdit widget

The basic controls are provided by the `AdminPanel` class, so we now need a data-bound widget for editing a `book` object. This class is similar to the user-editing class we saw in chapter 4, but there are a few things to take into account here. In this class, much like a Swing or AWT class, a lot of code is spent simply creating widgets, which makes for a very long constructor method. We'll just examine small sections of the constructor.

Listing 9.12 shows the beginning of the `BookEdit` constructor, where the initial values are set.

Listing 9.12 The first part of the `BookEdit` class lays out widgets and sets initial values

```
public BookEdit(final Book book) {
        this.book = book;
        main.add(new Label(CONSTANTS.title()));      <-- An il8n constants implementation
        main.add(title);                             <-- Add elements to panel
        title.setText(book.getTitle());              <-- Initialize values to Book object
        main.add(new Label(CONSTANTS.description()));
        main.add(description);
        description.setText(book.getDescription());
        catPanel.add(new Label(CONSTANTS.categories()));
        catPanel.add(newCategory);
        catPanel.add(cats);
        catsAndAuthors.add(catPanel);                <-- (1) Lay these out across screen
        authorPanel.add(new Label(CONSTANTS.authors()));
        authorPanel.add(newAuthor);
        authorPanel.add(auths);
        catsAndAuthors.add(authorPanel);
        main.add(catsAndAuthors);
        cats.setSelectedCategories(
            book.getCategories());
        auths.setSelectedAuthors(book.getAuthors());  (2) Initialize selections to current value
```

This is very standard code. The `title` and `description` are just basic `TextBox` and `TextArea` fields. There is also a little bit of layout work done (1).

The first thing that might be new to you is setting the selected values on the `cats` and `auths` boxes (2). Since these have a many-to-many relationship with `Book` objects, we need to do a little bit of work to support selection. You saw in listing 9.11 that the global values are being stored on the `ModelState` class and initialized on the controller. We need to create two `ListBox` children to support this. These are both functionally the same, so we'll just examine the `CategorySelect` class in listing 9.13.

Listing 9.13 `CategorySelect` selects a subset of the global `Category` objects

```
public class CategorySelect extends ListBox {
    private List categories;
```

```
private PropertyChangeListener l = new PropertyChangeListenerProxy(
      "categories",
      new PropertyChangeListener() {          // 1 Set up ModelState listener
         public void propertyChange(
            PropertyChangeEvent propertyChangeEvent) {
             categories = (List) propertyChangeEvent.getNewValue();
             if (categories == null) {
                 categories = new ArrayList();
             }
             update();
         }
     };

public CategorySelect() {
    ModelState model = ModelState.getInstance();
    model.addPropertyChangeListener(l);
    this.categories = model.getCategories();
    this.update();
    this.setMultipleSelect(true);
    this.setVisibleItemCount(5);
    this.setStyleName("categorySelect");
}

public void cleanup() {                       // 2 Clear listener when done
    ModelState.getInstance()
        .removePropertyChangeListener("categories", l);
}

public List getSelectedCategories() {        // 3 Loop to get current selection
    List values = new ArrayList();
    for (int i = 0; i < this.getItemCount(); i++) {
        if (this.isItemSelected(i)) {
            values.add(categories.get(i));
        }
    }
    return values;
}

public void setSelectedCategories(List categories) {
    for (int i = 0; i < this.getItemCount(); i++) {
        boolean selected = false;
        for (int j = 0;
            (categories != null) &&
            (j < categories.size());
            j++) {
            Category c = (Category) categories.get(j);

            if (this
               .getItemText(i)
               .equals(c.getName())) {        // 4 Note the first generalization point
                selected = true;
                break;
            }
        }
        this.setItemSelected(i, selected);
    }
}
```

```
    private void update() {
        List selectedCategories =
            this.getSelectedCategories();       // 5 Hold on to current selections
        this.clear();                           // Clear current list
        if (categories == null) {
            return;
        }
        for (Iterator it = categories.iterator();
             it.hasNext();) {                   // Loop through new categories list
            Category c = (Category) it.next();
            this.addItem(c.getName());          // 6 Note the second point for generalization
        }
        this.setSelectedCategories(selectedCategories);   // 7 Restore user's selections
    }
}
```

This is a class that could be generalized into a more specific class with a little work. We'll talk about how you might build that class in a bit, but first let's look at the core functionality here. First we have a `PropertyChangeListener` that we're going to bind to the `ModelState` object to get the list of all categories in the current state ❶ and a `cleanup()` method that releases the reference for garbage collection ❷. Next we use the `selectedCategories` property on the model object to set the selection state. In the getter method ❸, we cycle through the current set of values on the `ListBox` parent and determine the selections, building a new `List` based on the indexes from the current global list. On the setter method, we perform the same operation in reverse. When determining whether two objects are equivalent, we need to use the `name` property on the `Category`, since instance equality is not guaranteed ❹. In general, you'll want to compare primary key values in this operation, since the actual values in an object might have changed on a different object instance elsewhere in the application. This is the first place where we might generalize this class.

In the `update()` method, there's an important bit of logic: we capture the current selected objects ❺ and then restore them ❼ as the update happens. This ensures that if the call to the controller to get the categories in `AdminPanel` comes back after the selections are set, the values are not lost.

The second place we could generalize this class is in this method as well. When we're adding the `String` values to the `ListBox` ❻, we need to determine a value for the object. In Swing, the standard behavior is to use the `toString()` method to do this. If you have done Swing development, however, you know that this can be a problematic solution. Often you want the `toString()` method to be a full representation of the object's value for debugging or logging purposes. In many cases, you might want different `String` representations of the same class. For instance, in the `AuthorSelect` class, we don't use a single property to create this value, but the `lastName` and `firstName` properties:

```
public void setSelectedAuthors(List authors) {
        for (int i = 0; i < this.getItemCount(); i++) {
            boolean selected = false;
            for (int j = 0;
```

```
                (authors != null) &&
                (j < authors.size());
                j++) {
                Author a = (Author) authors.get(j);
                if (this.getItemText(i)
                        .equals(a.getLastName() + ", " +
                                a.getFirstName())) {
                    selected = true;
                    break;
                }
            }
            this.setItemSelected(i, selected);
        }
    }

    private void update() {
        this.clear();
        if (authors == null) {
            return;
        }
        for (Iterator it = authors.iterator(); it.hasNext();) {
            Author a = (Author) it.next();
            this.addItem(a.getLastName() + ", " + a.getFirstName());
        }
    }
```

In this case, you could construct a set of Strategy pattern options to perform these operations: a custom `Comparator` implementation and an interface to provide a customizable `String` value. This can make your classes harder to use, though. For our purposes here, we'll simply create two very similar classes.

Once we have these two many-to-many `ListBox` implementations, we need to bind them to our `Book` object. We'll take care of that in the `BookEdit` constructor, where we have the long run of `PropertyChangeListener` bindings. Listing 9.14 shows some of these bindings.

Listing 9.14 A block of property bindings in the `BookEdit` constructor

```
listeners[1] = new PropertyChangeListenerProxy(
    "description",
    new PropertyChangeListener() {
       public void propertyChange(
           PropertyChangeEvent propertyChangeEvent) {
           description.setText((String)
               propertyChangeEvent.getNewValue());
       }
    });
book.addPropertyChangeListener(listeners[1]);
description.addChangeListener(new ChangeListener() {
       public void onChange(Widget sender) {
           book.setDescription(
               description.getText());
       }
   });
```

Create binding for text field

```
listeners[2] = new PropertyChangeListenerProxy(
        "categories",
        new PropertyChangeListener() {
           public void propertyChange(
               PropertyChangeEvent propertyChangeEvent) {
               cats.setSelectedCategories((List)              <-
                         propertyChangeEvent.getNewValue());
           }
        };                                                     Bind categories'
book.addPropertyChangeListener(listeners[2]);                  properties
cats.addChangeListener(new ChangeListener() {
        public void onChange(Widget sender) {
            book.setCategories(
                     cats.getSelectedCategories());           <-
        }
    });
```

Now we have a ListBox for maintaining the many-to-many relationship and a binding, but we still need a way to create new categories. For this we're going to use a DialogBox class and a New button. Since this is fairly basic, we'll simply add this into the BookEdit constructor. Listing 9.15 shows the creation of the dialog box for making a new category.

Listing 9.15 Using a DialogBox to create a new category within BookEdit

```
newCategory.addClickListener(new ClickListener() {      <- Add listener to New
        public void onClick(Widget widget) {               category button
            final DialogBox box = new DialogBox();
            box.setPopupPosition(
                widget.getAbsoluteLeft(),             (1) Place dialog
                widget.getAbsoluteTop());                 above button
            box.setText(CONSTANTS.categoryName());

            VerticalPanel edit = new VerticalPanel();            Create Save
            final TextBox name = new TextBox();                  button
            Button save = new Button(CONSTANTS.save());      <-
            edit.add(name);

            HorizontalPanel buttons = new HorizontalPanel();
            buttons.add(save);
            buttons.add(new Button(CONSTANTS.cancel(),
                    new ClickListener() {
                    public void onClick(Widget widget) {
                        box.hide();
                    }
                }));
            edit.add(buttons);

            final Category c = new Category();
            name.addChangeListener(
               new ChangeListener() {
                public void onChange(Widget widget) {      (2) Create binding for
                    c.setName(name.getText());                 name property
                }
            });
```

```
            save.addClickListener(new ClickListener() {
                public void onClick(Widget widget) {
                    List selected =
                        new ArrayList(cats.getSelectedCategories());
                    selected.add(c);
                    List catlist = ModelState.getInstance()
                                            .getCategories();
                    if (catlist == null) {
                        catlist = new ArrayList();
                    }
                    catlist.add(c);
                    ModelState.getInstance()
                            .setCategories(catlist);
                    cats.setSelectedCategories(selected);
                    book.setCategories(selected);
                    box.hide();
                }
            });
            box.setWidget(edit);
            box.show();
        }
    });
```

❸ Add category to selected categories

❹ Add category to global list

Close dialog box

Although this is all done with anonymous classes, it shouldn't look too alien. We use a standard listener pattern to bind the `name` property ❷. We make sure to store the new category in both the book's categories and the global one on `ModelState` ❸ ❹. This category, however, doesn't get inserted into the database until the book is stored. In listing 9.5 we took care to create or merge the categories as they come in with a book.

You'll notice the positioning of the dialog box ❶. By using the `absoluteLeft` and `absoluteTop` properties on the `Button`, we can make the dialog box pop up where the user's eye is already focused. This gives us the effect seen in figure 9.4.

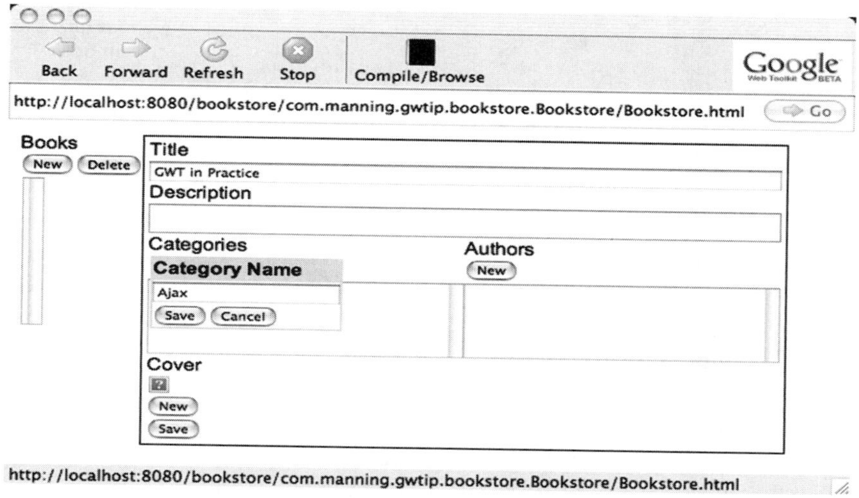

Figure 9.4 The new category `DialogBox` pops up over the button, keeping the user focused on the same point.

The final special point concerns the dialog box for the cover photo. `FileUpload` elements have special requirements for use in GWT. Since you obviously can't read a file into the Ajax environment, and there is no standard file handling methodology, you must use a traditional submit form. In the GWT world, this is done with a `FormPanel`. Listing 9.16 shows the cover-image upload `DialogBox`. It is similar to the previous listing but has some important differences.

Listing 9.16 The cover-image upload `DialogBox` in the `BookEdit` constructor

```
newImage.addClickListener(new ClickListener() {
      public void onClick(Widget widget) {
          final DialogBox box = new DialogBox();
          box.setPopupPosition(widget.getAbsoluteLeft(),
              widget.getAbsoluteTop());
          box.setText(CONSTANTS.cover());

          final FormPanel form = new FormPanel();
          form.setAction(GWT.getModuleBaseURL() +
                     "CoverUpload");
          form.setEncoding(
              FormPanel
                 .ENCODING_MULTIPART);
          form.setMethod(FormPanel.METHOD_POST);
          form.addFormHandler(new FormHandler() {
                  public void onSubmitComplete(
                      FormSubmitCompleteEvent completeEvent) {
                      String url = completeEvent.getResults();

                      if (url.indexOf("<pre>") != -1) {
                          url =
                              url.substring(url.indexOf(">") + 1,
                              url.lastIndexOf("<"));
                      }

                      book.setImage(
                          GWT.getModuleBaseURL() +
                          ".." + url);
                      cover.setUrl(book.getImage());
                      box.hide();
                  }

                  public void onSubmit(FormSubmitEvent submit) {
                      ;
                  }
          });

          VerticalPanel inner = new VerticalPanel();
          form.setWidget(inner);

          FileUpload upload = new FileUpload();
          upload.setName("cover");
          inner.add(upload);

          Button save = new Button(CONSTANTS.save(),
                  new ClickListener() {
                      public void onClick(Widget widget) {
```

1. Set action, like an HTML form
2. Use multipart/form-data encoding
3. Use FormHandler to capture results
4. Handle special problem with Safari
5. Set final URL on Book

Perform null operation on Submit

```
                form.submit();                                    <- ❻ Submit form
            }                                                          when clicked
        });
    HorizontalPanel buttons = new HorizontalPanel();
    buttons.add(save);

    inner.add(buttons);
    box.setWidget(form);
    box.show();
  }
});
```

If you have handled file uploads from HTML or JSP pages before, this will all look fairly straightforward. We set up the `<form>` tag in the `FormPanel` object as we would for any other web application ❶ ❷, and we submit the form when the Save button is clicked ❻. Because we aren't going to send the user's browser to a new page when this form is submitted, we need a way to handle the returned results. Here we're using a `FormHandler` ❸.

One special thing to pay attention to here is that when the image is uploaded, our servlet returns text/plain as the location of the URL. Safari, however, takes the results that come back and formats them for viewing in a web page by wrapping them in a `<pre>` tag. Your application needs to check for this and strip it out if you just want a plain text value back from a server, as we're doing here ❹.

After we get the value back, we construct the real URL using the base path from the GWT application root and set it on the `Book` object ❺.

With the file upload element covered, we have completed our tour of this basic CRUD application.

9.5 Summary

You have already seen the basics of application construction patterns, but in this chapter we looked at some new issues you'll need to address in your applications. We looked at creating a set of client-enabled DTOs and mapping them to server-side classes to make sure our service JPA beans are not serialized to our GWT client. There are several important reasons for this, as we noted:

- serialization of JPA entities breaks down in some instances
- you'll often want support for `PropertyChangeEvents` in your client model and not on the server
- you'll often want to be able to share your server-side model with other server-side projects without having GWTisms attached

In this chapter we used a method whereby the JPA-enabled data access beans, DAOs, and service can be used by other applications, not just our GWT web app, unlike the direct JPA example in chapter 4. In this chapter we also looked at configuring Spring within the scope of a GWT application, and using the `RemoteServiceServlet` as a proxy into the Spring-configured application for the client-side application. Finally, we looked at some common cases in the client application, including dealing with many-to-many relationships in a CRUD application and handling file uploads from the client browser.

In practice, this part of the Bookstore application is most useful for administrators. In the next chapter we'll examine the customer-facing client application and look at how Java EE security constructs can affect a GWT application.

10 Building the Storefront

This chapter covers

- Securing GWT applications
- Dealing with security in the client
- Building a drag-and-drop system

A bookstore is one of the only pieces of evidence we have that people are still thinking.

—Jerry Seinfeld

In the last chapter, we looked at a basic CRUD application for a database of books. In this chapter, we're going to take that application and turn it into the basis of an Ajax storefront that can sell the books listed in the database. While a basic database of books is OK, you'll likely have multiple interfaces to your data—a customer-facing storefront for buying the books in the database is a good example.

There are a few things we need to do to the chapter 9 application to make this happen. First, we need to secure our administration tool and create a separate service for customers. Next, we need to build a drag-and-drop system using only the GWT APIs. Also, because the storefront is the customer-facing portion of our application, it should be pretty—we'll look at adapting a JavaScript library to create reflections for our cover images, as if they were sitting on a reflective surface (see figure 10.3). Finally, we'll bring it all together and construct a basic shopping cart system.

10.1 Securing GWT applications

Providing security for your application you're building is generally of critical importance. In terms of GWT applications, security usually means securing the service. In the last chapter, we built a simple CRUD service for updating books in the database. Now we need to secure that service and the page using it. One of the most common ways to manage identity in the enterprise is with a Lightweight Directory Access Protocol (LDAP) server, so that's what we'll use to secure our application.

In the sample application, we'll use ApacheDS, the directory server from the Apache Software Foundation. You could, of course, use Microsoft Active Directory, Fedora or Red Hat Directory Server, or OpenLDAP. We'll pass over the setup of the LDAP server—if you're interested in such details, check out the links in table 10.1.

Table 10.1 More information on setting up LDAP environments

Environment	URL
ApacheDS	http://www.screaming-penguin.com/node/5677
OpenLDAP	http://today.java.net/pub/a/today/2005/05/31/tomcatldap.html
Microsoft Active Directory	http://jspwiki.org/wiki/ActiveDirectoryIntegration

In our web app, we have two URLs we must secure: the entry page and the service. First we need to set up the LDAP queries in the context.xml file. Listing 10.1 shows how this is done.

Listing 10.1 Adding the LDAP queries to Context.xml

```
<?xml version="1.0" encoding="UTF-8"?>
<Context path="">
<Realm className="org.apache.catalina.realm.JNDIRealm"
    debug="99"
    connectionName="uid=admin,ou=system"           ❶
    connectionPassword="secret"
    connectionURL="ldap://localhost:389"
    roleBase="ou=roles,dc=manning,dc=com"          ❷
    roleName="cn"
    roleSearch="(uniqueMember={0})"
    roleSubtree="false"
    userSearch="(uid={0})"                         ❸
    userPassword="userPassword"                    ❹
    userPattern="uid={0},ou=users,dc=manning,dc=com"  ❺
    digest="MD5"
/>
</Context>
```

❶ Specify user used to perform query
❷ Match groupOfUniqueNames and field
❸ Check field to determine if user is present
❹ Specify password field
❺ Search pattern for user's global entry
Define encoding scheme for password

Even if you're unfamiliar with LDAP, this example should still be fairly straightforward. First we specify the identity of the root user we'll use to log in to the LDAP server ❶. Here we're using the default ApacheDS password of `secret`, but you'll want to change that. Next we specify the skeleton of a query we'll use to identify a `role` node ❷. Roles here are LDAP objects of `groupOfUniqueNames` type that contain `uniqueMembers` that point to users in that role ❸. Finally we specify the query base ❺ and the password field we'll match ❹. Figure 10.1 shows the administrator role for our test application in JXplorer.

TIP JXplorer is a handy Java-based LDAP client available for pretty much any platform. It's available for free from http://www.jxplorer.org/.

Now that the `Realm` is configured for Tomcat, we need to go back to the web.xml file and define the security settings. First, we want to secure the administration page and the administration service. We'll do that with the `<security-constraint>` element. Listing 10.2 shows how we'll configure this element.

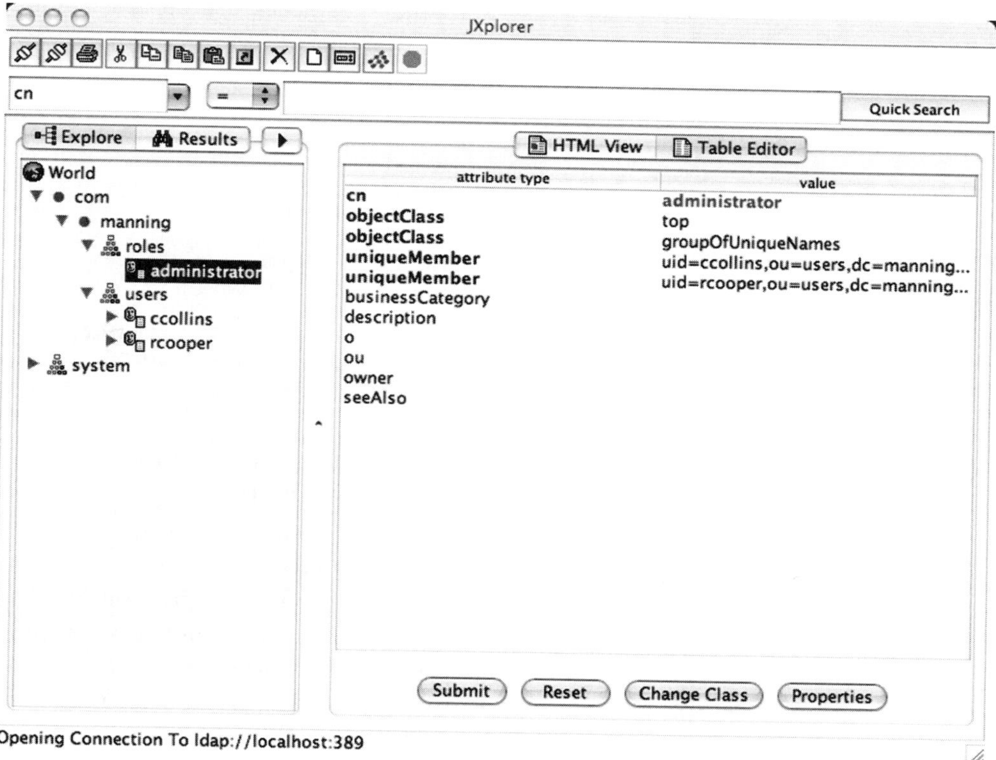

Figure 10.1 Two `uniqueMember` attributes point to the users defined as being in the administrator role.

Listing 10.2 The <security-constraint> element locks up the Administration page

```
<security-constraint>
        <display-name>Administration</display-name>
        <web-resource-collection>
            <web-resource-name>BookstoreService</web-resource-name>
            <description>The Administration Service</description>
            <url-pattern>
   com.manning.gwtip.bookstore/BookstoreService
            </url-pattern>
            <http-method>GET</http-method>
            <http-method>POST</http-method>
            <http-method>HEAD</http-method>
            <http-method>PUT</http-method>
            <http-method>OPTIONS</http-method>
            <http-method>TRACE</http-method>
            <http-method>DELETE</http-method>
        </web-resource-collection>
        <web-resource-collection>
            <web-resource-name>Administration Page</web-resource-name>
            <description>The GWT page that hosts the app</description>
            <url-pattern>
   com.manning.gwtip.bookstore.Bookstore.jsp
             </url-pattern>
            <http-method>GET</http-method>
            <http-method>POST</http-method>
            <http-method>HEAD</http-method>
            <http-method>PUT</http-method>
            <http-method>OPTIONS</http-method>
            <http-method>TRACE</http-method>
            <http-method>DELETE</http-method>
        </web-resource-collection>
        <auth-constraint>
            <description/>
            <role-name>administrator</role-name>
        </auth-constraint>
    </security-constraint>
```

❶ Define path to BookstoreService servlet

❷ Secure HTTP calls to service

Change HTML to JSP

Restrict to role

Here we're specifying the service URL ❶ and the host page URL ❷.

You might be asking why we need to secure the host page, and not the scripts themselves. Well, obviously the host page won't work without the service. However, you want to secure the host page so that the user is prompted to log in before this page is reached. While using `HTTP Basic` authentication might prompt the user when the service connection is made, this can be cumbersome, and most people are more attuned to having a customized login page in a web form these days.

The Servlet specification supports this: we need to create a form that submits the user credentials to the special `j_security_check` URL, and an error page for when the login fails. Listing 10.3 shows the remaining bits of the web.xml deployment descriptor we must set up to facilitate this.

Listing 10.3 The <login-config> and <security-role> elements in web.xml

```
<login-config>
    <auth-method>FORM</auth-method>
    <realm-name/>
    <form-login-config>
        <form-login-page>/login.jsp</form-login-page>
        <form-error-page>
               /login-error.jsp
           </form-error-page>      </form-login-config>
</login-config>
<security-role>
    <description/>
    <role-name>administrator</role-name>
</security-role>
```

❶ Specify FORM-based authentication

❷ Specify page with login form

❸ Error page for failed logins

❹ Define administrator role

Here we're specifying that we're using FORM-based authentication ❶, as opposed to BASIC for HTTP Basic authentication. Next, we specify the two special JSP pages ❷ ❸. Finally, we include a <security-role> element for each role our application needs to support. Since we only have one, we specify administrator ❹.

Now that we have taken care of the plumbing in our web app, we need to create the special JSP pages. We'll just look at the login.jsp page, in listing 10.4, as it demonstrates the special login form for using form-based authentication in our application.

Listing 10.4 The login.jsp page submitting the credentials to j_security_check

```
<!DOCTYPE HTML PUBLIC "-//W3C//DTD HTML 4.01 Transitional//EN"
   "http://www.w3.org/TR/html4/loose.dtd">

<html>
    <head>
        <meta http-equiv="Content-Type"
              content="text/html; charset=UTF-8">
        <title>Login Page</title>
    </head>
    <body>

    <h1>Login Page</h1>

    <form method="POST"
        action="<%=response.encodeURL(
                     request.getContextPath()+
                     "/j_security_check")%>">
        <input type="text" name="j_username" />
        <br />
        <input type="password" name="j_password" />
        <br />
        <input type="submit" />
    </form>
    </body>
</html>
```

❶ Set action to j_security_check URL

Here we have a very basic HTML form in a JSP page. The action is set to the special j_security_check path as mandated by the Servlet specification ❶. We need two

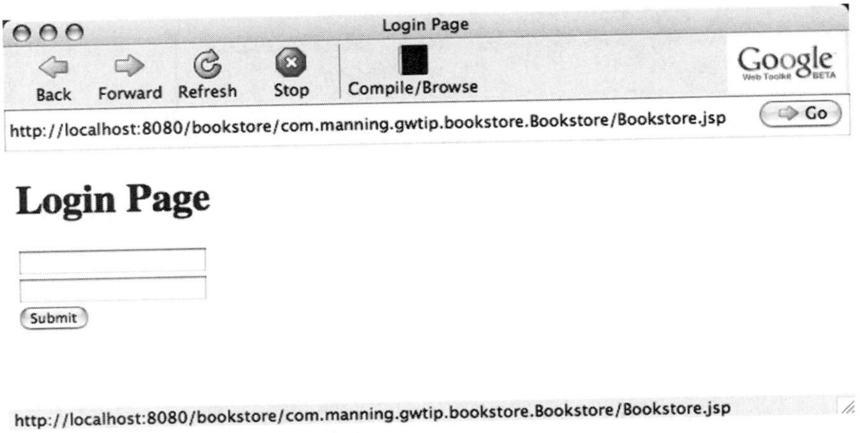

Figure 10.2 Bookstore.jsp is now intercepted by the login.jsp page, requiring authentication.

form fields, `j_username` and `j_password`, which contain the obvious data. Now when we visit the new HTML host page, which we have turned into a JSP page, we're first prompted with the login form based on the container-managed security settings. Figure 10.2 shows this prompt in the hosted mode browser.

It might seem that we're done! The authentication prompt comes up, the user is validated against the LDAP server, and we're passed into a working version of our CRUD application. So what's wrong? Well, when you're using form-based authentication, the user authentication information is stored in the HTTP session, which is, by default, a cookie-based system. If the user's browser doesn't accept cookies, or if you're prevented from using them by policy (such as in government agency websites), you have a problem. The session information is lost, and authentication fails when calls to the `BookstoreService` are made. Once again, the Servlet specification has a means of working around this: `HttpServletResponse.encodeURL()`.

The `encodeURL()` method will take a path in the application and append the session identifier into the URL string so the server can determine the user authentication information from the URL and not from a cookie. The problem is that the URLs for our service are now part of the monolithic script compilation for the GWT application, so we need a way to pass in the proper service URL to our application. This is where having the host page as a JSP page comes in.

First, we need to modify the host page to include the session information. Listing 10.5 demonstrates how we'll do this, creating a JavaScript object to hold that information.

Listing 10.5 The new JSP host page with the properly encoded service URL

```
<!DOCTYPE HTML PUBLIC "-//W3C//DTD HTML 4.01 Transitional//EN"
"http://www.w3.org/TR/html4/loose.dtd">

<html>
  <head>
```

```
    <script type="text/javascript">
        var services = {
          bookstoreService :
               "<%=response.encodeURL(
    "/com.manning.gwtip.bookstore.Bookstore/BookstoreService"
               ) %>"
        };
    </script>
  <title></title>
  <meta name='gwt:module'
     content='com.manning.gwtip.bookstore.Bookstore'>
  </head>
 <body>
  <script language="javascript" src="gwt.js"></script>
  <iframe id="__gwt_historyFrame" style="width:0;height:0;border:0;">
  </iframe>
 </body>
</html>
```

Wrap path with session info

This is not a big change. The important thing is that once this is evaluated on the server, the path will be encoded with the session information, like this:

```
/com.manning.gwtip.bookstore.Bookstore/BookstoreService;
jsessionid=A3667E9D89E1A15B5BBD1F4F7791B395
```

Now we just need to get this information into our application. While it's not designed for this purpose, there is a GWT class that will do just this. In chapter 1 you saw the `Dictionary` class in the internationalization package. It is designed to get internationalization data from the host page, but we can also use it to get configuration information, such as the encoded service URL. We'll go back to the constructor for the `Controller` class and change the way we assign the service endpoint. Listing 10.6 shows the new constructor.

Listing 10.6 The new `Controller` constructor gets the service URL from the dictionary

```
private Controller() {
     super();
     Dictionary dict = Dictionary
        .getDictionary("services");
     ServiceDefTarget endpoint = (ServiceDefTarget) service;
     endpoint.setServiceEntryPoint(
        dict.get("bookstoreService"));
}
```

❶ Get Dictionary from the services object

❷ Get value of the bookstoreService attribute

First, we get the object we defined in the host page as `services` ❶, and then we get the value of the `bookstoreService` property and bind that to the endpoint of our service ❷. Now our service works automagically! The browser will make subsequent requests to the service using the same `jsessionid` value.

We have now secured the `BookstoreServiceServlet` from unauthenticated users. Since we cannot use this system to get method-level security, we need to go back and create a customer service interface that exposes only the methods that unauthenticated or public users should be able to access. Listing 10.7 shows this new interface.

Listing 10.7 The CustomerService interface

```
package com.manning.gwtip.bookstore.client.remote;

import com.google.gwt.user.client.rpc.RemoteService;

import com.manning.gwtip.bookstore.client.model.Author;
import com.manning.gwtip.bookstore.client.model.Book;
import com.manning.gwtip.bookstore.client.model.Review;

import java.util.List;

public interface CustomerService extends RemoteService{

    Review createReview(int bookId, Review review)
        throws BookstoreRemoteException;

    /**
     * @gwt.typeArgs <com.manning.gwtip.bookstore.client.model.Book>
     */
    List findAllBooks()
        throws BookstoreRemoteException;

    /**
     * @gwt.typeArgs <com.manning.gwtip.bookstore.client.model.Category>
     */
    List findAllCategories()
       throws BookstoreRemoteException;

     /**
     * @gwt.typeArgs <com.manning.gwtip.bookstore.client.model.Author>
     */
    List findAllAuthors()
        throws BookstoreRemoteException;
    /**
     * @gwt.typeArgs <com.manning.gwtip.bookstore.client.model.Author>
     */
    List findAuthorsByName(String firstName, String lastName)
        throws BookstoreRemoteException;

    Book findBookById(int bookId)
        throws BookstoreRemoteException;

    /**
     * @gwt.typeArgs <com.manning.gwtip.bookstore.client.model.Book>
     */
    List findBooksByAuthor(int authorId)
      throws BookstoreRemoteException;

     List findBooksByCategory(String categoryName)
        throws BookstoreRemoteException;
}
```

Reuse client beans, define service

Define only exposed write method

Define read-only methods

Since this service is stateless and unsecured, we have nothing else to do here. The application now has two services exposed, one secured and one unsecured. We have defined the access privileges, configured our web application to enforce them, and modified our class to support cookie-less users.

Now that we have both sides of our security defined, we'll move on to adding a little coolness to our client-side application. The first thing we want to do is build in support for drag-and-drop shopping.

10.2 Building a drag-and-drop system

When we were looking at JSNI in chapter 6, we used the Script.aculo.us drag-and-drop system as an integration example. While this does work, it has certain drawbacks. First, it uses a separate JavaScript file that must be updated with new versions to support new browsers. One of the big advantages of using GWT is that when new versions are released, a simple recompile brings in all the new browser compatibility tweaks without changing or updating files. The second drawback is that those Script.aculo.us JavaScript files aren't optimized by the GWT compiler, which includes obfuscation and compression. Since we depend on friendly named JavaScript methods, they can't be compressed into bandwidth-friendly but non-human-readable versions. The obvious solution is to build a drag-and-drop system with GWT.

We'll break this task down into two large and blindingly obvious steps: dragging and dropping. Figure 10.3 shows us dragging a book we created with chapter 9's CRUD application to the shopping cart widget, outlined in red.

We'll start by implementing the drag system.

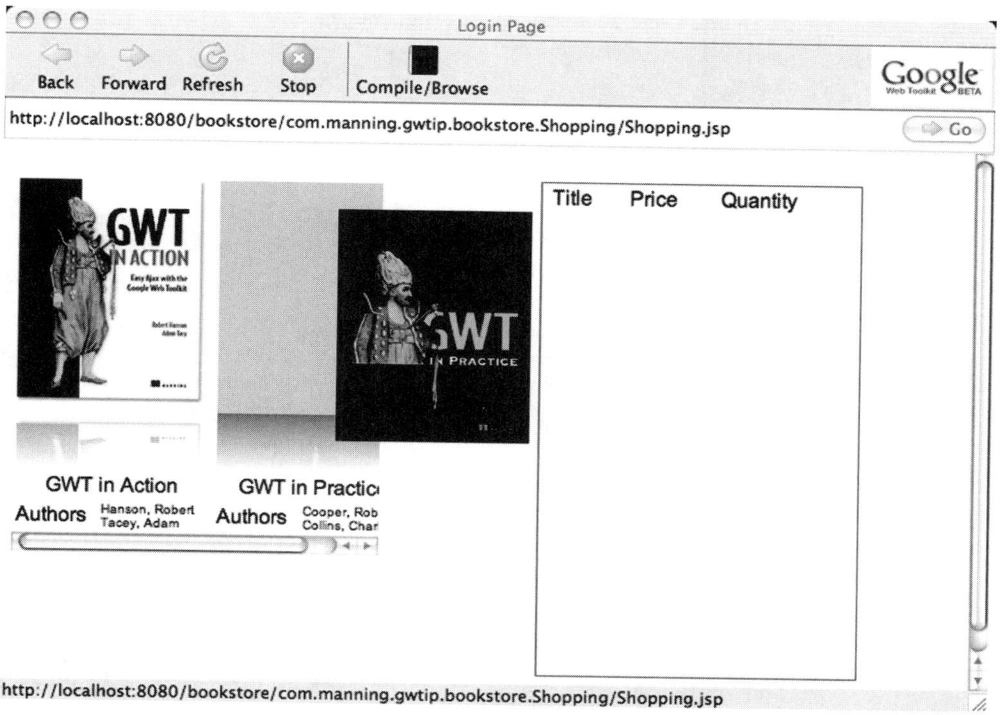

Figure 10.3 The cover of the book being dragged to the shopping cart

10.2.1 Enabling dragging

Dragging is based on mouse presses and mouse movements. This means, in the GWT world, using a class that implements `SourcesMouseEvents`. Images implement this interface, and other classes can be wrapped inside a `FocusPanel` that will provide the mouse events.

Our drag-and-drop controller will need to add a mouse listener to whatever it is we need to drag, so unlike the JSNI example in chapter 6 that worked directly on the DOM, we'll use the `SourcesMouseEvents` interface to define the draggables on screen. Listing 10.8 shows the beginnings of our new `DragAndDrop` class.

Listing 10.8 Enabling dragging in the `DragAndDrop` class, part 1

```
public class DragAndDrop {
    private static final DragAndDrop instance = new DragAndDrop();
    private Draggable dragging;
    private Element placeholder;
    private Map draggables = new HashMap();
    private Map dropListeners = new HashMap();
    private List dropTargets;

    private DragAndDrop() {
    }

    public static DragAndDrop getInstance() {
        return instance;
    }

    public void makeDraggable(SourcesMouseEvents w, boolean revert) {
        Draggable d = new Draggable();
        d.widget = (Widget) w;
        d.listener = new DragSupportListener(
                           (Widget) w, revert);          <-- 1 Cast to Widget to get properties
        w.addMouseListener(d.listener);
        draggables.put(w, d);
    }

    class DragSupportListener extends MouseListenerAdapter {
        private String startFlow;                 | Hold original
        private String startZ;                    | DOM settings
        private int startX;                       |
        private int startY;                       |
        private boolean revert;
        private int offsetX;
        private int offsetY;

        public DragSupportListener(Widget w, boolean revert) {
            this.revert = revert;
            DOM.addEventPreview(new EventPreview() {          |
                public boolean onEventPreview(                |
                      Event event) {                          | 2 Override native
                    switch(DOM.eventGetType(event)) {         |   drag handling
                    case Event.ONMOUSEDOWN:                   |
                      DOM.eventPreventDefault(event);         |
                    }                                         |
```

```
                return true;
            }
        });
    }

    public void onMouseDown(Widget sender, int x, int y) {
        super.onMouseDown(sender, x, y);
        if (dragging != null) {
            dragging.listener.onMouseUp(dragging.widget, 0, 0);
        }
        dragging = (Draggable) draggables.get(sender);
        startFlow = DOM.getStyleAttribute(
                dragging.widget.getElement(),
                "position");
        startX = dragging.widget.getAbsoluteLeft();
        startY = dragging.widget.getAbsoluteTop();
        offsetX = x;
        offsetY = y;
        startZ = DOM.getStyleAttribute(
                dragging.widget.getElement(),
                "z-index");
        DOM.setStyleAttribute(
                dragging.widget.getElement(),
                "position",
                "absolute");
        DOM.setStyleAttribute(
                dragging.widget.getElement(), "top",
            "" + startY);
        DOM.setStyleAttribute(
            dragging.widget.getElement(), "left",
            "" + startX);
        DOM.setStyleAttribute(
            dragging.widget.getElement(),
            "z-index",
            "" + 10000);
        placeholder = DOM.createDiv();
        DOM.setStyleAttribute(placeholder, "width",
            dragging.widget.getOffsetWidth() + "px");
        DOM.setStyleAttribute(placeholder, "height",
            dragging.widget.getOffsetHeight() + "px");
        DOM.setStyleAttribute(placeholder, "background", "#CCCCCC");
        int index = DOM.getChildIndex(DOM.getParent(
                    dragging.widget.getElement()),
                dragging.widget.getElement());
        DOM.insertChild(DOM.getParent(dragging.widget.getElement()),
            placeholder, index);
    }
```

❸ Make sure we aren't dragging

Get original style attributes

❹ Pull element into absolute space

Hold page flow

Here we can see the beginnings of dragging. Our support listener holds the basic state data we need to preserve for the element ❶. When the element is pressed on, we move the widget into absolute space on the page, still in the same location as it was originally ❹. Finally, we create a simple gray placeholder <div> to make sure the page flow doesn't change around our now *floating* `Widget`. There is also a special case we need to deal with: what if we're already dragging something? ❸

One of the problems you can run into when making an Ajax drag-and-drop system is the loss of mouse events. If you move the mouse outside the screen or the observable area of the GWT app, the drag state will remain, but the movement is no longer being tracked. We need to clean up and make sure the release state is handled properly in this situation.

The other gotcha we need to handle is the native drag event support in Safari and Mozilla. These browsers expect drag events to become "operating system reference drag events" for the image, rather than just a simple set of mouse events ❷. We'll take care of that by handling the native mouse events at a level below the `SourcesMouseEvents` level.

Listing 10.9 shows the last part of the mouse eventing for dragging.

Listing 10.9 Enabling dragging in the `DragAndDrop` class, part 2

```
public void onMouseMove(Widget sender, int x, int y) {
    super.onMouseMove(sender, x, y);

    if(dragging != null) {                          ❶ If dragging, move to new position
        DOM.setStyleAttribute(dragging.widget.getElement(), "top",
            Integer.toString(sender.getAbsoluteTop()
                - offsetY + y));
        DOM.setStyleAttribute(dragging.widget.getElement(),
            "left",
            Integer.toString(sender.getAbsoluteLeft()
                - offsetX + x));
    }
}

public void onMouseUp(Widget sender, int x, int y) {
    super.onMouseUp(sender, x, y);
    DOM.setStyleAttribute(dragging.widget.getElement(), "z-index",
        startZ);

    if (revert) {
        DOM.setStyleAttribute(
            dragging.widget.getElement(),
           "position",
            startFlow);
        DOM.setStyleAttribute(                       ❷ Restore Widget to original state
            dragging.widget.getElement(), "top",
            "" + startY);
        DOM.setStyleAttribute(
           dragging.widget.getElement(),
           "left",
            "" + startX);
        DOM.removeChild(
            DOM.getParent(
               dragging.widget.getElement()),        ❸ Remove placeholder
            placeholder);
        placeholder = null;
```

```
            }
            dragging = null;
        }
    }
                                                        Define data class
    private class Draggable {                    <--    to hold position
        public DragSupportListener listener;
        public Widget widget;
    }
}
```

Here we have completed the basics of dragging, though the `onMouseUp()` method is abbreviated—we'll see the rest of it in the next section. In this example, we're listening for move events and repositioning the widget to the new location ❶. Then we check the `revert` state, and if it's `true`, we reset the `Widget` to its original DOM positioning ❷, and finally remove the placeholder `<div>` we created previously ❸.

Now that the dragging elements are following the mouse around, we need to look into adding drop targets.

10.2.2 Handling drops

The other side of drag and drop is, of course, drop. When items are being dragged around the screen and released, we want to determine whether they are being dropped onto something that should trigger a drop event. There are two aspects to doing this: First, we must set up the listeners we need for sending drop notifications to our application. Second, we need to determine when a dragged item is actually dropped onto an item.

Listing 10.10 shows the setup of the listeners we need.

Listing 10.10 Setting up for drop listeners

```
public void addDropListener(Widget w, DropListener dl) {
    List listeners = (dropListeners.get(w) != null)
        ? (List) dropListeners.get(w) : new ArrayList();      <-- Create
    listeners.add(dl);                                          listener list,
    dropListeners.put(w, listeners);                         ❶ store listener
}                                              ❷ Make widget a
public void makeDroppable(Widget w) {       <--   drop target
    dropTargets = (dropTargets == null) ?
                  new ArrayList() : dropTargets;
    dropTargets.add(w);
}                                                      ❸ Remove
                                                          listener from
public void removeDropListener(SourcesMouseEvents w,  <-- drop target
    DropListener dl) {
    List listeners = (dropListeners.get(w) != null)
        ? (List) dropListeners.get(w) : new ArrayList();
    listeners.remove(dl);
}
```

This is a really simplistic way to create drop targets. We aren't actually making a new widget, we're simply storing the state of drop targets in the drag-and-drop controller. This makes using drag and drop much easier than in a lot of other systems, since it can be instrumented into almost any existing widget. So we need to store a widget as a drop target ❷, and be able to add ❶ and remove ❸ listeners for that widget.

We still need to fire events on those listeners. Listing 10.11 shows modifications to the `onMouseUp()` method in the `DragSupportListener` inner class we'll use to determine when a drop event has happened. It's inserted just before the `revert` logic.

Listing 10.11 Determining when a drop event has happened

```
int top = dragging.widget.getAbsoluteTop();
int left = dragging.widget.getAbsoluteLeft();

int centerY = top +
    (int) ((float) dragging.widget.getOffsetHeight()
           / (float) 2);
int centerX = left +
    (int) ((float) dragging.widget.getOffsetWidth()
           / (float) 2);

for (int i = 0;
        (dropTargets != null) && (i < dropTargets.size());
        i++) {
    Widget w = (Widget) dropTargets.get(i);

    if ((centerY >= w.getAbsoluteTop()) &&
            (centerY <= (w.getAbsoluteTop() + w.getOffsetHeight())) &&
            (centerX >= w.getAbsoluteLeft()) &&
            (centerX <= (w.getAbsoluteLeft() + w.getOffsetWidth()))) {
        List listeners = (List) dropListeners.get(w);

        for (int j = 0;
                (listeners != null) && (j < listeners.size());
                j++) {
            DropListener l = (DropListener) listeners.get(j);

            if (l.onDrop(dragging.widget)) {
                break;
            }
        }
    }
}
```

❶ Find center point of widget
❷ Loop through drop targets
❸ Check if widget is over target
❹ If true, stop looping through listeners

This example includes a bunch of DOM math, but the logic remains fairly simple. Find the center point of the dragged widget ❶ and loop over the drop listeners ❷. If the drag widget is inside the drop target ❸, call the `onDrop` event ❹ and terminate if `true` is returned.

Obviously, if you have a great many drop targets, breaking them up into regions so you can contain the loop and limit the amount of mouseover checking that has to be done would be a good optimization here. This method has the advantage of working no matter what the flow or position state of all the drop targets happens to be at the time a drop is handled. Working with this method becomes very simple. For instance, our `Cart` class catches book covers dropped on them:

```
public class Cart extends FlexTable implements DropListener {
// ... some code omitted for brevity
    public boolean onDrop(Widget dropped) {
        if (dropped instanceof CoverImage) {
            CoverImage cover = (CoverImage) dropped;
            boolean found = false;
            for (Iterator it = lineItems.iterator(); it.hasNext();) {
                LineItem item = (LineItem) it.next();
                If (item.book.getId().equals(cover.book.getId())) {
                    item.quantity++;
                    found = true;
                    break;
                }
            }
            if (!found) {
                LineItem item = new LineItem();
                item.book = cover.book;
                item.quantity = 1;
                lineItems.add(item);
            }
            update();
        }
        return true;
    }
// ...
```

Here we simply have to detect the drop event and determine whether the item is already in the cart. If it is, increment the quantity. If it's not, add it.

Similarly, instrumenting the `CoverImage` to be draggable is just as easy. In our `BookSummary` class you can see this being done:

```
public class BookSummary extends FlowPanel {
    private static final BookstoreConstants CONSTANTS =
        (BookstoreConstants) GWT.create(BookstoreConstants.class);
    private Book book;
    CoverImage cover = new CoverImage();
    FlexTable summary = new FlexTable();
    public BookSummary(Book b) {
        super();
        book = b;
        this.add(cover);
        cover.setUrl(b.getImage());
        cover.book = b;
        DragAndDrop.getInstance().makeDraggable(cover, true);
// ...
```

We simply call the `makeDraggable()` method and our cover image is automatically draggable.

Speaking of the cover image, you may have noticed in figure 10.3 the neat little Apple-style reflections appearing under the cover images. This comes from the `ReflectedImage` class, which we'll look at next.

10.3 JSNI special effects

Once again, we fall back to using the JSNI to create pretty image effects. Here we'll use either a `<canvas>` element or a Microsoft DirectX `DXImageTransform` to produce a faded reflection of an image. The core of this JavaScript logic comes from Neon-Dragon.net (http://cow.neondragon.net) and is available under an MIT-style license. The problems we ran into while making this class support image reflection demonstrate some interesting things about images in GWT in general, which we'll talk about after we look at the code.

Listing 10.12 shows the code for our `ReflectedImage` class.

Listing 10.12 The `ReflectedImage` class using JSNI for image effects

```
public class ReflectedImage extends Image {
    public ReflectedImage() {
        super();
        addLoadListener(new LoadListener(){
            public void onLoad(Widget widget) {
                reflect(getElement(), (float) 0.25, (float) 0.5,
                188, 150);
            }

            public void onError(Widget widget) {
            }
        });
    }

    public native void reflect(Element image,
       float height, float opacity,
       int offsetHeight, int offsetWidth)/*-{
            var d = document.createElement('div');
            var p = image;

            var classes = p.className.split(' ');
            var newClasses = '';
            for (int j = 0; j < classes.length; j++) {
                if (classes[j]!= "reflect") {
                    if (newClasses) {
                        newClasses += ' ';
                    }

                    newClasses += classes[j];
                }
            }

            var reflectionHeight = Math.floor(offsetHeight * height);
            var divHeight = Math.floor(p.height * (1 + height));

            var reflectionWidth = offsetWidth;

            if (document.all && !window.opera) {
```

❶ Specify reflection size in constructor

❷ Create <div> tag to hold image and reflection

```
                d.className = newClasses;
                p.className = 'reflected';
// ....
                reflection.style.marginBottom =
                   "-"+(p.height-reflectionHeight)+'px';
                reflection.style.filter = 'flipv'+
               'progid:DXImageTransform.Microsoft.Alpha('+
            'opacity='+(opacity*100)+
            ', style=1,
            finishOpacity=0, startx=0, starty=0, '+
            ' finishx=0, finishy='+(height*100)+')';
// ...
                d.appendChild(p);
                d.appendChild(reflection);
            } else {
                              var canvas =
                                  document.createElement('canvas');
// ...
                    d.appendChild(p);
                                            d.appendChild(canvas);

                    context.save();

                    context.translate(0, image.height-1);
                    context.scale(1, -1);

                    context.drawImage(image, 0, 0,
                                    reflectionWidth, offsetHeight);

                    context.restore();
// ...
                    context.fillStyle = gradient;
// ...
                }
            }
    }-*/;

    public native void unreflect(Element image)/*-{
        if ("reflected".equals(image.className)) {
                image.className = image.parentNode.className;
                image.parentNode
                     .parentNode
                     .replaceChild(image,
                                   image.parentNode);
        }
    }-*/;
}
```

Use DXImageTransform to create reflection ❸

❹ **Create <canvas> element for reflection**

Swap image positions

A lot of code has been omitted to save space but, skipping over the ugly part for a moment, we start by creating a new `<div>` tag to hold the original image and its reflection ❷. Then we `split` to determine whether we should use the DirectX API ❸ or the standard `<canvas>` element ❹, and we position the reflection and its image into the appropriate position in the document. Figure 10.4 shows the Safari DOM inspector view of the results.

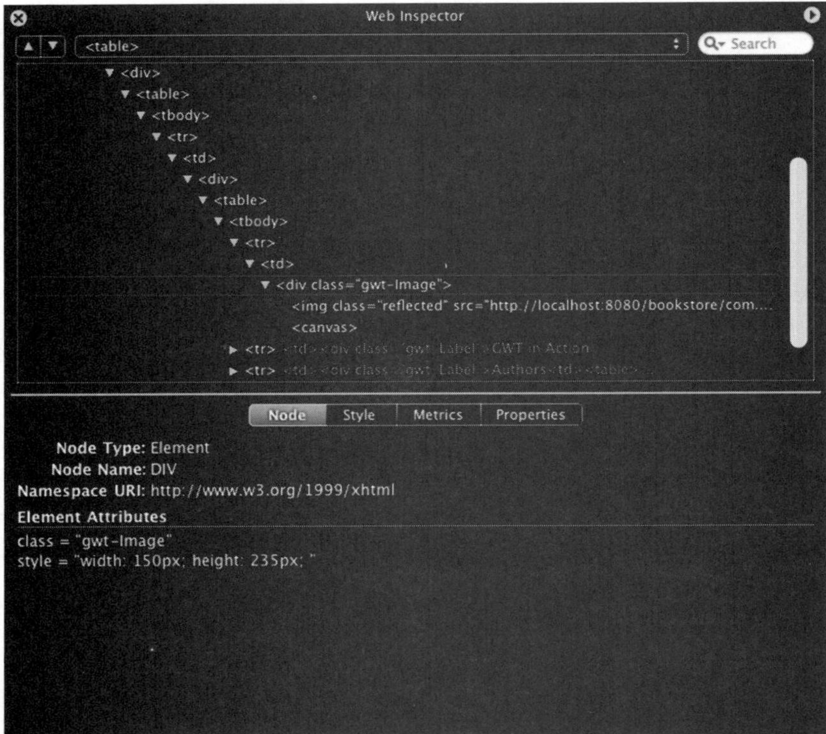

Figure 10.4 The `<div>` gets assigned the same class as the original image (`gwt-Image`) with the original image and the nested `<canvas>` tag inside.

There is a bit of hackery involved in this example, but this code is not too out-there. What's the object lesson here? The important thing to note, is that we have hard-coded the reflection size ❶. That seems silly—why have we done that? Unfortunately in Safari and Opera, the `offsetWidth` and `offsetHeight` properties on the image don't seem to be available when the `onLoad` event is fired! We have actually changed the script's execution from the original author's intentions.

The original function of this script was to look for images with a `reflected` class name and instrument them with reflections in the body's `onLoad` event. This works well for standard HTML pages you just want to add an effect to, but for GWT's dynamic pages, we need to be able to do this on demand. Since all the images in our sample bookstore are of the same size, this isn't a problem, but it does mean that at image creation time, you need to know the sizes if you intend to do calculations based on them. Even in GWT, you can't completely escape testing in all browsers.

10.4 Summary

In this chapter, we ran the gamut of things to consider in your GWT application: using the Java EE specification to secure your services and pages against an enterprise directory, implementing a basic shopping cart using a drag-and-drop system, and creating reflections on images. While these are disparate parts of the bookstore application, they have one important aspect in common: you can't escape understanding core web development principles and testing in multiple browsers and with multiple configurations.

Whether it's working with security in a cookie-free environment, or overriding some browsers' native element dragging, GWT won't do all the work for you. Recall that we said in chapter 1, GWT is a toolkit, not a framework. It won't replace good old know-how in web development, but hopefully we have given you some clues to help you avoid obvious traps. This isn't all of what's involved in web development, however.

Building up data in the client side is only a part of what you'll need to do. Another side is managing the state of the application in both the client and the server. In the next chapter, we'll look at our final application, which shows you more about using the tools GWT gives you for managing state.

11 Managing Application State

This chapter covers

- Building an enhanced Comet service
- Working with the GWT history system
- Using standard servlet state

Everything is in a state of flux, including the status quo.

—Robert Byrne

In this chapter we're going to examine an example application we call "State of the Union." This application demonstrates state management in a long-lived fashion, using log files to capture state on the server with the standard Java Servlet API. This will be done in the context of a GWT application, and within the GWT history system we introduced in chapter 1.

We'll cover using the `History` class to update the client state as the model changes, as well as deal with state on the server, representing state in the client, and exploring the possible cases where handling user actions is important. Before we get there, though, we'll take a look at implementing a publisher-subscriber messaging system on the server, and at using XML as a non-RPC data representation. All the while, we'll emphasize the placement of these techniques in the context of an MVC pattern on the client.

11.1 Overview of the sample application

State of the Union is a web-based presentation system with two parts. The first is a Swing desktop application that captures an area of your screen and shares it on the web with other people (see figure 11.2). This program is available in both source and binary forms from the Manning website. Since it's only tangential to our GWT example, we're not going to walk through all the code, but feel free to look at it on your own.

Figure 11.1 shows a UML diagram of the application and the relationships in the client classes that we'll examine in this chapter.

The other part of State of the Union is, of course, our GWT application. This application enables users to watch the presentations as they are given and provides a chat area so the presenter and users can discuss the presentation. Additionally, we'll record each presentation and allow the user to bookmark a presentation and come back to it. By returning to it, users can see it played back in real time as it occurred from the moment it was bookmarked, or they can send the link to someone else who can see the presentation after the fact.

Figure 11.2 shows the screen-sharing box surrounding a portion of a desktop window and the GWT shell providing access to the chat area of the application. The area within the box on the left is shared to the Internet Explorer client pictured in figure 11.3.

The first section of this chapter will provide an overview of the application and lay out its structure. Then we'll take a selective tour of important sections of the code, showing how the features and principles we looked at in earlier chapters can be integrated into a large working application.

In building the State of the Union application, we'll also use an enhanced version of the Comet streaming technique we introduced in chapter 5. Since conversations are taking place in real time, we want the server to *push* data to the client, and the Comet technique is an ideal solution. We'll use Luca Masini's GWT Comet implementation, which we looked at in chapter 5 (from http://jroller.com/masini/entry/updated_comet_implementation_for_gwt), as a base and expand it into a more robust solution with multiple channels, some basic permissions, and security.

After creating the Comet implementation, we'll construct a primitive file-based recording mechanism and then use the `History` class to preserve the momentary state. Once we have built a local service implementation for messaging, we need to expose it to GWT clients. To do this, we will use the plain old `javax.servlet.http.HttpSession` class in a `RemoteServiceServlet` implementation. Lastly, we take a brief look at the controller and view layers of the State of the Union application.

To begin, we'll look at the `ConversationServiceLocal` class, which provides the basis for our messaging system.

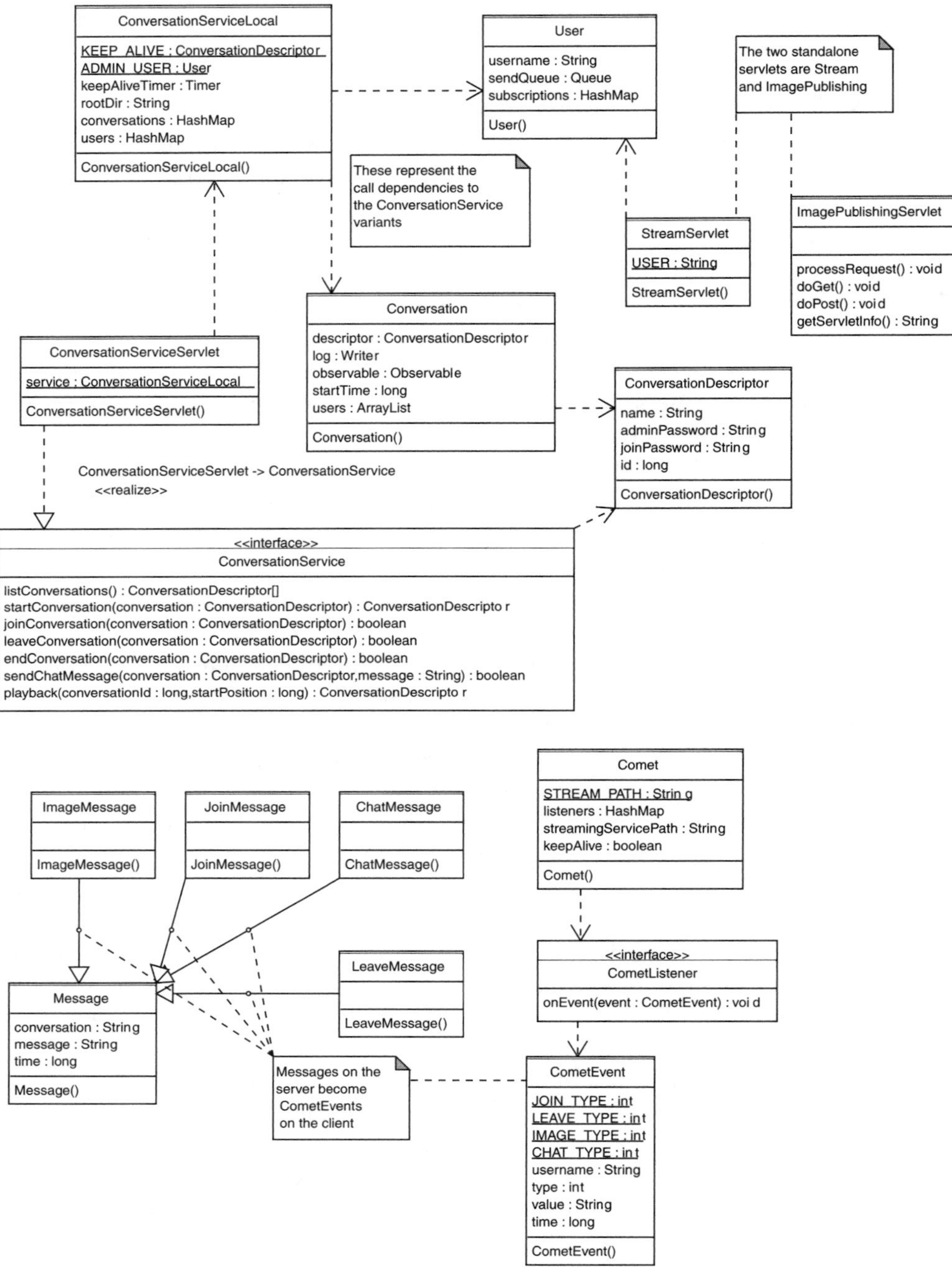

Figure 11.1 A UML class diagram of the core classes we'll look at in State of the Union

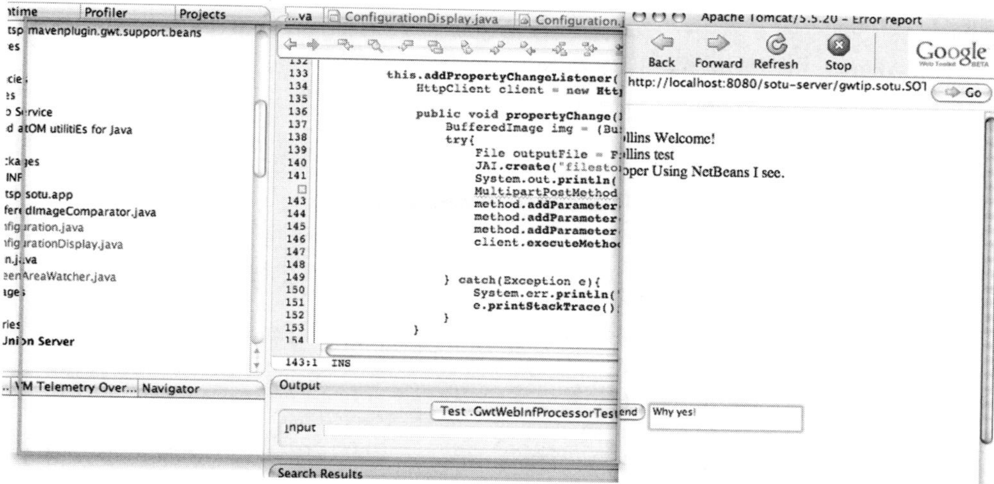

Figure 11.2 The screen-sharing application uploads the framed portion of the screen to the server.

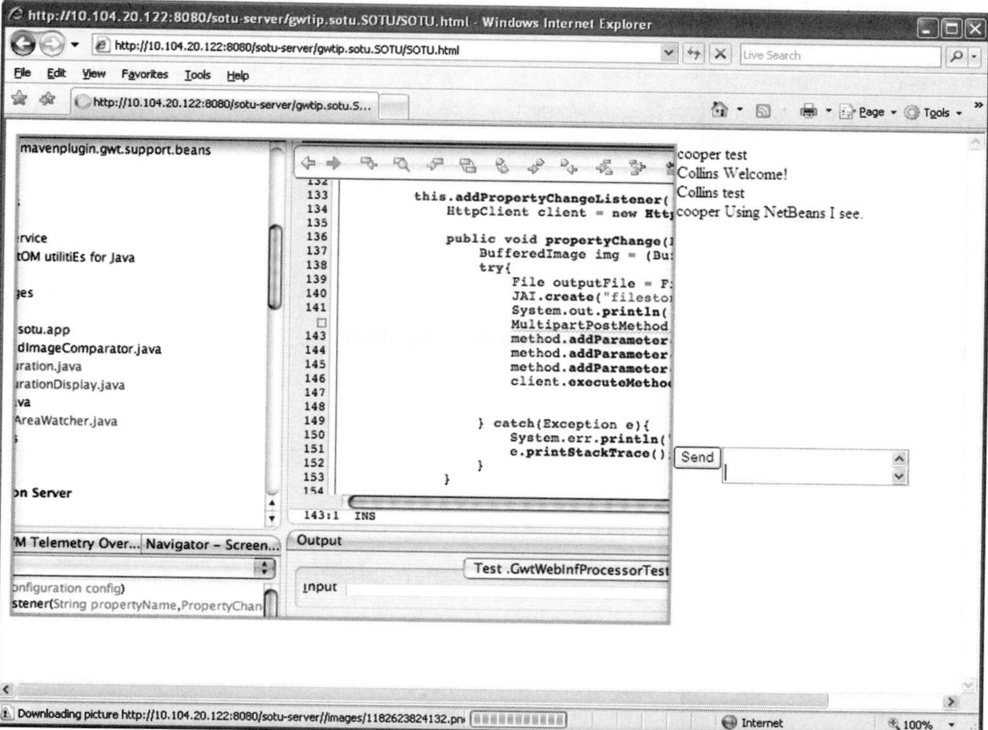

Figure 11.3 Client users can chat and see updated images from the capture application.

11.2 Creating a basic messaging service

While the Comet implementation presented in chapter 5 demonstrates the technique, the messaging system shown there was fairly rudimentary. There was only one channel shared with the whole server through the `java.util.Observable` class. In this application, we want to discretely isolate each conversation so the user doesn't receive every message that passes through the server. As we have stated before, it's usually a best practice to implement your basic service outside the scope of GWT for better code reuse. To that end, we'll start with the `com.manning.gwtip.sotu.server.ConversationServiceLocal` class and its counterparts on both the client and server.

First we need a user object. This is a basic POJO for holding the outbound message queue for each user, the channel subscriptions the user has, and a username to display in the conversations. Listing 11.1 shows our representation of a person.

Listing 11.1 User.java: the server-side user representation

```
public class User {

    public String username;
    public Queue<Message> sendQueue =
        new LinkedList<Message>();
    Map<String, SubscriptionObserver> subscriptions =
        new HashMap<String, SubscriptionObserver>();

    public User() {
        super();
    }

    public User(String username){
        super();
        this.username = username;
    }

    SubscriptionObserver createObserver(String name){
        SubscriptionObserver o = new SubscriptionObserver(name);
        subscriptions.put(name, o);
        return o;
    }

    public class SubscriptionObserver
        implements Observer {

        public String name;

        protected SubscriptionObserver(String name){
            this.name = name;
        }

        public void update(Observable observable, Object object) {
            Message m = (Message) object;
            if (m.conversation.equals(this.name)) {
                sendQueue.add((Message) object);
            }
        }
    }
}
```

Create queue of messages

Map subscription observers to conversation name

Create observer for Observable

(1) Create Observer that adds messages to the queue

Add message to send queue

Nothing too complicated here. We're simply using the `Observable` to form a queue to send to the user ❶. Unlike Masini's implementation, we're using multiple `Observables` and cannot block the `Servlet` thread waiting for notifications on all of them, so we form a queue of `Message` objects that need to go out to the user. The map of `SubscriptionObservers` keeps track of the conversations to which the user is currently subscribed.

Next we need our actual service. We'll look at this code in sections, one step at a time. Listing 11.2 shows the first part of `ConversationServiceLocal`.

Listing 11.2 ConversationServiceLocal.java, part 1: setting up the keep-alive channel

```
public class ConversationServiceLocal {
    public static final ConversationDescriptor KEEP_ALIVE =
        new ConversationDescriptor();
    private static final User ADMIN_USER = new User();
    private final Timer keepAliveTimer =
        new Timer(true);
    private String rootDir;
    static {
        Random r = new Random();
        KEEP_ALIVE.name = "keepAlive";
        KEEP_ALIVE.adminPassword =
            Long.toString(r.nextLong());
        ADMIN_USER.username =
            Long.toString(r.nextLong());
    }

    Map<String, Conversation> conversations =
new HashMap<String, Conversation>();
    Map<String, User> users = new HashMap<String, User>();
```

❶ Create keep-alive conversation

❷ Create Administrator user to join conversation

❸ Create timer that will send to conversation

Populate with random data

In this first section, we create our keep-alive conversation ❶. We start by creating a `ConversationDescriptor` for the keep-alive conversation and an artificial user to send messages to the conversation ❷ at times determined by the `Timer` ❸. While these basic data values are static, we still need to set up the elements for this service implementation. We do this in the `init()` method, shown in listing 11.3.

Listing 11.3 ConversationServiceLocal.java, part 2: initializing the service

```
public ConversationServiceLocal() {
        super();
    }

    public void init(String rootDir) throws IOException {
        if (this.rootDir == null) {
            File root = new File(rootDir +
                    File.separator + "conversations");
            root.mkdirs();
            this.rootDir = root.getAbsolutePath();

            try {
                this.createConversation(ADMIN_USER, KEEP_ALIVE);
            } catch(Exception ae) {
```

Ensure recordings directory exists

```
            ae.printStackTrace(); // this should never happen
        }
        keepAliveTimer.schedule(new TimerTask(){          ❶ Make ADMIN_USER
            public void run(){                                send messages with
                sendChatMessage(ADMIN_USER,                   TimerTask
                                KEEP_ALIVE, "ping");

                while (ADMIN_USER.sendQueue.poll()
                        != null) {                          Clear ADMIN_USER's
                    int i= 0;                               queue to save
                    i++;                                  ❷ memory
                }
            }                        Set recurring TimerTask
        }, 500, 3000);               for 3 seconds
    }
}
```

As you can see, we're using a `TimerTask` to have our admin user send a chat message of `ping` every three seconds ❶. This will keep our Comet stream open to the browser without timing out. We're also going through the `ADMIN_USER`'s send queue and clearing it out to make sure it doesn't take up memory ❷. Notice the inclusion of a dummy operation inside the `while` loop. This makes sure that the loop won't be optimized out by the compiler, as if it weren't doing anything.

In the next section, listing 11.4, are the basic beginnings you'd expect to see in the service's public interface.

Listing 11.4 ConversationServiceLocal.java, part 3: creating a conversation

```
public ConversationDescriptor createConversation(
        User user, ConversationDescriptor descriptor)
        throws AccessException, SystemException {

    Conversation check = conversations.get(descriptor.name);
    String finalName = descriptor.name;

    for (int i = 0; check != null; i++) {             Ensure unique
        finalName = descriptor.name + i;            ❶ name
        check = conversations.get(finalName);
    }

    descriptor.name = finalName;                        Set unique name
    try {                                             ❷ to descriptor
        Conversation conversation =
           new Conversation(descriptor, this.rootDir);
        conversations.put(descriptor.name, conversation);
        this.joinConversation(user, descriptor);          Automatically
                                                          join user to
    } catch(IOException ioe) {                            channel
        throw new SystemException(
            "Unable to open log file:"
            +ioe.toString());
    }
    return descriptor;
}
```

This bit of code creates conversations. It's also worth noting the use of the `Conversation-Descriptor` class here, which we guarantee to have a unique name ❶ ❷ when we create the conversation. This is a simple data class that we'll pass around to the GWT clients. It's mostly used as a data structure to contain arguments that would otherwise have to expand the method signatures of all of our service methods. The conversation itself contains the authoritative conversation descriptor we'll use to identify conversations for comparisons later. Listing 11.5 shows these comparisons to the authoritative `ConversationDescriptors` for ending and joining conversations.

Listing 11.5 ConversationServiceLocal.java, part 4: ending and joining

```
    public void endConversation(User user,
                ConversationDescriptor descriptor)
            throws AccessException {
        Conversation conversation = conversations.get(descriptor.name);

        if (
          (conversation
                .descriptor
                .adminPassword != null) &&                          ❶ Verify admin
          !conversation.descriptor.adminPassword.equals(               password
                descriptor.adminPassword
)
) {
            throw new AccessException(
                "Administration password rejected.");
        }

        try {
            conversation.log.flush();
            conversation.log.close();
        } catch(IOException e) {
            e.printStackTrace();
        }
        conversations.remove(descriptor.name);

        for (User u : conversation.users) {
            this.leaveConversation(u, conversation.descriptor);
        }
    }

    public void joinConversation(User user,
                ConversationDescriptor descriptor)
            throws AccessException {
        Conversation join = conversations.get(descriptor.name);
        if (
             (join.descriptor.joinPassword != null) &&              Verify join
                !join.descriptor.joinPassword.equals(               password
                        descriptor.joinPassword)                  ❷ as needed
) {
            throw new AccessException(
                    "Incorrect password to join this channel."
);
        }
```

```
        User.SubscriptionObserver observer =
            user.createObserver(                          Add observer
                descriptor.name                           to observable
);
        join.observable.addObserver(observer);
        join.users.add(user);
        this.sendMessage(new JoinMessage(user, join));
    }
```

Here we associate two passwords with a conversation: a `joinPassword` and an `adminPassword`. The `adminPassword` ❶, passed in on the `ConversationDescriptor` when the conversation is created, controls whether a user has permission to end a conversation while users are still joined, and it is also used to verify the image upload client, which we'll look at in more detail later. The `joinPassword` ❷ is optional but establishes whether a user can join a conversation, providing for private chats.

In listing 11.6, we can see the housekeeping involved in leaving conversations and a simple listing method.

Listing 11.6 ConversationServiceLocal.java, part 5: leaving and listing conversations

```
    public void leaveConversation(User user,
                        ConversationDescriptor descriptor) {
        Conversation leave = conversations.get(descriptor.name);
        User.SubscriptionObserver observer = user.subscriptions.remove(
                descriptor.name
);
        leave.observable.deleteObserver(observer);
        leave.users.remove(user);

        Message message = new LeaveMessage(user, leave);        Automatically
        this.sendMessage(message);                              end empty
        if (users.size() == 0) {                                conversations
            try{
                this.endConversation(user, leave.descriptor);
            } catch (AccessException e) {
                ;// this shouldn't happen;
            }
        }
    }

    public ConversationDescriptor[] listConversations() {
        Collection<Conversation> values = conversations.values();
        ConversationDescriptor[] results = new
            ConversationDescriptor[values.size() - 1];
        int count = 0;

        for (Conversation c : values) {
            if (c.descriptor == ConversationServiceLocal.KEEP_ALIVE) {
                continue;
            }
            results[count] = new ConversationDescriptor();
            results[count].name = c.descriptor.name;

            if (c.descriptor.joinPassword != null) {
                results[count].joinPassword =
```

```
                "private";                    Don't return
        }                                     joinPassword
                                           ❶  with the list
        count++;
    }
    return results;
}
```

You can see in the `listConversations()` method that we're not returning the authoritative versions of the `ConversationDescriptor` objects, since they contain the password data. We're creating new instances with only the names duplicated. If there is a `joinPassword` specified, we set that to an arbitrary value (`private`) so the clients can know that this is a password-protected channel ❶.

If you're thinking ahead to how this might work, you're already wondering how we'll deal with users that drop. Since their observers remain in the channel and in the system's object graph, if they never call `leaveConversation()`, they'll never get garbage collected. Moreover, their queues will continue to fill up as messages are added, potentially causing memory problems on the server. But don't worry. We have that covered, and we'll show you how when we look at our `HttpSession` usage.

In the final part of `ConversationServiceLocal`, shown in Listing 11.7, we finish the rest of the basic messaging functions.

Listing 11.7 ConversationServiceLocal.java, part 6: sending messages

```
    public boolean sendChatMessage(
            User user, ConversationDescriptor descriptor, String text
) {
        Conversation conversation =
                conversations.get(descriptor.name);
        if (conversation.users.contains(user)) {           ❶ Send basic
            this.sendMessage(                                 chat message
                    new ChatMessage(user, conversation, text));
            return true;
        } else {
            return false;
        }
    }

    boolean sendImageMessage(
            ConversationDescriptor descriptor, String url
) {
        Conversation conversation =
                conversations.get(descriptor.name);
        this.sendMessage(
            new ImageMessage(conversation, url));      Send updated screen
        return true;                                ❷  image message
    }

    void sendMessage(Message message) {
        Conversation conversation =
                conversations.get(message.conversation);
```

```
        conversation.observable.notifyObservers(message);
        //...                                         Part of method is
    }                                               ❸ omitted for now

    public void signOff(User user) {
        for (String name :                               ❹ Unsubscribe user
                user.subscriptions.keySet()) {             from all channels
            ConversationDescriptor d = new ConversationDescriptor();
            d.name = name;
            this.leaveConversation(user, d);
        }
        users.remove(user.username);
    }

    public User signOn(String username) {
        User user = new User();
        user.username = username;
        users.put(username, user);

        return user;
    }
```

This final bit of code shows the basics of sending messages. There is the standard chat message ❶ and a special message containing an update to the screen image display ❷. Finally it shows the basic messages for signing a user on and off from the service ❸, ❹.

This concludes our messaging service for now. You'll notice that the tail end of the code has been omitted as well as part of the `sendMessage()` method ❸. We'll take a look at this code when we visit the playback methodology we're going to use in section 11.4. For now, we're only focusing on the basics of the service.

You'll notice we're using several `Message` subclasses. These are basic classes that simply format an XML message for our GWT clients. In the `signOff()` method, you can see why we kept the hash of observers around in the user: so we can clean them all up when the user signs off the system.

Now that we have our basic publisher-subscriber system in place, we need to expose it to the GWT clients as a Comet service and move messages from the server to the client.

11.3 Handling messages on the client and server

While the `Comet` class in the `com.manning.gwtip.sotu.client.remote` package doesn't look markedly different from what you saw in chapter 5, the `Message` classes on the server get translated into `CometEvents` on the client with an XML payload that must be parsed. We also need a slightly different flow to our streaming servlet. We'll look at both of these now.

11.3.1 Messages and CometEvents

There are two sides to this equation: `Messages` and `CometEvents`. We'll use `Messages` on the server to create XML payloads that will be sent by the streaming service. Once received on the client, we'll use CometEvents to parse the XML and put it into a more usable, albeit simple, data structure.

We'll look at the Message subclasses first. Listing 11.8 shows the ChatMessage class because it's representative of the other three types.

Listing 11.8 ChatMessage.java

```
public class ChatMessage extends Message {

    public ChatMessage(User user,
                       Conversation conversation,
                       String text) {
        this.time=                                              <-- Calculate offset from the start of the conversation
          System.currentTimeMillis() - conversation.startTime;
        StringBuffer message =
            new StringBuffer("<chat>");                         <-- (1) Build StringBuffer of XML
        message.append("<user><![CDATA[");                      <-- (2) Catch special characters
        message.append(user.username);
        message.append("]]></user>");
        message.append("<time>");
        message.append( this.time );
        message.append("</time>");
        message.append("<value><![CDATA[");
        message.append(text);
        message.append("]]></value>");
        message.append("</chat>");
        this.message = message.toString();
        this.conversation =                                     <-- Carry the conversation name with the message
            conversation.descriptor.name;
    }
}
```

This class provides a pretty simplistic way of building an XML message. We're using a StringBuffer to build the message ❶, but you could use a true XML API to do the same thing. We take care that potential special character problems are handled by the CDATA sections ❷.

Once we have this XML, we need to parse it into something a little more workable on the client side. This is where the CometEvent shown in listing 11.9 comes into play.

Listing 11.9 CometEvent.java

```
public class CometEvent {

    public static final int JOIN_TYPE = 0;          <-- (1) Establish type using a constant
    public static final int LEAVE_TYPE = 1;
    public static final int IMAGE_TYPE = 2;
    public static final int CHAT_TYPE = 3;

    public String username;
    public int type;
    public String value;
    public long time;

    public CometEvent(String xml) {
```

```
        Document doc = XMLParser.parse(xml);              <-❷ Parse XML payload
        Element root = (Element) doc.getFirstChild();
        username =
          root.getElementsByTagName("user")                  <-┐ Aah! The joys of
          .item(0).getFirstChild().getNodeValue();             │ working with
        time = Long.parseLong(                               ❸ DOM code
                  root.getElementsByTagName("time")
                  .item(0).getFirstChild().getNodeValue());
        NodeList messages = root.getElementsByTagName("value");
        if (messages!= null && messages.getLength() > 0){
            this.value = messages.item(0).getFirstChild().getNodeValue();
        }
        if (root.getNodeName().equals("join")){               <-┐ Use ifs in
            this.type = CometEvent.JOIN_TYPE;                    │ Java rather
        } else if (root.getNodeName().equals("image")) {       ❹ than switch
            this.type = CometEvent.IMAGE_TYPE;
        } else if (root.getNodeName().equals("leave")) {
            this.type = CometEvent.LEAVE_TYPE;
        } else if (root.getNodeName().equals("chat")) {
            this.type = CometEvent.CHAT_TYPE;
        } else {
            throw new RuntimeException("Unknown type.");
        }

    }
}
```

While it has all the ugliness of DOM code ❷ ❸, this is where we take the payload and turn it into the proper `CometEvent`. We use a fixed set of constants to determine the type of message that's being sent ❶, and then we parse out what kind of event we're using ❹. Yes, you could pass this information in the callback JSNI method used by the `<script>` pushes in the streaming servlet, but this XML step makes it easier to expand the number of types and potentially even alter the data sent with requests. It's also fairly lightweight on the client side, since XML parsing is done natively by the browser.

Of course, the XML has to get to the browser in the first place, and for this we need to revisit the streaming `Servlet` implementation.

11.3.2 Streaming messages to the client

Our streaming servlet must be slightly different from the one presented in chapter 5. Because our service has individual users and isolates what's sent to each of them, we need to maintain these users. This is one of the functions that the `StreamServlet` has to provide. The other is to watch the user's queue and send messages as they are needed by the client.

As you saw in listing 11.3, our local service class takes care of keep-alives, so that code doesn't appear here. We're also not blocking on the `Observables` because we're actually monitoring multiple conversations at the same time rather than one broadcast channel across the whole application. The modified `StreamServlet` is presented in listings 11.10 and 11.11.

Listing 11.10 StreamServlet.java, part 1: setup and utility methods

```
public class StreamServlet extends HttpServlet {

   public static final String USER = "User";

   public StreamServlet() {
        super();
   }

   public void init(ServletConfig config) throws ServletException {
        super.init(config);
        try {
            ConversationServiceServlet.service.init(
                    config.getServletContext()
                    .getRealPath("/") );
        } catch (IOException ioe) {
            throw new ServletException("Unable to init directories", ioe);
        }
   }

    private void writeAndFlush(
        OutputStream out, String value)
            throws IOException {
        out.write(value.getBytes());
        out.write(new byte[500 % value.length()]);
        out.flush();
    }
```

❶ **Initialize with WAR path for writing logs**

Define utility method for writing to output stream

In listing 11.10 we're just resolving the real path to the deployed context directory and passing it to the static `ConversationServiceLocal` reference on the RPC servlet ❶. We also have a utility method that writes some bytes to the output stream and pads it with empty bytes so at least 500 bytes are sent. This makes sure that any buffers between the servlet and the client get flushed and the client sees the messages in real time.

Next, in listing 11.11, we'll examine the core of the stream servlet. It's a long method implementing the servlet's service call.

Listing 11.11 StreamServlet.java, part 2: the Comet stream manager

```
public void service(ServletRequest req, ServletResponse res)
            throws ServletException, IOException {
        HttpServletRequest request = (HttpServletRequest) req;
        ServletContext application = this.getServletContext();
        HttpSession session = request.getSession();

        res.setContentType("text/html;charset=UTF-8");
        OutputStream out = res.getOutputStream();
        this.writeAndFlush(out, "<html>");

        User user = (User) session.getAttribute(StreamServlet.USER);
        if (user == null) {
            user = new User(request.getParameter("username"));
            System.out.println("Setting user");
            session.setAttribute(StreamServlet.USER, user);
        }
```

Create user if there isn't one ❶

```
            try {
                ConversationServiceServlet
                    .service
                    .joinConversation(
                        user,
                        ConversationServiceServlet.service.KEEP_ALIVE);
            } catch (AccessException ae) {
                ;// this should never happen;
            }
            while (true) {
                try {
                    Message m =
                        (Message) user.sendQueue.poll();

                    while (m != null) {

                        StringBuffer write =
                                new StringBuffer(
                        "<script type=\"text/javascript\">" );
                        write.append("\twindow.parent.cometCallback('"+
                                m.conversation+"',unescape('"+
                                URLEncoder.encode(
                                m.message, "UTF-8")
                                .replaceAll("\\x2B","%20")+
                                "'));\n");
                        write.append("</script>\n");
                        this.writeAndFlush(out, write.toString());
                        m =
                            (Message) user.sendQueue.poll();
                    }

                } catch (IOException e) {
                    e.printStackTrace();
                    throw e;
                }
                try {
                    Thread.sleep(500);
                } catch (InterruptedException e) {

                }
            }
        }
    }
```

❷ Join the keep-alive conversation for new users

❸ Check user's send queue for messages

Ensure special characters work in JavaScript

❹ Poll again for loop

❺ Wait before polling queue again

This implementation isn't terribly different from Masini's, but there are a few differences. First, we need to make sure we have a `User` object and that the user is on the keep-alive conversation ❶ ❷. We're then storing the user in the `HttpSession` object (more on this later). Next, we go into a loop to poll the user's outbound message queued ❸ ❹ and send any pending messages, followed by a half second `sleep()` ❺.

Doing our polling this way has some advantages and disadvantages that you should take into consideration when you use Comet streaming. The user's outbound message could have been implemented as another `Observable`, which the servlet could block on and then send the messages as they are ready to go out. This would have the advantage of reducing the possible half-second delay between the time a message hits the conversation and the time it's sent to the user. For our purposes, however, a half-second delay isn't too bad. The disadvantage would be that once a message is ready to go out, like messages in our keep-alive conversation, all the outbound stream servlet threads will want to wake up at once. Add heavy user load to this burst behavior, and you can see how this design could cause problems on the server. The staggered `sleep()` cycle of all the threads calling into `StreamServlet` #6 reduces this risk. It also gives your servlet container the option to be a little smarter about how it handles thread pooling and I/O operations to the clients. The send workers monitoring the output stream can be recycled across connections while the executions sleep. If they all woke up at once, it might flood the send workers that are translating the `ServletOutputStream` into `java.nio` calls. At any rate, your mileage may vary, so keep this in mind when designing your applications.

Now that we have the servlet to stream the Comet messages, we need a servlet to receive images from the admin, which we'll look at in the next section.

11.3.3 Receiving images

The last part of State of the Union is another really basic class. This is a simple servlet that uses the Apache Commons FileUpload (http://commons.apache.org/fileupload/) module to take images from our Swing application and push them out to the clients. You'll notice two things about this servlet in our sample project: First, it's the only servlet that isn't defined in the gwt.xml file. We want the GWT messaging module to be reusable by other applications without rebuilding the whole system, so we'll keep the FileUpload module isolated from the rest of the servlets. Second, the fact that FileUpload has no dependencies on any GWT-specific code highlights the importance of separating your *true* service class from your GWT service class. In many cases, you might want to provide non-GWT UIs that interact with the same service. By keeping this separation clean, it's possible to use regular Java servlets with the service in the same context as your GWT application.

Listing 11.12 shows the `ImagePublishingServlet` code for turning `multipart/form-data` submissions into image messages for the GWT clients.

Listing 11.12 ImagePublishingServlet.java: sending messages from outside GWT

```
public class ImagePublishingServlet extends HttpServlet {

    protected void processRequest(
            HttpServletRequest request, HttpServletResponse response)
                throws ServletException, IOException {
        response.setContentType("text/plain;charset=UTF-8");
        PrintWriter out = response.getWriter();
        boolean isMultipart = ServletFileUpload
                .isMultipartContent(request);
        if (!isMultipart) {
            throw new ServletException(
                "What are you thinking?");          ❶ Expect a multipart upload
        }
```

```
        FileItemFactory factory = new DiskFileItemFactory();
        ServletFileUpload upload = new ServletFileUpload(factory);

        try {
            List<FileItem> items = upload.parseRequest(request);
            String conversation = null;
            String adminPassword = null;
            FileItem image = null;
            for (FileItem item : items ) {
                if (item.isFormField() &&
                        "adminPassword".equals(item.getFieldName())){
                    adminPassword = item.getString();
                } else if (item.isFormField() &&
                        "conversation".equals(item.getFieldName())){
                    conversation = item.getString();
                } else {
                    image = item;
                }
            }
            if (conversation == null ||
                    adminPassword == null ||
                    image == null) {
                throw new ServletException("No data.");
            }
            String filename = "/images/"+
                    System.currentTimeMillis() +
                    ".png";
            FileOutputStream fos = new FileOutputStream(
                    this.getServletContext()
                    .getRealPath(filename));
            CopyUtils.copy(
               image.getInputStream(), fos);
            Conversation conv = ConversationServiceServlet
                    .service.conversations
                    .get(conversation);
        if (adminPassword.equals(adminPassword)){
            ConversationServiceServlet
                .service
                .sendImageMessage(conv.descriptor,
                    request.getServletPath()+
                    "/"+filename);
            out.println("OK");
            out.close();
        } else {
            response.setStatus(response.SC_FORBIDDEN);
            new File(this.getServletContext()
                    .getRealPath(filename)).delete();
            out.close();
        }
        } catch (Exception e) {
            throw new ServletException(e);
        }
    }
    // regular servlet methods omitted for brevity
}
```

Parse incoming data

Make sure required data is present

2 Write uploaded file

3 Accept images only with admin password

Tell client everything is fine

4 If password failed, clean up image file

Again, nothing too complex here. We're taking a form upload of `multipart/form-data` ❶ and saving the image ❷. We confirm that the `adminPassword` matches the one for the channel for which the image is destined, and we call the `sendImageMessage()` method on the service ❸. If the password is wrong, we return an HTTP error and clean up the image ❹.

This is nothing fancy, but it is a servlet outside of the scope of our GWT classes, and we're taking advantage of the Maven plugin's merge feature so that this fairly standard JEE servlet gets included with the GWT application. If you have dealt with HTTP file uploads before, nothing here should seem too alien except the calls into our service, which you have already seen.

Next we'll explore the recording and playback of conversions.

11.4 Recording and playing back conversations

As you saw earlier, the `rootDir` value is initialized during the `init()` call of `ConversationServiceLocal`, but it's still incomplete. With listing 11.13, we'll backtrack to the `sendMessage()` method we skipped over in listing 11.7, and we'll look at the `Conversation` object to see how we're writing out the logs. We'll also look at the `playback()` method on the service and see some ramifications of how that works.

First, the complete `sendMessage()` method is shown in listing 11.13. What we're doing here is making sure that each of the messages sent to a conversation is written to the log file.

Listing 11.13 ConversationServiceLocal.sendMessage()

```
void sendMessage(Message message) {
      Conversation conversation =
              conversations.get(message.conversation);
      conversation.observable.notifyObservers(message);
      try {
          if (conversation.descriptor !=
          ConversationServiceLocal.KEEP_ALIVE) {          <-- Don't record keep-alives
              conversation.log.write("#"+
                  (message.time) +                     <-- ❶ Record time index
                      "#"+
                      message.message +
                      "\n");
              conversation.log.flush();                 <-- Flush so we don't lose anything
          }
      } catch (Exception e) {
          e.printStackTrace();
      }
}
```

You may have already noticed that we closed the `Conversation.log` attribute in listing 11.5, but now you know why. This is an open file inside the exploded WAR file in which we're recording every call to `sendMessage()` ❶. We're also starting each message with the time the message was sent. This information is in the XML payload as well, so this is just a convenience to keep the server from having to parse the XML during playback.

Playback is the other part of the `ConversationServiceLocal` class, and it warrants some discussion. Once we have these logs, we want to be able to play them back in real time, simulating the original conversation flow. To this end, we have the `playback()` method and a nested class in the `ConversationServiceLocal` class, as shown in listings 11.14 and 11.15.

Listing 11.14 ConversationServiceLocal.java, part 7: adding playback support

```
public ConversationDescriptor playback(
            User user,
            long conversationId,
            long startPosition)                    ❶ Begin playback for ID and time index
throws AccessException, SystemException {
        ConversationDescriptor d = new ConversationDescriptor();
        try {
            File log = new File(rootDir,
                conversationId + ".txt");          ❷ Find log
            if (!log.exists()) {
                throw new SystemException("Conversation does not exist.");
            }
            List<String> lines = FileUtils.readLines(log , "UTF-8");
            d.name = "Playback "+
                System.currentTimeMillis();        ❸ Create playback conversation
            Random r = new Random();
            d.joinPassword = Long.toString(r.nextLong());
            d.adminPassword = Long.toString(r.nextLong());
            this.createConversation(                         ❹ Create channel with Admin user
                    ConversationServiceLocal.ADMIN_USER, d);
            this.joinConversation(user, d);                  ❺ Join user to channel
            PlaybackThread playback = new PlaybackThread(
                    startPosition, d, lines);
            playback.start();                      ❻ Start playback and return descriptor
            return d;
        } catch (IOException ioe) {
            ioe.printStackTrace();
            throw new SystemException("Unable to read conversation log.");
        }
}
```

So what have we done here? The `playback()` method takes a previous conversation ID and a start time ❶. It then reads the log file for that conversation ❷, creates a new playback conversation ❸ ❻ with the `ADMIN_USER` ❹, and joins the user to the conversation ❺.

By now you might be asking yourself how this works. For instance, why does the `ADMIN_USER` create the channel, and not the person who initiated the playback? Doesn't the new conversation start a whole new log? Isn't that wasteful? The answers to all these questions is the old coders' saw, "That's not a bug, that's a feature!"

You see, rather than add a new level of control and not let the user chat in the conversation, come up with a special-case `History` management routine, or figure out how to add the user's chat to the prerecorded conversation log, we just start a new log. As the conversation plays back, the user can chat into the conversation, almost as though she is taking notes, and can bookmark the new conversation and send it to friends as she would for a real-time conversation. Because the `ADMIN_USER` starts and is a member of the conversation—though his send queue is forever ignored, and he only talks into the keep-alive conversation—the conversation is not ended until the complete playback thread has executed. This means bookmarks to the new conversation preserve the rest of the original conversation, which plays back in hyperspeed at the beginning, preserving the conversation log.

The speed of playback is controlled by the `PlaybackThread` in listing 11.15.

Listing 11.15 ConversationServiceLocal.java, part 8: the PlaybackThread

```
private class PlaybackThread extends Thread {
        private ConversationDescriptor descriptor;
        private List<String> lines;
      private long startPosition;

        PlaybackThread(long startPosition,
             ConversationDescriptor descriptor,
             List<String> lines) {
            this.descriptor = descriptor;
        this.lines = lines;
        this.startPosition = startPosition;
        }

        public void run() {
            StringBuffer currentMessage = new StringBuffer();
            String nextLine = null;
            Iterator<String> lit = lines.iterator();
            Message previousMessage = new Message();
            previousMessage.time = 0;
            if (lit.hasNext()) {
                currentMessage.append(lit.next());
            }
            while (lit.hasNext() &&
                 conversations.get(descriptor.name)
                     != null) {
                nextLine = lit.next();
                while (!nextLine.startsWith("#")) {
                    currentMessage.append(nextLine);
                    nextLine = lit.hasNext() ? lit.next() : nextLine;
                }
                String parse = currentMessage.toString();

                Message send = new Message();
                send.conversation = descriptor.name;
                send.message = parse.substring(
                          parse.indexOf("#", 2) + 1,
                          parse.length());
                send.time = Long.parseLong(
                          parse.substring(1,
                          parse.indexOf("#", 2)));
                if (send.time > startPosition) {
```

❶ **Ensure the right message**

Determine timestamp of message

```
                try {
                    Thread.sleep(send.time =
                        previousMessage.time);            <-- ❷ Sleep till message was sent
                } catch (InterruptedException e) {
                    ;//do nothing
                }
                  }
                  sendMessage(send);

                  previousMessage = send;
              }
              try {                                   <-- End conversation
                  endConversation(
                     ConversationServiceLocal.ADMIN_USER, descriptor);
              } catch (Exception e) {
                  e.printStackTrace();
              }
          }
      }
  }
```

The PlaybackThread class spins through the messages in the log file ❶ until it gets to the time index specified. Then it sends a message and takes a nap until the subsequent message was sent in the original conversation ❷, giving us the real-time playback from the original recording.

That's a good bit of server-side plumbing to support this feature. We now have a mechanism for playing back a stream from the past and recording the time index at which we bookmarked it. The question now is how to get this information to pass into the service from the client? For that, we'll jump over to the client side and look at how we're capturing this historical information in our Controller class.

The Controller class on the client side is pretty simple. We don't have a whole lot of state on the application, but we do want our bookmarking and linking to work as advertised. In the MVC design of our Comet application, our Comet object really serves as the model layer of our application: it is what our view classes watch and render, and what our Controller manipulates based on user input. While the Comet object is not a simple set of data or an object graph, it serves the same purpose.

With that in mind, our goal for our history is to preserve enough data to restore the model to the appropriate state and allow the view layer to render it as it normally would.

11.4.1 Capturing changes to the model layer

Since we have already looked at the playback() method on our service, we know how to get a replay of our model sent to the client. Here we're going to look at our Controller class, which provides this functionality (listings 11.16 through 11.18). In traditional controller layer form, it also handles calls from UI events back to our service to effect these changes on the model. It also contains basic state for our application, to make sure the proper UI elements are displayed at the appropriate times.

For the sake of simplicity, we're containing this all in a singleton to simplify accessing it from our UI classes. Listing 11.16 shows the first part of the `Controller` class.

Listing 11.16 Controller.java, part 1: setting up the client controller

```
public class Controller {
    private static Controller instance;
    public static ConversationServiceAsync service;
    public static Comet comet;
    private ConversationPanel conversation;
    private LobbyPanel lobby;
    public ConversationDescriptor currentConversation;
    private boolean ignoreHistory = false;

    private Controller() {
        super();
        service =
(ConversationServiceAsync)
               GWT.create(ConversationService.class);      ❶ Get remote service instance

        ServiceDefTarget endpoint = (ServiceDefTarget) service;
        endpoint.setServiceEntryPoint(
                GWT.getModuleBaseURL() +
                "/conversationService");

        History.addHistoryListener(                          ❷ Add history listener for changes
           new HistoryListener() {
            public void onHistoryChanged(String token) {
                   if (!ignoreHistory)
                       handleToken(token);
                }
            }
        });
    }

    void handleToken(String token){
        if (token != null &&
                token.indexOf("|") != -1) {
            long conversationId = Long.parseLong(
                    token.substring(0,
                    token.indexOf("|")));
            if (currentConversation == null ||
                    currentConversation.id == conversationId) {
                long startPosition = Long.parseLong(
                        token.substring(
                        token.indexOf("|") + 1,
                        token.length()));
                if (currentConversation != null)
                    leaveConversation(                      ❸ Leave current, start new conversation
                        currentConversation);
                playback(
                    conversationId, startPosition);
            }
        }
    }
    public static Controller getInstance() {
```

```
        return instance =
            (instance == null) ?
            new Controller() : instance;
    }
```

This bit of code just establishes our `Controller` singleton. It gets a reference to the remote `ConversationService` ❶ and sets up a `HistoryListener` for capturing linked events ❷.

The `HistoryListener` needs to check whether the change to the history is just an update to the current conversation we're already watching. If it is, we can ignore it. If there isn't a current conversation, or if the update to the history token is for a different conversation, we leave the current one where applicable and start playing back the new one ❸.

The history token is updated in code we'll look at later. This is an important function, as your browser won't reload a page if you're watching one conversation and you open a bookmark to an archived conversation. It will simply change the anchor portion of the URL, which is what we use for our history token.

The other important case comes in when someone links blindly to a conversation. We'll take care of that after looking at the `Controller` class.

Next we move on to adding our calls to the service methods, as shown in listing 11.17.

Listing 11.17 Controller.java, part 2: mirroring the service methods

```
    public void createConversation(ConversationDescriptor descriptor) {
        RootPanel p = RootPanel.get();
        p.remove(this.lobby);                               ❶ Note lack of
        service.startConversation(descriptor,                  User object

                new AsyncCallback() {
            public void onSuccess(Object result) {
                ConversationDescriptor d =
(ConversationDescriptor) result;
                conversation = new ConversationPanel(d, comet);
                RootPanel.get().add(conversation);
            }

            public void onFailure(Throwable caught) {
                Window.alert(caught.getMessage());
            }
        );

    }

    public void joinConversation(ConversationDescriptor descriptor) {

        service.joinConversation(
descriptor,
                new AsyncCallback() {
            public void onSuccess(Object result) {
                displayConversation((ConversationDescriptor) result);
            }

            public void onFailure(Throwable caught) {
```

```
                Window.alert(caught.getMessage());
            }
        });
    }

    public void leaveConversation(final ConversationDescriptor descriptor)
   {
        service.leaveConversation(
descriptor,
                new AsyncCallback() {
            public void onSuccess(Object result) {
                RootPanel.get().remove(conversation);
                conversation = null;
                comet.clearCometListeners(
                    descriptor.name);                    <-- Clear comet listeners
                selectConversation();
            }

            public void onFailure(Throwable caught) {
                Window.alert(caught.getMessage());
            }
                }
 );
    }

    public void sendChatMessage(ConversationDescriptor descriptor,
String text) {
        service.sendChatMessage(
descriptor, text,
                new AsyncCallback() {
            public void onSuccess(Object result) {
                // do nothing.
            }

            public void onFailure(Throwable caught) {
                Window.alert("Failed to send message: " +
                caught.toString());
            }
                }
 );
    }

    public void listConversations(AsyncCallback callback) {
        service.listConversations(callback);
    }

    public void playback(long conversationId, long startPosition) {
        initComet("playback-quest");

        service.playback(
            conversationId,
            startPosition,
           new AsyncCallback() {
            public void onSuccess(Object result) {
                displayConversation((ConversationDescriptor) result);
            }

            public void onFailure(Throwable caught) {
```

```
            Window.alert(caught.getMessage());
        }
    });
}
```

The most noticeable aspect of this code is the lack of `User` object being passed to the service methods ❶. As you saw in our implementation of the messaging service, a user is an argument for almost every method. In this case, it will come in when we look at maintaining our server state. When we looked at the `StreamServlet` class in listing 11.11, you saw that the user is created on the initial connection to the Comet stream. This application doesn't provide any user-level authentication, since the user name is just used as a display for messages.

Next, in listing 11.18, are the methods that set up the Comet stream and move through the UI states.

Listing 11.18 Controller.java, part 3: controlling the UI state

```
private void displayConversation(
    final ConversationDescriptor descriptor){
    RootPanel p = RootPanel.get();
    p.remove(this.lobby);
    if (conversation != null) {
        p.remove(conversation);
    }
    conversation = new ConversationPanel(descriptor, comet);
    currentConversation = descriptor;
    comet.addCometListener(descriptor.name,
        new CometListener() {
            public void onEvent(CometEvent evt) {
                History.newItem(
                  descriptor.id + "|" + evt.time);          ❶ Update history token
            }
    });

    RootPanel.get().add(conversation);
}
                                                    Take user into the channel list
public void login() {
    final DialogBox dialog = new DialogBox();
    dialog.setText("Login");

    VerticalPanel panel = new VerticalPanel();
    dialog.setWidget(panel);

    final Label label = new Label("Enter Username");
    panel.add(label);

    final TextBox text = new TextBox();
    panel.add(text);

    Button button = new Button(
            "Login",
            new ClickListener() {
        public void onClick(Widget sender) {
            initComet(text.getText().trim());
```

```
                dialog.hide();
                selectConversation();
            }
        });
        panel.add( button );
        dialog.show();
    }

    private void initComet(String username){
        comet = (comet == null) ? new Comet(username) : comet;
    }

    public void selectConversation() {
        this.lobby = (this.lobby == null) ? new LobbyPanel() : lobby;
        RootPanel.get().add(lobby);
    }
}
```

The part you need to pay attention to in this code takes place in the displayConversation() method. Here we add the CometListener that creates our new history token and updates it ❶. Since we're inside the display conversation method here, we know that the HistoryListener we created (in listing 11.16) will ignore the event because we set the currentConversation attribute.

There are a few other things you might notice about this class that aren't related to our History usage. There isn't a guarantee of a unique user name here, but that would not be hard to add. For instance, you could replace the whole step of the login() dialog with HTTP basic authentication, and have the StreamServlet fetch the user name from the HttpServletRequest object.

Now that the client is keeping the History in sync with changes to the model, we have to handle the case where someone deep-links to a specific point in a conversation from outside the application.

11.4.2 Handling deep links

The last part of the history management we need to deal with is the support for blind deep-linking into the GWT application, since we have already implemented the functionality in our controller to handle playback of channels. All that remains to be done is to check, when the application first loads, whether there is a history token provided, and if so to pass it into the handleToken() method. We can do this in the EntryPoint class, as shown in listing 11.19.

Listing 11.19 EntryPoint.java

```
public class EntryPoint implements EntryPoint{

    public EntryPoint() {
        super();
    }

    public void onModuleLoad() {
        Controller c = Controller.getInstance();
```

```
                String token = History.getToken();
                if (token == null || !c.handleToken(token)) {     ❶ If token exists, process it
                    c.login();    ❷ Otherwise, call login()
                }
            }
        }
```

Once again, this is pretty simple. If there isn't a history token, or if the `handleToken()` method doesn't like it, log in ❷. Otherwise, the `handleToken()` method will start playback of the conversation ❶.

This completes the client-side business logic, and we have seen the `ConversationServiceLocal` class already. Now we need a `RemoteServiceServlet` to bridge the gap from our `Controller` to the service implementation.

We should acknowledge that there are a few easily imaginable features that we haven't implemented in this application. For example, what if you wanted to adapt the application to support multiple channels simultaneously for the user? That's actually pretty easy. Instead of using the `History` marker, you could provide a bookmarkable `Hyperlink`. We'll look at that quickly in the next section.

11.4.3 When to use hyperlinks rather than history

The Comet implementation registers and clears listeners based on the conversation name. The `ChatDisplay`, which we'll look at in the final section of this chapter, is bound to one conversation. You could simply adapt the `displayConversation()` method to create a new tab in a `TabPanel` and have the `leaveConversation()` method remove the tab where appropriate. The problem with this, however, is that we don't want our `History` tokens to try to serialize the state of a whole bunch of conversations.

One way to resolve this quandary is to borrow a page from the Google Maps playbook. Just as Google Maps provides a small link above a map view that you can copy or bookmark, we can provide a `Hyperlink` on each tab and have the `CometListener` created in the `displayConversation()` method alter the link value. The user can then use this link as a bookmark. This is really a design decision about how the application works. While there is no correct answer, we will take the approach presented here because this maintains the natural operation of the address bar and the CTRL/Command-D bookmarking idiom most people know.

Another design option for preserving state across complex user interfaces, such as those that display different models or different aspects of a model, is to pass the model configuration back to the server and persist it there. Then, upon initial connection, the state can be loaded from a database by a simple token that's a key to a preserved display state. While this approach really wouldn't serve the user well in almost any use case, it's something to keep in mind for your database-centric applications.

Another aspect of server-side state is the regular old `HttpSession`. We'll fill in the missing pieces of our business logic next, by seeing how `HttpSession` is used in the State of the Union application.

11.5 Dealing with state on the server side

You have seen that the ConversationServiceLocal class requires a user that isn't exposed by the Conversation service we send to the client. While GWT on the server uses a different programming metaphor, you still have access to the server-side state tools (Context, Session, Request) that you have used in traditional Java web applications. We'll explore how to get access to them.

To bridge the gap between our ConversationServiceLocal implementation and our Controller, we still need a RemoteServiceServlet. Although this servlet does implement the ConversationService interface, it's still a servlet. That means we can use all the features of a servlet in our service.

Of course, for code reuse purposes, tying your service implementation to the GWT library can be a bad thing. Indeed, in the case of web services or other services outside of your application, it may be impossible. As you saw in chapter 3, making a servlet that simply proxies into the service is generally a good practice. In the case of the State of the Union application, we want even more than that. We want our servlet to get the User and pass that into the service.

The StreamServlet created our User object and added it to the session, but how do we get to it? The answer is in our RemoteServiceServlet implementation, shown in listing 11.20.

Listing 11.20 ConversationServiceServlet.java: handling session state for service class

```
public class ConversationServiceServlet extends RemoteServiceServlet
        implements ConversationService {

    static final ConversationServiceLocal service =
                new ConversationServiceLocal();      <-- 1 Create ConversationServiceLocal class
    public ConversationServiceServlet() {
        super();
    }

    public boolean sendChatMessage(
    ConversationDescriptor conversation, String message) {
        User u = (User) this.getThreadLocalRequest()          <-- 2 Get the user from the session
                        .getSession()
                        .getAttribute(StreamServlet.USER);
        return ConversationServiceServlet.service.sendChatMessage(
                      u, conversation, message);
    }

    public ConversationDescriptor startConversation(
          ConversationDescriptor conversation)
            throws AccessException, SystemException {
        User u = (User) this.getThreadLocalRequest()          <-- 2
                        .getSession()
                        .getAttribute(StreamServlet.USER);
        try {
            return ConversationServiceServlet.service.createConversation(
                         u, conversation);
        } catch (AccessException ae){
```

```
            return null; //this shouldn't happen.
        }
    }

    public ConversationDescriptor[] listConversations() {
        return ConversationServiceServlet.service
                .listConversations();
    }

    public boolean joinConversation(ConversationDescriptor conversation)
throws AccessException {
        User u = (User) this.getThreadLocalRequest()      ❷ Get the user from the session
                        .getSession()
                        .getAttribute(StreamServlet.USER);
        ConversationServiceServlet.service.joinConversation(
                    u, conversation);
        return true;
    }

    public boolean endConversation(ConversationDescriptor conversation)
throws AccessException {
        User u = (User) this.getThreadLocalRequest()
                        .getSession()
                        .getAttribute(StreamServlet.USER);
        ConversationServiceServlet.service.endConversation(
                    u, conversation);
        return true;
    }

    public boolean leaveConversation(ConversationDescriptor conversation)
throws SystemException {
        User u = (User) this.getThreadLocalRequest()
                        .getSession()
                        .getAttribute(StreamServlet.USER);
        ConversationServiceServlet.service.leaveConversation(
                    u, conversation);
        return true;
    }

    public ConversationDescriptor playback(
        long conversationId, long startPosition)
        throws AccessException, SystemException{
          User u = (User) this.getThreadLocalRequest()
                       .getSession()
                       .getAttribute(StreamServlet.USER);
         return ConversationServiceServlet.service.playback(
                    u, conversationId, startPosition);

    }

    public void init(ServletConfig config) throws ServletException {
        super.init(config);
        try {
            ConversationServiceServlet.service.init(
                        config                          ❸ Init service here and in Comet servlet
                        .getServletContext()
                        .getRealPath("/"));
```

```
            } catch (IOException ioe) {
                throw new ServletException("Unable to init directories", ioe);
            }
        }
    }
```

You understand that the service methods of the RemoteServiceServlet make reflective calls to the appropriate implementation methods on the servlet, but what if you actually want to use Servlet features in your service methods? Well, as you're no doubt aware, each request to a servlet on a container takes place on a single object and in multiple threads. Because method executions take place in this environment, the service request thread wraps around the service methods. Java has a class for isolating attributes to a specific thread: the ThreadLocal class. GWT's RemoteServiceServlet utilized this feature to give us the getThreadLocalRequest() and getThreadLocalResponse() methods. These provide access to the full suite of javax.servlet.http.* features we might have otherwise been denied.

Since the RemoteServiceServlet class in this application is but a veneer over the ConversationServiceLocal class, we can access these features, including the session, from our RemoteService methods. As you saw in the Controller, the Comet stream is opened before any service methods can be called by the Controller. That means we know a User object has been populated to the session. In each service method, we retrieve the User object ❷ and pass it, where appropriate, to the ConversationServiceLocal class, which was created with the servlet ❶.

Of course, many service implementations won't follow this pattern. If you were using a single sign-on system such as Java Open Single Sign-On (http://www.josso.org/) or an LDAP server like ApacheDS (http://directory.apache.org/) to authenticate both the web application and a web service proxied by your RemoteService, you might want to create a new service instance for each call. Or you might create the service on the first call and store it in the HttpSession with the authentication credentials provided by the HttpServletRequest. In almost all but the simplest green-field development efforts, isolating the actual service code from the RemoteServiceServlet is a good idea.

The last part of this code worth calling to your attention is the init() method. You might recall that we also initialized the service in the StreamServlet ❸. The service ignores second init() calls, but the real reasoning here is that you can't really control the order in which servlets in your gwt.xml file are created or initialized. In a traditional web application, you'd specify "load on startup" and an order. The GWT shell's universal servlet, however, denies you this option. While it's generally true that the first connection should be to the StreamServlet, you should always obey that first rule of network programming: never trust the client. We don't want to gamble the state of our service on the order in which the first client connects.

Now that our servlet is in place and we've got our User object from the HttpSession, we're almost done with the application. The last part is putting a UI on this beast and making sure we clean up after ourselves when a user leaves the application.

11.6 Adding a UI and cleaning up

You have seen a number of GWT user interfaces, from the simple to the data-bound and complex. There are several classes in the `com.manning.gwtip.sotu.client.ui` package, and most of them follow the patterns you have already seen. We're not going to look into each of them here, but we'll look at the `ChatDisplay` class briefly, since it demonstrates the use of the Comet class as a model, the `ChatEntry` class as it handles user input, and our `ImagePublishingServlet`, which sends the `IMAGE` Comet events.

11.6.1 Displaying events

First up is the simple `ChatDisplay` class in listing 11.21. This is a panel that displays chat messages to the user, watches the Comet class as the model, and renders events. It also implements the `CometListener` interface to capture the events. It's added as a listener to the Comet instance by the `ConversationPanel` class, not listed here. (See the full source listing available from the Manning website.)

Listing 11.21 ChatDisplay.java

```
public class ChatDisplay extends ScrollPanel
        implements CometListener {          <- Implement CometListener to catch events

    private VerticalPanel innerPanel =
        new VerticalPanel();                <- (1) Create inner panel for ScrollPanel

    public ChatDisplay() {
        super();
        this.add(innerPanel);
        this.setStyleName("chat-display");
        this.setHeight("300px");
        this.setWidth("720px");
    }

    public void onEvent(CometEvent event) {

            HTML html = new HTML(           <- (2) Format each message for styling
                    "<span class='user'>"+
                     event.username +
                    "</span> " +
                    "<span class='value'>" +
                     event.value +
                    "</span>");
            switch(event.type){             <- Switch on event type
                case CometEvent.CHAT_TYPE:
                    html.setStyleName("chat");
                    break;
                case CometEvent.JOIN_TYPE:
                    html.setStyleName("join");
                    break;
                case CometEvent.LEAVE_TYPE:
                    html.setStyleName("leave");
                    break;
                case CometEvent.IMAGE_TYPE:
                    return;                 <- Handle IMAGE_TYPE events with CometImage
```

```
            }
            innerPanel.add(html);
            this.setScrollPosition(
                innerPanel.getOffsetHeight());     ❸ Set scroll position
        }                                            to lowermost point
    }
```

This simple class handles most of the view to our Comet model. For almost every `CometEvent` fired, we create a simple HTML object with `<span>` elements for style purposes ❷ and add it to a `VerticalPanel`. By extending `ScrollPanel`, we're giving ourselves limited functionality, because `ScrollPanel`, much like Swing's `JScrollPane`, is just a wrapper for providing scroll functionality ❶. After each of the HTML widgets is added to the `innerPanel` property, we call `setScrollPosition()` to make sure the scroll pane sits at the bottom, allowing the user to see the newest message ❸.

HINT If you wanted to control the call to set scroll position to not interrupt people looking at the backlog in the `ScrollPanel`, you can compare the value of `getScrollPosition()` to the previous `offsetHeight()` of the `innerPanel` at the top of the method, and only call `setScrollPostion()` if the `ScrollPanel` was already at or near the bottom of its display.

Now that we're rendering messages from the server, we need to send messages to the server.

11.6.2 Sending events

We're displaying our model, and we want to make changes to it through the controller. An example of this appears in the `ChatEntry` class, shown in listing 11.22. This is another simple panel that we use to send chat messages back to the server via the controller.

Listing 11.22 ChatEntry.java: passing user events to the controller layer

```
public class ChatEntry extends DockPanel {

    private Controller controller =                Get reference
        Controller.getInstance();                  to controller
    private ConversationDescriptor descriptor;
    private TextArea entry;
    private Button send;

    public ChatEntry(ConversationDescriptor descriptor) {
        super();
        this.setStyleName("chat-entry");
        this.descriptor = descriptor;
        this.entry = new TextArea();
        this.entry.setStyleName("entry-box");
        this.entry.addKeyboardListener(
          new KeyboardListener(){
            public void onKeyPress(
                   Widget sender, char keyCode, int modifiers) {
```

```
                if (keyCode == KeyboardListener.KEY_ENTER &&
                   (modifiers &
                    KeyboardListener.KEY_SHIFT)
                        != KeyboardListener.KEY_SHIFT) {
                    send();
                }
    }

            public void onKeyUp(
                    Widget sender, char keyCode, int modifiers) {
                //do nothing;
            }

            public void onKeyDown(
                Widget sender, char keyCode, int modifiers) {
                //do nothing;
            }

        });
        this.send = new Button("Send",
            new ClickListener(){
            public void onClick(Widget sender) {
                send();
            }

        });
        this.add(this.entry, CENTER);
        this.add(this.send, WEST);
    }

    private void send() {
        if (entry.getText().trim().length() != 0) {
            controller.sendChatMessage(
                descriptor, entry.getText());
            entry.setText("");
            entry.focus(true);
        }
    }
}
```

Add KeyboardListener to TextBox ❶

Add ClickListener for Send button

Position widgets

❷ Send message, empty TextBox

ChatEntry extends DockPanel, and it contains two child widgets: a TextBox and a Button. We add a KeyboardListener ❶ to the TextBox, so when a user presses return (or enter) we send the message unless it's modified by the Shift key—the convention for most instant-messaging clients. The Send Button can also be used to send a message. Both of these methods make a call to the send() method that calls the controller and then clears the value of the entry text area so that the next message is ready to send; send() also focuses the entry element so the user can continue typing if the Send Button was clicked ❷.

This concludes our brief tour of the view level of the application. It's fairly simplistic, as there are no elements that both render model elements and make update calls to the controller level. However, we're not quite done. We still have one problem with our application.

11.6.3 Cleaning up

Because the `ConversationServiceLocal` object contains listeners that are local parts of the `User` object, even though the `User` is stored in the session, the `User` won't be cleaned up when the session ends because the static (to the context `ClassLoader`, anyway) service retains references to the listeners. We want to make sure the user makes a clean logout, and we'll do this with the elderly but little-used `HttpSessionListener` interface. This is one of the parts of our application where having the GWT Maven module merge our web.xml files really pays off. We want to make sure that when a session dies, taking the `User` with it, it cleans up the listeners after itself.

Ah, the `HttpSessionListener`. A Java developer can go almost a lifetime without using one, since most of the time a request is an atomic action, and the `HttpSession` object just stores simple data values that die an unnoticed death when the JRE garbage collection wipes them away. In this case, however, we want to actually use one. We need to make sure a `User` gets cleaned out of the service when it is no longer connected.

Of course, the `StreamServlet` will throw an `IOException` when the client resets its Comet connection, but that doesn't mean we want to create a new `User` and rejoin all the conversation subscriptions. Instead, we'll take advantage of the fact that the Comet client reconnects to the server in short intervals (or, in the case of the Lobby, refreshes the list of active conversations). Since each of these requests kicks back the can marking the end of the user's `HttpSession` time, we can set a very low threshold for session timeouts and define an `HttpSessionListener` in the web.xml to clean up after the user. Listing 11.23 shows the session listener that will clean up the `User`.

Listing 11.23 SessionListener.java

```
public class SessionListener implements HttpSessionListener {

    public SessionListener() {
        super();
    }

    public void sessionDestroyed(HttpSessionEvent httpSessionEvent) {
        User u =
                (User) httpSessionEvent          ❶ Get User from session
                    .getSession()
                    .getAttribute(StreamServlet.USER);
        ConversationServiceServlet.service.signOff(u);     ❷ Sign off user and
    }                                                         remove listeners

    public void sessionCreated(HttpSessionEvent httpSessionEvent) {
        ;//Do nothing.

    }
}
```

Here we're simply getting the user from the session before it's killed ❶ and signing the user off ❷. As you saw back at the beginning of the chapter, keeping the subscription list on the `User` is useful because it lets us gracefully clean up the `User` when the session dies. With the `User` object's subscriptions successfully removed, the `HttpSession` can end, as does this tour of the State of the Union application.

11.7 Summary

Our tour of the State of the Union application is now complete. It is our sincere hope that you find at least the Comet implementation useful in one of your applications. Even if you don't, we have now pulled together concepts you were introduced to earlier in the book. We have used a Comet data source as our model, and generated and parsed XML using the GWT XML API (triple TLA!). We have looked at how to integrate `History` management into a controller layer and looked at using the `RemoteServiceServlet` to control session state at the server. Hopefully you have come away with a better understanding of the issues around both client-side and server-side state in your applications.

In the last three chapters, we have presented sample code that illustrates the issues surrounding real-world application development with GWT. While writing code is part of every developer's job description, there are other things that factor into real-world development. Designing your application to take best advantage of the tools available is important, and we have highlighted the design decisions we made in these applications, and places where you might make other decisions to fit your application.

With that, we have reached the conclusion of *GWT in Practice*. We have covered a lot of ground here, from details on how GWT deals with projects, to how your team can deal with projects, to some techniques and technologies that make building your GWT applications easier. We hope you have increased your own bag of tools and have some great ideas for building your own GWT applications.

A Notable GWT Projects

This appendix lists notable GWT resources, including add-on modules, applications, and tools. The projects listed here generally came to our attention through the GWT user group (http://groups.google.com/group/Google-Web-Toolkit) or the GWT contributor group (http://groups.google.com/group/Google-Web-Toolkit-Contributors). These groups are themselves an invaluable resource; they are where the creators and users of GWT share ideas, discuss problems, and in general learn about GWT happenings.

GWT incubator

The GWT incubator (http://code.google.com/p/google-web-toolkit-incubator/) is a sibling to GWT that's managed by the GWT team and is "used as a place to share, discuss, and vet speculative GWT features and documentation additions." New features that future GWT releases may incorporate show up here first.

GWT Google APIs

The GWT Google APIs package (http://code.google.com/p/gwt-google-apis/) is a collection of libraries for integrating GWT with other Google APIs, such as Google Gears. It was created by the GWT team and is maintained by a collection of contributors.

GWTx

GWTx (http://code.google.com/p/gwtx/) is an extended set of the standard Java library classes on top of what's provided by the GWT distribution. It currently includes `PropertyChangeSupport`, `StringTokenizer`, and more. It was created by Sandy McArthur.

GWT Tk

GWT Tk (http://www.asquare.net/gwttk/) is a library of reusable components for GWT and includes UI widgets, utilities, debugging tools, and several well-presented examples. It was created by Mat Gessel.

GWT Widget Library

The GWT Widget Library (http://gwt-widget.sourceforge.net) is a library of many GWT widgets, including UI components such as a graphics panel, Google search elements, Script.aculo.us support, Calendar, Calculator, and utility items such as CookieUtils, ArrayUtils, pagination support, and more. It was created by Robert Hanson and is maintained by contributors.

GWT Server Library

The GWT Server Library (http://gwt-widget.sourceforge.net/?q=node/39) is a library of server-side components for GWT and Spring integration. As the general overview states, it is a collection of Java server-side components for GWT with a focus on integrating the Spring framework to support RPC services. It simplifies a lot of the server configuration required for GWT-RPC. It was created by George Georgovassilis.

GWT Window Manager

GWT Window Manager (http://www.gwtwindowmanager.org/) is a high-level windowing system for GWT. It includes draggable free-floating windows that can be maximized, minimized, opened, and closed. It was created by Luciano Broussal and is maintained by a group of contributors.

Bouwkamp GWT

The Bouwkamp GWT project (http://gwt.bouwkamp.com/) provides a RoundedPanel widget, a panel with support for rounded corners. It was created by Hilbrand Bouwkamp.

Rocket GWT

The Rocket GWT library (http://code.google.com/p/rocket-gwt/) provides a wide variety of useful GWT components. Included are many UI widgets, including drag-and-drop support, many server-side support components, code-generation components, support for Comet, various browser utilities, and more. It was created by Miroslav Pokorny.

GWT-Ext

GWT-Ext (http://code.google.com/p/gwt-ext/) is a library that integrates GWT with Ext JS. It was created by Sanjiv Jivan.

MyGWT

MyGWT (http://mygwt.net/) is a collection of GWT widgets and utilities built around the Ext JS library. It was created by Darrell Meyer.

GWT-Maven

GWT-Maven (http://code.google.com/p/gwt-maven) provides Maven 1 and 2 support for GWT. It was created by Robert Cooper, Charlie Collins, and Will Pugh and is maintained by a community of contributors.

GWT4NB (NetBeans)

GWT4NB (https://gwt4nb.dev.java.net/) provides NetBeans IDE support for GWT. It was created by Prem Kumar, Tomasz Slota, and Tomas Zezula.

Cypal Studio For GWT (Eclipse)

Cypal Studio for GWT (http://www.cypal.in/studio), formerly Googlipse, is an Eclipse IDE plugin for GWT support.

GWT Studio (IDEA)

GWT Studio (http://www.jetbrains.net/confluence/display/IDEADEV/GWT+Studio+plugin) is an IntelliJ IDEA IDE plugin for GWT.

B Quick Reference

This appendix provides a set of GWT quick-reference items. The main sections are tools and options, module and host-page configuration elements, supported JRE emulation classes, serializable type information, common UI elements and properties, and event-handling interfaces. You should find this to be a useful quick reference for commonly needed GWT information.

Command-line tools (and options)

GWT provides a set of command-line tools that help with the creation and maintenance of projects and are shortcuts for running the compiler and shell. These tools, and the arguments they take as input, are outlined here for reference.

GWTShell

`GWTShell` is a Java class (`com.google.gwt.dev.GWTShell`) that provides the environment for GWT to support hosted-mode (Java to JavaScript bridge) development. The arguments it supports are listed in table B.1.

Table B.1 `GWTShell` options

Argument	Purpose
`-port <[number]>`	Runs an embedded Tomcat instance on the specified port.
`-noserver`	Prevents the embedded Tomcat server from running, even if a port is specified.
`-whitelist`	Allows the user to browse URLs that match the specified regular expressions (comma or space separated).

Table B.1 `GWTShell` options *(continued)*

Argument	Purpose
`-blacklist`	Prevents the user from browsing URLs that match the specified regular expressions.
`-logLevel`	Specifies the level of logging detail: `ERROR`, `WARN`, `INFO`, `TRACE`, `DEBUG`, `SPAM`, or `ALL`.
`-gen`	Specifies the directory into which generated files will be written for review.
`-out`	Specifies the directory output files will be written into (defaults to current).
`-style`	Specifies the script output style: `OBF`[uscated], `PRETTY`, or `DETAILED` (defaults to `OBF`).
`<url>`	Automatically launches the specified URL.

JUnitShell

`JUnitShell` is an extension of `GWTShell` that is useful for testing. It supports all of the options of `GWTShell` except for `-noserver`. It also supports the additional options shown in table B.2. To pass arguments to `JUnitShell`, you need to use the special `-Dgwt.args=[options]` system property when you invoke a test runner.

Table B.2 `JUnitShell` options

Argument	Purpose
`-web`	Causes your test to run in web (compiled) mode (defaults to hosted mode).
`-notHeadless`	Causes the log window and browser windows to be displayed, which is useful for debugging.

GWTCompiler

`GWTCompiler` is a Java class (`com.google.gwt.dev.GWTCompiler`) that facilitates the compiling of Java source into JavaScript. It supports the arguments shown in table B.3.

Table B.3 `GWTCompiler` options

Argument	Purpose
`-logLevel`	Specifies the level of logging detail: `ERROR`, `WARN`, `INFO`, `TRACE`, `DEBUG`, `SPAM`, or `ALL`.
`-gen`	Specifies the directory into which generated files will be written for review.
`-out`	Specifies the directory output files will be written into (defaults to current).
`-treeLogger`	Logs output in a graphical tree view.

Table B.3 GWTCompiler options *(continued)*

Argument	Purpose
-style	Specifies the script output style: OBF[uscated], PRETTY, or DETAILED (defaults to OBF).
<module>	Specifies the name of the module to compile.

ApplicationCreator

ApplicationCreator is both the name of a Java class (com.google.gwt.user.tools.ApplicationCreator) and a shortcut script. ApplicationCreator is used to generate GWT project stub files and structure. It supports the options shown in table B.4.

Table B.4 ApplicationCreator options

Argument	Purpose
-eclipse	Creates a debug launch config for the named eclipse project.
-out	Specifies the directory output files will be written into (defaults to current).
-overwrite	Overwrites any existing files.
-ignore	Ignores any existing files; does not overwrite.
<class name>	Specifies the fully qualified name of the application class to create.

ProjectCreator

ProjectCreator is both the name of a Java class (com.google.gwt.user.tools.ProjectCreator) and a shortcut shell script. ProjectCreator is used to create project-related files for Ant and Eclipse. It supports the options shown in table B.5.

Table B.5 ProjectCreator options

Argument	Purpose
-ant	Generates an Ant build file to compile source (*.ant.xml* will be appended).
-eclipse	Generates an Eclipse project.
-out	Specifies the directory output files will be written into (defaults to current).
-overwrite	Overwrites any existing files.
-ignore	Ignores any existing files; does not overwrite.

JUnitCreator

`JUnitCreator` is both the name of a Java class (`com.google.gwt.junit.tools.JUnitCreator`) and a shortcut shell script. `JUnitCreator` is used to generate stub test classes. It supports the options shown in table B.6.

Table B.6 `JUnitCreator` options

Argument	Purpose
`-junit`	Specifies the path to your junit.jar (required).
`-module`	Specifies the name of the GWT module to use (required).
`-eclipse`	Creates a debug launch config for the named Eclipse project.
`-out`	Specifies the directory output files will be written into (defaults to current).
`-overwrite`	Overwrites any existing files.
`-ignore`	Ignores any existing files; does not overwrite.
`<classname>`	Specifies the fully qualified name of the test class to create.

I18NCreator

`I18NCreator` is both the name of a Java class (`com.google.gwt.i18n.tools.I18NCreator`) and a shortcut shell script. `I18NCreator` is used to generate or update `Constants` and `Messages` interfaces based on resource bundles. It supports the options shown in table B.7.

Table B.7 `I18NCreator` options

Argument	Purpose
`-eclipse`	Creates a i18n update launch config for the named Eclipse project.
`-out`	Specifies the directory output files will be written into (defaults to current).
`-overwrite`	Overwrites any existing files.
`-createMessages`	Creates scripts for a `Messages` interface rather than a `Constants` one.
`-ignore`	Ignores any existing files; does not overwrite.
`<interfacename>`	Specifies the fully qualified name of the interface to create.

Module descriptor elements

The GWT module descriptor (Project.gwt.xml) file provides configuration information to `GWTCompiler` and other tools. It supports the options shown in table B.8.

Table B.8 Module descriptor elements

Element	Purpose
`<inherits name="logical-module-name"/>`	Inherits all the settings from the specified module as if the contents of the inherited module's XML were copied verbatim.
`<entry-point class="classname"/>`	Specifies an entry point class.
`<source path="path"/>`	Specifies the path for translatable Java source code. It defaults to the client package of the current module but can be customized and can specify more than one location.
`<public path="path"/>`	Specifies the path for non-translatable resources to be included with the module, such as CSS, images, and existing JavaScript.
`<servlet path="url-path" class="classname"/>`	Loads a servlet class mounted at the specified URL path (for convenient RPC testing).
`<script src="js-url|css-url"/>`	Automatically injects the external JavaScript/CSS file located at the location specified by `src`.
`<set-property name="client-property-name" values="comma-separated-values"/>`	Sets the values for an existing client property.
`<define-property name="client-property-name" value="value"/>`	Defines a set of properties. This is useful for deferred-binding and the additional `<replace-with>` module element.
`<extend-property name="client-property-name" values="comma-separated-values"/>`	Extends the set of values for an existing client property.

Host page entries

A GWT host page is an HTML file that includes references to a GWT module and optional metatags for purposes relating to properties, as shown in table B.9.

Table B.9 Host page entries

Host page entry	Syntax	Purpose
`<script> reference`	`<script language="javascript" src="package.Module.nocache.js"></script>`	Invokes module to be loaded; the `nocache` script determines runtime settings and in turn invokes a cache script.
`gwt:module`	`<meta name="gwt:module" content="_module-name_">`	Legacy pre-GWT 1.4 means of specifying the module to be loaded.

Table B.9 Host page entries *(continued)*

Host page entry	Syntax	Purpose
`gwt:property`	`<meta name="gwt:property" content="_name_= _value_">`	Statically defines a deferred binding client property.
`gwt:onPropertyErrorFn`	`<meta name="gwt: onPropertyErrorFn" content="_fnName_">`	Specifies the name of a function to call if a client property is set to an invalid value (meaning that no matching compilation will be found).
`gwt:onLoadErrorFn`	`<meta name="gwt: onLoadErrorFn" content="_fnName_">`	Specifies the name of a function to call if an exception happens during bootstrapping or if a module throws an exception out of `onModuleLoad()`; the function should take a message parameter.

JRE library classes

GWT includes emulation for a core set of the standard Java Runtime Environment (JRE) classes, as shown in table B.10. Most of these classes work in much the same way that they do in Java, but several, such as `Object`, `Class`, `Exception`, and `Serializable`, have notable differences relating to the restrictions present in the JavaScript environment.

Table B.10 JRE emulation classes

Package	Class
`java.lang`	`ArrayStoreException`, `AssertionError`, `Boolean`, `Byte`, `CharSequence`, `Character`, `Class`, `ClassCastException`, `Cloneable`, `Comparable`, `Double`, `Error`, `Exception`, `Float`, `IllegalArgumentException`, `IllegalStateException`, `IndexOutOfBoundsExcetpion`, `Integer`, `Long`, `Math`, `NegativeArraySizeException`, `NullPointerException`, `Number`, `NumberFormatException`, `Object`, `RuntimeException`, `Short`, `String`, `StringBuffer`, `StringIndexOutOfBoundsException`, `System`, `Throwable`, `UnsupportedOperationException`
`java.utl`	`AbstractCollection`, `AbstractList`, `AbstractMap`, `AbstractSet`, `ArrayList`, `Arrays`, `Collection`, `Collections`, `Comparator`, `ConcurentModificationException`, `Date`, `EmptyStackException`, `EventListener`, `HashMap`, `HashSet`, `Iterator`, `List`, `ListIterator`, `Map`, `MissingResourceException`, `NoSuchElementException`, `RandomAccess`, `Set`, `Stack`, `TooManyListenersException`, `Vector`
`java.io`	`Serializable`

Serializable types

GWT includes support for specific classes to be serializable and sent across the wire to and from server and client using Remote Procedure Calls (RPCs). The types shown in table B.11 are those that are `Serializable`; the annotations required for `Serializable Collections` are also shown.

Table B.11 Serializable types

Type	Details
`char`, `byte`, `short`, `int`, `long`, `boolean`, `float`, `double`	Java primitive types are allowed.
`Character`, `Byte`, `Short`, `Integer`, `Long`, `Boolean`, `Float`, `Double`	Primitive wrapper types are allowed.
`String`	`String` is allowed.
`Date`	`Date` is allowed.
User-defined	Custom user-defined types that implement the GWT `IsSerializable` or `Serializable` interfaces are allowed. Custom types must also have a no-args constructor and must not contain any instance fields that are not also serializable (unless they are transient or final, as these are not transmitted).
`Collections`	`Collections` within the JRE emulated library (shown in table B.10) are allowed but must be annotated with `@gwt.typeArgs` to include type information. Fields, parameters, and return types should be annotated (when `Collections` are involved).

UI components and properties

The `com.google.gwt.user.client.ui` package provides the core UI components. Table B.12 lists the most common elements and their properties.

Table B.12 UI components and properties

Class	Usage	Default style	Event handling
`Horizontal-Panel`	Basic horizontal layout panel	None	Supports low-level browser events by implementing the `EventListener` interface.
`Vertical-Panel`	Basic vertical lay-out panel	None	Supports low-level browser events by implementing the `EventListener` interface.

Table B.12 UI components and properties *(continued)*

Class	Usage	Default style	Event handling
DockPanel	Basic layout panel that inserts indexed elements into defined sections	None	Supports low-level browser events by implementing the EventListener interface.
FlowPanel	Basic layout panel that inserts indexed elements into sections that are allowed to flow	None	Supports low-level browser events by implementing the EventListener interface.
StackPanel	Basic layout panel that inserts indexed elements directly on top of each other in a stack	.gwt-StackPanel { the panel itself } .gwt-StackPanel .gwt-StackPanelItem { unselected items } .gwt-StackPanel .gwt-StackPanelItem-selected { selected items }	Provides handling of the header for each element, which when clicked displays the associated element.
TabPanel	Composite layout panel that is made up of DeckPanel and TabBar subcomponents; it inserts indexed elements directly on top of each other in a deck	.gwt-TabPanel { the tab panel itself } .gwt-TabPanelBottom { the bottom section of the tab panel } .gwt-TabBar { the tab bar itself } .gwt-TabBar .gwt-TabBarFirst { the left edge of the bar } .gwt-TabBar .gwt-TabBarRest { the right edge of the bar } .gwt-TabBar .gwt-TabBarItem { unselected tabs } .gwt-TabBar .gwt-TabBarItem-selected { additional style for selected tabs }	Implements SourcesTabEvents, which allows a TabListener to attach.

Table B.12 UI components and properties *(continued)*

Class	Usage	Default style	Event handling
`HTMLTable`	Panel that acts as a base providing HTML type table support	None, but subclasses `HTMLTableCell-Formatter` and `HTMLTableRow-Formatter` providing access to cell- and row-level styling	Implements `SourcesTableEvents`, which allows a `TableListener` to attach.
`FlexTable`	`HTMLTable`-derived panel that supports dynamically created non-balanced rows and cells	Provides its own specialized subclass of `HTMLCellFormatter`, `FlexCellFormatter`	Implements `SourcesTableEvents` through `HTMLTable` parent.
`Grid`	`HTMLTable`-derived panel that supports rigidly defined rows and cells	None, but can utilize the parent `HTMLTable` subclasses for styling	Implements `SourcesTableEvents` through `HTMLTable` parent.
`FocusPanel`	Simple functional panel that supports focus events	None	Implements `SourcesClickEvents`, `SourcesFocusEvents`, `SourcesKeyboardEvents`, `SourcesMouseEvents`, and `SourcesMouseWheelEvents`; these allow `ClickListener`, `FocusListener`, `KeyboardListener`, `MouseListener`, and `MouseWheelListener` to attach.
`ScrollPanel`	Simple functional panel that supports scroll events	None	Implements `SourcesScrollEvents`, which allows a `ScrollListener` to attach.
`PopupPanel`	Popup panel	None	Implements `SourcesPopupEvents`, which allows a `PopupListener` to attach.
`DialogBox`	`PopupPanel` that allows for small draggable informational areas to be placed in panels that are pop-ups over other widgets	`.gwt-DialogBox { the outside of the dialog }` `.gwt-DialogBox .Caption { the caption }`	Subclass of `PopupPanel` that implements `SourcesPopupEvents` and `MouseListener` (allows a `PopupListener` to attach and directly supports mouse events).

Table B.12 UI components and properties *(continued)*

Class	Usage	Default style	Event handling
MenuBar	Menu widget that can contain submenus or fire commands when an element is chosen	.gwt-MenuBar { the menu bar itself } .gwt-MenuBar .gwt-MenuItem { menu items } .gwt-MenuBar .gwt-MenuItem-selected { selected menu items }	Implements PopupListener.
MenuItem	A class representing an item placed inside a MenuBar	None	Supports either a submenu or a command (which has an execute method) when selected.
Tree	A tree widget that presents nodes in expandable and collapsible sections	.gwt-Tree { the tree itself } .gwt-Tree .gwt-TreeItem { a tree item } .gwt-Tree .gwt-TreeItem-selected { a selected tree item }	Implements SourcesFocusEvents, SourcesKeyboardEvents, and SourcesMouseEvents; these allow FocusListener, KeyboardListener, and MouseListener to attach.
TreeItem	A class representing an item placed inside a Tree	None	None.
Button	A ButtonBase subclass that implements a clickable button	.gwt-Button { }	Implements SourcesClickEvents, SourcesFocusEvents, and SourcesKeyboardEvents; these allow ClickListener, FocusListener, and KeyboardListener to attach.
CheckBox	A ButtonBase subclass that implements a checkbox	.gwt-CheckBox { }	Implements SourcesClickEvents, SourcesFocusEvents, and SourcesKeyboardEvents; these allow ClickListener, FocusListener, and KeyboardListener to attach.

Table B.12 UI components and properties *(continued)*

Class	Usage	Default style	Event handling
`RadioButton`	A `CheckBox` subclass that implements a radio button	`.gwt-RadioButton { }`	Implements `SourcesClickEvents`, `SourcesFocusEvents`, and `SourcesKeyboardEvents`; these allow `ClickListener`, `FocusListener`, and `KeyboardListener` to attach.
`ListBox`	A class that presents a list of choices to the user	`.gwt-ListBox { }`	Implements `SourcesChangeEvents`, `SourcesClickEvents`, `SourcesFocusEvents`, and `SourcesKeyboardEvents`; these allow `ChangeListener`, `ClickListener`, `FocusListener`, and `KeyboardListener` to attach.
`TextArea`	A `TextBoxBase` subclass that implements a multiline text input widget	`.gwt-TextArea { }`	Implements `SourcesChangeEvents`, `SourcesClickEvents`, `SourcesFocusEvents`, and `SourcesKeyboardEvents`; these allow `ChangeListener`, `ClickListener`, `FocusListener`, and `KeyboardListener` to attach.
`TextBox`	A `TextBoxBase` subclass that implements a single-line text entry	`.gwt-TextBox { }`	Implements `SourcesChangeEvents`, `SourcesClickEvents`, `SourcesFocusEvents`, and `SourcesKeyboardEvents`; these allow `ChangeListener`, `ClickListener`, `FocusListener`, and `KeyboardListener` to attach.
`PasswordTextBox`	A `TextBoxBase` subclass that implements a single-line password (hidden text) entry	`.gwt-PasswordTextBox { }`	Implements `SourcesChangeEvents`, `SourcesClickEvents`, `SourcesFocusEvents`, and `SourcesKeyboardEvents`; these allow `ChangeListener`, `ClickListener`, `FocusListener`, and `KeyboardListener` to attach.

Table B.12 UI components and properties *(continued)*

Class	Usage	Default style	Event handling
`FormPanel`	A class used to group input elements for use with an HTML form submission	None	Implements `FiresFormEvents`, which allows a `FormHandler` to attach.
`FileUpload`	A class used to support the HTML `<input type='file'>` element; must be used within a `FormPanel`	None	Supports low-level browser events by implementing the `EventListener` interface.

Listener and source interfaces

The `com.google.gwt.user.client.ui` package provides interfaces related to event handling for various GWT components. Table B.13 lists the most common of these listener and source interfaces.

Table B.13 Event source and listener interfaces

Listener interface	Source interface	Description	Methods
`ChangeListener`	`SourcesChangeEvents`	Used when a component changes, such as the elements in a list being updated.	`onChange()`
`ClickListener`	`SourcesClickEvents`	Used when a mouse button is clicked.	`onClick()`
`FocusListener`	`SourcesFocusEvents`	Used when a widget gains or loses focus.	`onFocus()` `onLostFocus()`

`Keyboard-Listener`	`SourcesKeyboard-Events`	Used when keys on the keyboard are pressed.	`onKeyDown()`
			`onKeyPress()`
			`onKeyUp()`

`LoadListener`	`SourcesLoadEvents`	Used when a widget completes loading, typically for images.	`onError()` `onLoad()`

`MouseListener`	`SourcesMouseEvents`	Used when the mouse is moved.	`onMouseDown()`
			`onMouseUp()`
			`onMouseEnter()`
			`onMouseLeave()`
			`onMouseMove()`

`MouseWheel-Listener`	`SourcesMouse-WheelEvents`	Used then the mouse wheel is moved.	`onMouseWheel()`

Table B.13 Event source and listener interfaces *(continued)*

Listener interface	Source interface	Description	Methods
PopupListener	SourcesPopupEvents	Used when a popup window is closed.	onPopupClosed()
ScrollListener	SourcesScrollEvents	Used when a scroll bar is moved.	onScroll()
TabListener	SourcesTabEvents	Used directly before and when a navigation tab is selected.	onBeforeTab-Selected() onTabSelected()
TableListener	SourcesTableEvents	Used when a table cell is clicked.	onCellClicked()
TreeListener	SourcesTreeEvents	Used when an item in a tree is selected, or when a tree node is opened or closed.	onTreeItem-Selected() onTreeItem-StateChanged()

index

Symbols

.NET 19, 131
$doc 152
$wnd 152

Numerics

1...n relationship 262

A

absoluteLeft 277
absoluteTop 277
Abstract Windowing Toolkit 8, 272
acceptance testing 213, 226
Action 99
ActionScript 121–123
ActiveDirectory 282
ActiveX 151
addStyleName 56
Adobe 121
Ajax environment 278
AJAX. *See* Asynchronous JavaScript and XML
allowScriptAccess 127
Amazon 108
anchor 322
annotation 19, 23, 101, 108, 117
anonymous inner class 46
Ant 59, 77, 184, 191, 194–195, 238
  build file 186
Apache JMeter 224
Apache Software Foundation 195
Apache Tomcat 12, 58, 62, 75, 77, 100, 130, 200, 205–206, 209
ApacheDS 282, 329
appendChild 152
applet 131, 135, 137
applicationContext.xml 263
ApplicationCreator 34, 36, 56, 59, 62, 147, 217, 340
Array 179
ArrayList 167
arrays 150, 173
artifact 199–200
AsyncCallback 66, 68, 71, 110, 126, 141, 233
asyncGet 113
asynchronous 66, 68, 110
Asynchronous JavaScript and XML 3, 6, 68, 108
asyncPost 113
Atom Publishing Protocol 112
Autocomplete 162
automated build 212
AWT. *See* Abstract Windowing Toolkit
Axis 131, 257

B

Bamboo 244
BeanMapping 257, 259
Benchmark 226–227
  begin 228
  end 228
benchmarking 212
binding, deferred 26, 214
bookmarks 7
boolean 150
bootstrap 13, 40
Bouwkamp GWT 336
box model 10
build 77, 200
  file 184
  GWT 231
  phase 195, 235
  queue 243
  tool 184, 187, 191, 233
building 59, 183
Button 44, 49, 56, 71, 332
byte 150

C

cache 15
CalculatorWidget 43
callback 68, 70, 74, 110, 122, 156, 179
canvas tag 296–297
Cascading Style Sheets 5, 33, 35, 54
CATALINA_HOME 130
catalina.base 79
CDATA 152, 311
certificate 136
change
  events 88
  notifier 47
ChangeListener 97
char 150

checkpoints 213
Checkstyle 7
CI. *See* continuous integration
ClassLoader 333
classpath 196
ClickListener 45, 49, 71, 95, 161, 212
client 14, 39
client.ui 90
closure 110, 168
code coverage 221, 226, 233
  patch 231
code generation 26, 178
com.google.gwt.junit.reportPath 228
com.google.gwt.xml.client.Document 116
Comet 108, 304, 310, 320, 329
  callback 314
  pushing data to the client 301
  setting up the stream 324
  streaming to the browser 137–141, 304
  support for 336
CometEvent 310, 331
CometListener 326
Commons-Collections 200
Commons-DBCP 78, 200
Commons-Pool 78, 200
Comparator 275
compile 186
compiler lifecycle 24
compileTarget 200, 236
component oriented 30, 45
Composite 43, 93
concurrency 110
ConcurrentHashMap 146
Constants 27
container 188
Context 327
context configuration 75
context.xml 78, 205–206, 209, 282
ContextListener 263
continuous integration 11, 212, 221, 234, 239, 242–243
Continuum 244
controller 41, 49, 51, 53, 86, 98, 178, 212, 223
cookie 286, 288
coverage report 239
coverage.ec 233
coverage.em 233
Create Read Update Delete 112, 250, 282, 289
Cross Site Scripting 15, 108
crossdomain.xml 130
CRUD. *See* Create Read Update Delete
Cruise Control 244
CSS. *See* Cascading Style Sheets
Cypal Studio for GWT 337

D

DamageControl 244
DAO. *See* Data Access Object
dashboard 243
data
  binding 86
  validation 98, 100
Data Access Object 260, 263
Data Transfer Object 65, 100, 251, 256, 259, 279
database 98, 100
DataSource 78, 80, 102, 200
debugger 7, 23, 58, 80
deferred binding 26, 214
define-property 24, 39
delay test 221
delayTestFinish 221, 223
DELETE 110, 112, 114–115
dependencies 186, 196
  scope 199
deploying 59, 183
deployment 13, 187
  descriptor 75, 206
deserialization 10, 117
design patterns 31, 42
  See also Model View Controller
DHTML 108, 137
DialogBox 276, 278
Dictionary 27, 287
Direct Web Remoting 4
directory structure 34
DirectX 297
distribute 186
div 291, 293, 297
DockPanel 332
document 115, 152
Document Object Model 8, 10, 25, 116, 151
  changing attributes 155
  drop event 294
  messaging 312
  SourceMouseEvents interface 290
  toggle() method 161–162
Dojo 3, 131
DOM. *See* Document Object Model
double 150
Dozer 259
drag and drop 162, 177, 281, 289
dragdrop.js 162
Draggable 162, 166
DragListener 168
DragSupportListener 294
DTO. *See* Data Transfer Object
DWR. *See* Direct Web Remoting

E

Echo2 4
Eclipse 58, 62, 70, 147, 153, 189, 215, 337
ECMAScript 121
Effect parent class 156
EJB. *See* Enterprise JavaBean
Element 116, 162, 170
embed 126–127
EMMA 231–233, 236–237
  Ant 238
  report 233, 238
encodeURL 285–286
Enterprise JavaBean 67, 110
entity 103
Entity (annotation) 251
EntityExistsException 105
EntityManagerFactory 105, 263
entry 112
  point 13–14, 16, 36, 38, 40, 71–72, 186
EntryPoint 15, 40, 70, 127, 160, 165, 325
equals 151
eval 123
event 53, 168
  driven 45, 53
  handling 46, 212, 349
exported annotation 180
Ext JS 3, 336
extend-property 27, 39
extensible 50, 53
ExternalInterface 121, 123, 131

F

Fedora Directory Server 282
file upload 279
FileUpload 278, 315
filter tests 223
FindBugs 7
finish test 221

finishTest 221, 223
Firebug 224
Firefox 8, 58, 110, 230
firePropertyChange 89, 267
FLA 121
Flash 6, 108–109, 121, 123, 130–131
Flash 8 121, 131
Flash MX 2004 121
flexibility 50
FlexTable 92
float 150
FocusPanel 290
form 285
  tag 279
formatting 154
form-based authentication 285–286
FormHandler 279
FormPanel 278–279
frame 108
fully qualified 55

G

garbage collection 98
generateClientBeans 256
generate-with 27
generator 24
generics 23, 117, 119, 256
GET 110, 112, 115
getElement 93, 158
getElementsByTagName 116
getModuleName 213
getScrollPosition 331
getText 97
getThreadLocalRequest 329
getWidget 93
Glassfish 130
Glick, Brian 74, 152
goal 200
Google Maps 110
  API 109
Google Web Toolkit 4, 9
  See also GWT
google.webtoolkit.extrajvmargs 202
google.webtoolkit.home 202
Grid 44, 56, 92
group 199
groupOfUniqueNames 283
GWT
  compiler 118, 188, 215
  contributor group 335
  coverage JAR 231–232, 236
  Google APIs 335
  incubator 335
  module descriptor 341
  Rocket library 336
  Server Library 336
  Studio 337
  third party related projects 187
  Tk 336
  user group 335
  Widget Library 336
  Window Manager 336
GWT Studio 337
GWT_HOME 34, 112
gwt:module 37
gwt:onLoadErrorFn 38
gwt:onPropertyErrorFn 37
gwt:property 37
gwt.args 230
  system property 213
gwt.beanProperties 180
gwt.benchmark.param 228
gwt.constructor 180
gwt.coverage.enable 232–233
GWT.create 70
GWT.create() 26
gwt.exported 180
gwt.fieldName 180
gwt.global 180
gwt.imported 180–181
gwt.namePolicy 181
gwt.noIdentity 181
gwt.readOnly 181
gwt.typeArgs 179
gwt.xml 151, 159
GWT4NB 111, 337
GWT-API-Interop 178
GWTCompiler 9, 19, 36, 56, 58, 62, 67, 116, 118, 149, 194, 339
gwt-dev-mac.jar 153
GWT-Ext 336
GWTHandler 265
GWT-Maven 196–197, 200, 209, 221, 264
  benefits 205
  generating GWT client beans 256
  goals 196
  properties 202
  support 337
  testing concepts 235
GWTRPCServiceExporter 264
gwt-servlet.jar 189, 200
GWTShell 56–57, 62, 72, 105, 196, 200
  and Hibernate 102
  and JUnit 213, 219
  list of arguments 338
  and Maven 204
  overview 12–16
  shortcut scripts 36
  and SOAP 130
  and Tomcat 75
GWTShellServlet 75–76, 188, 208–209
GWT-SL 264
GwtTest 223, 235
gwtTest 237
GWTTestCase 196, 212–213, 216, 218–220, 223, 235
GwtTestCase 205
gwt-user.jar 200
GWTx 86, 256, 335

H

hashCode 151
HashMap 119, 170
height 155, 158
Hello World 36, 62
hexadecimal 72
Hibernate 100, 102, 104
highlighting 154
History 11, 300, 318, 325–326
  bookmarking 326
  token 322
HistoryListener 322, 325
HorizontalPanel 93
host page 13–14, 36–37, 55, 80, 151–152, 342
hosted mode 12, 19, 80, 188–189, 205
  browser 16, 57
  GWT testing 212, 216
  GWTShellServlet 75
  running in 72
  and web mode 59
  web.xml file 208
HostedModeException 151
HTML 5, 35, 37, 54, 92, 109
  Host Page 284
  table 44
HTMLTable 92
HTTP 40, 110, 113–114, 188, 224
HTTP Basic authentication 284–285
HTTPRequest 108, 110, 112, 115

HttpServlet 189
HttpServletRequest 325, 329
HttpSession 301, 309, 314, 326, 329, 333–334
HttpSessionListener 333
Hudson 240–243
  Job 241
  workspace 243
Hyperlink 326

I

I18N. *See* internationalization
I18NCreator 341
IDE. *See* Integrated Development Environment
IDEA. *See* IntelliJ IDEA
IDENTITY 103
iframe 138, 144
ImageBundle 10
import 186
inheritance 13, 40, 118, 186
inherits 14, 38, 72, 153, 159
  element 115
initWidget 93
injected stylesheet 39
input elements 42
instrumenting classloader 233
int 150
Integrated Development Environment 7, 23, 33, 59, 108, 153, 221
IntelliJ IDEA 153, 337
internationalization 11, 27
Internet Explorer 8, 58, 127, 133, 230
IntRange 228
InvocationException 265
IOException 333
iPhone 6
IsSerializable 64, 88, 117, 179

J

j_password 286
j_security_check 284–285
j_username 286
J2SE 23
Jakarta Commons 78
Jakarta Commons-Collections 200
Jakarta Commons-DBCP 78, 200
JAR 184
jarsigner 136–137
Java 4, 19, 62
Java API for XML Web Services 74, 131, 134, 257
Java Applet 108
  Plugin 6, 132
Java Application Archive 184, 196, 200
Java Archive. *See* JAR
Java bytecode 212
Java Community Process 190
Java Enterprise Edition 81, 105, 250, 260, 263, 299
Java Naming and Directory Interface 77–78
Java Native Interface 150
Java Open Single Sign-on 329
Java Persistence API 80, 86, 100, 220, 251, 253, 279
Java Platform Debugger Architecture 58
Java Runtime Environment 23, 100, 136
  library classes 343
Java Servlet
  API 300
  Specifications 189
JAVA_HOME 133
java.nio 315
java.util 117
java.util.Observable 304
javac 186, 194, 218
JavaDoc 19, 23, 108, 117–118
  style annotation 228
JavaScript 4, 6, 19, 29, 35, 54, 62, 116, 212, 216, 281
  Native Interface 23, 29, 121, 138, 148, 159
  Object Notation 62, 72, 108, 119, 151–152, 188
JavaScriptDecorator 128
JavaScriptObject 128, 135, 150–151, 164, 176, 181
JavaScriptObjectDecorator 128–129
JavaServer Faces 6, 86, 105
JavaServer Pages 285
JAX-RPC 257
JAX-WS. *See* Java API for XML Web Services
JDBC 78, 100
JEE. *See* Java Enterprise Edition
JNDI. *See* Java Naming and Directory Interface
JNDIRealm 282
JNI. *See* Java Native Interface
JOSSO. *See* Java Open Single Sign-on
JPA. *See* Java Persistence API
JPDA. *See* Java Platform Debugger Architecture
JRE. *See* Java Runtime Environment
jsessionid 287
JSF. *See* JavaServer Faces
JSFunction 179
JSIO 178–179
JSList 179
JSNI 121, 128, 148, 184, 296, 312
JSNI. *See* JavaScript Native Interface
JSObject 134
JSON 108, 116
JSON. *See* JavaScript Object Notation
JSONObject 119
JSONParser 119
JSONString 120
JSONValue 120
JSP. *See* JavaServer Pages
JSR-181 131
JSWrapper 178–180
JUnit 7, 12, 212–213, 223–224, 228, 232
  module 213
JUnitCreator 217–219, 221, 341
JUnitHost 214
JUnitRunner 218
JUnitShell 196, 213, 216, 219, 221, 230, 235, 339
JVM arguments 235
JXplorer 283

K

KeyboardListener 45, 97, 331–332
keytool 136
Kodo 100

L

Label 93
layout 14, 33, 42
  panels 42
lazy loading 251
LDAP 282–283, 286, 329
limited JRE environment 221
List 179, 274

ListBox 93, 98, 271, 274
listener 45, 47, 89, 349
LiveConnect 127, 132
locale 29
Localizable 29
LocalizableGenerator 29
logging 17
  console 16, 57
logic 53
logLevel 17, 20, 74
long 150
look and feel 54
loose coupling 56

M

map-null 260
Masini, Luca 138, 301
Maven 36, 59, 77, 191, 212, 219, 221, 241
  AntRun plugin 237
  automating GWT builds 195–197, 234–236
  configuring Maven WAR plugin 200
  generateClientBeans settings 256
  layout 201
  merge feature 317
  reports 239
  repository 199
  site documentation 238
  site plugin 237
  support 337
  WAR plugin 200
Maven 1 196
Maven 2 196
media 54
Meebo.com 137
mergewebxml 209
message-based programming 74
Messages 27
meta tag 29, 37
META-INF 209
metaprogramming 24, 27
Microsoft Direct X 296
MIME-type 76
model 41, 46, 53, 86, 89, 94, 212, 223
Model View Controller 6, 33, 40, 46, 49, 61, 111, 213, 265, 320
Model View Presenter 42
module 9, 38, 72, 80, 151, 184, 186, 194, 200, 205
module definition 36
module descriptor 38, 40
module file 38
Moo.fx 149, 155–156, 158, 184
mouseover 294
Mozilla 127, 292
  Firefox 58, 110, 230
  Foundation 109
multipart/form-data 278, 315
MVC. *See* Model View Controller
MVP. *See* Model View Presenter
MyGWT 337
MySQL 103

N

NamedQueries (annotation) 253
native 149, 170
navigation 95
NetBeans 58, 111, 132, 147, 153, 337
Netscape 6, 108, 127
nocache script 40
nocache.js 15, 37
non-serializable 88
noserver 19, 79, 209

O

OBFuscated 21
object 126
Object notation 119
object oriented 40, 49, 100
Observable 146, 314
Observer 40–41, 46, 86, 110, 144, 166, 168, 171, 180
observer/observable 46
offestWidth 298
offsetHeight 298, 331
onBeforeRequestDeserialized 224
onChange 47, 97, 168
OnChangeListener 45
onClick 212
onDrag 166
onDrop 294
onEnd 166
onFault 123
onLoad 298
onModuleLoad 16
onMouseUp 293–294
onResult 123
onStart 166
onSuccess 100
OO. *See* object oriented
opacity 155
OpenJPA 100, 104
OpenLDAP 282
Opera 8, 298
operator 48
  buttons 53
org.w3c.dom.Document 116
ORM 251
orm.xml 101, 103–104, 251

P

PAC. *See* Presentation Abstraction Control
packaging 183–184, 196, 199
page 95
  based 86
Panel 56
parse 116
PCS 89
PendingCall 123
persistence unit 101, 263
persistence.xml 101
PersistenceContext 105
phase 200
PHP 19, 131
plain old Java object 68, 251, 304
plain old XML over HTTP 112, 188
plugin.jar 133
PMD 7
POJO. *See* plain old Java object
POM. *See* Project Object Model
pom.xml 201
POST 110, 112, 115
POX. *See* XML over HTTP
Presentation Abstraction Control 42
Primary Key 274
processCall 70
profile 202
profiler 58
Project Object Model 197, 199–200, 235
ProjectCreator 62, 147, 185–186, 217, 340
property 27
propertyChange 223
PropertyChangeEvent 86, 95, 253, 279
PropertyChangeListener 86, 96, 223, 274–275

PropertyChangeListenerProxy 97, 275
PropertyChangeSupport 46, 86, 335
property-provider 25
Prototype 159
public 14, 39
  path 35, 39, 55–56, 188
PUT 110, 112, 114–115

R

ReadyCallback 127, 135
Realm 283
rebind 14
Reenskaug, Trygve 41
ReflectedImage 296
Reflection 96
refresh 58
Remote Method Invocation 110, 230
remote package 230
Remote Procedure Call 4, 9–10, 107, 112, 225, 257, 344
  building and deploying applications 187–189
  creating with GWT 61–62, 66, 72, 79
  payload 226
  testing GWT RPC 212, 219
remote testing 226
RemoteBrowserManager 230
RemoteService 66, 68, 329
RemoteServiceServlet 66, 68–69, 200, 264, 279, 301
  database 104
  getThreadLocalRequest method 329
  getThreadLocalResponse method 329
  managing application state 326–327, 329
  testing GWT 224
remoteweb 230
removePropertyChange-Listener 97
replace-with 25, 39
reporting dashboard 239
ReportViewer 228
Representational State Transfer 62, 108, 112, 114, 188
Request 70, 327
RequestBuilder 114–115
RequestCallback 114
request-response cycle 53
resource
  bundle 27
  injection 39, 54–55
ResponseTextHandler 110, 113
REST. *See* Representational State Transfer
RIA. *See* Rich Internet Application
Rich Internet Application 5
RMI. *See* Remote Method Invocation
Rocket GWT 336
role 283
RollBackException 105
ROOT.xml 205, 209
RootPanel 16, 40
RPC. *See* Remote Procedure Call
Ruderman, Jesse 109
runTarget 200, 236

S

Safari 8, 58, 127, 133, 279, 297–298
  advanced HTTP support 114–115
  drag events 292
  testing GWT 230
Same Origin Policy 15, 109, 121, 130–131, 136
schema 104
SCM 241
scope 95
script 39, 141, 151–152
  tag 37, 156, 312
Script.aculo.us 3, 149, 155, 162, 166, 168, 184, 289
ScrollPanel 331
  setScrollPosition method 331
Seam 6
search engine 9
security 136
  context 137
  realm 205
security-constraint tag 283
security-role tag 285
SelectedIndex 98
selector names 56
Selenium 226
serialize 10, 19, 35, 64, 67, 88, 117, 219, 344
server 14
  communication 147
  path 35
server side 188
server-push animation 137
ServerSerializationStream-Reader 70
service servlet 69, 98, 188, 209, 224
Service-oriented Architecture 121
Servlet 284–285, 305, 312
servlet 39, 72, 77, 104, 189, 209
Servlet API 75
servlet container 75, 79, 188
servlet filter 205
ServletContext 264
ServletFilter 208
servlet-mapping 189, 209
ServletOutputStream 315
Session 95, 327
Set 118
setHeight 56
set-property 39
setScrollPostion 331
setStyleName 56
settings.xml 201–202, 236
setUp() 216
setVisible 56
setWidget 93
setWidth 56
Shift key 332
shopping cart 282
short 150
Silverlight 6
Simple Object Access Protocol 62, 67, 70, 120–121, 131, 220
SimpleUrlHandlerMapping 264
single-state model 53
Singleton 322
singleton 266
sinoidal transition 155
site.xml 238
sleep() 314
Slider 162
Smalltalk 41
SOA. *See* Service-oriented Architecture
SOAP. *See* Simple Object Access Protocol
SOAPFlashClient 128
source 39, 349
  control management 241–242
  path 35, 39, 68, 188, 215
SourcesChangeEvents 95
SourcesClickEvents 95